DAY BY DAY

BIBLE QUESTIONS

From
Bertie & Thoma
with Christian love

Christmas 2010

Day by Day Bible Questions

Edited by
KEN TOTTON

PRECIOUS SEED PUBLICATIONS

The Glebe House, Stanton Drew, Bristol, UK, BS39 4EH

First published September 2010

ISBN 978 1 871642 30 8

This is the thirteenth book in the Day by Day series.

The others are:

Day by Day through the Old Testament
Day by Day through the New Testament
Day by Day in the Psalms
Day by Day Moments with the Master
Day by Day in Prayer
Day by Day with Bible Characters
Day by Day Christ Foreshadowed
Day by Day Bible Promises
Day by Day Divine Titles
Day by Day Bible Commands
Day by Day Paradise to the Promised Land
Day by Day Bible Pictures and Parables

Printed in China

Contents

Acknowledgements

It is now twenty-nine years since the first volume in this popular Day by Day series was produced, and Bible Questions is now the thirteenth volume. There can be no more wholesome and vital activity than daily reading and meditation in the word of God, Ps. 119. 97, and the Precious Seed Committee is united in wishing to promote this objective.

'Day by Day Bible Questions' is *not* a book addressing Bible difficulties – there are many excellent volumes which meet that need. Rather, this latest volume encourages daily reading and meditation by focusing on a significant scripture question, that is, a question actually asked in the Bible, and providing an exposition with application. As with the earlier books in the series, we are once more indebted to an international team of contributors, all of whom are already busy in the service of God.

They have sought to handle each question contextually, but at the same time to relate the timeless truths of scripture to the needs of God's people today. Their greatest motivation is the hope that their labours might be used by the Lord to stimulate others in the prayerful study of His word.

In addition to the authors' contributions, the book's production would not have been possible without the efforts of a well-established team. The idea for this title was first posed in 2007. Howard Coles provided encouragement and direction in the compilation of the questions and their associated readings. John Bennett, a veteran of the Day by Day series, provided much valuable advice and support at every stage, but especially with proof reading, assisted by John Scarsbrook and Brian Clatworthy. Derek Hill once again carried out the typesetting efficiently, while the cover design is the work of Barney Trevivian. Roy Hill, in addition to helping with proof reading, managed the printing aspects. All are deserving of our thanks for their valued commitment and contributions.

On behalf of the Precious Seed Committee
Ken Totton
July 2010

The Contributors and their Contributions

Wesley Ferguson	Northern Ireland	January 1 – 16
Mark Kolchin	USA	January 17 – 31
Lindsay Parks	USA	February 1 – 14
John Scarsbrook	England	February 15 – 29
John Salisbury	England	March 1 – 15
Richard Catchpole	England	March 16 – 31
Brian Clatworthy	England	April 1 – 15
Malcolm Horlock	Wales	April 16 – 30
Ken Totton	England	May 1 – 15
Ian Rees	England	May 16 – 31
Richard Collings	Wales	June 1 – 15
William Burnett	Canada	June 16 – 30
Paul Richardson	England	July 1 – 15
Alistair Sinclair	Scotland	July 16 – 31
Boushra Mikhael	Canada	August 1 – 15
Tom Meekin	Northern Ireland	August 16 – 31
Howard Coles	England	September 1 – 15
Brian Gunning	Canada	September 16 – 30
Robert Thomson	Scotland	October 1 – 15
Keith Keyser	USA	October 16 – 31
Roy Hill	England	November 1 – 15
Alan Gamble	Scotland	November 16 – 30
Philip Coulson	Scotland	December 1 – 15
Ian Jackson	England	December 16 – 31

Biographies of the Contributors

Wesley Ferguson is an elder in the assembly in Antrim in Northern Ireland. He ministers the word throughout the Province and the UK and is the author of numerous magazine articles, and recently authored *Genesis* in the Ritchie series *'What the Bible Teaches'*. He was a teacher and a schools' inspector.

Mark Kolchin, along with his wife Cynthia, was commended to the Lord's work in 1993 by the assembly in Toms River, New Jersey, USA. He is currently engaged in an itinerant Bible teaching and conference ministry and maintains an evangelistic and Bible teaching web site, www.knowtheword.com. He has written on a variety of topics in the Christian life.

Lindsay Parks is an elder in the assembly meeting in the Gospel Hall, Indiana, PA, USA. He has been a family practice physician for over thirty-three years, married to Diane, with three children, and ten grandchildren. He has preached the gospel and ministered the word in a number of assemblies in the USA, Canada, and Northern Ireland. He has a special exercise for assembly young people, and has participated in a number of conferences designed to help young believers.

John Scarsbrook is an elder in the Killamarsh assembly, Derbyshire, England. He is active in ministry throughout the UK. He is a self-employed financial broker, married to Ruth, with four married sons and ten grandchildren, and is Secretary to the *Precious Seed Trust*.

John Salisbury has served as an elder in the Spencer Bridge Road assembly, Northampton, UK for many years, supported by his wife, Wendy. Retired from business, he is active in ministry in the UK. He has two married sons and seven grandchildren.

Richard Catchpole lives in South Norwood, London, with his wife Judith. He is in fellowship in the Clifton Hall assembly. He was commended in 1989 to the grace of God for the work of the Lord. He travels extensively in the UK in a Bible teaching ministry and engages in children's and school work in his home locality. He has also made visits to Poland and India.

Brian Clatworthy is an elder in an assembly in Newton Abbot, Devon. He retired from secular employment in 2008 after a career in HM Revenue and Customs. He is a member of the *Precious Seed Trust*, and has written a number of articles for the magazine. He has a teaching ministry mainly, but not exclusively in Devon and Cornwall. He is married with two grown-up children.

Malcolm Horlock is an elder in the Bethesda assembly at Rhiwbina, Cardiff, Wales. Married with four children and eight grandchildren, he is active in Bible teaching, both orally and in writing.

Ken Totton is in fellowship at Roseford Chapel, Cambridge, England. Following a career in the telecommunications industry, he devotes his time to Bible teaching, both locally and further afield. He is Books Editor for *Precious Seed Publications*. He is married to Kate and has two sons.

Ian Rees saw an assembly planted in Francistown, Botswana, having served the Lord there for thirteen years. Now based in the UK, he continues in fellowship in Manvers Hall, Bath, one of his commending assemblies. He is currently a Publications Editor for *Precious Seed Publications*. He is married and has seven children.

Richard Collings is in fellowship in the assembly at Caerphilly, Wales and is a committee member of *Precious Seed Trust*.

William Burnett was born and raised in Scotland, and spent his professional life in the oil refining business. His employer seconded him to Canada in 1972, and he accepted early retirement in 1994. He has been a 'tentmaker' among the assemblies since his late teen years, and now ministers throughout North America, and abroad. He also sits on the board of Counsel Magazine, and contributes regularly to various assembly publications. He has recently written a book entitled, *Daniel – Godly living in a hostile world*. He and his wife Beth reside in Oakville, Ontario, Canada, where they are in happy fellowship in Hopedale assembly. They have three married sons, and eight grandchildren.

Paul Richardson is actively involved in the Lord's work at Woodfield Gospel Hall, Harrogate, England. He has spent most of his career in the financial services industry. Paul is married to Elizabeth and has four sons.

Alastair Sinclair is in fellowship with the assembly at Crosshouse, Ayrshire, Scotland, and is active in oral ministry throughout the UK. He writes regularly for assembly magazines and is married with a son and two daughters. He works in the IT industry.

Boushra Mikhael is a retired surgeon, who served as an elder for over twenty-five years at Rideauview Bible Chapel in Ottawa, Ontario, Canada. Now he is commended by two Ottawa area assemblies to a full time teaching ministry involving an itinerant ministry in North America and overseas. He is active in camp work and he is involved in writing for various assembly publications. He is married to Nadia and they have two sons who are also physicians involved in the Lord's work. They have three grand-daughters.

Tom Meekin was a full time worker in Brazil (1972-1981) who on his return to N. Ireland resumed secular employment, still keeping busy in gospel work in UK. He has since travelled widely abroad giving help both in gospel and ministry and is now correspondent of his former commending assembly at Glengormley. Now retired, he spends more time giving help locally. Married to Sally, a true helpmeet for forty years, he has three married daughters and six grandchildren.

Howard Coles is a Treasurer of *Precious Seed Trust*. He is a qualified accountant, running a small manufacturing business. He is married with three grown-up children and is an elder in the Coleford assembly, near Bath, England. His ministry is mainly amongst assemblies in the south west of England.

Brian Gunning is in fellowship in the Brockview assembly in St. Catharines, Ontario, Canada, and is a self-employed accountant. He is married to Marlene, with four daughters, three married, and a grandson. He is an elder in the local assembly. He is editor of *Counsel* magazine and a director of Gospel Folio Press. He has an active itinerant preaching ministry throughout North America.

Robert Thomson is in fellowship at Bishopton Gospel Hall, Renfrewshire, Scotland. He is married with three children.

Keith Keyser is a commended full-time worker and is in fellowship in the assembly meeting at Gilbertsville, Pennsylvania. He ministers throughout North America and spent some time in Spain. He has also written material for assembly magazines.

Roy Hill is in fellowship in the assembly at Pensford Gospel Hall, near Bristol, and is well known as an international Bible teacher. He is married with five children and nine grandchildren. Having spent his life in the printing trade he is currently chairman of *Precious Seed Trust* and a board member of Gospel Folio Press in Canada. He also writes extensively for assembly magazines.

Alan Gamble is in fellowship in the assembly at Bethesda, Linthouse, Glasgow, Scotland. He is active in Bible teaching in the UK and North America. He serves as a trustee of Interlink, a missionary service group. Married to Elizabeth, they have three adult children and one grandson. His professional background is in law.

Philip Coulson and his wife Rachel were commended to a full-time preaching and teaching ministry by the Forres assembly in 1999. Since then Phil has moved widely amongst the assemblies in the UK and abroad, particularly in SE Asia. He continues to visit India, Sri Lanka and Burma with a desire to establish and strengthen assemblies of Christians gathering in obedience to the word of God. Phil and Rachel have two children and three grandchildren, all living in Forres.

Ian Jackson is in fellowship with the assembly meeting at Marine Hall, Eastbourne, England. He is married with three children, two married, and four grandchildren. He is a commended full-time worker travelling widely as an evangelist and Bible teacher.

Introduction

Questions are part of our normal everyday interactions as human beings. We ask questions to seek information, advice, and help. It has been observed that in many fields of human endeavour success depends largely on asking the *right* questions. As FRANCIS BACON put it, 'A prudent question is one-half of wisdom'. Sometimes also we ask questions to challenge the status quo or highlight complacency. Asking and answering questions goes to the heart of normal human enquiry and learning. Concerning the child Jesus we read, 'They found him in the temple, sitting in the midst of the doctors, both hearing them, and asking them questions', Luke 2. 46.

Many of the questions of the Bible are ordinary enough, but beyond the mundane interactions lie the big questions of life and existence, issues of identity and purpose, 'Who am I? How did I get here? Why am I suffering?' Instinctively, as believers we turn to the word of God for answers and we are not disappointed! 'What is man, that thou art mindful of him?' Ps. 8. 4, is a reminder of our lowliness, yet also of our incredible human dignity and destiny in the purposes of God, forfeited in Adam, yet to be realized in union with Christ, the Last Adam.

As we might expect, Bible questions reflect the entire round of human *experience*. The Books of Job and the Psalms are particularly rich in the 'Why?' and 'How long?' questions as the righteous wrestle with suffering in contrast to the apparent prosperity of the wicked. The Book of Job records the sufferings of a righteous man, sufferings compounded in many instances by the faulty assumptions and theories of his 'friends'. Job's anguish is mirrored in his vexed questioning and searching of the ways of God. Fittingly, the book concludes with the Almighty humbling Job with a majestic series of unanswerable questions of His own, Job 40-41.

Many of the Bible's questions are *rhetorical* – ones that require no answers because the answers are obvious and do not need to be stated. 'A question is often put not to elicit information, but as a more striking substitute for a statement. The assumption is that only one answer is possible, and that if the hearer is compelled to make it mentally himself it will impress him more than the speaker's statement', *Fowler's Modern English Usage*. 'The LORD is my light and my salvation; whom shall I fear?' Ps. 27. 1;

'Where shall the ungodly and the sinner appear?' 1 Pet. 4. 18; both are examples of rhetorical questions – in both cases the answers are clear.

Some Bible questions are truly *famous* having arrested readers over the centuries and supplied texts for innumerable sermons. Many a sinner has been asked the question, 'Wilt thou be made whole?' John 5. 6. We do not have far to read in the Old Testament before we encounter the sad question asked of fallen Adam by the Lord God, 'Where art thou?' Gen. 3. 9. God knew exactly where Adam was hiding, but what tragedy, destruction, and universal misery was linked with that simple question!

Yet, by contrast the New Testament opens with an enquiry full of hope asked by the Magi from the east, 'Where is he that is born King of the Jews?' Thus right at the beginning of his Gospel, Matthew signals that He who is the fulfilment of all Messianic promise has come not simply to fulfil the promises to Israel, but in order to bring untold blessing to the Gentile world too.

Many of our Lord's questions to His disciples are deeply challenging and timeless, 'Is not the life more than meat, and the body than raiment?' Matt. 6. 25, or in some instances utterly incisive, 'O generation of vipers, how can ye, being evil, speak good things?' Matt. 12. 34.

As opposition grew, the Lord faced many objections from opponents. Late in His ministry Pharisees, Sadducees, and a lawyer ply our Lord with crafty questions designed to compromise Him, Matt. 22. 17, 28, 36, before the Lord silences His critics with a few of His own, questions which went to the heart of His Messianic identity, David's Son and David's Lord, vv. 42-45. Other notable questions of the Gospels include: the *most pivotal* – 'What shall I do then with Jesus which is called Christ?' Matt. 27. 22; the *most searching* – 'For what shall it profit a man, if he shall gain the whole world, and lose his own soul?' Mark 8. 36; the *most mysterious* – 'My God, my God, why has thou forsaken me?' Ps. 22. 1.

The attentive reader will quickly discover that questions are not uniformly distributed in the Bible. Some books are conspicuously rich in questions. The Letter to the Romans, Paul's great treatise on the gospel, is brim-full of logic and questions. Believers all through the ages have revelled in the security implied by the triumphal divine challenge to the moral universe, 'Who shall lay any thing to the charge of God's elect?' Rom. 8. 33, and the sublime comfort of 'Who shall separate us from the love of Christ?' v. 35.

The Book of the Revelation fitly supplies crucial questions addressing the consummation of the divine programme of the ages, none more momentous than the challenge, 'Who is worthy to open the book, and to loose the seals thereof?' Rev. 5. 2. Praise God, the slain Lamb in the midst of the throne has conquered, and is uniquely qualified to bring to fulfilment the manifold purposes of God!

Thus, from Genesis to Revelation the questions of scripture form a worthy storehouse for our meditation and instruction. We will find much to challenge, inform, inspire, and comfort, for truly 'the things written aforetime were written for our learning'. To be sure, the answers to some of our deepest questions await that time when our vision is no longer as 'in a mirror dimly, but then face to face', 1 Cor. 13. 12 ESV. Until then we rejoice that 'the secret things belong unto the LORD our God: but those things which are revealed belong unto us and to our children for ever', Deut. 29. 29.

January 1st

Genesis 3. 6-10

WHERE ART THOU?

When David considered the greatness of God, the Creator, he marvelled that such a God was 'mindful' of mere man, or 'visited' him. Genesis chapter 3 tells of God walking in the garden in the cool of the day. Did He do this habitually to enjoy with Adam the paradise He had created? On this occasion there could be no sharing with Adam, for he had disobeyed the one prohibition given him by God.

So Adam was afraid to walk with God, and he hid. God's call, 'Where art thou?' is not a request for information. God knew exactly where Adam was. But God was not satisfied to abandon him, even when he had failed. Adam must realize where his sin had placed him. Amazingly, God always takes the initiative in seeking the lost. We would never act first, so He acts to bring us to Himself. He does seek us! Amazing grace!

Adam must be confronted with his plight. He must ask himself where he is. It is good that we habitually take stock of where we are in relation to walking with God.

He confesses that he hid because he was afraid. Psalm 139 tells us that we cannot get away from God's presence. As our Judge, He sees our sins, but as our Saviour He watches to bring us into blessing. We see God's care in His question.

Adam's first reaction to his sin was to involve, perhaps even to blame, Eve – she gave him the forbidden fruit. But he finally confessed, 'And I did eat'. He had taken the first positive step toward recovery.

In John chapter 4 the Lord Jesus wanted to create in the Samaritan woman a thirst for living water. It was the gift of God, and Jesus, the Son of God, delighted to give the gift. But first, there was the awkward question of her husbands. Her sin must be brought to her conscience so that she will be ready to be forgiven. Adam's sin brought in a curse, but the Genesis story is of blessing at the end. Adam would have a coat of skin.

Are we prepared today to ask, 'Where am I?' It may be the first step to spiritual recovery of lost fellowship with our loving God. He who sees us where we are hiding from Him has plans for us of grace and blessing beyond our imagining.

January 2nd

Genesis 4. 3-10

WHERE IS ABEL THY BROTHER?

When Adam disobeyed God in Eden, his action had implications beyond his imagining. If our relations with God are damaged, our relations with other people will be damaged too. 'Thou shalt love the Lord thy God' has a second part, 'and thy neighbour as thyself'; the two laws are inseparable.

Cain and Abel had the same parental training, the same family background. The courses they travelled differed according to their choices. Their lifestyles differed. Their values differed.

John states that Cain 'was of that wicked one, and slew his brother. And wherefore slew he him? Because his own works were evil, and his brother's righteous', 1 John 3. 12. This was the basis of the problem between Cain and his brother Abel.

They did different kinds of work. They offered different sacrifices. But their differences were fundamentally in their attitudes to God. Hence, the animosity of Cain toward Abel.

The summary of the law of God in the New Testament consists of two parts: love of God and of one's neighbour. Cain's behaviour showed that he lacked love or respect for God. It is not surprising, then, that he did not love or respect his brother.

In Romans chapter 1 Paul analyzes the depraved state of Gentile society in his day. He traces it back to their failure to acknowledge God as Creator. The climax is the general breakdown of human relations in violence and hatred. A society in which God is not acknowledged will finally become dysfunctional. The seeds of this are seen in Cain in Genesis chapter 4.

The Epistle to the Hebrews says that it was by faith that Abel offered to God a more acceptable sacrifice than Cain. This would seem to imply that there was an explicit instruction from God about the way of approach to Him. The Epistle normally represents faith as believing, obedient response to a word from God. The fact that Abel offered the best of his lambs may indicate that blood-sacrifice was essential. It may be significant that Cain is not said to have offered the best of his crop.

Cain's attitude comes out in his sneering question, 'Am I my brother's keeper?' With this attitude, how could he possibly offer an acceptable sacrifice?

January 3rd

Genesis 12. 10-20

WHY DIDST THOU NOT TELL SHE WAS THY WIFE?

Verse 5 of this chapter records the arrival of Abram and his family in Canaan. God then promised him the land, and Abram built an altar in gratitude to God, 'calling on the name of the Lord'. So far, his faith was prospering.

Then, verse 10, his faith was tested by a grievous famine, and abruptly Abram went to Egypt. Equally abruptly, his faith was replaced by fear. This focused on Sarai, his beautiful wife, who was also his half-sister. The Egyptians would be quick to notice her beauty and Abram feared they would kill him, to leave her helpless in their hands. He had not considered that she might attract the attention of the Pharaoh's officials. But she was taken into Pharaoh's palace, with a view, no doubt, to being added to his harem.

Abram had hoped, v. 13, that all would 'be well' with him. And Pharaoh did treat him well, v. 16. So all was going well. Or was it? There was one problem: throughout the chapter the refrain is 'Abram's wife', not 'sister'. This intervention of Pharaoh's was not part of Abram's plan, and Abram had no answer to the problem.

Genesis records the onward movement of God's purposes, not those of the people He linked to Himself through grace. So now, with Abram perplexed, God acted, upset Pharaoh's intentions and delivered Sarai. God was going to give Abram descendants through Sarai, 'his wife'.

Abram called Sarai his sister, probably to ensure his own survival so that the promise of descendants might be assured, for he was still childless. This is one example among a number in Genesis, of people trying to devise ways of helping God out of His supposed difficulties. But God is never in difficulties.

Pharaoh, ignorant of Abram's destiny, rebuked him sharply. How sad to see a man, whom God had promised to bless, being rebuked by a heathen king! Abram told a half-truth, a whole lie. God had to rescue him. What a contrast we find in Jacob, who in his last days blessed the Pharaoh – and 'the lesser is blessed by the greater'. So Abram was 'driven out' of Egypt, as Adam and Eve were 'driven out' of paradise (the same word is used).

January 4th

Genesis 15. 7-11

WHEREBY SHALL I KNOW THAT I SHALL INHERIT?

In chapter 14 Abram won a great victory against a marauding force led by four kings from the north. They had passed right through the land, as far as Sodom in the south. Abram defeated them, released Lot and drove them northwards to Dan, the northern boundary of the land; a token of his right to the land? On his return to the south, he was met by Melchizedek, with whom he shared a faith in the living God, the Creator of heaven and earth. After this, God came to Abram in a vision, assuring him that, in relation to his victory God was his shield. More than this, He was also Abram's 'exceeding great reward'.

This prompted Abram to reply that he had no offspring to inherit any reward that had been promised him, far less a numerous progeny. God renewed the promise of numerous offspring, as numerous as the stars in heaven. He believed God and so he was accounted righteous; so he would inherit the land.

But how was he to know this? What token would God give him? In answer God instructed him to provide victims to seal a covenant between him and God.

The mysterious ceremony, described in verses 10 to 17, was God's way of showing that He, the living God whom Abram trusted, was binding Himself, solemnly and formally, to give the land to Abram's descendants. There would be a delay, for the time had not yet come to oust the inhabitants of Canaan. This covenant brings together God's intention to give Abram possession of the land (foreshadowed in chapter 14), with His intention to grant him innumerable descendants.

To those who trust Him God gives indications along the way to assure them that He, the living God, can preserve His own – He is their shield. He also gives them patience to wait for His time to fulfil His promises. When Israel went after God in the journey to Canaan, they journeyed part of the time, but there were periods of waiting for the cloud to move. In some ways these static periods tested faith more than the actual days of travel. God's path for us contains indications of our duty to be active and decisive. The more advanced part of the course consists of knowing when to wait, so as not to run ahead of God.

January 5th

Genesis 16. 7-14

HAGAR . . . WHENCE CAMEST THOU?

Sarai's plan, to overcome her barrenness by using her handmaid as a sort of surrogate mother, had misfired. She had thought it would be easy to follow a common practice in such cases and claim the child, if one were born, as her own son. But Sarai's plan changed Hagar's relationship to her; for Hagar conceived, it seems, quickly, and her success undermined Sarai's confidence in her status as Abram's wife.

Hagar's flight from Sarai's pressure may have seemed to solve the problem. Abram sidestepped the issue and he left Hagar, in his words to Sarai, 'in thy hands'. For the second time in this episode he had 'hearkened to his wife'.

But when God has plans for a family or a person, sidestepping never solves problems. So, 'the angel of the Lord' met Hagar by a wilderness well. Sarai never calls Hagar by her name in this whole story, but God tells us her name, for her child was Abram's son, and Abram was God's friend. 'The angel of the Lord' addressed Hagar by name, and by her true title, 'Sarai's handmaid', not 'Abram's second wife'. The question of where she was coming from was important, for she was Sarai's handmaid, and her place was where Sarai was. It would be to her child's advantage to have years in the home of a man of God.

As to where she was going, she seems to have been heading in the direction of Egypt. But her place in the divine purpose for Abram was not Egypt, but Canaan. For the present, Sarai was her mistress, v. 9, and to her she must submit – 'under her hands', not just 'in' them. And God had plans for her seed.

God had a place, not only for His chosen seed of Abram, but also to bless others through them. God heard the cry of Hagar's son in chapter 21 verse 17. God saw and heard even the son of a bondwoman. He would be a desert-dweller, but he would be father of a great race and be able to fight his corner.

Hagar was amazed that God took notice of her, 'Thou God (so great!) seest me (so puny!)'. The God of vision, who saw, was also the God of provision. He saw her! He provided for her! Wonderful grace! And He still sees and provides for us.

January 6th

Genesis 17. 15-21

A CHILD BORN TO A MAN A HUNDRED YEARS OLD?

In chapter 15, Abram had needed assurance about the delay in his having a son. Sarai's use of Hagar to solve the problem had failed disastrously. At the end of chapter 16 it is repeatedly stated that Ishmael was Hagar's son. Now, in chapter 17, God appears to Abram, after a further delay of thirteen years. The promise of descendants is repeated. The covenant of circumcision is instituted. Abram is now to be called Abraham, a new beginning. Moreover, Sarai also receives a new name, Sarah. And Sarah will bear the promised son! Can this be possible?

Abraham knew that, humanly speaking, this was impossible. He had felt his years passing, his strength and virility waning. He had seen Sarah clearly no longer capable of bearing a child. Yet he had a word from God. If only God would accept Ishmael it would be simple. God graciously granted him a repetition of the promise: the son born would be Abraham's son, and Sarah's. It all seemed so impossible.

In chapter 18 he received yet another repetition of the promise from his heavenly visitors. Sarah overheard the promise and laughed. In the face of such an impossibility, ought one to laugh or cry?

Abraham and Sarah were being granted an opportunity sometimes granted to those who trust God and believe His word: they would see how the impossible can, in God's hands, become possible. God is the Source of all life. He grants us the privilege of becoming parents. He gives us the physical potential. At the point of our helplessness, He can grant us a manifestation of His divine power. This is true both in the physical and in the spiritual realm. God 'quickeneth the dead, and calleth those things which be not as though they were', Rom. 4. 17.

Zechariah and Elizabeth learnt this in Luke chapter 1. The word to them was, 'With God nothing shall be impossible'; a paraphrase of, 'Is anything too hard for the Lord?' Mary and Martha reached despair before the Lord called, 'Lazarus, come forth!' They feared the stench of corruption, but the dead heard the voice of the Son of God and came forth. This kind of experience is for those who trust a word from God above all else.

January 7th

Genesis 18. 16-21

SHALL I HIDE FROM ABRAHAM THAT WHICH I DO?

We can trace the life of this man Abraham from his origins in Ur down to this point in the story. First, he had a word from God when he was called to leave Ur and go to a place which God would show him. Then, when he and Lot had to part, in chapter 13, he allowed Lot (though younger) to choose an area. Abraham himself was content with what God chose for him. He would have the land and descendants to populate it. He had had dealings with God on several occasions to sustain his faith through the long years of waiting. His life was marked by his faith in God. God's promises would be fulfilled.

Lot, by contrast, followed Abraham, rather than obeying a word from God. When he must part from Abraham he chose on the basis of what he could see, and he chose what reminded him of Egypt. Yet Lot was a righteous man, 2 Pet. 2. 7, 8. He gave the heavenly visitors hospitality. The lawlessness of Sodom grieved him daily, but his compromise had radically reduced his influence for good. Hence his inability to persuade his prospective sons-in-law to leave Sodom.

Abraham's hospitality to the heavenly visitors can be contrasted with Lot's. The atmosphere in Abraham's tent was very unlike that in Lot's house in Sodom. The tension in the story of the judgement on Sodom is seen in Abraham drawing near to the Lord to plead for Sodom – in reality to plead for Lot. Sodom's violent, perverted society demanded immediate judgement – their 'iniquity was full'. But if God destroyed Sodom, how could righteous, but compromised, Lot escape?

God acted as one would expect towards a man described in scripture as His friend. He would advise him of His intention to destroy Sodom. God had no problem about rescuing Lot, for He is the Judge of all the earth. Abraham saw only the destruction of the city, with all in it; God would deliver the righteous out of it. 'God remembered Abraham and sent Lot out', Gen. 19. 29.

God answers our prayers according to His wisdom, grace and power. He does not always give us what we ask, but He may well have plans to answer by doing something greater than what we asked. He reads our hearts, not just our lips.

January 8th

Genesis 18. 22-33

SHALL NOT THE JUDGE OF ALL THE EARTH DO RIGHT?

Abraham drew near to the Lord to plead for Sodom. The ground of his plea was that there were righteous people there who did not deserve the summary justice which must fall. His pleading about what number of such people would avert the judgement is based on this argument.

A more fundamental basis for his pleading was what he knew of the character of God, the Judge of all. A corrupt judge may be bribed, a weak judge may be intimidated, but He whose character is the touchstone of judicial integrity cannot be diverted from doing justice. The criterion for assessing all administration of justice is, 'How would God judge this case?' Therefore, reasoned Abraham, God must spare Sodom for even a few righteous people in it. But how many were needed?

Abraham did not realize that God was going to destroy Sodom at this time, because the evil in the city demanded it. He would be in possession of all the facts, knowing that it was as bad as it had been reported to Him. Note the word 'altogether' in verse 21. So, regardless of what reasoning Abraham produced, Sodom was doomed, for the Judge of all the earth must do right. Israel's occupation of Canaan was kept on hold, until the iniquity of the Amorites was full, Gen. 15. 16. When their iniquity had reached the point where God could tolerate no more, they must be punished.

What God could do, and actually did, was to remember Abraham and deliver Lot. In a future day, when God judges corrupt 'Babylon', the call to the faithful will be, 'Come out of her, my people', Rev. 18. 4. It is a sad commentary on Lot's condition that he and his nearest kin had to be dragged out, but even so they did come out. Two angels had four hands, one for each of those dragged out to safety. Lot was, as it were, 'saved . . . through the fire', 1 Cor. 3. 15 JND. He himself escaped, but what he had lived for was burned up.

What Abraham was sure of was that God would do right. He had not guessed how it would be done. God's methods of answering our prayers are more wonderful than our expectation.

January 9th

Genesis 21. 8-21

WHAT AILETH THEE, HAGAR?

Hagar had had previous experience of God when He sent her back to her mistress, Sarah. She had learned that the living God knew her name and circumstances. He also cared about her. He had found her by a spring well and she realized that He saw and provided for her. Moreover, He had given promises about her as yet unborn son and his descendants.

Back in Abraham's house there was rejoicing thirteen years later when Sarah bore a son and called him Isaac, a name that told of laughter. But problems arose: when Isaac was weaned, Ishmael, Hagar's son, was probably a lad in his mid-teens. At the ceremonies to mark Isaac's weaning Ishmael mocked him. Sarah's rejoicing at the birth and progress of Isaac was turned to fierce indignation against Ishmael and his mother.

Sarah insisted that 'this bondwoman and her son' should be driven out, in effect exiled. Her mind was focused on the issue of inheritance, the possession of the Promised Land. The seed and the land were closely connected. It is ironic that the distress felt by Sarah at this time had its roots in her own decision to press Abraham to seek offspring through Hagar. However, the promise and purpose of God demanded that Isaac be established as son and heir to faithful Abraham. He was son of both Abraham and Sarah, as God had stipulated. Interestingly, Sarah's pronouncement, 'Cast out the bondwoman', is quoted in the New Testament, Gal. 4. 30, as 'scripture'.

Therefore, Hagar must go. Abraham, who loved Ishmael, made reluctant provision for Hagar's departure with her son. The skin-bottle of water would last some time but would run out. Hagar went off, carrying the bottle and leading her son. So Abraham and Sarah were rid of an irritant in their marriage.

Inevitably, the water ran out, but God had not forgotten Hagar. She thought Ishmael must die, but God heard his voice. God knew where they were. His providence brought her again beside a spring well. God assured Hagar that Ishmael would survive and thrive. God cares for all His creatures, sees our needs and hears our cries. He is 'the Saviour of all men, specially of those that believe', 1 Tim. 4. 10. Hagar need not fear.

January 10th

Genesis 22. 1-14

WHERE IS THE LAMB FOR A BURNT OFFERING?

Abraham rose up early in the morning, ready to go the full distance to accomplish God's will for him and Isaac. Isaac went with him, willingly but unwittingly, to the place of sacrifice. The three-day journey gave ample time for thought and for wrestling with the question – how to balance God's promises regarding the son of promise with the demand to give him up in sacrifice. He had already given up Ishmael despite his affection for him – 'O that Ishmael might live before thee!'

Then, the young men were left with the ass and the two, father and son, went together. And still Isaac was ignorant of his own central part in this drama. But he was puzzled – fire and wood, but no lamb! Then he articulated his question, 'Where is the lamb for a burnt offering?'

Now Hebrews chapter 11 verse 19 tells us that Abraham reckoned that God could raise Isaac from the dead. Did he, then, consider that Isaac was the lamb that God provided? He had said to the young men, 'I and the lad will go yonder and worship, and come again to you'. So he was confident that they would both return. Had not God told him that his descendants would spring from Isaac? Yes, they would both return.

The harmony between father and son, as they went both together, is moving. Isaac was bound on the altar, evidently unresisting. Abraham lifted the knife to sacrifice his own beloved son, his only son now that Ishmael had been renounced. In the words of Hebrews chapter 11 verse 17b RV, he 'was offering up his only begotten son'. God accepted the will for the deed and did not demand the full execution of the deed.

Our minds cannot but go to another scene, another Father and another Son. John's Gospel traces the harmony between God the Father and His Son Jesus as they moved to the sacrifice at Calvary. This was the same location as where Abraham offered up Isaac. But Jesus knew all along where the journey was to end. And there would be no ram to replace Him. God 'spared not his own Son', Rom. 8. 32, and, in the Septuagint translation of Genesis chapter 22 verse 16b, God says to Abraham, '(Thou) hast not spared thy son, thine only son'. What an echo!

January 11th

Genesis 24. 1-21

MUST I NEEDS BRING THY SON AGAIN?

The two main strands in the Genesis story blend in this episode: first, Abraham and his descendants, and second, the land which God was going to give them.

Abraham was adamant that a bride for his son must not be sought in Canaan. Had he not been told, in chapter 15, verse 16, there would come a time when the continued godlessness of the Amorites would demand that God should act in judgement – the iniquity of the Amorites would be full? So Abraham made the servant to swear solemnly not to seek a bride in Canaan. Abraham decided that the bride for Isaac must be sought among his own people in Mesopotamia. But she must come to where Abraham and the chosen people were; Isaac must not go to the place from which God had called out Abraham. The seed and the land are inseparably linked.

This episode is a beautiful depiction of the behaviour of a faithful servant, a true steward, careful of his master's interests and instructions. Acquiring a wife, for oneself or another, is a serious undertaking, calling for care and thought. This bride would be married to a special son, born through divine intervention and destined to father a special race.

He was to seek a wife from among Abraham's own people. That was clear and simple. He was not to agree to take Isaac to the young woman's country, for Abraham had been called to leave it. That also was very clear. He understood clearly that she must be a suitable person for his master's special son. That required special consideration. Character is not necessarily produced by a suitable bloodline! Then there was also the need for her to be willing to go to Canaan.

Wisely, the servant prayed for God's guidance in his search. This did not cause him to go unthinkingly. He knew where people from a community visited every day, the well where they had to draw water. He would meet people there and could use his intelligence to see where God was directing him. In his prayer he told God what kind of behaviour would indicate a suitable young woman. Asking God for guidance does not require that we cease to use common sense.

January 12th

Genesis 24. 50-67

WILT THOU GO WITH THIS MAN?

Abraham's faithful steward has fulfilled his responsibility: he established contact with a suitable bride for Isaac, one who met the criteria which he had drawn up. Her family were Abraham's kinsfolk, as required. They were happy with the proposal that Rebekah go to be Isaac's bride. The steward was now confirmed in his conviction that God was prospering his mission, and he gave Him thanks.

This stage in the transaction is marked by the giving of lavish gifts to Rebekah, as was fitting in view of Abraham's wealth. Valuable gifts were also given to her family. Only then did the steward and his men accept the food and drink which had been offered them before negotiations began.

His mission, however, was not fully accomplished, until he had conveyed the bride to Isaac. He was therefore keen to leave on his return journey the next morning. Her family were in no hurry to bid her farewell. Those urging delay were her brother Laban and her mother. Her father, evidently, took no part in the proceedings.

All were agreed that the match had the Lord's blessing. The servant argued, therefore, that they should act promptly to let him complete his mission. At this late stage in the negotiation, the bride was asked for her own feelings.

How did she feel? She doubtless took note of the wealth of Isaac. She must have noted the courtesy and propriety of the steward's approach. She knew that her family were happy about the arrangements. The question was: did she feel as happy to go now, without prolonging the farewells? She almost certainly understood the obvious insincerity of Laban's words to the steward. Later events show us how mercenary most of his thoughts tended to be. Was this a happy home?

She agreed that there should be no delay. Thus, she placed herself on a path to be part of a divine plan to bless her and her descendants. Do we look back with joy to a day when we began a path of blessing beyond our ability then to comprehend? Have we an ambition to help others to join us on such a path? Have we the same sense of urgency as the steward had that day?

January 13th

Genesis 25. 29-34; Hebrews 12. 16

WHAT PROFIT SHALL THIS BIRTHRIGHT DO TO ME?

God had fulfilled His promise to Abraham that Sarah would bear him a son. Isaac's birth assured him of the covenant's continuance. A suitable bride for Isaac gave hope of offspring to continue the covenant line. But Rebekah was barren for twenty years. Any question of the birthright of the eldest son was abstract, for they had no son. Then Isaac's prayer was answered and Rebekah became pregnant. Her difficult pregnancy symbolized the rivalry between the two sons she was going to bear.

The inspired account tells of God's dealings in grace within His covenant with Abraham. The two sons differed in their personalities and pursuits, but also in their values. Esau was an outdoor person, fond of hunting and such pursuits. He had no interest in the covenant – Hebrews chapter 12 calls him 'a profane person'. Isaac loved him because he brought him venison. Jacob, on the other hand, valued the covenant. Rebekah, whom God had told that the elder would serve the younger, must have implanted in Jacob ambitions of power. She cherished the prospect of the exaltation of her home-loving, quiet Jacob. The birthright involved both spiritual and material benefits.

Isaac loved good food, and so did Esau. Isaac had faith, but Esau did not acquire this value as he did the love of good food. So, one day, Esau, ravenous and tired, returned from the hunt. Short-term need made him vulnerable. Jacob, who had made a tasty meal, exploited his short-term thinking: he offered to sell Esau the meal in exchange for the birthright. The birthright was of little interest to a ravenous young hunter. The inspired writer sums up the transaction, 'Thus Esau despised his birthright'. Some people auction ornaments inherited from their parents; to the older generation they were heirlooms, but the offspring just do not like them – 'What good are they to us?'

Jacob and Rebekah seem to us cold and calculating, but they did value the covenant. Their means were devious, but their ends indicated that Jacob at least could be educated. Jacob was in a stern school. If we seek God's purposes by carnal means, we must expect to learn lessons as we reap what we sow.

January 14th

Genesis 27. 18-29

WHO ART THOU, MY SON?

The disunity in the home of Isaac and Rebekah was deep-seated. Favouritism was the norm, and some negative outcome was inevitable. Jacob had gained the birthright by devious means. Rebekah's ambitions for him remained undiminished.

Events came to a head one day when Isaac asked Esau to go out and hunt deer to make him his favourite meal. He promised that on his return Esau would be blessed. Isaac seems to have expected to die soon, or perhaps he was making sure that Esau would be specially blessed before someone forestalled his father's plans for him. But Rebekah heard Isaac make this request, and her fertile mind moved rapidly into action. She spoke to Jacob and explained how they could frustrate Isaac's intention. Jacob must pretend to be Esau.

She sent Jacob to take two kids. She would make a meal of these for Isaac. Jacob would present the meal to Isaac, pretending that he was Esau bringing venison. Jacob was willing to co-operate, but not confident of success. What if Isaac touched him? He would feel his smooth skin and think he was mocking him. This would bring down a curse instead of a blessing.

Rebekah was confident that they could deceive Isaac. She knew his lack of perception. The story is full of details of his gullibility. Goatskin would seem to his touch to be the skin of hairy Esau. Esau's cloak would make Jacob smell like Esau. Isaac's perceptions were no match for Rebekah's skill.

Jacob came in with the disguise and the mock-venison. Isaac had not expected Esau so soon. Hence his question, 'Who art thou, my son?' He said he was Esau, and he reminded Isaac of the blessing. He explained the speed of his 'success' by claiming divine help. The web of lies was spreading. His voice almost gave him away, for it was Jacob's voice.

Finally, Isaac was persuaded and bestowed the blessing. God would have blessed Jacob without the deception, but he must learn his own identity. He had to flee from home. He spent a difficult twenty-year exile. Laban's house taught him valuable lessons. He proved God there. He learnt about God, and himself, and in chapter 32 verse 27, he confessed, 'I am Jacob'.

January 15th

Genesis 29. 18-30

DID NOT I SERVE WITH THEE FOR RACHEL?

Jacob's first meeting with Rachel was in chapter 29. He discovered that she was a relative of his and, fittingly, greeted her with a kiss. He was, as he said, her father's 'brother'. Brothers should love each other, but it was sibling rivalry which had driven Jacob away from home.

Laban welcomed him to his home, gave him a month's probation, and then explained that it would be improper for him to continue working without pay. In effect, he would be happy to use his skills, but there was no question of his ever inheriting anything.

When Laban asked him what wages he wanted, he said he would serve him for seven years for the hand of Rachel, his younger daughter. Laban seemed to agree, though his words were rather vague for a business agreement. Jacob's terms, to serve for seven years, were generous, for he loved Rachel, as perhaps he never loved anyone else. So he was disposed to be, in this instance, uncharacteristically generous.

The years flew past because of his love. Do the words, that they 'seemed to him but a few days', recall Rebekah's words to him about the duration of his exile? We note in passing that Isaac's blessing had included the words, 'Let people(s) serve thee', but at this point it was Jacob who was the servant.

The time for the wedding came – it seems that Jacob had to remind Laban of the fact. The wedding ceremony seemed to go well. The bride was provided with her personal handmaid. There was just one problem: morning disclosed that it was the wrong bride! Custom forbade, said Laban, to marry the younger daughter first. Custom was the excuse to cheat Jacob, just as Jacob the younger brother had cheated the older. Jacob had begun to reap what he sowed. Laban suggested that Jacob could serve a second seven years, for Rachel this time.

Jacob's education was bringing him into stressful, tangled family situations, not of his making. He had rival wives, their handmaidens, and their offspring. There was barrenness, jealousy, and impatience. Added to all this, Laban dealt with him crookedly regarding wages. What a reaping all this was!

January 16th

Genesis 32. 22-32

WHAT IS THY NAME? AND HE SAID, 'JACOB'

God had encouraged Jacob with a dream at Bethel as he fled from Esau. After his years in God's school at Laban's house, God, speaking as the God of Bethel, told him to return. When he reached Mahanaim, God encouraged him again with the knowledge that he had an angelic host on his side.

Now, in chapter 32, the meeting with Esau, which Jacob must face, was imminent. Jacob had made progress, for he acknowledged that it was God's protection which saved him from Laban's guile, 31. 5, 7. But the meeting with Esau was the crucial test of God's presence with him, so God granted him an experience in preparation for that meeting. He sent placatory presents to Esau and was left alone at the Jabbok. A stranger approached him and wrestled with him through the night. As the struggle continued, Jacob realized that this was not just a man. He said finally that he had that night 'seen the face of God': it was 'the Angel of the Presence'.

Now Jacob struggled so valiantly that the heavenly Challenger could not subdue him. This must mean that to subdue Jacob would involve destroying him, and God had no intention of doing this. What God could do was convince Jacob that he could not by strength force God's hand. By putting his thigh, the seat of his strength, out of joint, God showed Jacob that He had power beyond that of any human combatant. Jacob's thinking is made clear in his words, 'I will not let thee go, except thou bless me'. This was an opportunity to gain a blessing to strengthen him for the imminent meeting with Esau.

The Angel asked, 'What is thy name?' This was the nub of the issue between Jacob and Esau, the identity of Jacob: Isaac could be deceived, but not God. Jacob wisely said, 'Jacob', and he received a new name, 'Israel' – a kind of celebration. We note that he did not get the blessing by defeating the Angel or by cunning. He could only *cling*. God blesses men through His grace, not for their superior strength, or cleverness, or holiness.

We do not put God under pressure to bless us by the earnestness of our prayers. He desires the best for us and we can, in our weakness, cling with confidence to Him.

January 17th

Genesis 37. 5-11

WHAT IS THIS DREAM?

No sooner does the extended narrative of Joseph's life appear in scripture than we see conflict immediately arise from his brethren. Loved by his father and highly favoured, Joseph incurred their disdain, who 'hated him and could not speak peaceably unto him', v. 4, a fitting picture of the One who came unto His own and His own received Him not. Joseph's first dream – drawn from the world of agriculture – angered his brothers who rejected the message and the obvious implication that it portrayed. The second dream – drawn from the world of astronomy – did much of the same, implying the whole family's submission as it depicted the sun, moon and stars also bowing down to him. Not only did it infuriate his brethren even more, but it also evoked the incredulous response and firm rebuke from his father. Certainly, it was beyond Jacob's understanding. Equally, it was beyond his brothers' thinking that Joseph would rise to such heights, as time would inevitably prove, Gen. 41. They envied him, but Jacob 'observed the saying', v. 11. He had come to know through personal experience that the Almighty God is sovereign and capable of accomplishing that which is beyond human comprehension and ordinary means.

How accurately the events of Joseph's early life portray that of our Lord Jesus! The One from whom the whole family in heaven and earth is named, and to whom many have already bowed the knee, will have a kingdom whose 'dominion will be from sea to sea', Zech. 9. 10. It will be a kingdom in which all will unhesitatingly bow to Him in acknowledgement of His divinely-prophesied rule. Though the well-beloved Son, He too is despised and rejected and that without cause. Collectively, humanity in general, and the nation in particular, have hidden their faces from Him, esteeming Him not and defiantly proclaiming, 'We will not have this man to reign over us'. Yet, there will come the day in which God's words will surely come to pass as they did with Joseph, but not before the deep-seated hatred and envy of His brethren are clearly addressed and resolved, so that those who rejected Him at first will be reconciled to Him at last to come under His beneficent rule.

January 18th

Genesis 37. 18-28

WHAT PROFIT IS IT IF WE SLAY OUR BROTHER?

These words of Judah, along with Reuben's, Gen. 37. 21, were the lone voices of 'reason' amidst the treachery of Joseph's brethren who conspired to slay him. Despite being sent by his father to determine the welfare of his brethren and his willing obedience to do so, vv. 13-14, the favoured son of Jacob met with only hatred and harsh treatment. Stripped of the garments and the coat that had evoked such jealousy, Joseph's brothers cast him into a pit and then sat down to eat a meal, vv. 23-25. Strange callousness among those of his own family! Yet hatred of this sort continues today and demonstrates the depravity of the human heart. Selling him to the Ishmaelites, they carried out their nefarious scheme to the full extent, sealing their deeds by concocting a plausible explanation to deceive their father, who suffered sorely at the distressing news, v. 34. It was the ultimate irony for Jacob who, some time before, duped his own father in a similar manner. The lesson is clear, 'what goes around comes around'. In the language of scripture, 'Be sure your sin will find you out', Num. 32. 23.

It was hypocrisy of the cruellest kind that Joseph's brothers arose to comfort their grieving father when all along their dulled consciences surely spoke to them of their actions. Yet, so deep was their hatred for Joseph that they continued with apparently no sense of guilt at all. How true the scripture, 'The heart is deceitful above all things, and desperately wicked: who can know it?' Jer. 17. 9. Indeed, it is! Tragic, that the heart of man is so vile in its imaginations and so deceitful in its operations – and apart from grace, hopelessly alienated from the life of God. Yet, by God's sovereign hand, Joseph's life was providentially spared to be reconciled in a future day to these same brethren. Not so with our Saviour, whom God spared not, but delivered Him up for us all, Rom. 8. 32, including those who sat down at Calvary and kept watch over Him there, Matt. 27. 36. This same favoured Son of the Father, sent to seek the welfare of His brethren, also met with harsh cruelty, was 'stripped' in humiliation, Isa. 53. 5, and dismissed. In spite of this, a penitent Israel will come to Him in the future, Zech. 12. 10.

January 19th

Genesis 39. 1-21

HOW CAN I DO THIS GREAT WICKEDNESS?

Brought to Egypt by Midianite traders, Joseph was immediately sold to Potiphar, Pharaoh's officer and captain of the guard, Gen. 37. 36. It would not be long, however, before the quality of Joseph's character would be manifest. Evidently the Lord was with him; Joseph was given great authority by his master in whose eyes he found favour and who prospered through Joseph's faithful stewardship. All was entrusted entirely to his care so that Potiphar took no account of that which was in his house, 39. 1-6. The demonstration of Joseph's commitment to Potiphar, and his faithfulness to God, would now be tested in another sphere. The faithful life will eventually be challenged, if not assaulted. Joseph would come to find favour of a different sort from Potiphar's wife, who cast longing glances at the handsome servant in her household. His refusal to yield to her amorous advances not only demonstrated faithfulness to his master Potiphar, but more importantly toward a greater Master, 'How can I do this great wickedness and sin against God?' Any sin is wickedness against God, but sin of this magnitude is particularly damaging and difficult to overcome. David the psalmist said, in regard to his adultery with Bathsheba, 'Against thee, thee only have I sinned and done this evil in thy sight', Ps. 51. 4. Sin, though unseen by the eye of man, is still witnessed by the eyes of God with whom we have to do. Potiphar might never have known about it, but Joseph knew that God did and the very thought of disobedience to the Lord was utterly abhorrent to him, despite the ill-treatment he received from his brethren. He of all people could have acted foolishly as a victim of a root of bitterness, but not so. Despite the negative turn of events in his life and the false allegations against him, Joseph maintained his personal integrity and godly convictions, which would later prove invaluable and underscore the faithfulness of God in honouring him – another example of how Joseph's life typifies that of our Saviour.

What a challenge and what an opportunity to glorify our God and reap great reward! 'Cast not away therefore your confidence, which hath great recompense of reward', Heb. 10. 35.

January 20th

Genesis 40. 5-19

DO NOT INTERPRETATIONS BELONG TO GOD?

Now in prison through the false accusations of Potiphar's wife, Joseph had yet another opportunity to prove the quality of his character and his devotedness to the Lord. As with Potiphar, Joseph incurred the favour of his superior, this time the keeper of the prison, who entrusted to him the care of his fellow prisoners. Faithfulness in private life often, though not always, opens the door of opportunity in other spheres. It is clear testimony to the unseen hand of God, working both to will and to do of His good pleasure, Phil. 2. 13, and ruling in the affairs of man, even from a lowly prison house. Then, in time, Pharaoh's chief butler and baker were also imprisoned, providentially coming under the charge of Joseph. Both were distressed over the dreams they had during the same night, which was reflected in their sad countenances. Inquiring about their sorrow, Joseph was told by both that they had no interpreter, to which he responded, 'Do not interpretations belong to God, tell me them, I pray thee'. Such is the sentiment and conviction of every true servant of the Lord: giving glory to his God while at the same time making himself available to serve others. The apostle Paul stated the principle similarly, 'What hast thou that thou didst not receive?', 1 Cor. 4. 7. It is the understanding and conviction of those who will genuinely be used of the Lord to truly make a difference in this world that one acknowledges the gifts and abilities that he possesses are from the grace received for service, Rom. 12. 3, and the ability which God gives, 1 Pet. 4. 10-11. Joseph affirmed this not only in his attitude as accepting his lot but also with his words, as he was faithful to declare the whole counsel of God to the baker and butler. To the one, it was a positive interpretation, Gen. 40. 13; to the other, a negative. Both had come from God, and the faithful steward and servant was obliged to deliver the message as he had received it from the Lord, despite its implications. Again, the apostle Paul reminds us, 'Moreover it is required in stewards, that a man be found faithful', 1 Cor. 4. 2. For Joseph, it proved to be true in his life. For every believer in Christ, it should also prove true, no matter what our situation may be.

January 21st

Genesis 50. 15-21

FEAR NOT: FOR AM I IN THE PLACE OF GOD?

A more poignant scene in the narrative of Joseph there could not be, save when Joseph made himself known to his brethren after his absence of many years, Gen. 45. 3. Their fear was understandable, the hateful attitude and ill-treatment meted out years before, the hardened indifference and complacency, the cover-up of their sordid deed to their father. All these memories and more flooded their now awakened consciences, prompting them to unitedly fall down and request forgiveness from the one they had treated so harshly. Joseph's answer is remarkable, 'Fear not: for am I in the place of God?' Joseph reassured them that it was not his prerogative to act in the place of God. Fear certainly was at the core of their concern. But it was not for him to repay evil for evil, nor to exact vengeance for their misdeeds done to him since that right belonged exclusively to God, Rom. 12. 17-19. Consequently, from his standpoint, they had nothing to fear. How they had sorely underestimated the love of their brother, who to them had become their saviour. Rather, he comforted them and spoke kindly to them, reminding them of the work of God on their behalf, despite the difficult experience he had gone through. All had worked together for their good, Rom. 8. 28, and produced a far more exceeding and eternal weight of glory, 2 Cor. 4. 17, as it does for all those who through faith and patience inherit the promises.

Their repentance was the necessary ingredient for the forgiveness extended to them and a pattern of the type of sorrow required to be reconciled to the Saviour, whose love is even greater. In contrast to Joseph, He is in the place of God and there is no restraint to His hand to act in judgement. Yet, in love, He readily extends it to those who acknowledge their guilt, speaking words of kindness and comfort to those who dealt so cruelly with Him. It is also a fitting picture of the remnant of Israel who having gone through the Tribulation will look upon Him whom they have pierced and mourn for Him, Zech. 12. 10. Only then will they be able to comprehend the measureless dimensions of the love of Christ in its all breadth, length, depth, and height, Eph. 3. 18. Amazing love!

January 22nd

Exodus 1. 8-21

WHY HAVE YE DONE THIS THING?

Firmly established in Egypt, the children of Israel had now become exceedingly prosperous, Joseph's lowly path having paved the way for the nation's later blessing and abundance. However, drawing the attention of a new king in Egypt, they soon found themselves under the stinging lash of the king's taskmasters, as Pharaoh dealt shrewdly with them in an effort to thwart their national progress, Exod. 1. 6-12. But the more he afflicted them, the more they grew, proving that persecution can have a positive effect upon God's people, Acts 8. 4. When it was decreed to kill all Hebrew males as a further strategy to suppress Israel, the Hebrew midwives, fearing God and not the king, rejected his command. The king's query was, 'Why have ye done this thing and saved the male children alive?'

The actions of the midwives is the hallmark of all those who share the same deep-seated faith. It rejects the decrees of man when in contradiction to the laws of God. When Peter and the other apostles were staring at the prospect of persecution from the Jerusalem Council they boldly declared, 'We ought to obey God, rather than men', Acts 5. 29. Whether it is with Israel in Egypt, or Daniel in Babylon, or the church in the last days, the godless laws of man and society progressively mount up to intimidate the people of God in their testimony for Him. The attempt of the world's governmental policies will, as then, be contrived to impede the progress of His people, if not to silence their voice altogether.

Like Moses' parents, the Hebrew midwives were not afraid of the king's commandment, Heb. 11. 23. As a result, God dealt well with them and provided for them households, Exod. 1. 20-21. Count on it – faith and obedience bring their rewards, one way or another, from the storehouse of God. Moses would also be spared the intended fate, to grow up to be the deliverer of his people.

Prophetically, the whole scene prefigures the wrath of the dragon at work to devour the Messiah upon His birth, Matt. 2. 16; Rev. 12. 4, and the divine protection of Him who will, in a future day, be both the Saviour and Deliverer of His people.

January 23rd

Exodus 2. 11-15

WHO MADE THEE A PRINCE AND A JUDGE?

These sarcastic words, uttered against Moses by one of the two quarrelling Hebrews, demonstrated the dilemma that faced this future leader. Despite being adopted by Pharaoh's daughter and raised in the opulence of the king's courts, Moses' inclination was nevertheless toward his brethren whom he sought to defend in one instance and mediate for in another. Identified as the perpetrator of a crime against the Egyptian the day before, Moses became frightened and later fled when he learned that the news of this had reached the ears of Pharaoh, Exod. 2. 14-15. He was compelled to run from the consequences of his well-meaning, but impulsive actions. He had attempted to cover up his crime, but soon learned to his utter dismay that he had been found out. The sentiment to defend his brethren might have been admirable, but the impulsive action was not, as he trusted in the arm of the flesh to achieve his goals. The misunderstanding received from among his own made matters worse, heightening his distress. How quickly our misdeeds are observed, pointed out to us, and made known to others! What hard lessons to learn! Yet, it would become another turning point in his life as his steps would lead him to the backside of the desert and continued training in the life of faith and the ways of God. Later, when the daughters of the priest of Midian were driven away by shepherds, Moses would once again stand up to defend them and help them by watering their flocks, v. 17. The unfolding of these events would eventually lead to his marriage with Zipporah and the birth of Gershom, who was so named by Moses who confessed, 'I am a stranger in a strange land', v. 22. It was verification that he esteemed the reproach of Christ greater riches than the treasures of Egypt, Heb. 11. 26, and a reminder of the adage, 'Failure can be the backdoor to success'. This episode in Moses' life, along with the debacle in Egypt, was both part and parcel of the Lord's personal cultivation of the life of His servant to prepare him for the greater task yet to come. He would defend and provide for an even larger flock in the wilderness, as eventually he would lead them to the brink of the Promised Land.

January 24th

Exodus 3. 1-12

WHO AM I THAT I SHOULD GO UNTO PHARAOH?

'Who am I?' is often the question asked by any true servant when contemplating his abilities for the service of the Lord; Moses was no exception. His experience in Egypt defending the people of God was both an inauspicious start and a sore reminder of his personal inadequacy in managing the issues that confronted him. Plainly, he was not equipped to deal with the pressures of leadership and the inevitable criticism that ensued, Exod. 2. 14. Yet God had another plan for His man Moses, whom He sent to the backside of the desert for forty years. The road to effectual service often leads down before it leads up. David understood this, 1 Sam. 17. 17, as did the great prophet Elijah, 1 Kgs. 17. 1ff. The apostle Paul substantiated this principle, Gal. 2. 1, and the Lord Jesus wonderfully exemplified it in His humiliation and exaltation, establishing the pattern for us, Phil. 2. 5-11; Jas. 4. 10.

Moses had undoubtedly learned many valuable lessons during this stage of his life and would learn many more. It stood in stark contrast to the lavish confines of Pharaoh's courts, hardly the place to glean the valuable lessons of life and of God. Though there would be more to his spiritual development, God had determined that it was sufficient to launch His servant into a new sphere of ministry. It represented yet another significant turning point in the life of this future deliverer of Israel whose humble occupation as a shepherd served as a prerequisite. God stated His past work, reminding Moses concisely, 'I have seen', 'I know', 'I have come down to deliver'. But Moses objected to the call with an 'I' of his own – 'Who am I?', questioning his own confidence and the validity of God's choice of him. But man's inadequacy only accentuates the sufficiency of God, 2 Cor. 12. 9. The Lord counters His wavering servant saying, 'I will certainly be with you', Exod. 3. 12. These are reassuring words that form the basis of useful service necessary to dispel all doubt. Yet Moses would need further convincing, but that did not stop the Lord placing His hand upon him. Neither should our doubts disable us from stepping out in faith when the Lord calls us to do some deed for Him, whether great or small.

January 25th

Exodus 4. 10-16

WHO HATH MADE MAN'S MOUTH?

This statement by the Lord to Moses was to refute his second objection against the call of God in his life. The first focused on the doubt and unbelief of the people; the second, on doubt and unbelief regarding himself. One dealt with the matter of authority, the other with the matter of ability. Three parts of Moses' person were consecrated: his hand, his heart, and his mouth, Exod. 4. 2, 6, 11. Issuing out of his experience at the burning bush, it would precede God's final word to him in dismissing each of his objections. Claiming that the people would question whether the Lord had appeared to him, v. 1, Moses was initially asked what was in his hand. When he responded, 'A rod', he was instructed to cast it to the ground, whereby it became a snake, a powerful symbol in Egypt. Taking it by the tail, Moses portrayed the power of God in transforming the instruments of a believer's livelihood for the glory of God. No surprise that what was called 'a rod', would later be called *'the* rod of God', v. 20; 17. 9. That which is ordinarily held in the hand and used for one's own purposes can and should be used for His. Otherwise, it is shown for what it is apart from the Lord – a dangerous 'serpent'. The same would be true with the next sign. When told to place his hand in his bosom, it became leprous, 4. 6. Even Moses' actions symbolized by his hands could spring from an unclean source symbolized by his bosom. But with God's grace, the heart can be renewed and restored, v. 7, and useful to Him. Both signs, along with the third sign of Nile water turning to blood, v. 9, would convey to the nation that Moses had been personally commissioned by the Lord and given authority to act on His behalf.

The last objection, however, concerned his lack of confidence and eloquence. The solitude of the past forty years no doubt contributed to this aversion to the public spotlight. When he complained that he was slow of speech, he was starkly reminded, 'Who hath made man's mouth?' v. 11. God can, and always will, enable His people to do the impossible, proving that His grace is sufficient despite weakness, as Moses would prove, 8. 9, 26, 29, and Stephen would affirm, Acts 7. 27.

January 26th

Exodus 5. 1-9

WHO IS THE LORD, THAT I SHOULD OBEY HIS VOICE?

The question of Pharaoh is ultimately the question of man in every generation. It highlights the defiance of the creature toward his Creator; the attitude of feeble man to Almighty God. What foolishness! To the one enlightened by mercy and grace, it is indeed folly, the evidence of the ignorance and sinfulness of man, accentuated by an air of arrogance and boastful independence. Despite God's obvious claims, mankind, like Pharaoh, persists, opposed to Him and unaware of His power, to his own demise. For Pharaoh, it occurred after Moses returned to Egypt following a forty-year absence. Now, equipped and empowered by God, Moses, along with Aaron, returns to the courts of Pharaoh, albeit with a different approach, fearlessly demanding that the king let God's people go. The years of obscurity in the desert had not lessened his desire to serve God's people, nor had it robbed him of the opportunity to do so again. The years spent learning lessons in the school of faith are never wasted time. Standing before the king, Moses declares God's demands and makes them plainly known. But it is not met without resistance by him who also represents the god of this world, who contests the release of any under his control. For Israel, it resulted in further distress to them as a nation as they suffered under the wrath of the king, an ominous foreshadowing of the time of Jacob's sorrow when they will experience severe persecution, Jer. 30. 7, under the reign of Antichrist. What sufferings Jerusalem (and all Israel) must go through in order to obtain the peace for which they were named!

Pharaoh's attitude typifies the heart of man as well as the nations who are so opposed to God's plan. Yet, pondering our past life outside of Christ, it can be said, 'And such were some of you!' 1 Cor. 6. 11. We too were dead, deceived, depraved, and disobedient, and the children of wrath even as others, Eph. 2. 1-3. The same words were upon our lips, 'Who is the Lord that I should obey His voice?' But God, who is rich in mercy, reversed our direction through His great love, so that we who once were so defiant, now come with hearts ready to obey.

January 27th

Exodus 6. 26-30

HOW SHALL PHARAOH HEARKEN UNTO ME?

Having been unsuccessful in his initial encounter with Pharaoh, Moses returned to voice his complaint before the Lord, Exod. 5. 22-23. He had expected events to turn out far differently than they had. To make matters worse, not only had Pharaoh rebuffed the command of Moses and Aaron, but he also intensified his persecution of Israel, which deepened Moses' own frustration and self-doubt. It would necessitate a second encounter with this formidable opponent, but not before the Lord would again deal with His inexperienced and wavering servant.

With firm, but reassuring words, God declared to Moses that Pharaoh would be compelled by the hand of the Lord to let His people go and drive them out of the land, 6. 1. Pharaoh's contesting of God's ways, though strong at first would be short-lived, as the Lord would later accomplish His purpose, proving that He can use the wrath of man to praise Him, while the remainder of wrath He will restrain, Ps. 76. 10. Foremost in His message to Moses is the phrase, 'I will', uttering it twice in verse 1 and seven times in verses 6-8. The words left no room for doubt and no reason for argument. Additionally, the Name of the Lord was highlighted, which though it had been used previously, Gen. 13. 2, now took on special significance as the *covenant-keeping* God who always keeps His promises to His people, Exod. 6. 3-4. Regardless, the latent uncertainty that resided within Moses quickly emerged as Israel failed to heed his words, vv. 9, 12, further adding to Moses' distress and lack of confidence, v. 30. But his objections were overcome, yet again, as God reminded him that he was His ambassador to Pharaoh to speak all that was commanded of him, 7. 1-2.

So it is with us. We, who have been enabled by the Spirit and empowered by the Son, are to go into all the world to preach the gospel – sent at the Lord's command to declare what we have seen and heard, even in the face of opposition. As His ambassadors, we are to speak as the oracles of God, 1 Pet. 4. 11, boldly proclaiming the truth of God. Our own inadequacy or lack of support from others should never eclipse the powerful words of Him who says to us, and through us, 'I will'.

January 28th

Exodus 12. 21-27

WHAT MEAN YE BY THIS SERVICE?

The Lord had given clear instruction regarding the observance of the Passover: a specific month which would become the beginning of the year for them, Exod. 12. 2; a specific mandate directed to all the congregation of Israel, v. 3; a specific manner, an unblemished male lamb of the first year, killed at twilight and the blood applied, vv. 5-7. A clearer picture of the life and death of our blessed Saviour, there could not be! Provided for each man's need, v. 4, the 'whole assembly' was responsible for His death, Luke 23. What could conjure up in the mind of the Christian and stir the heart even more than seeing in this event, a picture of the defenceless Lamb of God, giving His life a ransom for many? What a sight and what a Saviour!

But what value would the Passover be, apart from one generation, if it were not passed on to the next? When Moses explained to the elders of Israel their responsibilities, he reminded them to diligently observe and keep this ordinance, even after they had entered the land. It was to be a perpetual reminder of how the Lord had delivered them and brought them out with a high hand. When their children would inevitably ask the question, 'What mean ye by this service?', they were to respond by personally explaining the account of the Lord's dealings with them in the past, emphasizing His mercy in bringing them out of bondage, Exod. 12. 26-27. Each generation of believers is enjoined, in effect, to do the same. 'Christ, our Passover was sacrificed for us', Paul proclaimed, 1 Cor. 5. 7 NKJV. He is our Sacrifice, slain once for all and never to be repeated, perfecting forever them who are sanctified, Heb. 10. 12, 14. Nevertheless, this 'Passover' lives on in the hearts of His people, who week after week are reminded of His all-sufficient death, till He come, 1 Cor. 11. 26. His death, too, is 'according to each man's need' and commences a new calendar in the life of all those who apply the blood. But it does not stop there. What we have experienced by faith should never be withheld, 2 Kgs. 7. 9, from others or our offspring since, 'The promise is to you and to your children and to all who are afar off, as many as the Lord our God will call', Acts 2. 39 NKJV.

January 29th

Exodus 15. 1-18

WHO IS LIKE UNTO THEE O LORD AMONG THE GODS?

The song of Moses followed subsequently by the song of Miriam, Exod. 15. 20-21, attested the Lord's mighty work in the midst of His people. Both were songs of praise, acknowledging victory through Him. Israel's deliverance in Egypt was past; this deliverance at the Red Sea was similar, yet different. The former was a powerful and glorious proof of their redemption, declaring that they were indeed God's special people through the provision of blood. This redemption was equally a powerful and glorious proof that they were His special people. But it would not occur through the shedding of blood, as it was at the Passover, but, instead, through the working of His strong hand. Four times God's 'right hand' is identified in bringing about the victory, vv. 6, 9, 12. His 'arm' is cited in verse 16. It was to show to them that as His redeemed people there would be a new dynamic in their experience as a nation – His mighty hand, outstretched for them. This truth stirred up their grateful response, prompting them to sing, 'Who is like unto Thee, O Lord, among the gods, glorious in holiness, fearful in praises, doing wonders?' v. 11.

The New Testament shines the spotlight upon the Old Testament type. As Moses did for Israel, so our Lord does for His people, leading us in triumph, 2 Cor. 2. 14, in the song of praise saying, 'I will declare thy name unto my brethren in the midst of the church will I sing praise unto thee', Heb. 2. 12. Rightly so, for He has also triumphed gloriously since 'having spoiled principalities and powers, he made a show of them openly, triumphing over them in it', Col. 2. 15. As redeemed Israel stood by the sea, hearing the words, 'Stand still and see the salvation of the Lord', Exod. 14. 13, so we also are challenged to allow the Lord to work on our behalf without our interference, in faith and in full obedience to His word. Not only are we called to 'stand still', but to 'be still', Ps. 46. 10, and 'sit still', Ruth 3. 18. By this we prove that we are His and He is ours, and begin to enter into a fuller apprehension of what is 'the exceeding greatness of his power to us-ward who believe according to the working of his mighty power', Eph. 1. 19.

January 30th

Exodus 17. 1-7

WHEREFORE DO YE TEMPT THE LORD?

Setting out 'according to the commandment of the Lord', Israel soon found themselves in dire straits as they came to Rephidim, a place where there was no water to drink, Exod. 17. 1-2. They contended with Moses and complained vociferously, expressing their discontent for having been led out of Egypt into the wilderness where they concluded they would perish. At this trying juncture, Egypt in the past looked much better to them than their present surroundings and they made their feelings known. How soon they had forgotten the affliction they had suffered at the hand of Pharaoh! Little did they realize also that the complaint to their leader was actually a complaint against the Lord for leading them there. Even so, the Lord accommodated their request by instructing Moses to strike the rock at Horeb, which sustained them for the time. It is a tremendous picture of that Rock which is Christ, 1 Cor. 10. 4, providing living water to those who hardly deserve it!

It was yet another trial for the nation which had been tested previously with a similar experience prior to arriving at Marah, Exod. 15. 22. Their pathway then, as here, was plainly in the will of God, but their response clearly was not. Their disdain for their present situation only revealed their deep need to know better the One who had promised to 'bring them out that he might bring them in' to their inheritance in Canaan, Deut. 6. 23. As Moses would later explain, their sojourn in the wilderness was to humble and prove them in order to know what was in their heart, 8. 2. Their difficulties had in fact clouded their minds and caused them to forget what lay ahead.

'If thou faint in the day of adversity, thy strength is small', warned Solomon, Prov. 24. 10. The trying of our faith as James explains is to be welcomed and counted all joy that it might work in bringing about a faith that is perfect and entire, Jas. 1. 4, that brings glory to God and conforms us to the image of His Son, Rom. 8. 29. Our complaint under trial does indeed reveal to us all that is in our hearts, so that the necessary adjustments can be made to sharpen our focus on things future and the inheritance that is reserved for us in heaven, 1 Pet. 1. 4.

January 31st

Exodus 32. 25-29

WHO IS ON THE LORD'S SIDE?

This question by Moses drew a line in the sand for the erring nation, Exod. 32. 26. No sooner had Moses returned from the mount where he had been for forty days, than he witnessed rank departure by the company whom God had wonderfully and powerfully redeemed from the land of Egypt. Yet the idolatry of that country had apparently lingered with them as they bowed to the calf Aaron had fashioned at their bidding, vv. 2-4. Evidently the wait was so long, and the temptation so strong, that they chose to replace the worship of the true God with that of a four-footed beast and assign to it the source of their glorious deliverance, v. 4. Amazing! It was only Moses' intercession that prevented God's hand of judgement from coming down upon the woeful scene. Yet it proved too much even for him as he smashed the tablets containing the commandments and served Israel an ultimatum to show their allegiance.

Sadly, Moses' absence on the mountain manifested the tie they still had to the things of this world. The subsequent pressure that Israel put upon Aaron and his pitiful capitulation only catered to their fleshly appetites. It speaks all too well of the latent evidences of 'Egypt' that are resident within us, waiting to be stirred up when certain conditions prevail – and they will. It is a fair warning to mortify the deeds of the flesh, Col. 3. 5, and to lay aside all filthiness of the flesh, the overflow of the old life that dies hard, Jas. 1. 21. Sin lies at the door and waits for every opportunity to spring up and mar the testimony and to bring reproach upon the work of God.

It is sad that it can be so in the life of the redeemed who are new creatures in Christ; sadder still that it should characterize the church of God, 'which he has purchased with the blood of his own', Acts 20. 28 JND. Even sadder is the picture that it presents of the widespread departure and apostasy that will be extant at the Lord's return and afterwards, answering the question, 'When the son of man cometh shall he find faith on the earth?' Luke 18. 8. But commitment has its rewards, as the Levites would discover, Exod. 32. 28, and those also who maintain single-mindedness as they wait for the Lord's return.

February 1st

Numbers 16. 1-11

SEEK YE THE PRIESTHOOD ALSO?

This question, asked by Moses of Korah and the sons of Levi, was posed on a dark day in the history of the nation. The end result of the sins of this chapter was catastrophe. Three men, Korah, Dathan, and Abiram, were swallowed alive into the pit, with all of their families accompanying them. Two hundred and fifty would-be priests were burned alive by the fire of the Lord. The resultant plague that swept the camp, because of the wrath of the Lord, caused the death of another fourteen thousand seven hundred people.

It all began with discontent in hearts against the Lord, and then pride – wanting a place that was not given them from on high. Korah and those with him spoke against the Lord, and against Moses and Aaron. Questioning their authority, they essentially demanded the priesthood. Their act of rebellion demanded what the Lord had neither fitted nor chosen them for.

The Lord created, by Moses' decree, a 'new thing', and opened the earth to swallow the guilty out of sight. But Moses and Aaron interceded for the entire congregation and their intercession saved many other lives that day.

The lessons here for our consideration are several. We must never seek place or position beyond that for which the Lord has fitted and enabled us. His way is perfect, 2 Sam. 22. 31, and His ways are not our ways, Isa. 55. 8. Further, in God's assembly, rebellion against those the Lord has placed in authority is never warranted or approved by the Lord. Rebellion may be the very spirit of the day in which we live, but it is *never* God's way.

We are a 'kingdom of priests', Rev. 1. 5-6, and a 'holy priesthood, to offer up spiritual sacrifices acceptable to God through Jesus Christ', 1 Pet. 2. 5. What Korah and his fellow-rebels wanted and could never have under the law, what they died trying to gain, we now enjoy as a gift through grace. What a place! What a position! Let us never take lightly these offices we have, purchased by the blood of Calvary's Lamb. As believers, we can enter His presence unafraid, bidden to come, invited to stay, because of the finished work of the Saviour. May we never take this for granted!

February 2nd

Numbers 20. 2-13

HEAR NOW YE REBELS; MUST WE FETCH YOU WATER OUT OF THIS ROCK?

The need for water was a perennial issue during the years in the wilderness. The Lord met Israel's need numerous times. Here, they again murmured against the Lord, contending with Moses and Aaron. The two sought the Lord, and His glory shone before them. The Lord told them that the rod, familiar to the people, and used by Moses as directed by the Lord, was to be used again. Moses was to speak to the rock, and God would provide them water.

Moses led the people to the rock, but in the emotion of the moment, instead of speaking to the rock, he angrily asked them the above question. Then he lifted the rod and smote the rock twice. The grace of God allowed water to flow to a needy people, but the damage was done.

The Lord immediately spoke to both men, and told them that not only had they disbelieved Him, they had failed to treat Him as holy before the people. Their punishment was that their leadership would not be used in securing the land of Canaan.

By calling the people 'rebels', Moses joined in their rebellion, Num. 27. 14. He disobeyed the Lord, and failed to hallow the Lord before the people. Part of his sin was that he struck the rock twice; in Horeb, Exod. 17. 1-7, and again in error here. Considering the Rock as a type of Christ, Moses spoiled the type by striking it twice. God only ever planned to 'strike the Rock' once, as His judgement against man's sin would only require the Saviour to go to Calvary once.

Our lessons here are important. Total obedience to the word of the Lord is mandatory. Many years of faithfulness to God can be undone by one incident in which we act in arrogance and self-centeredness. Though Moses led Israel for some time after this, his future was sealed by this question, and what he did in the moments after. The Lord took him up to Mount Nebo, and showed him the glories of Canaan shortly before he died. But He could not go back on His word. One unguarded moment could ruin years of testimony. May God give us grace each moment to simply obey Him!

February 3rd

Numbers 23. 1-12; Deuteronomy 23. 5

WHAT HAST THOU DONE UNTO ME?

Balaam is one of the great enigmas of the Bible. A false prophet, Balaam was slain with the enemies of Israel, Num. 31. 8. He was hired by them to bring a curse against God's people. Divine providence overruled in several remarkable ways and, in the end, Balaam understood clearly that he could never curse what God had blessed. He uttered a number of amazing statements about the purposes and power of the Lord; in fact, some of the more memorable words of the Old Testament came from this man.

The Midianites had arrayed themselves against Israel. Their leader, Balak, tried to get Balaam to curse Israel. But the more Balaam learned of this people and their God, the more he understood that he could never succeed. He gave four different orations, each of them declaring the greatness of God, as shown to, and through, His earthly people. He even offered forty-two animals in sacrifice, to honour the Lord.

During one of these offerings Balak angrily asked him this question. He accused Balaam of blessing the very people he had hired him to curse. Balaam answered him, 'Must I not take care to speak what the Lord puts in my mouth?' Num. 23. 12.

When we read Deuteronomy chapter 23 verse 5, we fully understand God's purposes through this man. Balaam's order was to curse God's people; the Lord turned it into a blessing. This parallels the words of Joseph to his brothers, 'Ye meant it unto me for evil, but God meant it for good', Gen. 50. 19.

Dear believer, your life may seem oppressed, and you may feel that you are being attacked by enemies on every side, but never lose hope in the providence of God. He who knows and understands the end from the beginning, has thoughts only of peace towards us. He has our best interests in His heart. He will not permit our enemies to overcome us, and will always undertake our cause. And most importantly, He can and will turn what we first perceive as a curse, into an amazing blessing.

Balaam apparently did not get his wish to 'die the death of the righteous'. But God will never allow His righteous people to be confounded.

February 4th

Deuteronomy 30. 11-20; Romans 10. 6-8

WHO SHALL GO UP FOR US TO HEAVEN, AND BRING IT UNTO US?

Here, Moses gives Israel the stark contrasts of life and death, blessing and cursing, and challenges them to make the right choice. He had been the mediator before God for the nation of Israel, repeatedly pleading with Him to spare a rebellious people. Now, nearing his own death, Moses sets before the people the rewards of obedience, and the sad consequences of further rebellion. He knew how often they had disobeyed, and he gave to them many wonderful promises from the Lord, *if* only they would obey.

But how would Israel obey without Moses there on their behalf? How could they be sure they were doing all God wanted of them? God's word was neither hidden to them, nor distant from them; not in heaven, nor in the depths of the sea. It was near to them – not just in their mouths to be mindlessly repeated; but in their hearts, so that they could easily obey. They could choose life and good, or death and evil.

What about the present day of grace? God still longs to dwell with, and within, His people. He has gone to the ultimate, in allowing men and women to put their faith in Him. God has, in amazing love, sent the very Word down to us in the incarnation. This is the essence of the gospel and from this very perspective Paul reasons, Rom. 10. Israel is now set aside as a nation for rejecting their Messiah. But Paul writes words of hope and promise, longing to see Israel saved. He quotes these words of Moses, but adds truth the Old Testament predicted, and the New Testament fulfilled. Any who might seek to scale heaven's heights, looking for the answer, would not need to do so to bring Christ down from on high. He had already come here.

Have we ever thanked the Lord that He allowed us to be born in the day of grace? We have never lived through the shadows that Israel had to. Instead of simply giving us His spoken word, He allowed His Son, the living Word, to come down to us, and go to a cross, bearing sin's curse, that we might be saved. And once saved, this Word comes to live within us. Amazing grace!

February 5th

Deuteronomy 32. 28-38

HOW SHOULD ONE CHASE A THOUSAND, EXCEPT THEIR ROCK HAD SOLD THEM?

The words of this song contain some of the last words of Moses. Shortly, the Lord gives him a glimpse of the Promised Land, forbidden to him because of his disobedience. This great leader was susceptible to sin, as was Israel as a nation. Yet, in this wonderful song of praise, poetry, prophecy, promise and power, he left for us some of the greatest words in scripture. Nine times in this song, Moses uses the word 'rock', a common Old Testament title of God.

Moses uses this metaphor to underscore this entire song. In context, these are words of warning, as Moses knew the people would become even more disobedient after his death. He reminded them repeatedly of God's faithfulness, and their repeated failure. Verse 4 actually starts with the title 'The Rock' – God is perfect, without iniquity, just, right, and a righteous Judge. In verse 15, he reminds Israel that while they considered themselves 'righteous', *Jeshurun*, they had actually forgotten the Rock of their salvation. Then, in verse 18, he chastises the people for being unmindful of the Rock that had begotten them, and forgetting the God who had formed them.

But it is when he contrasts Israel's Rock with whatever 'rock' the pagans called their gods, that the supremacy of the Lord of hosts is magnified to Israel. God had not yet sold or surrendered them as a nation, but He would let them suffer unimaginable defeats, due to rebellion and disobedience. Even then, Israel's Rock is greater than any pagan idol.

He is not only our everlasting Saviour, but also the very foundation upon which we stand. All around us is shifting sand. The ideas and doctrines of men are changing constantly, from generation to generation. But this unchanging Rock stands firm. The hymn-writer said it best, 'Often on the Rock I tremble – faint of heart, and weak of knee; But the mighty Rock of Ages never trembles under me'. He is still the unchanging God. Any foe could overpower us were He not the Rock of our salvation. 'He is the Rock, his work is perfect . . . just and right is he', Deut. 32. 4. Thank God we stand in Him!

February 6th

Joshua 5. 13-15; Exodus 3. 5

ART THOU FOR US, OR FOR OUR ADVERSARIES?

Joshua was on holy ground, as the Lord, perhaps even the pre-incarnate Christ, appeared to him and empowered him as the new leader of Israel, for the imminent conquest of Jericho.

Joshua fell on his face and worshipped. What of our reverence for the Almighty God? Sadly, modern Christianity has become far too casual. In the Revelation, everyone who came face to face with the risen Lord fell on their faces before Him. Far too often, we do not show Him the respect and reverence He commands and deserves.

Joshua's question was a fair one. He was stirred by fear of the task before him as leader of Israel, and the apparition he was facing. The Lord's Messenger assured him that He was on Israel's side, and would fight for them.

'For us': Joshua would remember these words many times in the days ahead. Each time he faced an adversary, he would remember, 'The Lord is for us'. What strength; what comfort; what encouragement! For us today, these same two words still hold true.

Paul asks this question, 'If God be for us, who can be against us?' Rom. 8. 31. But he immediately links this great truth with the reason that God is on the side of the believer, in this day of grace, 'He spared not His own Son, but delivered Him up for us all'. For God to be for us, He had to be *against* His Son, as Christ suffered for sin on Calvary. In one of the great Messianic passages in the Old Testament, Jeremiah writes words which came fully true during Christ's suffering as sin-bearer, 'Surely against me he turns his hand again and again the whole day long', Lam. 3. 3 ESV. God is now 'for us', because, at Calvary, He turned His hand against the Lord Jesus.

In every situation we face, no matter the adversary, no matter how daunting the circumstances, God is for us. Why should this even be possible? Because He turned His hand against a lonely Man at Calvary, suffering there for our sins. What love, peace, and assurance! God is for us. He will never be against us, Jas. 1. 17. He will always be on our side, and will battle our adversaries with and for us. God is *for us*.

February 7th

Joshua 18. 1-10

HOW LONG ARE YE SLACK TO GO TO POSSESS THE LAND?

This question essentially introduces the second half of the book of Judges. The first half is summed up in the end of verse 1, 'the land lay subdued before them', ESV. Through many battles, God had fought with and for Israel, and had conquered their enemies for them. Here, the entire population of Israel gathered before the tabernacle, assembling at Shiloh. This is the first mention in scripture of Shiloh, which city was to be the central location for the people, once they had taken occupancy of Canaan. It would eventually be replaced by Jerusalem, which would play a central role in the rest of human history.

The land had been conquered. The obstacles had been removed, but seven tribes of Israel had yet to take possession of what the Lord had provided for them, through His mighty wonders. Joshua challenged them with this question.

We should be challenged by this question as well. The apostle Paul, summing up his life lived for the honour of his Saviour, addresses this question spiritually, 'Not that I have already obtained this or have already reached the goal; but I press on to make it my own, because Christ Jesus has made me his own. Beloved, I do not consider that I have made it my own; but this one thing I do: forgetting what lies behind and straining forward to what lies ahead, I press on toward the goal for the prize of the heavenly call of God in Christ Jesus', Phil. 3. 12-14 NRSV.

It had not always been so. The great apostle had, in today's terms, 'a lot of baggage', many things in his past that could drag him down. After all, he had been responsible for the deaths of many of the early Christians! How would each of us live with that past? But he did not let his past spoil his present. He looked ahead, and strained forward, with every ounce of his spiritual ability. His goal, his prize, was Christ.

Oh that we might go in for apprehending HIM! The more we learn of the manifold glories of the risen Saviour, the closer we will get to the prize God has in store for us.

February 8th

Judges 1. 1-7

WHO SHALL GO UP FOR US AGAINST THE CANAANITES FIRST, TO FIGHT AGAINST THEM?

This was the first recorded question asked of the Lord by Israel after the death of Joshua. After this courageous leader died, Israel went through a period of national decline and apostasy. The Book of Judges details this sad state of affairs, and describes it twice in this way, 'In those days there was no king in Israel, but every man did that which was right in his own eyes', Judg. 17. 6; 21. 25. The immediate answer to our question was 'the children of Judah'. As leaders, both civil and military, their exploits essentially set the stage for the performance of most of the judges that followed. While Judah and Simeon had some successes, they failed to rid Israel of some of its most nefarious enemies, 1. 19, 21. Their failure to completely eradicate the enemy led directly to the sad failure and apostasy of this era. Israel ended up joining themselves to the very people they were to destroy. As a result, God's truth was compromised and failure resulted.

Today, New Age philosophy has made men and women each their own 'god'. Thinking that they are accountable to themselves alone, mankind lives 'right in their own eyes'. We cannot live like them, nor even think like them! Satan's ways are not God's ways. Our enemies *must* be defeated. Sins that so easily beset us must be vanquished. We must gain control over them, with His help. We can leave none unconquered, for if we do, the seeds of failure are planted.

Believers have many clearly-stated commandments in the New Testament, and the Spirit of God wants them to be our guides for life. Our warfare is not physical, but spiritual. We are commanded to battle against 'the schemes of the devil', Eph. 6. 11 ESV. The whole armour of God is provided, for both offence and defence. There is nothing for the back of the warrior, as we are not to retreat in battle. We must face the foe, meet him and his evil devices head on, and be ruthless!

May God help us to say, as did Paul, 'I have fought a good fight, I have finished my course, I have kept the faith', 2 Tim. 4. 7! Oh that we might have complete victories, for His glory!

February 9th

Judges 6. 1-18

IF THE LORD BE WITH US, WHY THEN IS ALL THIS BEFALLEN US?

This question represents the first recorded words of Gideon. Israel had once again disobeyed God and the Lord had delivered them into the hands of the Midianites, who had overpowered them, and brought them low. An angel appeared to Gideon at the outset of his selection as a judge and deliverer of Israel.

The direct answer to this question was the deliberate sin of Israel. Sin always carries with it retribution from God. Even the Lord's people must remember this; it overtook the Corinthians, 1 Cor. 11. 27-33, and Ananias and Sapphira, Acts 5. 1-11.

But what of those who seek to live their lives in subjection and obedience to God, and who suffer untold heartache and sorrow? This was a repetitive theme of the psalmists, who saw the wicked prosper, while the godly endured calamity. The Lord is with us, but often 'all of this' has befallen us.

Most importantly, no believer can look at the lives of others, and pass judgement that the Lord is visiting them with trials because of their sin. This prerogative belongs only to God.

Sadness abounds because of sin that has touched the entire race, and indeed all of creation, Rom. 8. 18-23; 1 Pet. 5. 6-11. There is no guarantee that the lives of believers will be spared heartbreak and sorrow. But, as the Lord twice answered Gideon, the Lord will be with us. He will never leave us, nor forsake us.

But we enjoy a blessing neither Gideon nor Israel ever had. The favour of God came upon Gideon and others; but the grace of God *indwells* us. The very Godhead has taken up residence within us. This wonderful experience did not happen to any in the Old Testament.

The child of God can take comfort in these wonderful assurances. Not only is God for us, nothing can separate us from His love, Rom. 8. 31-39. He will be with us in every trial, 1 Cor. 10. 13. He knows exactly what we need, even before we pray, Matt. 6. 8. Our Great High Priest is able to sympathize with us, in any difficulty that we may pass through, Heb. 4. 14-16. Dear child of God, take courage! No matter what has befallen you, the Lord understands, and will never forsake His own!

February 10th

Judges 13. 15-25

WHY ASKEST THOU THUS AFTER MY NAME, SEEING IT IS SECRET?

During another period of Israel's apostasy, the Angel of the Lord appeared unto Manoah and his wife. This is yet another example of the Lord drawing near to His earthly people. He spoke to Moses from a burning bush. He led Israel by a pillar of fire, and a hovering cloud. He answered Job from a whirlwind. He spoke to Elijah in a still, small voice. He called the young boy Samuel four times, in the still of the night. And He often spoke to men and women, by appearing in angelic form.

In this account, during the dark days of the judges, the heavenly Messenger promised to this barren couple, a son. Samson would be consecrated to God, a Nazarite from the womb. He would become another judge, another brief hope to lead Israel through these days of declension and failure. Sadly, he himself would fail, as Israel so often did.

This visit troubled Manoah and his wife. They offered a sacrifice to the Lord at the request of the Angel, but thought that they would be struck dead for seeing God.

How would we have done, living in these times? An austere and awesome God, upon whom no one could look. No real opportunity to draw near, no closeness, no companionship. Manoah asked the Messenger His name, and was given the above response. His name was secret, too wonderful to understand, Judg. 13. 18 ESV.

But to us, in this day of grace, He has spoken finally, by His Son. Even before Christ came, His name was proclaimed, 'Jehovah the Saviour', 'Emmanuel' – God with us.

When considering all the ways chosen by the Lord to reveal Himself to Israel in the Old Testament, they pale into insignificance when compared to what He had in mind for His final act. He came to where we were, in the person of His only begotten Son. And the beauties in this One, in His many names and titles, bring to us hope, joy, peace, salvation, forgiveness, assurance, comfort, and spiritual stability. There is no longer a fear of His presence. Through the Lord Jesus, we are as near to God as He is. What wonders grace has wrought!

February 11th

Ruth 1. 1-14

TURN AGAIN, MY DAUGHTERS: WHY WILL YE GO WITH ME?

Naomi and her family had left a place of famine, to move to a place that seemed more prosperous and fruitful. But where they left, was where the Lord had placed them.

They had left Bethlehem, and had moved to Moab, to a people that did not follow the God of Israel. A move of only sixty miles brought real heartbreak. Her husband died; then, sometime later, both boys got married. What were the fears of her heart, as she beheld her boys, sons of Israel, marry daughters of Moab? But after another ten years, both boys died. Naomi was left without any of her men, in a strange foreign land, and now with two daughters-in-law who did not know her God.

Word from home spoke of food and plenty, and Naomi resolved to return. As she left, we can see her looking at the girls in grace and love, and asking them this question. She called them her 'daughters', for they had stayed with her after their husbands' deaths, and had grown close. Naomi hoped they could find husbands in the families of their people. In this most caring and selfless of questions, she entreated them, three times, to return. They wept together along that road that day.

Orpah decided to return to her people. But Ruth answered with words that will live forever. Naomi's spirit rose, as she heard this young woman of pagan origin, personally accept *her* God! And this may be one of the most memorable lessons of this lovely story. For over ten years, through unspeakable sadness and heartache, in a strange land, surrounded by people of other gods, Naomi had lived for her Lord. Her testimony in the home and family had been unshakeable. In times of great personal loss, she had never lost her faith in God. And none of this remarkable testimony had been lost on Ruth.

We never know who is looking, who is watching, who is listening. We are surrounded daily by those who know not our Lord Jesus. But if we can live as Naomi did, faithfully as in a foreign land, we will never need to ask a question like the one Naomi asked. Instead, we will be able to bring others 'home' with us.

February 12th

Ruth 1. 15-22

AND THEY SAID, IS THIS NAOMI?

The journey was almost ended; Bethlehem was in sight. Naomi and Ruth had travelled together from Moab, and a journey of almost ten days had given Naomi time to talk with Ruth, about her choice of trusting the God of Israel.

The men were in the fields, busy with the barley harvest. The women of the city were moved with great excitement at what they saw. One of their own, gone for years, was coming home, bringing someone with her. Perhaps they did not fully recognize her. Had the sorrows of the past affected Naomi's countenance? She answered, 'Call me not Naomi, call me Mara: for the Almighty hath dealt very bitterly with me'. Naomi had been changed from 'pleasant' to 'bitterness'. She wanted her name to reflect the discouragement of her heart. In two verses, she said four negative things about the Lord, and His dealings with her. Had her faith in God gone, her confidence in Him been shaken?

Actually, it would seem that despite her grief and loss, she still had an unshakeable trust in her God. After all, she *was* coming home. She *had* brought Ruth back with her. And she chose her return to coincide with the barley harvest. How much had the Lord told her of His plan to procure a kinsman-redeemer for Ruth? In her response, she called God *El Shaddai* – the Almighty. This was the God of all provision, who had been with her for all the years of sadness in a faraway land. Hers was a deeply rooted faith that could not be shaken. Even coming home in sorrow and bitterness she had not lost faith in the unchanging character and promises of God.

How well do we do in this regard? Most of us have not faced the tragedies Naomi faced; reverently stated, God forbid we ever should! But some of our dear fellow-saints have, and have been asked to pass through very deep waters. While these trials may change us in various ways, they should never change our faith in the God who never changes. He always has a plan, and He always knows what He is doing. He always has our best interests at heart, and His thoughts are always precious towards us. We must *always* trust Him.

February 13th

Ruth 2. 1-13

WHY HAVE I FOUND GRACE IN THINE EYES . . . SEEING I AM A STRANGER?

One of the most beautiful aspects of the Old Testament, often filled with the harsh demands and swift judgements of the law, are the many little pictures of grace, and this is one of the more lovely ones.

Ruth asked to glean in the fields of Boaz, a wealthy relative of Naomi's husband Elimelech. His name means 'man of valour'. Boaz noticed the young woman working in his fields, but had already learned her story; her kindness to Naomi, the desire of her heart to leave her homeland, come to Bethlehem, and live for the God of Israel. He kindly asked for her attention, then requested that she would glean only in his field. He asked her to stay with his younger women, promised that his young men would not touch her, and offered her his full protection. She fell down before him, owned her place as stranger, and asked, 'Why have I found grace in thine eyes?'

His answer to her was exceptional. He mentioned her exodus, her kindness to Naomi, and that she had chosen to trust alone in the God of Israel. At this moment, little could she have known that this kind man, extending his grace and favour to her, would one day make her his bride! But the greater miracle of this grace, would not be realized for centuries, for this young pagan woman would be named in the genealogy of the very One who would bring God's saving grace to a fallen world.

We too, as strangers, have been shown God's marvellous grace. The God of Israel is not only our God, but our 'heavenly Father'. The Kinsman-redeemer, who has purchased us as His bride, is His own dear Son. We've been afforded eternal protection and safety, through the finished work of the cross. We are not only able to find refuge beneath His wings; we are sheltered by the Saviour's precious blood. Far more than servants, we have been adopted into the very family of God.

As we consider this wonderful story of the grace of God extended to one so undeserving, may we pause, and thank Him again, for the wonderful grace of Jesus, truly greater than all our sins!

February 14th

Ruth 2. 14-23

AND HER MOTHER IN LAW SAID UNTO HER, WHERE HAST THOU GLEANED TODAY?

Where *have* we gleaned today? What have we read? What have we seen? Have we harvested more of the world, or more of the things of God? Naomi, with great love for Ruth, directed her to Boaz, who would not only become her kinsman-redeemer, but her husband. The fields of Boaz provided for Ruth protection and safety. His young men would protect her, and not harm her. There was work to occupy her time, and reward for her toil and labour. She had fed well, and had extra left over. What had been provided for her that first day in Boaz's fields was personally and specifically for her.

The lessons here are vital. What we allow our minds to feed upon becomes part of us, and will assuredly shape our character. It has been said that 'a man is never what he thinks he is: but what he thinks, he is', cp. Prov. 23. 7. The human mind is the devil's playground. Paul warns, 'Don't give the devil that sort of foothold', Eph. 4. 27 PHILLIPS. Have we done this by where we have gleaned today? Satan is always looking for ways to get an advantage over us, and he attacks our minds first. May we be always on guard against harvesting that which will pollute our minds, sadden our souls, and poison our characters.

This thought also applies to those in God's assemblies. Paul also tells us the assembly is 'God's tilled field', 1 Cor. 3. 9, a place bought for us by a greater Kinsman-redeemer. It is a place of provision, protection, and safety. In each assembly, the truth of God's word is to be guarded, defended, and kept. Christendom today is discarding the doctrines of the New Testament, desiring to unite all shades of opinion. It is important to understand that scriptural doctrines *do* set lines of demarcation and separation. Scriptural assemblies maintain their uniqueness to God by obeying the biblical doctrines. We must always be careful where we glean, and do nothing to weaken or compromise the truths of God. Satan's prime objective is to destabilize the testimony of God, including the assemblies. The 'dumbing down of doctrine' is one of his chief weapons. May we always jealously guard the truths of the faith!

February 15th

Ruth 3. 1-13

AND (BOAZ) SAID, 'WHO ART THOU?'

Once again the scene changes and Ruth is not now on the highway as in chapter 1, nor yet in the harvest field of chapter 2. She is now in the threshing floor, and it is night. Later, in the closing chapter, the events take place in the gate of the city; each succeeding location having its attendant and appropriate lessons.

Threshing floors, where wheat is separated from chaff, speak to us of times of trial and testing, when that which is of value is distinguished from that which is worthless. Add to this the night season where consciousness is intensified and in chapter 3 we are at a critical stage in the story of Ruth.

The events of this chapter should not be viewed in the context of Western society and culture but in the light of Leviticus chapter 25 and Deuteronomy chapter 25, the law concerning inheritance and the continuation of a family name. Naomi now sees the opportunity of putting that law to the test and thus providing security and prosperity for Ruth. In Naomi's mind there is only one man to whom she will turn; repeatedly she refers to him as 'the man', and, at the appropriate time, with all due preparations made and guidance given, Ruth enters the threshing floor. She comes softly, Ruth 3. 7, not that she was ashamed, but as the virtuous woman she was, not wishing to embarrass Boaz in any way, she takes her place at his feet. At midnight, Boaz turns in his sleep and is startled. One of those disturbed nights in scripture with important consequences, cp. Esther 6. 1ff. Almost involuntarily the question is asked, 'Who art thou?' Ruth's reply is precious, as she clearly makes known her desire. 'I am Ruth thine handmaid (lit. 'bondslave'): spread therefore thy skirt (thy wings) . . . thou art a near kinsman (a redeemer)'. Boaz must have rejoiced to hear Ruth's voice! This was not a one-sided attraction, Boaz had already made enquiry regarding Ruth and made provision for her in chapter 2. He had also established where he stood in the line of responsibility in anticipation of this moment, Ruth 3. 12. Now he could legitimately bring the law to bear on the situation in order to claim his bride. As Naomi perceptively observed, 'The man will not be in rest, until he have finished the thing this day, v. 18.

February 16th

1 Samuel 1. 1-11

THEN SAID ELKANAH HER HUSBAND TO HER, 'HANNAH, WHY WEEPEST THOU?'

As we move from Ruth into 1 Samuel it is important to remember that the moral conditions which prevail are largely those seen in the Book of Judges. 1 Samuel opens with a Levite practising bigamy, a priest who is seated, a barren woman, a faltering lamp of testimony and the word of the Lord deemed 'precious' in view of its scarcity.

In such circumstances it is so encouraging to find a woman who in spite of her divinely-imposed barrenness, is burdened with the welfare of the people of God. It would be only natural to expect her desire to be for a child. Yet her prayers were not just for a child on which to bestow motherly affection, but for a man child whom she could dedicate to the Lord, that he might have a godly influence on the amorality of the nation.

Elkanah, although a Levite, did not appear to dwell in one of the cities allocated to his family, Josh. 20. However, he did seek to maintain a contact with the house of the Lord, the tabernacle, then situated at Shiloh, and it is in connection with one of these annual visits that we first read of Hannah's tears. Such was her distress that she refused to partake in the offerer's portion of the peace offering. She doubtless felt that as she had nothing to bring by way of sacrifice, and she was certainly not experiencing peace in her soul, to share in the sacrificial meal would be hypocritical. To Elkanah, the annual sacrifice was maybe little more than a ritual, but to Hannah it was a reality and she was prepared to give sacrificially if the Lord would provide.

Both Elkanah and Eli saw her tears, but neither saw her heart. The one offered sympathy, the other censure. Elkanah was concerned that she would not eat; Eli's concern was what he thought she had drunk! Only the Lord understood the weight of the burden she carried, His gracious heart responded and Samuel was born. How good to see that when Hannah had weaned her son she fulfilled her vow and brought him to the Lord! Now she has much to offer and, with her son and her sacrifice, she brings wine, a beautiful expression and outpouring of her joy!

February 17th

1 Samuel 3. 1-21

AND (ELI) SAID 'WHAT IS THE THING THAT THE LORD HATH SAID UNTO THEE?'

It would not be difficult to find reasons to be critical of Eli, the priest at Shiloh. There is no doubt that he withheld discipline from his sons, which in turn compromised his priestly duties. He also lacked discernment as he observed Hannah in prayer before God and thought she was drunk. However, before being too disparaging, we need to remember the days in which he lived and the situation in which he found himself.

The line of descent for the high priesthood was from Aaron through Eleazar. Somewhere, in the chaotic days of the Judges, appointments to this office had become confused and Eli was a descendant of Ithamar, Aaron's other son. The line did not revert back to the preferred order until the dismissal of Abiathar and the appointment of Zadok in the days of Solomon.

Responsibility had been thrust upon him and now, as an old man of ninety-eight years, he trod a lonely path, trying to retain some vestige of authority and piety amidst a backslidden people constantly prone to idolatry.

Eli saw in Samuel the son he would have loved as his own. In contrast to Hophni and Phineas who 'made themselves vile', Samuel 'ministered before the Lord'. Solemn warning came to Eli through a 'man of God', leaving him in no doubt that his leniency toward his sons would bear bitter fruits. It was, however, to Samuel that the Lord spoke directly.

It is quite touching to see the young lad who 'did not yet know the Lord', responding commendably to the three-fold call. Eli, on his part, realized that the Lord had passed him by, yet without bitterness he instructs Samuel how to reply with due reverence and obedience. The weight of the divine communication robbed Samuel of sleep as he 'lay until the morning', fearing to tell old Eli what the Lord had imparted to him. Eli, however, was already resigned to accepting the Lord's judgement upon his house and when his questioning of Samuel receives an answer there is something very creditable in his response, 'It is the Lord: let him do what seemeth him good'. Do we in turn bow to the Lord's authority in our lives and circumstances?

February 18th

1 Samuel 4. 12-22

WHAT MEANETH THE NOISE OF THIS TUMULT?

Some years had passed since the purposes of God had been made known to Samuel. It was now evident to all that the young man who had faithfully ministered before the Lord in Shiloh was 'established to be a prophet of the Lord', 1 Sam. 3. 20.

In the chapters which follow, the Philistines take centre stage. These were an immigrant people occupying the south western part of the land. They had their own national identity and religion, with cities, lords and kings. They were, however, even from patriarchal days at best an irritant and at worst an adversary to the people of God. Now, in 1 Samuel chapter 4, they faced Israel for the first time in a pitched battle.

After the first day of fighting, Israel's elders counted their losses and realized that the battle was going against them. In a desperate effort to reverse their fortunes they called for the ark of the covenant to be carried before them into battle. This action shows the appalling ignorance and the spiritual bankruptcy of the nation. To think that the representation of the Lord's presence, with its mercy seat and cherubim, should be considered a mere talisman, something to bring good fortune when the nation would have been better occupied crying to the Lord in repentance! The ark's arrival appeared initially to have the desired effect, until a Philistine commander rallied his troops with words reminiscent of the apostle Paul's to the Corinthians, 'Stand fast . . . quit you like men, be strong', 1 Cor. 16. 13. The battle was won, the ark was lost, and Israel's army fled.

Poor Eli! With failing sight and feeble limbs he sat by the wayside, no doubt gazing dimly in the direction the ark had been taken. When the messenger came with sad tidings, Eli heard the cry of anguish. In response to his enquiry came news which would break any parent's heart, 'Thy two sons . . . are dead'. Yet it was not this fact which dealt the final crushing blow to Eli; it was 'when he made mention of the ark of God'. The old man's heart had followed the ark when he saw it lifted from the sanctuary and its loss was too much to bear. Eli, like each one of us, had his faults. But he had, in spite of it all, a care for the things of God. Do not judge him too harshly!

February 19th

1 Samuel 5. 1-12

WHAT SHALL WE DO WITH THE ARK OF THE GOD OF ISRAEL?

The focus of attention in chapters 5 and 6 is no longer Israel but the land of the Philistines. Interest must always centre where the presence of God is, and the ark was the symbol of His presence.

The Philistines had a dilemma. On the one hand, they had defeated Israel and had captured a significant trophy of war. On the other hand, however, celebration became consternation as, wherever they took the ark, disaster followed! Little did they realize that the victory owed nothing to their fish-god Dagon, but everything to the permissive will of the God of Israel. The Philistines were but a scourge in His hand to chastise His own wayward people.

The ark had been taken from Ebenezer, the place of help, to Ashdod, the place of oppression. It was, however, the 'victors' who were being oppressed in order for them to learn that the God of Israel would defend His own honour; He would vindicate His own righteousness, and no idolatrous deity could possibly stand in His presence; Dagon must be forced to bow at His feet! The Philistines set up the image again, only to find on the morrow that not only was Dagon prostrate again before the ark, but the head and hands, those parts which would give some semblance of intellect and power were broken off, leaving a formless stump.

Such is the blindness and intransigence of ungodly men that they presume by moving the ark to another location they will avoid the retribution brought upon Ashdod. 'Maybe it was just coincidence', they would reason, 'there must be a natural explanation'! Yet divine judgement followed them to Gath and then to Ekron. Painful swellings afflicted the people and death resulted for many.

Eventually, they realized that the ark must be returned to its rightful place. Even the pagan priests acknowledged that glory must be given to 'the God of Israel', 1 Sam. 6. 5. We are reminded that 'our God is a consuming fire' and it is 'a fearful thing' to fall into His hands, Heb. 10. 31; 12. 29. We can be assured that all who oppose Him will be defeated.

February 20th

1 Samuel 12. 1-18

BEHOLD . . . WHOSE OX HAVE I TAKEN? OR WHOSE ASS HAVE I TAKEN?

The verses before us today record an important watershed in the history of the nation. Authority and responsibility for leading and guiding the people of God passes from the hands of the judges and becomes the duty of the newly inaugurated monarchy. Israel had demanded a king that they might be 'like all the nations', 1 Sam. 8. 5. A longsuffering God had provided a king with all the apparent potential to fulfil their desires so that at the end of chapter 11, the people 'made Saul king before the Lord in Gilgal; and . . . rejoiced greatly'.

Samuel, though now advanced in years, still had the best interests of the nation at heart. He felt grieved that they had slighted his authority and he took the matter to the Lord, 8. 6. But the Lord saw a deeper malaise in His people as evidenced by the poignant response from the divine heart, 'They have not rejected thee, but they have rejected me'.

It takes a man of rare character and courage to stand before those who have known him best over many years and challenge them to reflect on his integrity. A man's oxen and asses represented both his wealth and his ability to work; Samuel had never displayed a covetous spirit in relation to the material goods of others, nor had he caused hardship to any. He had never been partial in his judgements or avaricious in his dealings. So, with the Lord as witness, the people can do no other than acknowledge the truthfulness of Samuel's words.

Samuel had subjected himself to the scrutiny of others: many years later, in the days of Jeremiah, the Lord would hold up Samuel as an outstanding example of one who, in his day, stood before God on behalf of the people, Jer. 15. 1. Now, in the remaining verses of chapter 12, the nation is given a history lesson to remind them of their persistent disobedience. This is followed by a display of God's power in sending the unseasonal thunderstorm as an indication of His displeasure with His people. Samuel's final appeal is very challenging, 'Only fear the Lord, and serve him in truth with all your heart: for consider how great things he hath done for you', 1 Sam. 12. 24.

February 21st

1 Samuel 15. 17-31

HATH THE LORD AS GREAT DELIGHT IN BURNT OFFERINGS . . . AS IN OBEYING THE VOICE OF THE LORD?

Obedience is all that the Lord asks of mankind. Yet, down the course of history, man's fallen nature has led him on a pathway of disobedience in spite of the constant evidence of God's love, mercy and goodness. Disobedience closed Eden's gates to him; it brought the judgement of the flood. Disobedience left Israel wandering in the wilderness and later brought retribution in the days of the Judges. It repeatedly reared its head throughout the years of the monarchy and led the nation captive to Babylon.

What a contrast, when for some thirty-three years this earth was graced with One who could say without fear of contradiction, 'The Father hath not left me alone; for I do always those things that please him', John 8. 29! One who trod a pathway of complete obedience even though it led to 'the death of the cross', Phil. 2. 8.

The word of God to Saul through Samuel was, 'Now go and smite Amalek, and utterly destroy all that they have, and spare them not' – unambiguous, precise instructions. Saul had the authority and with an army of 210,000 men he had the ability! But incomplete obedience amounts to *disobedience* and by sparing Agag and the best of the cattle, Saul effectively ended his reign as king, 1 Sam. 15. 26. True it is that his death is not recorded until chapter 31, but the kingdom would pass to a man after God's own heart and Samuel would not speak to Saul again, save only to pronounce his death from beyond the grave!

All the excuses and proposed good intentions of Saul amounted to nothing, obedience is everything. Sacrifices are worthless; offerings are meaningless, if the heart is rebellious. The Lord Jesus made it very clear to his disciples, 'If ye love me, ye will keep my commandments', John 14. 15 RV. Obedience to the word of God brings us to salvation; it keeps us on the pathway of discipleship and ensures our awareness of His leading and guiding hand day by day. The apostle recognized obedience as an evidence of reality, 'that I might know the proof of you, whether ye be obedient in all things', 2 Cor. 2. 9.

February 22nd

1 Samuel 16. 1-13

AND THE LORD SAID UNTO SAMUEL, 'HOW LONG WILT THOU MOURN FOR SAUL?'

Samuel the prophet was a man of admirable moral qualities. He found no satisfaction in the downfall of Saul, one in whom both as a man and a king, he saw potential. Yet now, at the end of chapter 15, there is a parting of the ways and Samuel returns to Ramah with a heavy heart.

In chapter 10, Saul had followed the instructions given to him and in his obedience 'God gave him another heart . . . and the Spirit of God came upon him', vv. 9-10. The change in Saul was noticed by others and soon it was asked, 'Is Saul also among the prophets?' v. 11.

Testing times followed Saul's coronation, as Ammonites, Philistines and Amalekites in turn challenged his authority and tested his mettle. On each occasion there was an element of victory for Israel, but with each succeeding trial, the influence and the character of Saul were diminished.

Saul's initial reluctance to take a prominent place, 1 Sam. 10. 21-23, was soon overcome with the prospect of position and power before him. His presumptuous sacrifice in chapter 13, his foolish oath in chapter 14, and his act of disobedience in chapter 15, all led to his ultimate rejection and removal. Samuel revealed that the root of Saul's problem was pride! 'When thou wast little in thine own sight . . . the Lord anointed thee king over Israel', 15. 17. Even after the condemning indictment which effectively ended his authority, v. 23, Saul's main concern was that he might save face and be honoured 'before the elders . . . and before Israel', v. 30.

It is a sad reality that the majority of the record of Saul's life is of the years following his rejection; a life lived with nothing for God! The compassionate heart of Samuel mourns the loss of Saul to the nation, but God already has a man prepared 'that is better than' Saul, v. 28.

Ultimately, Saul will write his own epitaph, 'Behold, I have played the fool, and have erred exceedingly', 1 Sam. 26. 21. A sad end for a man who, though given privilege and opportunity, threw it all away; a salutary lesson to all!

February 23rd

1 Samuel 17. 28-37

AND DAVID SAID, 'WHAT HAVE I NOW DONE? IS THERE NOT A CAUSE?'

Eliab would never forget the day when Samuel visited the house of his father Jesse. It was very evident that the prophet had come with an important purpose to fulfil and who better to take responsibility than he, Eliab the firstborn, the fine-looking man of stature. But Eliab failed to appreciate that although Samuel was impressed with his height, God was not impressed with his heart, and his words to David in our reading today fully vindicate the Lord's decision to refuse him.

David was not the first in scripture to experience the hostility of those nearest to him. The coals of envy smouldered in the hearts of Joseph's brothers when it was evident that the father's favour shone upon him. Later, through David, the Spirit of God would speak prophetically of Another who knew rejection, 'For thy sake I have borne reproach . . . I am become a stranger unto my brethren, and an alien unto my mother's children', Ps. 69. 7-8.

Yet, whether it be Joseph, David, or the Lord Himself, each undertook a journey seeking only the welfare of their brethren; in each one, integrity was inviolate and conscience was void of offence. In each case also, under the sovereign hand of God, there was a cause. For Joseph, it was a step along the pathway which would ultimately 'preserve life', not just for a family but for a nation. For David, his journey to the camp of Israel was a step nearer the throne, though first he must face and overcome the adversary in single combat. For the Lord Jesus, the 'despised and rejected' Man, whose own 'received him not', His journey was undertaken with the greatest cause in mind; not only the wellbeing of one nation, 'but that the world through him might be saved', John 3. 17.

David's enquiries that day brought him to the attention of the king. Saul, as leader of the Lord's people, knew it should be he who faced the giant. Yet, he was prepared to relinquish his armour while promising riches, a bride and freedom to another. How good to know that our Saviour defeated the foe, won His bride, and gave freedom and riches in abundance to His own.

February 24th

1 Samuel 18. 17-29

WHO AM I? . . . THAT I SHOULD BE SON IN LAW TO THE KING?

The wise man in Proverbs could well have had Saul in mind when he wrote, 'Wrath is cruel, and anger is outrageous; but who is able to stand before envy?' Prov. 27. 4, for it was envy which overflowed in anger against David. Yet, while Saul behaved foolishly and without reason, four times it is recorded of David that 'he behaved himself wisely'.

Following his victory over Goliath, David was acclaimed by the nation and attributed with triumphs ten times greater than those of Saul, 1 Sam. 18. 7. In his wrath, 'Saul eyed David from that day', and began to plot his downfall. One of the rewards promised by Saul to the man who overcame the giant, was the hand of his daughter; thus David had a rightful claim. Saul, however, planned to use his apparent generosity to his own advantage, and thereby remove the threat he perceived in David.

Saul's first move was to distance David from the court and give him a military commission, hoping that in time he would fall in battle. This ruse failed and served only to enhance David's reputation. It would seem that preparations were being made for the forthcoming marriage when David asked the question before us today. There was neither pride in his heart nor unseemly ambition in his mind. He realized it was an honour and a privilege to be so closely linked with the monarch, having come from such a humble background. Saul, however, saw David's modesty as an opportunity to humiliate him, and blatantly gave his daughter to another man!

Later, Saul would give Michal his younger daughter to David, not by obligation or favour, but because he hoped she would be 'a snare to him'; how devious is man's heart when he rejects the counsels of God!

Do we, as believers, really appreciate our privileges, having been brought into relationship with our God? We have a Saviour who, in defeating the foe, justly won His bride. We are now sons of God, not just sons-in-law, or even by the law, but by sovereign grace, true 'children of God: and if children then heirs; heirs of God, and joint-heirs with Christ', Rom. 8. 16-17.

February 25th

1 Samuel 21. 1-15

IS NOT THIS DAVID THE KING OF THE LAND?

Reference was made yesterday to the question raised in Proverbs chapter 27 verse 4, 'Who is able to stand before envy?' It is very evident from David's actions that he found it unbearable and from 1 Samuel chapter 19 verse 10 we read on no fewer than five occasions that 'David fled' in order to escape the harmful intentions of Saul. In chapter 22 he comes to the cave of Adullam, from where he commences his wilderness experience in the school of God.

On leaving the court of Saul, his first flight was to his own house. With Saul's 'messengers' hot on his heels he fled to Samuel at Ramah, where he found a measure of sanctuary with the man of God. Again, however, those sent to take him are not far behind and David felt compelled to flee, this time seeking the company of Jonathan. Such proximity to the house of Saul made him vulnerable, so from there he took his journey to Ahimelech the priest, with dire consequences for the whole priestly family! Then, fortified with the shewbread and bearing the sword of Goliath, David fled to Achish the king of Gath. Each step of his journey has attendant practical lessons and will reward careful study, but now he was seeking refuge among Israel's enemies – surely a questionable shelter for the man who could write, 'In the time of trouble he shall hide me in his pavilion', Ps. 27. 5; but who later, having learned the lesson, will pen the words of Psalm 34 as a direct result of this experience in Philistine country, 'This poor man cried, and the Lord heard him, and saved him out of all his troubles', Ps. 34. 6.

But note particularly in these verses the response and the words of the servants of Achish when David appears in their midst. There was no doubting who they recognized as the one with authority and ability in Israel; it was not Saul! David was on the horns of a dilemma and resorted to deception in order to extricate himself. As A. McShane so succinctly expresses it in his *Lessons for Leaders*, 'Is it not sad that the man who acted so wisely in the court of Saul now acts the fool in the court of Achish?' How careful we need to be in our behaviour before unbelievers, that the testimony be not compromised!

February 26th

1 Samuel 26. 1-12

WHO CAN STRETCH FORTH HIS HAND AGAINST THE LORD'S ANOINTED, AND BE GUILTLESS?

Our verses today record the second occasion when David is given what appears to be an opportune moment to remove the threat of Saul and seize the kingdom. In chapter 24, David spared Saul's life in the cave, even though the circumstances appeared in his favour and his men sought to persuade him to take advantage of the situation. Why, then, is he confronted with a similar choice in chapter 26?

Two possible explanations come to mind. First, we note that throughout these times of wilderness experience David is being tested and trained to lead the nation. Among those many lessons, he must learn that to rule the people of God he should not act on instinct or impulse, nor be impatient; and his judgement must be consistent.

We are a little surprised, therefore, when, having passed the test in chapter 24, his response to the churlish Nabal in chapter 25 appears inconsistent. On the one hand he spared Saul, the man who sought his life, but then prepared to slay the man who refused him bread! So, in chapter 26, he re-sits the test and this time passes with honours.

It may be, however, that the Lord was teaching him (and us) that favourable circumstances in themselves do not necessarily indicate that we are acting according to the Lord's will. David's men clearly saw that since opportunity had twice been given, this was God's way of bringing him to the throne. David, however, the man after God's own heart, would wait for God to remove Saul in His own good time. He would acknowledge Saul as the Lord's anointed right to the end, 2 Sam. 1. 21.

David, together with the loyal and fearless Abishai, entered Saul's camp by night and removed his spear and cruse. In Abishai's mind there was still only one solution, 'Let me smite him', adding that just one stroke from his strong hand would be sufficient! David, however, moved in the spirit of words written many years later by the apostle Paul, 'The weapons of our warfare are not carnal, but mighty through God to the pulling down of strong holds', 2 Cor. 10. 4. David would wait for God's time!

February 27th

1 Samuel 28. 7-19

BE NOT AFRAID: FOR WHAT SAWEST THOU?

It would be a very callous heart that did not feel a degree of sympathy and sadness for Saul as he stumbled on towards his end, with the pathway growing darker and darker.

Already we have been told that the Spirit of the Lord had 'departed from Saul', 1 Sam. 16. 14; 18. 12. He had known for some time that his kingdom had been given to another, 'better than' him, 15. 28. Samuel's last word to him some twenty years before had been one of judgement, and now Samuel was dead. Vainly he had pursued David, knowing in his heart that his efforts were futile, 26. 25. And, to add to his troubles, the Philistines were amassing an army well within his borders, and, when he saw it, 'he was afraid, and his heart greatly trembled'. How true the words of the wise man, 'The way of transgressors is hard', Prov. 13. 15.

Some years before, Saul, in the early zeal of his reign, had sought to rid the land of those who involved themselves with the dark forces of the spirit world, 1 Sam. 28. 3. Now, the heavens are brass, earth's prophets are silent; in desperation Saul appeals to the powers of darkness; O pity the man, weep for the soul to whom God no longer speaks!

Saul, disguised, distressed and in darkness, made his way to En-dor. What follows is shrouded in the mystery which belongs to an unseen, intangible spirit world which from time to time is briefly unveiled in scripture. Saul, in an outrageous moment of hypocrisy, swears to the woman in the Lord's Name that no punishment will result from her actions, and demands that Samuel be brought up; Samuel's voice is heard and a form appears. Not, I suggest, invoked by the woman who, herself, seemed to be taken by surprise, nor indeed was the apparition from the realm of darkness since Samuel was a man of God. But rather, a sovereign God, the 'Father of spirits', places on record a rare example of the dead speaking to the living, as a confirmation to Saul that his fate was sealed! There was no call for repentance, no parole granted, not even a plea of mitigation offered. A sad end for a man who promised much in his early days, yet lived as S. Ridout so appropriately called him, 'the man after the flesh'.

February 28th

2 Samuel 7. 1-17

THUS SAITH THE LORD, SHALT THOU BUILD ME AN HOUSE FOR ME TO DWELL IN?

The parallel verses to these in 1 Chronicles chapter 17 make the word of God to David through Nathan to be a statement rather than a question. 'Thou shalt not build me a house to dwell in', 1 Chr. 17. In each case the pronoun 'thou' is emphatic, as clearly indicated in NEWBERRY'S *Reference Bible*. This helps us to understand the weight of the Lord's words as He goes on to explain that it was not His purpose that David should build the Lord's house, that would be left for David's son, but rather, the Lord would build a house for David, 2 Sam. 7. 11. A house, a kingdom and a throne that 'shall be established for ever', v. 16.

The suggestion of a dwelling place for God on earth takes our thoughts back to the time when instruction was given to Moses for the construction of the tabernacle in the wilderness, 'Let them make me a sanctuary; that I may dwell among them', Exod. 25. 8. Throughout the succeeding years, the presence of God was known among His people, represented by the ark of the covenant. In chapter 6, David had brought the ark to Jerusalem and expressed his desire that it be given a more permanent resting place, suited to the greatness and majesty of the One signified by the ark.

David had to learn, however, that all he had, and all he was, depended upon the mercy and grace of a sovereign God, 2 Sam. 7. 8-9. David's God was no parochial deity to be confined within walls and doors! Later, when Solomon had built the temple under divine instruction, he acknowledged the magnitude of God in inspired language, 'But will God in very deed dwell with men on the earth? behold, heaven and the heaven of heavens cannot contain thee; how much less this house that I have built!' 2 Chr. 6. 18.

From the time when the Lord Jesus turned away from the temple mount in Jerusalem with the words, 'Your house is left unto you desolate', God has owned no building on earth as His house. The Spirit of God now indwells every believer, making our bodies His temple, 1 Cor. 6. 19; and the gathered company of His people He deigns to own as 'house of God', 1 Tim. 3. 15.

February 29th

2 Samuel 9. 1-13

IS THERE YET ANY THAT IS LEFT OF THE HOUSE OF SAUL, THAT I MAY SHOW HIM KINDNESS?

We thought in our reading yesterday of the house of God; a living, growing, enduring edifice. In contrast, today we read of the house of Saul. In so brief a time, through disobedience and self-will, the house of Saul, once having the potential to be 'established . . . for ever', 1 Sam. 13. 13, had now become so reduced that David had to enquire and search to determine if there were 'yet any that is left of the house of Saul'. How thankful we should be who are linked with the faithful, obedient Man, 'Christ as a son over his own house; whose house are we', Heb. 3. 6!

David was now established in his kingdom. All enemies had been subdued, the land had peace and his administration was ordered and prosperous, 2 Sam. 8. 15-18. Now his thoughts turn to his friend Jonathan and the promise made to him over twenty years earlier, 1 Sam. 20. 15. Jonathan had died alongside his father, fighting the Philistines on Mount Gilboa, some sixteen years previously, but David had not forgotten. The search for one who could benefit from David's kindness discovered Mephibosheth, lame on both his feet, dwelling in Lo-debar, the 'place of no pasture'. What an appropriate description of our helpless condition before 'the kindness and love of God our Saviour', reached out and lifted us to immeasurable heights! And, just as with Mephibosheth, our elevation was 'not by works of righteousness which we have done, but according to his mercy he saved us', Titus 3. 4-5. We notice too, that David did not ask Mephibosheth to meet him halfway; rather, he sent right to where he was and brought him to his table. Had our salvation depended on any ability or strength in us, we would never have known its blessings. Praise God for One who met our need 'when we were yet without strength', Rom. 5. 6!

Notice what David's kindness provided for Mephibosheth: lands restored, a *possession*; a place at the king's table, a *privilege*; bread continually, a *provision*; placed 'as one of the king's sons', a *position*. All these blessings and more are ours in Christ. May we 'walk worthy' of our calling!

March 1st

2 Samuel 13. 1-6

WHY ART THOU, BEING THE KING'S SON, LEAN FROM DAY TO DAY?

Today's question highlights the problem of secret sin. David had indulged in secret sin with Bathsheba, another man's wife. For probably twelve months he continued to conceal it and live as if everything was normal. But what a price he was paying! He aged physically, had no peace, couldn't sleep, and knew that God's hand of discipline was upon him, Ps. 32. 3-4. Although David repented, one of the consequences of his folly was that his family would indulge in violence and rebellion.

And it started with Amnon! He was secretly in love with his beautiful half-sister Tamar. Not as a brother, but in a lustful way as a lover. He would prove that lust conceived, results in sin and death, Jas. 1. 15.

Amnon knew that Tamar could never be his wife. Yet lust ruled his heart and affected his health to the extent that others saw him losing weight as the days went by.

And so his best friend, a cousin named Jonadab, noting his physical leanness enquired, 'Why art thou, being a king's son, lean from day to day?' We read that Jonadab, 'was a very subtil man'! Do you hear echoes of Eden? Eve was tempted by the 'subtil' serpent, and here Jonadab is complicit in the sin, as he tempts Amnon by submitting a plan that will ensure that his lust will be satisfied. The plan was put into action. Amnon defiled his half-sister Tamar just as his father had desired and taken Bathsheba. And just as his father had reaped the consequences of his sin, so did Amnon. He would be the victim of a revenge killing, instigated by Tamar's brother Absalom.

Consider the lessons of this tragic tale. A king's son, with all the privileges and possibilities of palace life is seen to be wasting away as a result of the burning lust in his heart.

How is it with us? As the children of God, 'Blessed . . . with all spiritual blessings in heavenly places in Christ', Eph. 1. 3, we are the most privileged people on earth! Are we prospering spiritually? Or is there a leanness of soul that needs to be addressed? Confession of sins brings forgiveness, and fellowship with God can be restored. Let us seek spiritual prosperity today.

March 2nd

2 Samuel 18. 19-33

IS THE YOUNG MAN ABSALOM SAFE?

Sense the anxiety in David's voice as he enquires about the well-being of his rebellious son. And no wonder! Since David's great sin in the matter of Uriah the Hittite, the family had fallen apart. Although David repented and was restored, his family never recovered. David's sins were repeated in his sons. The sword would not depart from his house. David had neither the moral ground nor courage to deal with the sins of his sons. And so he stood back as Amnon defiled his sister and Absalom avenged her. Absalom fled in fear and for three years there was no communication. David, for his part, loved Absalom and longed for him but did nothing either to rebuke or restore him.

Joab planned Absalom's return to Jerusalem and eventually, after two years, his reception into the king's presence. David received his son affectionately and, no doubt, thought that all would be well. But the son who caused such heartache went on to take the throne and now David was the one in exile. A family rift had become civil war and the armies of father and son were arrayed against each other. David instructed his army to deal gently with Absalom, for he still loved him unconditionally. Twenty thousand men died that day, but David's concern was his son's welfare, and so, as the messenger arrived with news of the battle, he asked, 'Is the young man Absalom safe?' 2 Sam. 18. 29. He was not, and David mourned the death of another son.

David's failure, after his great sin, was lack of communication with his sons. Parents often make mistakes which affect their children and they in turn sometimes cause heartache. But parents must love unconditionally. Such is God's unchanging love for rebellious children such as us. Samson's parents prayed for him before he was born. Moses' parents protected him after he was born. Timothy's grandmother and mother taught him the scriptures as a child. May those of us who are parents, grandparents, or who have an interest in the next generation generally, seek God's help in nurturing them in the fear and admonition of the Lord, and learn to love them unconditionally. We will make our mistakes, but remember, 'love never fails'!

March 3rd

1 Kings 3. 3-15

FOR WHO IS ABLE TO JUDGE THIS THY SO GREAT A PEOPLE?

Solomon stood in awe of God as he contemplated the enormous challenge of his high calling. His father had been the man after God's own heart and now he occupied the throne of Israel. God was now speaking with him, offering him whatever blessings he desired. What would he ask for? His choice would determine the character of his reign over God's people in years to come. Solomon asked for wisdom and God answered his request. The fame of his wisdom extended far beyond Israel and down through the centuries. Today, we speak of needing 'the wisdom of Solomon' to deal with difficult situations. We will never be called to the throne of Israel, but every believer is called to some service for God and wisdom is needed to successfully fulfil this ministry. Solomon's question provides valuable lessons in obtaining heavenly wisdom for earthly problems.

He loved the Lord. At his birth, we note that 'the Lord loved him'. But we read, 'Solomon loved the Lord', 1 Kgs. 3. 3. Only in the sense that we 'love him because he first loved us', will our service be of any value.

He knew his own weakness. He said, 'I am but a little child', v. 7. None of God's servants thought they were up to the task when called by God into service for Him. In effect, they all said like Isaiah, 'Woe is me!' Someone said, 'A man can be too big for God, but never too small'.

He had high regard for the people of God. He called them, 'Thy people which thou hast chosen, a great people', v. 8. We must be careful how we regard the people of God. That great leader Moses, when provoked once more by the Israelites, addressed them as, 'Ye rebels'. 'He spake unadvisedly with his lips' and God replaced him with a new leader.

He needed wisdom. He requested, 'Give therefore thy servant an understanding heart to judge thy people, that I may discern between good and bad'. How we too need wisdom!

The result. God exceeded his expectations! James tells us in chapter 1 verse 5 that if we need wisdom, our God will give liberally, providing we ask in faith, nothing wavering.

March 4th

1 Kings 8. 22-30

BUT WILL GOD INDEED DWELL ON THE EARTH?

What a day this was! God had communicated to Solomon His desire to 'dwell among the children of Israel', and so he had built the temple, furnishing it with vessels and establishing priestly order. Priests placed the ark of the covenant in the holiest of all, removing the staves as travelling days were over. As they retired, the glory cloud 'filled the house of the Lord'.

The heaven and the heaven of heavens cannot contain almighty God and yet He was dwelling with His people! But this was conditional. Back in Samuel's day, because of the sorry state of the people of God, the glory had departed from the house of God at Shiloh. Although the presence cloud had now returned, it would remain only as long as God's people walked before Him. The time would come when the presence of God would again remove from His people.

But will God indeed dwell on the earth? See the Babe in Bethlehem, Emmanuel, God with us! See Jesus of Nazareth walking the dusty roads of Galilee and Judea, and listen to John, 'We beheld his glory, the glory as of the only begotten of the Father, full of grace and truth', John 1. 14. Listen to the Master, 'He that hath seen me hath seen the Father'. God was indeed dwelling on earth!

But the Saviour has returned to the right hand of the Father by way of the cross. Has God changed His desire to dwell with His people? Listen again to the Saviour, 'Where two or three are gathered together in my name, there am I in the midst of them'. God dwells on the earth in the person of His Son wherever believers gather to His Name; He dwells in their midst!

But that is not all. God has determined that, after the resurrection and rapture of the saints to heaven, His Son will return in glory and reign a thousand years. Then, 'the earth shall be filled with the knowledge of the glory of the Lord, as the waters cover the sea', Hab. 2. 14. And beyond the millennial reign, in the eternal state, we hear the words, 'The tabernacle of God is with men . . . God himself shall be with them, and be their God', Rev. 21. 3. In the meantime, we have the privilege of gathering to His Name and sensing His presence in our midst.

March 5th

1 Kings 18. 7-19

AHAB SAID UNTO HIM, ART THOU HE THAT TROUBLETH ISRAEL?

These were dark days in Israel's history. Ahab was on the throne and Jezebel was queen. Never before had such an evil pair reigned over the ten northern tribes. God says of them, 'But there was none like unto Ahab, which did sell himself to work wickedness in the sight of the Lord, whom Jezebel his wife stirred up', 1 Kgs. 21. 25. Baal worship was now officially Israel's religion. The worship of the living God was illegal. All the priests had been slain with the exception of a hundred who were hiding in caves. Against this dark background we are introduced to an outstanding servant of God, the prophet Elijah. Elijah was a separated man. He had to be, to avoid the contamination of the sinful society in which he served God. Elijah was a man of prayer. James writes his epistle, and in chapter 5 verse 16 holds Elijah up as the example of the truth that, 'the effectual fervent prayer of a righteous man availeth much'. Elijah was a righteous man because he was separated from the corruption all around him. Reminding us of the Saviour in Gethsemane, he prayed 'earnestly', and 'he prayed again'. He prayed for famine, and then again for rain. How could he pray for complete opposites and be answered? Elijah knew the mind of God, so his prayers were in line with the will of God. These combined factors made his prayer life effectual.

Prayer in private gives power in public. Elijah, the man of prayer, on two occasions announced himself to Ahab as coming with the authority of the Lord God of Israel, 'before whom I stand'. The man living in the presence of God received a word from God. The time had come for the famine to end and Elijah must approach King Ahab. Elijah was the servant of the living God with the answer to the nation's immediate need. But Ahab had spent three years seeking to kill him and still regarded him as the cause of all the trouble. May we seek to live more like Elijah, to live in close communion with our God and walk in His ways, prove the power of effectual prayer and be an influence for God and for good, even though others might misunderstand us and even blame us for their circumstances!

March 6th

1 Kings 18. 20-40

HOW LONG HALT YE BETWEEN TWO OPINIONS?

It was decision day for God's people. Their rebellion against the Lord and their gross idolatry under wicked King Ahab had brought them to an all-time low. God was dealing with them as He sent famine and for three-and-a-half years they stubbornly endured the hardship of drought rather than repent and return to Him. Crops had failed, animals had died, the people were starving, but still they persisted in their evil ways.

Once again, God intervened. Elijah was sent to Ahab and the gathering on Mount Carmel was arranged. This was a national event. 'All Israel' was summoned, along with King Ahab, four hundred and fifty prophets of Baal, and four hundred prophets of the goddess Asherah. Carmel was to become a battlefield. It would be the battle of the gods. See on the one side the vast army of Baal and Asherah. All Israel, led by its king and eight hundred and fifty priests, were arrayed in support of these idol gods. Look for the opposing army and see one solitary man standing on the mountainside, the sole representative of the Lord of hosts. He approaches the people and throws out the challenge, 'How long halt ye between two opinions? If the Lord be God, follow him: but if Baal, then follow him'. There is a deathly silence; God is at work. Battle commences. The prophets of Baal are defeated and destroyed. The sight of fire from heaven consuming sacrifice, altar and water, prostrates the people confessing, 'The Lord, he is the God; the Lord, he is the God'. They no longer limp between two opinions. They confess that the Lord is *the* God, their God.

To limp between two opinions is fatal. The Lord Jesus spoke of two ways and their eternal destinies. The broad way, leading to destruction, and the narrow way, leading to life. Again, He spoke of two masters, and the impossibility of serving both. Listen to an earlier challenge in Israel's history. Joshua is saying, 'Choose you this day whom you will serve'. To halt between two opinions is dangerous. At best, it results in unhappiness. At worst, it results in eternal punishment with the lost.

May we respond as he did, 'But as for me and my house, we will serve the Lord', Josh. 24. 15.

March 7th

1 Kings 19. 1-18

WHAT DOEST THOU HERE, ELIJAH?

This was Elijah's darkest hour. Recently he had fearlessly faced the idolatrous masses on Mount Carmel as the sole representative of the living God. But the hero of Carmel had now descended into his darkest valley.

It happens to the best of God's servants. We are never more vulnerable than after a spiritual mountain-top experience. Elijah was now suffering depression as the result of 'burnout'.

Consider what brought Elijah here. Success on the mountain had been the pinnacle of his spiritual career. He had been publicly vindicated by the Lord of hosts. But the revival was short-lived and Jezebel had vowed to kill him. So, nothing had changed. His work had been in vain. Having no desire to die at the hand of Jezebel, he fled to the safety of Judah, leaving his servant there. After walking for a day into the wilderness, he sat under a juniper tree and prayed that God would take his life.

See the kindness of our God in His tender care of His servant! He knew that Elijah needed physical rest and refreshment. The Saviour provided this for His disciples as he instructed them to come apart and rest awhile. It is true that if we do not come apart and rest, we just 'come apart'! And so, when Elijah woke to the touch of an angel, he was not in heaven, as he had hoped, but still under the juniper tree. Food and drink, further sleep and another meal were provided to enable him to make the forty days' journey to Horeb, the Mount of God. It was here that God had conversed with Moses, and now He would speak with Elijah. The prophet was cowering in a cave when he heard the voice of God. The time had come to address the problem, 'What doest thou here, Elijah?' Elijah poured out his problem to God. His life's work had been useless and pointless. Nothing had changed! God sent a great wind and an earthquake with terrifying effects, but He was not in them. Then came a still small voice, which brought Elijah out of his cave, and again God spoke to him. There is a future for Elijah and the people of God. He will yet anoint kings and the prophet Elisha, soon to become his faithful servant. And, by the way, there are still seven thousand who have not bowed the knee to idols!

March 8th

2 Kings 2. 1-14

ASK WHAT I SHALL DO FOR THEE, BEFORE I BE TAKEN FROM THEE

In his darkest hour, Elijah thought that the work of God amongst His people was all down to him. And there, in the Mount of God, he had learned that God's purposes for His people were going to be fulfilled, and that although he had a role to play, he was only one of God's servants whom He would use.

The first stage in Elijah's rehabilitation had been for him to involve a younger man, Elisha, to share the work in which he was engaged. He would no longer be alone in his service for God. Elisha would become his constant companion and servant.

Elisha was to Elijah what Timothy would become to Paul. Elisha is the Old Testament character most often called a 'man of God'. Timothy is the only man in the New Testament so designated. Just as Elisha was introduced to encourage Elijah at a difficult time, so Timothy was introduced into the apostle Paul's life at a time when he was no doubt feeling low, having separated from Barnabas over the matter of John Mark.

God allowed Elijah to spend quiet years with Elisha, at the same time using other prophets in a public capacity. This completed the older man's rehabilitation and the younger man's preparation for his future ministry. God took Elijah up again to publicly announce the demise of another king of Israel, and now his work on earth was done. The old man and his young companion had crossed the Jordan. They stood side by side, anticipating Elijah's departure as the question came, 'Ask what I shall do for thee, before I be taken from thee'. Elisha asked for a double portion of his spirit. As Elijah was taken to heaven, his mantle fell upon the young man. His request was granted! The prophetic ministry would be continued and enlarged through Elisha, in a very different way amongst a different generation.

The apostle Paul was very concerned that the truth of God should be taught to succeeding generations. And so he wrote to Timothy, 'The things that thou hast heard of me among many witnesses, the same commit thou to faithful men, who shall be able to teach others also'. May God help us to work together, that His truth may be faithfully passed on to future generations!

March 9th

2 Kings 4. 1-7

WHAT SHALL I DO FOR THEE? TELL ME, WHAT HAST THOU IN THE HOUSE?

The need was dire. The poor widow was at her wits' end. Her beloved husband, a faithful servant of God, known to Elisha, had died, leaving her to raise two young sons. She was poverty-stricken to the extent that she faced bankruptcy and her boys faced bondage, as her creditor was about to take them as slaves to pay her debt. What could she do? In desperation she turned to Elisha and presented him with her situation. And so he asked, 'What shall I do for thee? Tell me, what hast thou in the house?' She looked around. There was nothing! She had sold everything of any value at all to meet the creditor's demands. Looking once more round her bare home she confessed that there was nothing left but a little pot of olive oil.

That which she least valued was, in fact, the answer to her need, but she did not know it! And so her faith was tested. Instructed by Elisha to go to her neighbours and borrow empty vessels, 'not a few', she sent her boys out and they returned with a collection of containers. They entered their empty home and shut the door. The miracle that was about to take place would be a transaction between them and God alone. The boys brought the first container and their mother poured oil from the little pot until it was full. Wide-eyed, they brought another, and another, and still the oil from the little pot was flowing, until the last vessel was filled. The only reason that the oil stopped flowing was a lack of empty vessels! What should she do now? Elisha instructed her, 'Go, sell the oil, and pay thy debt, and live thou and thy children of the rest', 2 Kgs. 4. 7.

Do we sense spiritual poverty? What have we in the house? There may be much that we rely on, but the only thing of value is that which the oil speaks of, the Holy Spirit. If we are to accomplish anything for God it will be, 'Not by might, nor by power, but by my Spirit', Zech. 4. 6. Do we believe that? Are we prepared to rely completely on the Holy Spirit, that He may empower us and make us a blessing? The need of the house was the need of the neighbourhood. Having experienced His blessing we can go out in His power to our neighbours.

March 10th

2 Kings 5. 1-14

ARE NOT ABANA AND PHARPAR . . . BETTER THAN ALL THE WATERS OF ISRAEL?

It was his moment of decision. The army commander with the fatal illness needed cleansing, and he knew it. All his bravery on the battlefield, his favour with the king of Syria, his wealth and fame counted for nothing as he saw the inroads of the killer disease affecting his body. Leprosy had infected his bloodstream. It was maiming him; it was incurable, progressive. It would separate him from society and turn him into an outcast. The man with everything had become the man with a great need; the need of cleansing and renewing. But this was impossible. He was hopeless and helpless. Until the news came; there was a prophet in Israel who could cure the disease! Here was a glimmer of hope in a dark situation. The king of Syria, devastated at the thought of losing his army commander, wrote a letter to the king of Israel sending Naaman with appropriate gifts to meet him and be cleansed of his leprosy. How wrong were their thoughts! Going to the wrong person, prepared to pay the wrong price, with the wrong presumption, as he confessed, 'I thought'. Naaman must learn that God's ways are not ours. He knew that he needed cleansing. But not in the way that he expected. Having failed to obtain the cure by his own efforts he finally stood at the prophet's door. Instead of a reception worthy of his status and a spectacular miracle at the hands of the prophet, he simply received the words of a messenger. He must wash seven times in Jordan and be clean. This was too much for proud Naaman! If he had to humiliate himself in this way, might he not do it in the rivers of Syria? In a rage he turned his chariot around, heading for home, still unclean. For the third time God used servants, messengers, to point Naaman in the right direction. They persuaded him to humbly obey the word from God, and in doing so, he was cleansed.

God's ways do not change. Proud sinners must still recognize their hopeless state and obey His word, 'Believe on the Lord Jesus Christ and thou shalt be saved', Acts 16. 31.

May we be faithful servants, used by the Master to point needy sinners like Naaman to the Saviour!

March 11th

2 Kings 20. 1-11

WHAT SHALL BE THE SIGN THAT THE LORD WILL HEAL ME?

Hezekiah was a great king of Judah. He is noted for cleaving to the Lord and obeying His commandments. He outlawed idolatry and destroyed the objects of worship. Above all, he had personal dealings with God; he was a man of prayer. In the matter of the siege of Jerusalem he prayed for deliverance and God answered him. One hundred and eighty-five thousand Assyrians died in their camp and their king was slain on returning home.

But earlier, Hezekiah had been seriously ill, almost to the point of death. Isaiah the prophet appeared with a message from God, 'Set thine house in order; for thou shalt die, and not live'. What a blow! After seeing God at work, delivering His people from oppression, Hezekiah must have thought that he would now enjoy a peaceful, prosperous time as king of Judah. What did he do in this circumstance? He prayed. No sooner had he prayed than God responded and Isaiah returned with the answer. His tears had been seen and his prayer had been heard. He would be healed and return to the house of the Lord to give thanks for his deliverance. Fifteen years would be added to his life; years of peace and safety, regardless of the intentions of his enemies.

Not content with that, Hezekiah asked for a sign to confirm God's promise. And his prayer, once again, was answered spectacularly. God, the 'Father of lights', ordered the shadow to reverse on the sundial by ten degrees!

Illness is often a mystery to the people of God. Why do the choicest saints seem to suffer the most? We pray when sickness and disease afflict us, but generally our God does not see fit to intervene. Unlike Hezekiah, we do not seek for a sign to confirm that we will be healed, for we do not, as he did, know God's plan for our life. However, we can confidently rest in the assurance that our God is working out His purpose in our lives 'for good', Rom. 8. 28. As 'the Lord that healeth thee', Exod. 15. 26, we understand that He *may* heal miraculously, but we bow to His sovereign purposes, wisdom, and love, and say, 'Thy will be done'.

March 12th

1 Chronicles 29. 1-9

AND WHO THEN IS WILLING TO CONSECRATE HIS SERVICE THIS DAY UNTO THE LORD?

Our God is the God who freely gives. He has given us His Holy Spirit, 'that we might know the things that are freely given to us of God', 1 Cor. 2. 12. God has freely given us all things at great cost to Himself, for His word tells us, 'He that spared not his own Son, but delivered him up for us all, how shall he not with him also freely give us all things?' Rom. 8. 32.

God, in turn, loves a cheerful giver, 2 Cor. 9. 7. He looks for people who, with willing hearts, will reciprocate His love by cheerfully rendering to Him that which is His by right. King David was such a man. He loved his God and the house of God. His great desire was to replace the temporary structure of the tabernacle with a permanent building where God would dwell with His people. God withheld this privilege from His servant but took account of what was in his heart. The thought was as good as the deed. Solomon his son would build the temple. And so David, enabled by God, gave Solomon the design of the structure along with the materials he had amassed for its construction. Now his work was over. His reign had run its course, and he spoke for the last time to his people. He led by example, telling them what he had willingly given for the building of the house of God, and then he challenged them, 'And who then is willing to consecrate his service this day unto the Lord?' The leaders responded; they 'offered willingly', 1 Chr. 19. 6. Then the people responded, 'They offered willingly', v. 9.

What was the result of such giving? Firstly, it brought joy to the hearts of those who gave, 'Then the people rejoiced, for that they offered willingly . . . and David the king also rejoiced with great joy', v. 9. Secondly, it brought glory to God as David, and then the people, 'blessed God', vv. 10, 20. They acknowledged that what they had given to God was His in any case! It was an act of worship as they consecrated their gift to the God who gave it in the first place.

Moved by God's love in Christ, may we willingly present not only our possessions but ourselves to Him, Rom. 12. 1-2! In doing so, we will have true joy and God will be glorified.

March 13th

2 Chronicles 20. 1-17

O OUR GOD, WILT THOU NOT JUDGE THEM? . . . OUR EYES ARE UPON THEE

What do we do when faced with a seemingly insurmountable problem?

This was the situation in which the people of God found themselves just now. Jehoshaphat had been a good king who brought about restoration and revival in Judah. God honoured him, and the surrounding nations feared him, because they saw that the Lord was with him, resulting in a peaceful time for the land of Judah. Then came an unwise alliance with Ahab, king of Israel, leading to warfare, Ahab's death, and Jehoshaphat's narrow escape. Jehoshaphat learned his lesson and continued his programme of restoration in the land, until one day the bad news came. A massive enemy army was approaching, led by the Ammonites and Moabites. What would Jehoshaphat do? He had recently experienced a personal crisis when in battle with Ahab. His chariot had been surrounded by enemy warriors seeking his death when he cried to the Lord and He saved him. Having proved God in this personal way, Jehoshaphat knew what to do in this new crisis. He proclaimed a fast and the people came to Jerusalem 'to ask help of the Lord', 2 Chr. 20. 4. They meant business. Jehoshaphat stood in the house of the Lord and led them in prayer, presenting their case to 'the God of our fathers', reminding Him that He was their God, too. Having prayed, 'Our eyes are upon thee', they stood there with their wives and children waiting for God's answer. They were not disappointed, the answer came quickly, 'Be not afraid nor dismayed . . . the battle is not yours, but God's . . . stand ye still, and see the salvation of the Lord'. And so they went out to meet the foe, not armed to the teeth, but singing praises to the God who had promised them victory. Their only task was to collect the spoil left by the defeated army. There was so much that it took them three days to do it!

The apostle Paul, veteran of many spiritual battles, encourages us, 'If God be for us, who can be against us?' Rom. 8. 31. No matter what our circumstance, we can be confident that God is for us and we need not fear as we commit our cause to Him.

March 14th

2 Chronicles 32. 9-23

WHEREON DO YE TRUST, THAT YE ABIDE IN THE SIEGE OF JERUSALEM?

Hezekiah was an outstanding king of Judah. There was 'none like him among all the kings of Judah'. He 'clave to the Lord', and, as a result, we read, 'The Lord was with him'. The man who loved the Lord demolished the centres of idolatry and drove back the Philistines. But the Assyrians were a different story. Having conquered Samaria and transported the people of Israel into captivity, they turned their attention to the southern kingdom of Judah. Sennacherib, king of Assyria took all the fortified cities. Hezekiah tried to buy him off and in doing so, emptied the temple coffers of silver and stripped the doors and posts of their gold. But Sennacherib was intent on taking Jerusalem and bringing Judah into subjection. He sent his commanders to Jerusalem demanding unconditional surrender. They taunted the people of God regarding their weak position as they faced insurmountable odds, 'What confidence is this wherein thou trustest?' It was the battle of the gods! Sennacherib praised his false gods and mocked the God of heaven as he viewed the weakness of His people. Laughing, he asks, 'Now on whom dost thou trust, that thou rebellest against me?'

Hezekiah's trust was in the Lord and he looked for His help through the words of His servant Isaiah. The word came, 'Be not afraid'. The oppressor was doomed. Further communication from the enemy prompted Hezekiah to spread the letter before the Lord and pray for deliverance. The answer to his prayer came again through Isaiah, 'I have heard'. The God who heard Hezekiah's prayer would answer in spectacular fashion. Sending a single angel one night He destroyed one hundred and eighty-five thousand soldiers! Sennacherib returned home and died at the hands of his sons.

No matter how great our enemy seems, be assured, 'It is better to trust in the Lord than to put confidence in man', Ps. 118. 8. We are encouraged to 'trust in the Lord with all thine heart . . . and he shall direct thy paths', Prov. 3. 5-6. We have no need to fear our enemy 'because greater is he that is in you, than he that is in the world', 1 John 4. 4. We are on the victory side!

March 15th

Ezra 1. 1-11

WHO IS THERE AMONG YOU OF ALL HIS PEOPLE? ... LET HIM GO UP TO JERUSALEM

These were amazing days. God, as always, was working out His purposes amidst the rise and fall of nations. Seventy years earlier, Nebuchadnezzar had taken the inhabitants of the southern kingdom of Judah captive into Babylon. Now his empire had fallen to the Persians and the inhabitants of Babylon must have wondered what would befall them under this new regime.

But God was working according to His timetable, and so, in fulfilment of Jeremiah's prophecy and in answer to Daniel's prayers, the seventy years of Judah's captivity were about to come to an end. The Spirit of God was at work in the heart of the Persian ruler and he made a public proclamation, 'Who is there among you of all his people? ... let him go up to Jerusalem'.

What a challenge for the people of God! Would they choose the prosperity of Babylon or the privation of Jerusalem? Babylon had become their comfort zone. The old folk had settled down there now, and the long journey back to a derelict Jerusalem seemed a daunting prospect. The young folk had been born into Babylon's culture and this was all that they knew. Tales of days of old in Jerusalem meant little to them; why would they leave? But there was a remnant, a small group, 'whose spirit God had raised', or stirred. This group was a small percentage of the people of Judah, numbering some fifty thousand, ranging from leaders to singers. But they all had one common aim: to reclaim their God-given inheritance and rebuild His house.

God took careful note of every individual who answered the call to return, and every item that had been stolen from His house that would accompany them. They set out, not knowing what dangers and difficulties lay ahead, but aware that their God was with them, meeting their weakness with His might.

God still calls for those who will leave their comfort zone in answer to the stirring of His Spirit, seeking to regain the vitality of New Testament Christianity and to build for God in the face of opposition and criticism. He notes with pleasure every individual who humbly seeks to obey His call.

March 16th

Nehemiah 2. 1-8

WHY IS THY COUNTENANCE SAD, SEEING THOU ART NOT SICK?

Nehemiah was a man with a burden. We learn that he was the 'king's cupbearer', Neh. 1. 11, in 'Shushan the palace', v. 1, one of three royal residences of the Persian monarch, Artaxerxes, his responsibility giving him regular access to the king's presence. With the arrival from Judea of Hanani, one of his kinsmen, Nehemiah inquired about the welfare of the Jews in the province and about the condition of Jerusalem, vv. 2-3. The report given to him caused him great distress and became a matter of earnest prayer, vv. 4-11; 2. 17. What of our response when we hear of difficulties, weakness and failure amongst the Lord's people? Do they become subjects for earnest prayer or are they simply matters of passing interest to us?

The events recorded in chapter 2 took place some four months later, 2. 1, months in which Nehemiah had prayed night and day, 1. 6. Is there such a consistency evident in our prayer life? Now Nehemiah could have prayed and then trusted that others would take up the work, something that would not have been unreasonable in light of the distance between Shushan and Jerusalem, but the situation so burdened him he desired to be practically involved himself in the work of rebuilding, 2. 5. It is evident that he gave careful thought to what it would involve, how long he would be gone and what would be needed if his mission was to be successful, vv. 6-8. Do we pray like that, giving thought to how we might become practically involved ourselves, whether locally or further afield? Or do we pray expecting others to do all the work?

Nehemiah knew that the king's permission was necessary before he could go and although he would have known that no sorrow was to be exhibited in the king's presence, Esther 4. 2, his concern and exercise was such that it could not be hid, Neh. 2. 2. God is not indifferent to the prayers or spiritual exercise of His people, and through the king's inquiry and subsequent approval He provided the opportunity for Nehemiah to realize his desire, v. 8. God greatly used Nehemiah; are your desires such that God could use you, Jas. 4. 3?

March 17th

Nehemiah 4. 1-14

WHAT DO THESE FEEBLE JEWS? WILL THEY FORTIFY THEMSELVES?

Any who undertake a work for God will, sooner or later, encounter opponents. Paul wrote, 'A great door and effectual is opened unto me, and there are many adversaries', 1 Cor. 16. 9. In the Book of Nehemiah, even as the work began, opponents were quick to ridicule and threaten, Neh. 2. 19, and that opposition intensified as the work progressed. In today's passage, the difficulties from the enemy without, 4. 1-9, eventually led to discouragement amongst the builders within, vv. 10-14.

While Sanballat was the spokesman, he was not alone in his contempt for the work of God and, supported by the company with him, he spoke contemptuously of the builders, calling them 'feeble Jews', and questioned the viability of their plans, v. 2. Four times he questioned, 'Will they?' each time inferring the impossibility of the task they had set themselves. Would they bring in an army of men to 'fortify themselves'? Did they hope that by offering sacrifices God would intervene on their behalf? Had they considered the time it would take? What would they use for materials? Finally, he dismissed their ability to build anything substantial or permanent, v. 3. These disparaging comments were spoken in the presence of 'the builders', v. 5. Despite this abuse the work continued, the people calling upon God, v. 4, and united in their desire to build, v. 6 – a testimony to what can be achieved, despite problems, when God's people are dependent upon Him and one in purpose.

The perseverance of the workers aroused increased opposition from their adversaries, v. 8, but the work continued, v. 9. As long as the people looked to God, progress was made, but as soon as their thoughts were focused elsewhere discouragement came. Looking at themselves and considering the task before them they soon began to conclude 'we are not able', v. 10. Others, repeating the threats of the enemy, added to the general sense of despondency, vv. 11-12. Against that background Nehemiah wisely said, 'Remember the Lord . . . great and terrible, and fight', v. 14. Remembering Him is ever the antidote to discouragement, Heb. 12. 3. In which direction are you looking?

March 18th

Nehemiah 5. 1-13

WILL YE EVEN SELL YOUR BRETHREN? OR SHALL THEY BE SOLD UNTO US?

In chapter 4, the problems and discouragements Nehemiah encountered were directly related to the activity and influence of the enemy without, but, in this chapter, the difficulties that arose came from within, from their nobles and rulers, Neh. 5. 1, 7. We should never forget that not all the problems that bring distress and division to the people of God necessarily have their source from the enemy without, sadly sometimes we can initiate them ourselves through personality clashes, carnal behaviour, proud and hurtful words, and many other things beside, 1 Cor. 1. 11; Gal. 5. 15.

The conduct of the nobles and rulers stands in marked contrast to Peter's exhortation to elders not to act as 'lords over God's heritage', 1 Pet. 5. 3. These leaders used the prevailing circumstances to their own material advantage, bringing their brethren, those redeemed from the heathen, into bondage again, Neh. 5. 8. The people needed food, v. 2, something not helped by the presence of a 'dearth', inflating prices, v. 3. In addition to that, the 'king's tribute' needed to be paid, v. 4. In order to address those needs these unscrupulous rulers had obliged the people to mortgage their land, v. 3, take out loans, v. 4, and deliver their children to servitude, v. 5. In reducing the people to such straits they transgressed specific commandments regarding the treatment of brethren, Exod. 22. 25; Lev. 25. 35-36. The law said one thing but these leaders did another. Their conduct was a denial of brotherly relationships, was inconsistent with walking in the fear of God, and exposed them to the reproach of their enemies, Neh. 5. 7-9. We are exhorted to add to our faith 'brotherly kindness'; to 'bear . . . one another's burdens', 2 Pet. 1. 7; Gal. 6. 2, but is that evident in our relationships? Or is our behaviour such as to attract just criticism? If right relations were to be restored change was necessary, Neh. 5. 10-12. The nobles obeyed Nehemiah, vv. 12-13, and a passage that began with complaints about brethren concludes with praise to God. Are there changes that we need to make in the interests of unity with brethren? If so, let us attend to it today, Matt. 5. 23-24!

March 19th

Esther 4. 1-17

WHO KNOWETH WHETHER THOU ART COME TO THE KINGDOM FOR SUCH A TIME AS THIS?

These were critical days. The king, Ahasuerus, had given a free hand to the wicked man Haman to destroy all the Jews in the kingdom, and the plan for their destruction was well advanced, Esther 3. 8-13, Christians likewise have a powerful enemy who 'as a roaring lion, walketh about seeking whom he may devour', 1 Pet. 5. 8. While Mordecai and the Jews throughout the provinces were aware of the danger, Esther the queen sheltered within the palace, and was oblivious to the situation. Though we live in a day of multimedia communications, one fears that all too often while some believers are found in circumstances where they face persecution and suffering, others live much as Esther was found, apparently oblivious to their plight. Do we daily 'remember them that are in bonds as bound with them; and them which suffer adversity', Heb. 13. 3?

When Mordecai informed Esther of the situation he exhorted her to personally appeal to the king on the Jews' behalf, Esther 4. 8, something that according to Persian law would be fraught with danger, v. 11. In his reply to this concern Mordecai indicated that Esther was unavoidably involved in this conflict between evil and good, 'Think not . . . thou shalt escape', v. 13, and to remain silent would result in a missed opportunity, v. 14.

Likewise, believers today are inextricably involved in the conflict between good and evil, Eph. 6. 12; are we ready and bold to speak up for the truth, or are we all too often silenced through fear of the consequences?

Mordecai had no doubt that God would bring deliverance, and he challenged Esther to consider if her place in the kingdom had not been overruled by God to that end, Esther 4. 14. Have we ever looked at our own life in that light, considering for what purpose God has placed us where we are? It was a desire of Paul to 'apprehend that for which also I am apprehended of Christ', Phil. 3. 12. God inevitably fulfils His purpose, but knowledge of that is no excuse for inactivity. Esther said, 'I go . . . if I perish, I perish', Esther 4. 16. May we display a similar resolve!

March 20th

Esther 6. 1-14

WHAT SHALL BE DONE UNTO THE MAN WHOM THE KING DELIGHTETH TO HONOUR?

Though the name of God is not directly mentioned in the Book of Esther, His providential hand is nevertheless clearly seen in His control of events and His care for His people. At the end of chapter 5 gallows are built, Haman intending to get a royal warrant to hang Mordecai the very next day. But other events were taking place to frustrate that intention: the king's sleepless night, the summons to bring the official chronicles, the portion selected to be read, the coming of Haman, the king's request, and the response of Haman were all overruled by God for the fulfilling of His purpose, Esther 6. 1-4. Even Haman's ignorance and pride were used by God to that end; if he had known the man to be honoured was Mordecai, would Haman have said the things that he did, vv. 8-9? How good to remember that God is sovereign, that His purpose embraces 'the whole earth' and none can 'disannul it', and His hand is stretched out upon all nations and none can 'turn it back', Isa. 14. 26-27.

It is surely impossible for believers in Christ to read the history of Mordecai and not think of Him. The experience of Mordecai, the way Haman hated him and his seed, Esther 3. 6; his sorrow, 4. 1; and his condemnation, 5. 14; all have ready parallels in the experience of the Lord Jesus, Rev. 12. 1-6; Luke 19. 41; John 19. 7. However, unlike Mordecai the Lord Jesus was to taste death in all its fullness, Heb. 2. 9. In his exaltation Mordecai was clothed in royal apparel and rode upon the king's horse, something we might view as anticipatory of the day when Christ will be manifest in glory, Rev. 19. 11-16. Added to that, the final view given to us of Mordecai's greatness can be seen as a foreshadowing of the millennial glory of the Lord, 'great among the Jews . . . accepted of the multitude of his brethren . . . speaking peace to all his seed', Esther 10. 2-3; Luke 1. 32; Zech. 12. 10; Isa. 54. 13. The despised man became the exalted ruler and so will it be with the Lord Jesus, Isa. 53. 3, 12. In response to what Mordecai had done, Esther 6. 2-3, the king took delight in honouring him, so God has taken delight in honouring Christ, Phil. 2. 8-11. But where do we find our delight?

March 21st

Job 1. 1-12

HAST THOU CONSIDERED MY SERVANT JOB?

Clearly God had considered him and there are few men who, when first mentioned in the scriptures, are commended as fully as Job is, 'perfect and upright, and one that feared God, and eschewed evil', a man of whom the Lord said, 'My servant . . . there is none like him in the earth', Job 1. 1, 8. Could such language even begin to be used in describing us? As to his *purity*, he was 'perfect', the word denoting not sinless perfection but rather 'maturity' a man of well-balanced character and conduct. He was 'upright', honest, trustworthy, beyond reproach and while reference is made in the book to those who 'said unto God, Depart from us' this man had a reverential fear of God, 22. 7. Although we read in subsequent chapters of 'evil doers' and 'evil men', Job 'eschewed' or 'abstained from' evil, 8. 20; 35. 12. Such were his *possessions* he was 'the greatest of all the men of the east' and one who used his wealth for the benefit of others, 29. 12-13. Concerned about the spiritual standing of his children, in his *piety*, Job acted in a priestly capacity before God, 1. 4-5, a man who clearly pleased God, v. 8, something that is the responsibility of every believer, 1 Thess. 4. 1.

Not only had God considered Job, it is evident that Satan had also considered him. When challenged, 'Hast thou considered my servant?', the adversary knew exactly of whom and of what the Lord was speaking and although not directly refuting the divine description of him, Satan nevertheless sought to malign Job's character, and to rob God of His pleasure in him, by suggesting that Job only served God for personal gain and if adversity came into his life the situation would be very different, Job 1. 9-11. These are solemn verses that reveal the *personality*, *activity* and *malignity* of the evil one and also suggest that Satan and his hosts, while not omniscient, nevertheless acquaint themselves with the godly, compare Acts 19. 15.

As we consider Job should not the description given of him challenge us? Have we such a godly character? Are we so godly in life that we might be the subject of conversation and commendation in heaven? Are Satan and his hosts likely to be aware of us because of the testimony we have?

March 22nd

Job 2. 1-13

DOST THOU STILL RETAIN THINE INTEGRITY? CURSE GOD AND DIE

In the latter part of chapter 1, in a single day, Job lost his wealth and his ten children. As that day unfolded, disaster quickly followed disaster and, in each case, one servant was spared to bring Job an eyewitness account, Job 1. 13-19. He had been faithful in days of prosperity and now, despite this dramatic change in circumstances, he is seen faithful in adversity, a worshipper of God, vv. 20-22. Could God trust us as he trusted Job, confident that even difficult days would witness no change in our devotion to Him?

Satan must have been surprised at Job's resolve, but when again challenged by God he suggested the trial had not gone far enough. He had complained that a three-fold hedge had been placed around Job, v. 10, two of which had already been removed, now the third is taken away and Satan 'smote Job with sore boils', 2. 7. It is at this point that we are introduced to Job's wife. It might surprise us that Satan had expressed no desire to hurt her; did he think that she might be of use to him, just as Eve had been? While she acknowledged her husband's faithfulness, using the same word 'integrity' as God had employed, her words were the counsel of despair and implied that recovery was impossible, that his only release would be through death, something that Job might hasten if he would but curse God. She encouraged him to do what Satan predicted he would do. While we cannot condone her words we should not forget the heavy loss that she had also experienced in the preceding events and yet no reference is made to her during that trying period. Not until her husband was touched did she speak out; the trial finally broke her. In rebuking his wife, Job asserted that as they had been ready to receive the good things God had given, so now they should accept the evil He had seen fit to bring upon them. What broke her faith manifested his. Peter, having spoken of 'the trial of . . . faith', said, 'Humble yourselves . . . under the mighty hand of God, that he may exalt you in due time', 1 Pet. 1. 7; 5. 6. Job humbled himself in these opening chapters of the book and at the end God exalted him, Job 42. 12.

March 23rd

Job 4. 17-21; 9. 2-12

SHALL MORTAL MAN BE MORE JUST THAN GOD?

In chapter 3, in his distress, Job cursed the day of his birth, questioned the point of his existence, and longed for death, comments that his friend Eliphaz interpreted, albeit unjustly, as a complaint against God. Speaking from the personal experience of a vision granted to him, Job 4. 12-16, Eliphaz contrasts the supremacy of God with the inherent frailty of men and questions if it is possible for a man to be 'more pure than his maker'. Even angelic beings are accountable to Him and in comparison with God are marked by imperfection. What then of men, made from dust, mortal and whose glory is transient? It is obviously unthinkable that men could be more righteous than God, so instead of complaining against God, as if He is at fault, Job is advised to seek after Him, 5. 8, and not despise 'the chastening of the Almighty', v. 17.

While Job would have readily acknowledged that a man could not be purer than God, in chapter 9 verse 2 he raises a rather different question, 'How should man be just with God'? The word 'just' is used here in a forensic sense, Job enquiring how a man could enter into debate with God with a view to being justified before Him, a question which went to the very heart of the issue between Job and his friends. They reasoned that suffering is a sign of sin, so Job must have sinned. Job, however, his conscience clear as to his own integrity, asks how a man can be vindicated by God. If a man attempted to argue his case before God the scales would be stacked against him, and he would be found unable to answer even one of a thousand questions God might demand of him, 9. 3. Such is His wisdom and strength, no man can prosper against Him, v. 4. Volcanoes, earthquakes, eclipses, sky, sea and constellations all testify to His wonderful works, vv. 5-10. He is invisible and invincible, vv. 11-12, leaving Job longing for one who could act as a mediator between himself and God, v. 33. It is surely with a thankful heart that we turn to the New Testament and read that 'there is one mediator between God and men, the man Christ Jesus', 1 Tim. 2. 5, through whom God is enabled to be 'just, and the justifier of him that believeth in Jesus', Rom. 3. 26.

March 24th

Job 11. 1-12

CANST THOU BY SEARCHING FIND OUT GOD?

Though all of Job's friends were irritated by his refusal to accept their proposition that his sufferings must be attributed to sin, and his insistence on being innocent, Job 10. 6-7; 11. 4, of the three men the words of Zophar were the harshest. He began by dismissing Job's expressions of anguish as being nothing more than a torrent of words from a man with too much to say, whose speech was empty of any substance or value. Far from placing any merit upon what Job said, Zophar actually accused him of mocking God, vv. 2-3. Though unable to substantiate his charge, Zophar nevertheless suggested that Job's sins were so great that what he was suffering was much less than he really deserved, v. 6. May we be preserved from ever having such a judgemental attitude towards our brethren, mindful of the warning of the Lord Jesus, 'Judge not, that ye be not judged', Matt. 7. 1, something that was to befall the three friends before the book concludes, Job 42. 7.

Convinced of Job's guilt, Zophar desired that God might speak, confident that with such a revelation Job would realize that God was indeed treating him leniently, 11. 5-6. Job's ignorance of that fact, as well as his persistent profession of innocence, was an indication to Zophar that Job had no concept of God's knowledge and wisdom, a wisdom the secrets of which lie beyond anything that men can imagine or know, vv. 6-7; a wisdom that is universal in its dimensions and scope, which men are powerless to prevail against, vv. 8-10. God's knowledge both of men and their wickedness is absolute, so that nothing can be hid from Him, v. 11. In reverential awe we must surely say with David, 'Such knowledge is too wonderful for me', Ps. 139. 6.

In view of what he has said, Zophar asserts that the wisest course for man 'born like a wild ass's colt', by nature headstrong and uncontrollable, is to consider and understand how great God is and then submit to Him, v. 12. May our prayer today be, 'Search me, O God, and know my heart: try me, and know my thoughts: And see if there be any wicked way in me, and lead me in the way everlasting', Ps. 139. 23-24!

March 25th

Job 14. 1-17; 19. 25-27.

IF A MAN DIE, SHALL HE LIVE AGAIN?

Zophar had suggested that despite his great suffering Job was not entirely without hope, that if he turned to God and repented his situation would be reversed, Job 11. 13-15. Job, however, saw little prospect of any deliverance from his trials and, in chapter 14, reveals his thoughts concerning life and death, concluding that his situation provided little ground for hope, 14. 19.

Regarding life, Job emphasizes its *brevity*, and as for death its *inevitability*. Man's life is of 'few days', akin to a flower that is soon cut down, a passing shadow, or an hireling that fulfils his labour and then is dispensed with, vv. 2, 6. Man's days are equally 'full of trouble', Job was forgetting the times of prosperity and blessing recorded in chapter 1. Since life is so brief and troubled, Job wonders why God should pay such attention to him. He will know that because man's heart is sinful it is impossible for men to be spotless in His sight, vv. 3-4; why then such intense judgement of him? Job knows the span of his life is set by God, men have no power to extend it, and he desires that God might leave him alone to allow him some period of rest before the inevitable happens, vv. 5-6. A tree that is felled might 'sprout again' but Job fears this cannot be said of men, destined to die and decompose, then 'where is he?' vv. 7-12. Job had no fear of death, indeed he saw it as offering relief from his trials, hiding him in the grave until God turns from His wrath. He would, however, like to think that death is not the end, that in divine purpose man shall live again, and the sufferings of the present time will issue in future vindication, vv. 13-15. Though Job longed for that, his present situation made such hopes but a dream. God apparently determined to remember nothing but his sins, vv. 16-17, a bleak prospect indeed. In chapter 19, Job's pessimism begins to disappear as in faith he confesses that he knows he has a 'Redeemer', who will 'appear' to vindicate him, and whom he will be raised to see.

The believer today knows what Job struggled to know. At death, 'Where is he?' we can answer, 'With the Lord', 2 Cor. 5. 8. 'Shall he live again?' Confidently, we reply that the Lord will come and 'the dead in Christ shall rise', 1 Thess. 4. 16.

March 26th

Job 15. 7-16

WHAT IS MAN, THAT HE SHOULD BE CLEAN?

This question, asked by Eliphaz, was not an inquiry as to how a man could be clean before God, but was rather a final challenge to Job, to demolish any claims he might continue to make of being innocent of the charge levelled against him, that his sufferings were linked to sins in his life. In the opening verses of the chapter, Job's arguments have again been dismissed as being empty, unprofitable and irreverent words that, to his friends, seemed to confirm the charges they had brought against him, Job 15. 1-6. Warming to his subject, Eliphaz then dismisses any profession Job might make to being wise. Earlier, Job had accused his friends of speaking as though they were the sole exponents of wisdom, 12. 2. Now, the tables are turned, and, with a series of questions, Eliphaz sarcastically asks if Job thought wisdom originated with him. Had he the advantage of longevity and precedence in existence? Not at all, there were others far older than Job, 15. 7, 10. Had he been made privy to the secret counsels of God, leaving him more knowledgeable than others? No, they were his equals in knowledge, vv. 8-9. Why, then, had he dismissed their earlier counsel, 'the consolations of God', advice that promised restoration if Job would only repent, v. 11? Why did he persist in his profession of innocence, and, in so doing, malign the justice of God, vv. 12-13? How could Job think he was innocent when the holiness of God is such that by comparison, the heavens are not clean in His sight, and angels are far inferior to Him? Where does that leave men, sinful in nature and conduct? Eliphaz is really saying, 'Far from being innocent, Job, you are abominable in God's sight'.

Can a man be clean in God's sight? Job has already said, 'Who can bring a clean thing out of an unclean? not one', 14. 4, but while that is impossible for men, it is not so for God. Although some of the Corinthians had formerly been 'fornicators, idolaters, adulterers' and many other things beside, Paul could say of them, 'Ye are washed', 1 Cor. 6. 9-11. How? John says, 'The blood of Jesus Christ his Son cleanseth us from all sin', 1 John 1. 9. Think today of the Person – 'His Son'; the price –'blood'; and the peace in knowing that it cleanses from 'all sin'.

March 27th

Job 19. 1-12; James 5. 11

HOW LONG WILL YE VEX MY SOUL, AND BREAK ME IN PIECES WITH WORDS?

Job's friends had but added to his distress and he appeals to be left alone. Contrary to any display of friendship, they turned against him, consistently accusing him of sin, though unable to provide evidence of it, Job 19. 3. If Job had inadvertently erred, then surely it was a matter between himself and God, and would not his own conscience convict him of it, v. 4? If they were, however, determined to persist in their charges, then he asks them to consider his position. Job had no doubt that God's hand was in his trials, but he could not find any rational explanation for them, vv. 6-7. In his perplexity, he had cried to God, even protested that his treatment was undeserved, but no answer had been afforded to him, v. 7. Amongst other things, he felt like a tree that had been uprooted, prostrate, and with his friends accusing him, with none to lift him up, v. 10; Eccles. 11. 3. Did they have no thought for his feelings? Job could have said, 'They persecute him whom thou hast smitten; and they talk to the grief of those whom thou hast wounded', Ps. 69. 26. What of our words toward those in distress? Are they helpful or hurtful? Is our speech 'always with grace seasoned with salt', Col. 4. 6? May God help us to be like the Saviour and 'know how to speak a word in season to him that is weary', Isa. 50. 4.

James chapter 5 provides the only direct reference to Job in the New Testament. Verse 11 asserts that those who endure trial, and come through with their faith in God intact, are admired and counted 'happy' by all who observe them. Job is such a man and his history explains why they are counted happy, for such will ultimately be vindicated and rewarded by God. Although Job did not understand his sufferings and his friends totally misinterpreted them, nevertheless their goal and outcome revealed that God was neither unjust in his dealings with Job, nor indifferent to his distress, but rather is 'full of tender compassion and pitiful'. Perhaps some reading this today are suffering and feel 'in darkness' with 'no light', much as Job did? Do not despair, but 'trust in the name of the Lord, and stay upon . . . God', just like God's Perfect Servant, Isa. 50. 10, 7.

March 28th

Job 20. 1-11; Psalm 73. 18-19

KNOWEST THOU NOT THIS OF OLD . . . THE TRIUMPHING OF THE WICKED IS SHORT?

Like Bildad and Eliphaz before him, Job 8. 11-19; 15. 20-35, Zophar speaks of the fate of the wicked and, akin to his two companions, infers that Job is such a man. Chapter 19 concluded with Job warning his friends to know that God judges men and they needed to fear Him. Zophar, offended at the suggestion that they required such a warning, and unable to contain himself, responds with words he felt Job needed to know, 20. 2-4. A truth that Zophar asserts has pervaded the whole of human history, and which has been summarized as, 'the happiness of the wicked is short lived, and their wrongdoing is self-destructive', F. I. ANDERSEN. They may 'triumph' but it is temporary; they may rejoice but it is momentary; there may be pride, even arrogance, but it is doomed to perish, vv. 5-7. Believers know that in the light of eternity the words of Zophar are true, the prosperity of the wicked is brief, but it does not always necessarily appear like that in life. Had Zophar, for instance, forgotten the history of Cain and Abel? Righteous Abel was slain but Cain went on to have children and build a city.

Over the centuries many saints have struggled to reconcile their faith in God with the problem that all too frequently the wicked prosper while the righteous are afflicted, Ps. 37; Jer. 12. 1-4; Hab. 1. 13. In Psalm 73 the writer speaks of the thoughts he had on this matter. Although the psalm begins on a confident note, 'Truly God is good to Israel', the author acknowledges that he was not always so certain. As he beheld the wicked, he had envied their prosperity and began to think that spiritual exercises were pointless, vv. 2-14. Yes, even godly men can be disturbed by such thoughts! But while that can become man's perspective on the wicked, when the psalmist went into the sanctuary he got God's view, v. 17. Though in demeanour confident, and apparently unshakeable, in the outworking of divine purpose, evil doers will be seen to be without foundation, and their final end is appointed to be speedy and complete, vv. 18-19. Do we at times envy the wicked? If so, we need to spend more time alone with God.

March 29th

Job 28. 12-28

BUT WHERE SHALL WISDOM BE FOUND? AND WHERE IS THE PLACE OF UNDERSTANDING?

This chapter opens with a graphic description of the industry and ingenuity of men in mining the treasures of gold, silver, brass and precious stones from the depths of the earth. But, having recorded the skill of men to accomplish such difficult and dangerous tasks, the question is twice raised as to where wisdom is to be found, Job 28. 12, 20. The 'wisdom' in view is seen, v. 28, to embrace the knowledge and understanding that produces within men a reverential and practical fear of God.

In connection with the first enquiry, the focus is upon where this wisdom is *not* found. Men do not value it and thus it is not to be gained from the world of men, v. 13; 1 Cor. 1. 21. Men can dig deep into the earth or go to the depths of the sea in search of material treasures, but such efforts, no matter how strenuously they might be pursued, cannot impart this wisdom to men, Job 28. 14. It cannot be purchased, for its value is beyond calculation, vv. 15-19; Prov. 3. 15. The question is repeated and now the focus is primarily upon where this wisdom *is* to be found. The source of it is not with men, nor with the fowls in the heights, and though the depths of destruction and death reveal the value of possessing it they are unable to impart it. But 'God understandeth . . . he knoweth', Job 28. 20-23. God's possession of wisdom is seen in His ability to do what is impossible for men and also in the order and power manifest in creation, vv. 24-27; Ps. 104. 24. God 'has the wisdom to adjust the pressure of the wind and measure the amount of water in the atmosphere' and 'to control the rain and guide the storm as it moves across the earth', W. W. Wiersbe. The first step for men in acquiring wisdom is to fear God, Job 28. 28; Prov. 1. 7.

Wisdom comes 'from above', Jas. 3. 17. It can be known only by divine revelation . . . 'by his spirit', 1 Cor. 2. 10. It is resident in Christ in 'whom are hid all the treasures of wisdom and knowledge', Col. 2. 3. Believers recognize the significance of the cross in relation to it, 1 Cor. 1. 24. Men go to great lengths to gather treasure from the earth; how diligent are we to gather this treasure from above? Read Proverbs 2 verses 3-7.

March 30th

Job 38. 1-11

WHO IS THIS THAT DARKENETH COUNSEL BY WORDS WITHOUT KNOWLEDGE?

In his controversy with his friends Job's final request was 'that the Almighty might answer me', Job 31. 35. That desire was now granted. Although today's verses are but a brief introductory section of the words of the Lord to him, surely we cannot fail to be impressed with both the privilege and majesty of the occasion. Consider the grace of the Lord in responding to the request of His servant. Apart from chapter 12 verse 9, this is the first use of the title 'Jehovah' since the opening two chapters. Despite all that had happened to Job the Lord was still the faithful covenant-keeping God, and His ways with Job involved no severance of, or inconsistency with, that relationship.

In verse 2, Job is not accused of speaking error but rather of obscuring divine truth in speaking words that conveyed his lack of knowledge and limited understanding of both God and His ways, something that the Lord proceeds to address. Contrary to what we might have expected, in His answer, instead of providing an explanation for Job's sufferings, the Lord unveiled to him His glory as manifest in regard to creation. In verses 4 to 7, in connection with the earth, the Lord took up the metaphor of a builder determining the dimensions of what he would construct, setting the cornerstone, laying the foundation. These verses have in view the initial creation and the question is raised, 'Where wast thou'? No man witnessed that process, Adam being made on the sixth day, the climax of God's work in creation. In verses 8 to 11, attention is drawn to the sea and now the metaphor is that of giving birth. Again, the record of creation is in view, Gen. 1. 2, 9-10. Who did this? Job knew, Job 26. 10.

Since no explanation is given for Job's sufferings we might wonder what significance this revelation had for him. The key is in verse 3 where the Lord commanded, 'Answer thou me'. Earlier Job had said, 'Call thou and I will answer, let me speak and answer thou me', as though he could address God as His equal, 13. 22. The unveiling of divine glory revealed Job's inability to do that. Paul would later write, 'O man, who art thou that repliest against God?', Rom. 9. 20.

March 31st

Job 40. 1-24

SHALL HE THAT CONTENDETH WITH THE ALMIGHTY INSTRUCT HIM?

The opening five verses are an interlude in the unveiling of the Lord's glory, Job being challenged to answer the questions the Lord had addressed to him in chapters 38 and 39. In his earlier controversy with his friends, Job's language implied God had treated him unjustly, and Elihu actually accused him of saying 'My righteousness is more than God's', Job 27. 2; 35. 2. Now, in light of the revelation of the Lord given to him, Job is commanded to state if he still feels confident to find fault. Confessing 'I am vile' (Heb. *qalal*), i.e. of no weight, insignificant, the one who had earlier said, 'Call thou and I will answer' is now silent in the presence of the Lord. Although previously he had much to say, and convinced of his argument even had repeated himself; now he has nothing further to add. God's revelation of Himself was fulfilling its intended purpose, but more remained to be done: Job is silenced but not yet submissive.

The Lord addresses Job again, 40. 6-7. In seeking to justify himself, Job's arguments had raised questions regarding the government, justice and competence of God, v. 8. In view of his complaints, the Lord challenges Job to consider if he was competent to assume the reins of government. Did Job have the power, majesty and attributes of the Lord, vv. 9-10? If he were to display his wrath could he humble 'every one that is proud', subdue evil and bring down the wicked, vv. 11-13? If Job could do all these, the Lord was ready to acknowledge that he was in a position where he could justly question His ways, v. 14. We might wonder why the Lord specifically mentions the 'proud'? Was pride at the heart of Job's arguments? As evidence of his ability to govern in the moral realm, let Job demonstrate his power to control in the natural realm, vv. 15-24. Could Job capture and domesticate 'behemoth', the largest of land animals, 'chief of the ways of God'? Job could not do any such thing and ultimately will say, 'I abhor myself and repent in dust and ashes', 42. 6. He has been brought to an end of himself, silent and submissive, overwhelmed by the glory and greatness of the Lord. May God find all of us thus humbled before Him!

April 1st

Psalm 2. 1-12

WHY DO THE HEATHEN RAGE, AND THE PEOPLE IMAGINE A VAIN THING?

This psalm is ascribed to David, Acts 4. 25 and is probably based on God's promise to Nathan, 2 Sam. 7. 11-16, that the Davidic throne would last for ever. Historically, it relates to the coronation of a king, possibly David, who is confronted by a confederation of rebellious states seeking his overthrow. They are characterized as being noisy and agitated, like the rolling and roaring of the sea, Ps. 2. 1-2. Not only do they conspire together, but they also stand up together, which suggests that they are resolved to reject their monarch. This reminds us of the citizens' delegation in the parable of the pounds, 'We will not have this man to reign over us', Luke 19. 14. The early church applied these texts directly to Herod, Pilate, *et al*, in their opposition to our Lord – God's Anointed, Acts 4. 25-28. Notice the use of the possessive pronouns – **His** anointed, **My** king and **My** Son – indicating God's total involvement, Acts 4. 28. God's initial response to His rejected king is to mock the conspirators, and then exercise wrath, Ps. 2. 4-5. But this is no laughing matter for the conspirators as God has already done what they tried to prevent. Whilst they were posturing, God has disposed of the matter by 'enthroning His king upon Zion' (i.e. Jerusalem), v. 6 NEB. Thus, verse 6 is pivotal, because verses 1-5 lead up to this declaration and in verses 7-12 the king expands on his mandate from God. Central to this mandate is the notion of sonship, v. 7ff. When David's descendents were enthroned, God renewed His covenant, and, in effect, adopted the king as His own son, see 2 Sam. 7. 14. Prophetically, this pointed to David's greater Son who would be declared the true Son of God through resurrection, Acts 13. 33; Rom. 1. 4; Heb. 1. 5. God now delegates His authority to His Son, Ps. 2. 8 who would ultimately triumph over His enemies, vv. 8-9. All conspirators are then called upon to serve the Lord by showing due deference to the Son, vv. 10-12. Failure to comply means destruction, but trusting in the Son brings blessing, v. 12. As we think today of all the forces that oppose Christ, let us rejoice in the fact that ultimately He will reign from shore to shore, Ps. 72. 1-19.

April 2nd

Psalm 8. 1-9

WHAT IS MAN, THAT THOU ART MINDFUL OF HIM?

This psalm is a hymn of unadulterated praise to God without any request on the part of the psalmist. Since the opening line is the same as the last line, the psalmist creates a literary device known as an *inclusio*. This confirms that the motif throughout the psalm is the revelation of God's Name and His majesty as revealed in creation. Everything in heaven and in earth is subservient to Him, and His splendour is celebrated throughout the whole universe. Even children, with all their inherent weaknesses, are strong when they take God's Name upon their lips, Ps. 8. 2; cp. Matt. 21. 16, utterly confounding the self-assertiveness of men, Ps. 8. 2. The psalmist informs us that it was sufficient for God simply to move His fingers to bring the heavens into existence, v. 3. Compared to this extraordinary feat, man is totally inconsequential, and the psalmist finds it difficult to think that man is of any importance to God whatsoever, vv. 4-5. Hence, the reasons for our question today, v. 4, see also Job 7. 17; 25. 6; Ps. 144. 3, and note their immediate contexts. And yet, the startling truth is that God is so interested in mortal man that He has bestowed upon him a position of strength and authority over the whole of His creation, vv. 6-9, cp. Ps. 21. 5. God made man in His own image, Gen. 1. 26, and only slightly inferior to the heavenly hosts, Ps. 8. 5. But man is not simply a cog in a complex universe, he has been given delegated authority from God to administer the whole earth, principally for the psalmist, the animal kingdom, vv. 8-9, cp. Jas. 3. 7. God, effectively, laid the world at man's feet, Ps. 8. 7, but sadly, man is not currently in charge of creation – man has lost dominion because of sin, Heb. 2. 5-8. Has God's purpose for man simply been thwarted then because of sin? By no means! In the Last Adam, the Second Man, 1 Cor. 15. 45-47, all that was lost by man has been gloriously restored in Christ through His death and resurrection, Rom. 5. 12-21. Praise God, we now see a *man* not only honoured, but crowned and exalted at God's right hand, Heb. 2. 9; Eph. 1. 19-22. Not only will creation be laid at His feet, but His enemies will become His footstool, Ps. 110. 1; 1 Cor. 15. 24-28. What a question then to reflect upon today!

April 3rd

Psalm 10. 1-12

WHY STANDEST THOU AFAR OFF, O LORD?

There are good reasons for thinking that this psalm was originally part of Psalm 9 as it has a common refrain, Pss. 9. 19; 10. 12. The psalmist is deeply perplexed and distressed to find that the wicked were prospering by exploiting the weak in society, vv. 2-3, as if God did not exist, vv. 4-5. God's inactivity seemed to vindicate their actions, that the world belonged to them, and nothing would shake their resolve to prosper, vv. 5-6. Their whole attitude towards others was evil, almost bestial as they lied, cheated, and resorted to murder to achieve their own selfish ends, vv. 7-10. Yet, God seemed to be the passive onlooker, almost an absentee landlord who simply observed from a distance their reprehensible conduct – notice the powerful imagery, v. 11; cp. Deut. 31. 18; Isa. 1. 15. Had God simply abandoned the weak and defenceless? Was His silence and inactivity evidence of His complicity?

To answer these questions we need to appreciate that lamentation in the Psalms was a powerful aspect of Israel's spirituality and arose out of the experience of dissonance. The problem for the psalmist was why was there injustice in the world? Why did God fail to put things right, and why was He perceived to be absent from the situation? But the question is not really about the passivity or absence of God at all in this situation. Rather, about how faith towards God responds to the experience of dissonance. In other words, how do we cope with a situation of injustice and where there are more questions than answers? This was Job's great dilemma as he sought answers to complex and, at times, overpowering circumstances. Despite these, however, he persevered. Not simply by gritting his teeth, but realizing that beyond the material and the visible was a God who, seemingly absent, was, nonetheless, ultimately in total control of his life, Job 23. 8-10; cp. Heb. 11. 27. Our psalmist arrives at this conclusion in verse 10 when he calls on God to publicly smite his enemies. The wicked may think that God ignores evil, but let us take heart today in knowing that God has set a day when He will judge the world with justice by the Man He has appointed – even our Lord Jesus Christ, Acts 17. 31.

April 4th

Psalm 22. 1-15; Matthew 27. 46

MY GOD, MY GOD, WHY HAST THOU FORSAKEN ME?

The title of this psalm includes the Hebrew expression *ayyeleth ha-shahar*, 'the hind of the dawn'. This may simply be a musical setting, but the Septuagint translates it as *'concerning the morning aid or help'*. We might therefore conclude that this gives us an early clue as to the theme of this psalm. Just as the hind waits for the dawn having endured the darkness of the night scene, so the suffering Servant of Jehovah waits for the deliverance of God at the break of day. The opening two verses reflect the divine abandonment of the Servant, hence the awful cry of dereliction, cp. Ps. 10. 1. No one could fail to see, however, that these words are prophetic since they are uttered by our dying Lord on Calvary, Matt. 27. 46; Mark 15. 34. Here, then, is the fulfilment of those servant songs, Isa. 52. 13-15; Isa. 53. Why, though, has God seemingly abandoned this faithful Servant when, in the past, He had delivered unfaithful Israel from captivity, Isa. 52. 2-3; Ps. 22. 3-5? Surely, it was because it pleased God to make His life an offering for (our) sin, Isa. 53. 10? Or, as the hymnwriter so aptly puts it, *'How great the pain of searing loss: the Father turns His face away, as wounds which mar the chosen One, bring many sons to glory'*. Notice the unique correlation with other biblical texts as the Servant discloses His predicament, Ps. 22. 6; Isa. 53. 3, 7; Matt. 27. 39. Eaton translates the Hebrew of verse 8 to almost parallel Matthew chapter 27 verse 43. Even in the depths of despair and suffering, the Servant remembers still that God had cared for Him during his lifetime, vv. 9-11. Whilst His mother gave Him comfort, it was God who had kept Him safe, and would ultimately deliver Him from trouble, cp. Pss. 2. 7; 89. 26. But trouble comes in battalions to this Servant as the hounds of hell surround Him in death, 22. 12-15. Who can ever measure the brutality of Calvary, and man's hatred towards the Saviour as He dies upon the cross? Yet as we think of the sufferings of Christ today let us not forget the subsequent glory that followed Him, 1 Pet. 1. 11. Let us also not forget that the darkest hour is always just before the dawn of a new and glorious day.

April 5th

Psalm 24. 1-10

WHO IS THIS KING OF GLORY?

This liturgical psalm was probably written to celebrate the triumphant entrance of the Ark into Jerusalem, 2 Sam. 6. The starting point for the psalmist is how God can be contained when He is the Creator of the universe, Ps. 24. 1-2. Solomon also faced this challenge at the dedication of the temple, hence the substance of his prayer, 1 Kgs. 8. 27. Paradoxically, Paul turns this on its head when he tells us that one of the great mysteries of the New Testament is Christ residing (contained?) in us, Col. 1. 27. The first test for the psalmist, Ps. 24. 3-6, is how does one approach the stronghold, no longer of men, but now constituted the hill of the Lord, and the sanctuary where God dwells? What does it mean to have clean hands, etc., v. 4? Does this not indicate the measure of moral fitness required of all to enter God's presence, cp. Ps. 15; John 4. 24, and note the privilege believers now enjoy, Heb. 10. 19-22? In verse 6 the psalmist seeks the face of the God of Jacob. Could this be a reminder to us that irrespective of how unfit we once were, like Jacob, God is always prepared to receive and bless us, Gen. 32. 29-30? Small wonder that the psalmist takes time to pause and reflect as inferred by the Hebrew word *Selah*, Ps. 24. 6. As the Ark neared the gates of the city of David, it was challenged, vv. 7-10, and one can envisage the scene as the huge gates of the city are ceremonially barred against the victorious king – cp. the state opening of the UK Parliament and the barring of Black Rod. The processional leaders call for the portcullis to be raised to admit the King of glory. Twice the gatekeepers ask, 'Who is the King of glory?', and twice the reply confirms that it is none other than the Lord of hosts. This is the first time that the title 'Lord of hosts' is used in the Psalter as an epithet for God. It emphasizes the power of God as He controls and leads the armies of heaven into battle. Ultimately, the gates are opened and the King of glory comes in. Whilst this scene may remind us of the ascension of Christ, Heb. 1. 3, the principal application points to that day when Christ will reign in millennial glory, Ps. 132. 13-14; Isa. 4. 5; Rev. 20. 4. What an inspiring thought for the day! Is the door of my heart still open to the King of glory?

April 6th

Psalm 27. 1-14

THE LORD IS MY LIGHT . . . WHOM SHALL I FEAR?

This rhetorical question is a fitting opening as its key theme is confidence in God. It is sandwiched between Psalms 26 and 28, which both express concern as to why God does not seem to be defending His servants despite their blameless lives. Psalm 27, however, moves us away from the plight of self-pity, and concentrates our minds on the power and presence of God to preserve us despite the strength of the enemy, v. 3. If the psalm is Davidic (the title 'of David' may simply mean that it was written for David) then it may relate to the time when David was being hunted by Saul. He portrays his adversary in terms of a wild animal seeking to devour his flesh, v. 2, or physically harm him, and slander his name, v. 12. But overriding his concern about self-preservation is the confidence he draws from the fact that God is on his side, almost like a defensive wall that surrounds his every action, v. 1. The psalmist has learnt from experience that no force or power can ultimately prevent his fellowship with God, and this reminds us of that confidence that we can enjoy daily in the love of God, Rom. 8. 38-39. This confidence in God leads the psalmist to express his keen desire to frequent the house of God, v. 4, where God's presence can be readily experienced. If we are to understand anything about God we must, of necessity, live in the light of His presence, Eph. 5. 8-10. Fellowship with God must be a priority in our lives if we are to grow in grace and become more Christ-like. The mood of the psalmist changes from verse 7 and reflects a state of anxiety rather than confidence. Because of this sudden mood swing, some commentators have suggested that the psalm consists of two parts either written by two different authors or by the same author at different times. It could, of course, simply be indicative of the highs and lows often experienced by believers, yet this is not what God intends for us! Our ambivalence is contrasted in this psalm with the steadfast character of God. Our psalm started with an assertion, but now ends with an exhortation. This is a call to stiffen our resolve in God, 2 Tim. 2. 1. As Joshua found his courage in God to enter the land, Josh. 1. 5-6, may we daily look to the Lord for strength and take heart!

April 7th

Psalm 42. 1-11; 43. 1-5

WHY ART THOU CAST DOWN, O MY SOUL? AND WHY ART THOU DISQUIETED IN ME?

Psalm 42 begins the second division of the Book of Psalms, which ends with Psalm 72. This division is often referred to as the Elohistic Psalter, because the Hebrew word *Elohim* is used when referring to God rather than the usual term of *Yahweh*. The divine title *Elohim* conveys the idea of exclusivity, confirming that Israel's God is essentially God of gods. Psalms 42 and 43 are considered to be one psalm united by a single superscription, and a number of common refrains, 42. 6, 12; 43. 5. Both reflect a theme of lament by an exiled writer who has an overwhelming desire to be in God's house again, 42. 1; 43. 3, 4. He compares his own wilderness experience to that of a hind which desperately seeks to assuage its thirst in a time of drought. Just as the hind strains all its sinews to find water, so the writer hungers and thirsts after righteousness, 42. 1-2. But instead of spiritual refreshment, his daily diet is his tears, and the constant taunt of his enemies who question the very existence of the living God, 42. 3; 43. 1. He is frustrated when he remembers the halcyon days of worship that he once enjoyed in fellowship with others, 42. 5. This leads to a sense of spiritual angst when he cross-examines his soul. Four times he concludes that he is spiritually depressed, 42. 5, 6, 11; 43. 5. Yet, when he takes himself in hand, he realizes that despite the overwhelming stresses and demands of the moment, he is still able to find the goodness of God encircling him, 42. 7-8. Hope in God becomes his clarion call as faith keeps asserting itself. This too is Jonah's experience in the depths of the sea, Jonah 2. 3-6, being a constant reminder of that greater journey of One who entered the throes of death for us, having endured such hostility against Himself from sinners, Heb. 12. 3. Spiritual depression is often experienced by believers as they allow personal circumstances to control their lives. Does this sound familiar? The solution presented in these texts is not to look inwards at our present circumstances nor even to find comfort in past experiences, but to daily look up to the living God. Is this not the continuing challenge of Hebrews chapter 12 verse 2?

April 8th

Psalm 73. 12-28

WHOM HAVE I IN HEAVEN BUT THEE?

This psalm deals with the recurrent Old Testament theme of theodicy. Why does God allow evil and injustice to exist in the world? Our psalmist gives vent to his frustration as he observes the prosperity and carefree lifestyle of the wicked, Ps. 73. 12. What was the point of serving God when the only reward for faithfulness was suffering, vv. 13-16? This reminds us of the modern tendency to evaluate everything by reference to whether it pays to be good, and that asks cynically, 'What's in it for me?' Satan applied this same reasoning to Job as he sought permission to test God's righteous servant, Job 1. 8-10. The psalmist was, however, reluctant to make his doubts public because of the effect this would have on the family of God, v. 15 NEB. How important it is to ensure that our own personal liberty does not become a stumbling block to others, 1 Cor. 8. 9!

When the psalmist turns away from his own personal despair and enters the sanctuary of God, everything becomes clear to him, Ps. 73. 17. He realizes that the true meaning of life is not found in the illusion of popular wisdom, a wisdom that would ultimately conspire to crucify the Lord of glory, 1 Cor. 2. 8. He now sees and understands things from God's perspective. What a difference this makes to our lives when we realize that God is not fazed or mocked by the wickedness in the world! Whatever a man sows that will he also reap, Gal. 6. 7; 1 Cor. 6. 9. While the wicked might seem to be getting away with things, pro-tem, their eternal destination is certain destruction, Ps. 73. 19, 27; cp. Ps. 37; Job 4. 8-9.

Our Lord warned his generation of a broad (easy) road that led to destruction, Matt. 7. 13, and how important it is for us to continue to present this message! The psalmist concludes his observations by chastising himself for being so silly about his earlier doubts, Ps. 73. 21-22. After all, God has not only helped him in the past, but is his only real hope for the future, vv. 23-28. Our question today, therefore, reminds us that we may often doubt and fail God, but He remains faithful, 1 Cor. 1. 9. It is in eternity, not time, that the justice of God will be fully vindicated.

April 9th

Psalm 77. 1-10

HATH GOD FORGOTTEN TO BE GRACIOUS?

This psalm of lament was written by someone who sees in his own personal grief and distress a mirror image of the sufferings of God's people in exile, vv. 1-9. Many commentators also see a correlation between this psalm and Habakkuk's prayer, Hab. 3. 3-15. The heartbreaking and powerful intercession of the psalmist on behalf of his people is intended to move God into action. And such is the intensity of the physical effort required – the stretched out hands in prayer, the groaning in spirit, and the sleepless nights, vv. 2-4a – that he is almost struck dumb like a man experiencing a stroke, v. 4. We are also reminded of our Lord's experience in Gethsemane, Luke 22. 44; Heb. 5. 7, and His vicarious sufferings on the cross for us, 1 Pet. 2. 24. The psalmist thinks about Israel's past blessing, Ps. 77. 6, which means the time of the exodus from Egypt, see also verses 14-20. But this leads only to frustration on his part, because he cannot understand why a faithful and merciful God, Exod. 34. 6, does not act to deliver His people from exile. All this pent-up emotion then makes him question whether God has in fact changed His nature, Ps. 77. 8-10. Can God still be relied upon to bless His people or has He simply abandoned them, v. 9? This is a sobering thought, and why he pauses for a deep intake of breath – *think of that – Selah*! We often blame God for our misfortunes, and also for failing to deliver us from them, cp. Ruth 1. 21. The turning point for the psalmist comes in verse 10, which is pivotal to the overall interpretation of the psalm. The Hebrew of this verse is unclear and difficult to translate. Most English translations lay emphasis on the despair felt by the psalmist, because God has seemingly failed to act. But a better rendering, and one in keeping with the later context, is to translate, as Eaton, 'But I say, this shall be my entreaty: to recite the deeds of the right hand of God Most High'. This verse then acts as a fitting precursor to the hymn of praise in verses 11-20, which centres on the saving grace of God. When God seems to be silent, one might be tempted to think that He has forgotten us. Let us, however, pause, and take time today to remember past blessings, and continue to trust Him with our future, 2 Cor. 5. 7.

April 10th

Psalm 77. 11-20

WHO IS SO GREAT A GOD AS OUR GOD?

For background to this psalm read again the meditation for yesterday. In this second part we move from lament into praise. This liturgy is not based though on any emotional outburst, but is rooted in sacred truth. It is a time, Eccles. 3. 1, to celebrate by remembering God's great deeds, especially His deliverance of Israel from Egyptian bondage, Ps. 77. 15-20. How important is the faculty of remembrance, because we so easily forget, Jas. 1. 23-24! What provision, therefore, God has made for us to remember His Son in the breaking of bread, 1 Cor. 11. 26! Why is the past so necessary to present experience? It is surely because it is the basis of present life and hope. For our psalmist, the recalling of the Exodus story provides assurance that God will deliver His people again.

Earlier, he had been extremely vociferous in complaining about God's inactivity, Ps. 77. 4, 7; now he praises God for who He is, and what He has done. Little surprise, then, that he concludes that God is incomparable, v. 13! Here are textual echoes of the words of Moses and the children of Israel as they celebrated God's triumph over Egypt at the Red Sea, Exod. 15. 11, cp. Jethro's comments, 18. 11. And the psalmist now realizes that this incomparable God, who dwells in holy splendour, Ps. 77. 13, is not passive or detached, but has, in fact, come down to redeem His *own* people out of bondage, v. 15; cp. Hos. 11. 1. What a picture this is of our Kinsman-redeemer who stepped down, entered human experience, Heb. 2. 14, and paid the price to deliver us from sin, Matt. 20. 28; 1 Tim. 2. 6. Here is something to meditate upon *today*; that is why the psalmist presses the pause button again – *think of that – Selah!*

From verses 16-20, the psalmist provides us with a graphic description of God's power over the elements at the Red Sea, cp. Mark 4. 41, and His fiery appearance later on Sinai. Who could now doubt that the psalmist's God was in control of all things? Yet, even more precious to him was the pastoral interest that God had in his life, Ps. 77. 20. Let us remember today our Shepherd who went through the deepest waters to rescue His flock, Heb. 13. 20.

April 11th

Psalm 85. 1-13

WILT THOU NOT REVIVE US AGAIN: THAT THY PEOPLE MAY REJOICE IN THEE?

This is one of eleven psalms where part of the superscription includes the statement, 'Of the Sons of Korah'. The name Korah was synonymous with rebellion in Israel, Num. 16, yet his descendents were spared judgement, 26. 11, and became praise leaders in temple services, 1 Chr. 9. 17-19. Therefore, these psalms speak to us of the grace and loving-kindness of God, and how it extends to those who are utterly undeserving. No wonder the psalmist uses the expression *Selah* in our psalm, Ps. 85. 2, meaning *'think of that!'*

Psalm 85 moves along these same lines as the psalmist calls for the restoration of Israel to their own land, and prays the faithful God to act at the present time, vv. 1-3. Twice in the psalm, Israel calls upon God to exercise His steadfast love towards them so that they might be saved, vv. 7, 10. It is because the psalmist has grasped that God is faithful to His covenant with Israel that he has the courage to ask God to respond to his entreaty, expecting a positive result, cp. 71. 20.

Revival and restoration in the spiritual realm always comes from God, Hab. 3. 2-3. They are linked with those who are contrite in spirit, Isa. 57. 15, and who recognize their own inadequacies, Ezra 9. 9. This is not something that can be worked up or stimulated by human emotion. But when God does send revival, our emotions are affected as our souls are enlightened by the spirit of a holy and righteous God, and we are freed from the fetters of apathy to truly praise God, Ezra 9. 8; Ps. 13. 3. Are we daily seeking revival or renewal in our hearts so that God's name might be again glorified in and through us? Can we today, in all sincerity, sing the words of J. Edwin Orr?

'O Holy Ghost, revival comes from Thee;
Send a revival, start the work in me;
Thy word declares Thou wilt supply our need;
For blessings now, O Lord, I humbly plead'.

Finally, when the psalmist thinks of the attributes of God in salvation, 85. 10, he previews the work of our Lord Jesus Christ as reconciling all these aspects in Himself at the cross.

April 12th

Psalm 137. 1-9

HOW SHALL WE SING THE LORD'S SONG IN A STRANGE LAND?

Decisions made in haste are often repented of at leisure, and this was undoubtedly Judah's experience in Babylonian exile. Hezekiah's unwise decision to show Babylonian envoys the treasures of Judah, 2 Kgs. 20. 12-19, ultimately led to the destruction of Jerusalem and exile for God's people. Now they had time to reflect upon their experiences as they sat down by the numerous canals that criss-crossed Babylon. Such a contrast to their homeland that depended on God for seasonal rainfall, Deut. 11. 14! Yet their tears were not for their present predicament, but for the memory of Jerusalem, and all that they had lost. Previously, the jibe of their adversaries had been, 'Where is your God', Ps. 79. 10, but now a more imaginative approach is evident, 'Sing us one of the songs of Zion'. Was this not a reasonable request by their captors? After all, how could one understand Judah's spiritual heritage without listening to her songs? But this was anathema to God's people. Sacred songs were not to be used simply for entertainment purposes or wrestled from their spiritual context. Pearls were not to be cast before the uncircumcised, Matt. 7. 6, and spiritual things could only be spiritually discerned, 1 Cor. 2. 14. Compromise always means playing into the hands of the enemy, but we should never be afraid to sing the songs of Zion in the right setting.

It was far better that Judah lost her dexterity with music and remained silent if it meant that Jerusalem and the cause of God were not forgotten. To make a decisive stand in the face of overwhelming odds is not easy, but sometimes the honour of God is far more important than life itself. Do we 'dare to be a Daniel' or have the waters of Babylon become too invasive in our lives? Is it, as Richard Niebuhr suggests, that 'the crisis of the church is not the church in the world, but the crisis of the church is the world in the church'?

The psalm ends with a call for God to take specific action against the enemies of His people. Let us take comfort today in the fact that irrespective of the verbal abuse of the enemy, God will, in the end, vindicate His people, Rom. 12. 17-19.

April 13th

Proverbs 1. 20-33

HOW LONG, YE SIMPLE ONES, WILL YE LOVE SIMPLICITY?

We are introduced today to Hebrew wisdom literature, which seeks to explain the meaning of life, and how it should be lived before God. An important feature of this viewpoint is that the choices that individuals make have a direct bearing on final outcomes. The wisdom in this passage, unlike any human wisdom, is directly linked to the knowledge of God, Prov. 1. 7. Here, wisdom is personified – it speaks to individuals rather than simply being a written text, cp. Luke 11. 49. It is not esoteric, but free to everyone and everywhere, Prov. 1. 20-21. Yet, even though it is available without restraint, individuals (simple ones) still ignore it, choosing rather to live their lives in ignorance (simplicity), as if God did not exist, v. 22. This is the reason for today's question, and reminds us that though God may appear to overlook man's ignorance, there will be a day of reckoning, 2 Pet. 3. 9-10. But people cry that this is not fair, and that God should not act in this way. Is there then injustice on God's part? The urgency of wisdom's appeal to the ignorant suggests otherwise. Time and again God had spoken and given individuals every opportunity to engage with Him only to find that His advice had been rejected as of no value, Prov. 1. 23-25. Consequently, they would find that when they most needed wisdom, it would be withheld from them, vv. 26-32. Not even prayer or diligent seeking after God would change matters, vv. 28-30, cp. Amos 8. 11. It would sadly be too late. God, in fact, would laugh at their disasters, because, in their folly, they had spurned His advice, Prov. 1. 25-26; cp. Ps. 2. 4. Ultimately, the punishment would fit the crime in that as they had chosen a particular way of life, they would be doomed to eat the calamitous fruit of their deeds, cp. Isa. 3.11; Ezek. 11. 21; Rom. 6. 21. By choice they had rejected wisdom's clear message, Prov. 1. 23, and turned away from God to their own foolish counsel, v. 31. Complacency and indifference would destroy them, v. 32. But what a different prospect awaits those who listen to wisdom's voice! Real spiritual prosperity without fear can be ours today as we respond positively to the word of God, Ps. 1. 1-3.

April 14th

Proverbs 8. 1-11

DOTH NOT WISDOM CRY?

We are again entering the realm of wisdom literature as we engage with this important passage. Once more the wisdom of God is *personified* as it calls for the attention of its hearers, Prov. 8. 1-4. This is the voice of God calling out to humanity, but what is emphasized on this occasion is that wisdom is someone to be pursued and embraced, unlike Lady Folly, 9. 13-18, whose invitation should be spurned. Wisdom is freely available to everyone, and provides guidance for dealing with the stresses and strains of everyday life, 8. 1-2. It also helps with the more complex issues of life, e.g., the many commercial, and legal transactions that were effected at the city gates in ancient Israel, v. 3; cp. Ruth 4. 1-12. Wisdom is universal in its comprehensiveness, and speaks truth to the whole of mankind, irrespective of status, Prov. 8. 4-5. Although wisdom is freely available to everyone, only those who are prepared to listen to her advice and grasp her message will benefit from it, v. 6; cp. Matt. 13. 14-16. Wisdom can rightly boast of certain inherent qualities such as uprightness, truth, and plain speaking, Prov. 8. 6-8, and these are all available to the individual who seeks this wisdom from God, cp. Jas. 1. 5. As the individual experiences these benefits, their value increases so that they become more precious than the price even of silver, or gold, or other precious jewels, Prov. 8. 9-11; cp. 3. 14-15; 16. 16. So here is an incredible paradox, because although these virtues are priceless, they remain accessible to everyone who is prepared to engage with God, and learn from His word. Sadly, we can often be very attracted to the tangible and material things of this world, but ultimately they will prove to be transient and valueless, 2 Cor. 4. 18. Contrast this, however, with the wisdom that comes from above that is non-combative, and produces a harvest of righteousness, Jas. 3. 17-18. If only political leaders today took time to embrace this wisdom, what a difference it would make to our world! So often we lack wisdom, and fail to appreciate that it cannot be found outside of God Himself, Job. 28. 20-23. But let us rejoice today in the fact that in Christ are hidden all the treasures of wisdom and knowledge, Col. 2. 3.

April 15th

Proverbs 23. 29-35; 24. 1-2

WHO HATH WOE? . . . WHO HATH CONTENTIONS?

Our questions today are linked with the dangers of drunkenness. How timely a reminder for us especially in today's society that regards alcohol as a remedy for many of life's problems! The drunkard is portrayed in a humorous fashion, but there is bitter irony to the whole proceedings. We are warned earlier that drunkenness leads to an impoverished state, Prov. 23. 20-21. We are now informed that excessive drinking leads to quarrelling, strife, self-inflicted wounds ('bruises', Septuagint), and blurred vision, v. 29. The drunkard is fully immersed in his drinking habit, but completely out of touch with reality, v. 30; cp. Isa. 5. 11. He has no discerning palate, and alcohol simply becomes an end in itself, v. 31. Sadly, there is a sting in this tale, because excessive alcohol leads to unconsciousness, 'such a one stretches himself out as one bitten by a serpent', v. 32, Septuagint. We might note Noah's drunken stupor, and reflect upon the danger that alcohol presents even to men of great faith, Gen. 9. 21-25. Drunkenness inflames passions, Gen. 19. 31-36, and can distort our judgement, Prov. 23. 33. Paul equates drunkenness with debauchery, Eph. 5. 18, as it is often connected with other vices, particularly sexual immorality, cp. 1 Cor. 5. 11. The influence of alcohol can also make us do totally stupid things. Two extreme examples are given: lying down in the middle of the sea or on top of a ship's rigging, Prov. 23. 34. We have all probably seen similar examples in society of such stupid and legless behaviour! We may also have observed that such individuals can become totally insensitive to any form of personal danger, v. 35. The continuous circle of drinking is then complete as once the latest hangover is finished, drinking starts again the next day, v. 35. How then do we avoid such foolish and harmful behaviour? The secret for the writer of Proverbs lies in not envying or consorting with evil men, 24. 1-2; cp. Ps. 37. 1. Even amongst the Corinthian believers there were those who had been drunkards, but had been saved and sanctified, 1 Cor. 6. 9-11. Therefore, let us remember today what we have been saved from and be sober, because the coming of the Lord is near, 1 Thess. 5. 6-8.

April 16th

Proverbs 30. 1-9

WHO HATH ASCENDED UP INTO HEAVEN?

Agur lamented his lack of understanding and wisdom, and, in particular, his lack of knowledge of God. Most likely, in its context, Agur's question meant, 'Who is there that has first ascended into heaven to acquire "the knowledge of the Holy One" RV, and then descended back to earth to declare that knowledge?' The answer was, of course, 'Nobody', any more than any mortal had ever gathered the wind in his fists or wrapped up the waters in a garment, or than he had fixed the remotest boundaries of the earth. If anybody should claim to know of such a man, then, Agur demands, let that person name him! And let that person identify the man beyond question by reference to his son's name, cp. Mark 15. 21. 'I should gladly sit at such a man's feet', Agur was saying, 'to learn of God from him'. But, as Agur knew, there was no such man.

True, many centuries before, Enoch had 'ascended up into heaven'; in that Enoch 'was not; for God took him', for he 'was translated that he should not see death', Gen. 5. 24; Heb. 11. 5. But Enoch had not subsequently descended so as to tell of anything he had seen, heard or learnt. Many years later, Elijah also would ascend to heaven, 2 Kgs. 2. 11, but no whirlwind and accompanying fiery chariot would bring him back to earth. Yes, some 900 years after Elijah's translation, the apostle Paul could speak of himself as 'a man' who had been 'caught up' to heaven, from whence he did, of course, come down again, 2 Cor. 12. 2-3. But the apostle made it clear that he was not in a position to reveal anything of the 'unspeakable words' he had heard while in 'the third heaven', v. 4.

And so, as our Lord told Nicodemus, no man has ever ascended to heaven, so as to come down again and to speak authoritatively of heavenly things. Ah, but the One who had ever been in heaven did not need first to mount up to heaven, as any ordinary man would. Rather, as having always enjoyed the fullness of heavenly knowledge, He had come down from heaven (and, indeed, as to His divine nature, dwelt there still), and was therefore perfectly equipped to testify of the things of heaven and of the Father, John 3. 13; cp. John 1. 18.

April 17th

Ecclesiastes 1. 1-11

WHAT PROFIT HATH A MAN . . . UNDER THE SUN?

The expression 'under the sun' occurs almost thirty times in Ecclesiastes and sets the tone of the book. And truly, viewed from a standpoint which does not reach beyond the horizon of this present world, man's arduous toil achieves relatively little.

Solomon recognized that what 'good' did come from man's labour was to be accepted and enjoyed as God's gift, Eccles. 2. 24; 5. 18; 8. 15. But, as he pondered man's 'labour at which he labours under the sun?' 1. 3 lit., he was constrained to ask on several occasions, 'What profit has he?' Eccles. 1. 3; 3. 9; 5. 16. The question Solomon posed was drawn from the world of business, the word translated 'profit' meaning 'that which is left over'. Solomon knew well that, in the end, all man's labour yielded him no 'surplus' on the 'profit and loss account' of the present life. Indeed, the thought of gaining nothing from one's life of hard work led him to write, 'I hated all my labour which I had taken under the sun: because I should leave it unto the man that shall be after me', 2. 18.

This lack of lasting value to one's work 'under the sun' was one factor which constrained 'the Preacher' to conclude, 'all is vanity', 1. 2-3; 2. 21. And the vast range of Solomon's own experience of power, riches, fame and pleasure equipped him better than any to deduce that man's life 'under the sun' was full of inexplicable, meaningless and unsatisfying events. This is one of the key themes of Ecclesiastes, which more or less opens and closes with the expression 'vanity of vanities . . . all is vanity', 1. 2; 12. 8. Against such a background, Solomon's 'conclusion' was that men should 'fear God, and keep his commandments . . . for God shall bring every work into judgment, with every secret thing, whether it be good, or whether it be evil', 12. 13-14; cp. 2 Cor. 5. 10. Here lies the real answer to the question, 'What profit hath a man of all his labour?' Because, for the believer, this present life is a time of probation leading to a day of review, which will, in a better world, give eternal value, meaning and significance to the present labour and toil – in a place, not 'under the sun', but where there will be no need of any sun, Rev. 21. 23; 22. 5!

April 18th

Ecclesiastes 7. 1-13

SAY NOT THOU, WHAT IS THE CAUSE THAT THE FORMER DAYS WERE BETTER THAN THESE?

It may appear strange that the Lord should, seemingly, forbid His people from considering the past and from analyzing the reasons why things in the present are no longer as they were then. Did not our Lord Himself counsel the church at Ephesus, 'Remember . . . from where you have fallen; repent and do the first works, or else I will . . . remove your lampstand', Rev. 2. 5 NKJV? Again, was it wrong for some to weep at the memory of better days when the second temple's foundation was laid, Ezra 3. 12? Of course not. Then what *does* today's question mean?

Any individual verse of scripture must be understood in its context. And this is no exception. The relevant section of Ecclesiastes commences in chapter 6 verse 12 with the question, 'Who knoweth what is good for man in this life?' The word translated 'good' then appears seven times in the first ten verses of chapter 7 – consistently translated 'better' and followed in each case by the word 'than'. The main thrust of the first half of chapter 7 is that good things can come out of suffering and affliction. For adversity is God's appointment ('the work of God'), permitted by Him to the end we might develop our sense of dependence on Him. 'In the day of adversity consider', v. 14.

One of the key lessons in times of trouble is to wait for God's timing (to be 'patient in spirit'), for 'better is the end of a thing than its beginning', v. 8. In the words of the New Testament, 'we count them happy which endure. Ye . . . have seen the end of the Lord; that the Lord is very pitiful, and of tender mercy', Jas. 5. 11. In contrast, it is arrogant ('proud in spirit') and foolish to be 'hasty in . . . spirit', to be fretful and angry with God and His providence, vv. 8-9. The godly person shows patience with the present, rather than, as our text forbids, longing wistfully for the past. Such a person will not murmur at God's ways by saying, in effect, as Job did, 'Oh that I were as in months past', Job 29. 2. To keep asking, 'Why were things so much better before?' is not, Solomon notes, to 'inquire wisely'. The wise person looks to the 'better' days which *lie before* rather than to the so-called 'better' days which *were before*!

April 19th

Song of Solomon 5. 9-16

WHAT IS THY BELOVED MORE THAN ANOTHER?

One interesting feature of the Song of Solomon is that, whereas the Shepherd-King spoke directly to his beloved of her beauty so as to assure her of his delight in her, S. of S. 4. 1-7; 6. 4-7; 7. 1-9, she spoke, not so much *to* him, as *of* him to others. So here. Following a period of estrangement, caused by her lethargy and lack of response to his love, the Shulamite maiden had sought her beloved, unsuccessfully, through the streets of Jerusalem. There, having suffered abuse from the city's watchmen, she had sought help from the 'daughters of Jerusalem'. It was these ladies who posed the question, 'What is thy beloved more than another beloved?' In response, the maiden painted a ten-point verbal portrait of her beloved, her glowing poetic description extending downwards from his head to his feet. Such is the historical setting of our question for today.

But surely, beyond the maiden's appreciation of her beloved, we can discern Israel's future appreciation of her King and Messiah – our Lord Jesus. The day is coming when His nation will confess, as they look back to their rejection of Him at His first advent, that they then saw 'no beauty' in Him that they 'should desire him', Isa. 53. 2. But not only so. For then, at His second advent, they will also exclaim, in striking contrast, 'He is altogether lovely', S. of S. 5. 16 (the word translated 'lovely' being closely related to that rendered 'desire' in Isaiah chapter 53). 'With her eyes and heart ravished by her Beloved, she (Israel) unfolds His loveliness', C. E. Hocking, *Rise Up My Love*, page 339. When Nebuchadnezzar dreamt of an imposing image which represented successive Gentile world empires, there was marked deterioration from its head 'of fine gold' to its feet 'part of iron and part of clay', Dan 2. 32-33. But there is no deterioration in our Lord Jesus; poetically expressed, He is 'fine gold' from the crown of His head to the sole of His feet! And not only His head and feet, for His hands also 'are as gold rings'. And to the believing heart the Saviour's preciousness is yet further enhanced by His sufferings and wounds. Well then do we sing with Isaac Watts, 'See from His head, His hands, His feet, sorrow and love flow mingled down!'

April 20th

Song of Solomon 8. 1-4

WHO IS THIS THAT COMETH UP FROM THE WILDERNESS, LEANING UPON HER BELOVED?

The Song of Solomon first traces the commencement and growth of the love between the Shulamite maiden and himself, culminating in their happy and glorious marriage. Sadly, the Song then describes a period of indifference on her part and of withdrawal on his part. But all that is now past. And, with renewed intimacy, the couple seemingly return to the place where their relationship had begun, passing near the very apple tree which had borne its silent witness to their 'first love'.

At the time of her forthcoming marriage to King Solomon, the maiden had been the centre of attention in the bridal procession which approached Jerusalem. The question had then been asked, 'Who is this that cometh out of the wilderness . . . perfumed with myrrh and frankincense', S. of S. 3. 6. Now, as the loving couple reach again the neighbourhood of the bride's home, not in royal state but in the simplicity of true affection, the question is again asked, 'Who is this that cometh up from the wilderness?' But on this occasion, the Shulamite is described, not as being 'perfumed with myrrh and frankincense', but, most beautifully, as 'leaning upon her beloved'.

How precious it is that we, in all our weakness and in spite of our past waning affection, can lean on our 'Beloved', on One immeasurably 'greater than Solomon'. And we rest in the knowledge that, leaning on Him (in all His wisdom, power, grace and faithfulness), even though we may stumble, He will not let us fall, and, even though we may grow faint and weary, He will uphold our tottering steps.

We lean on One who affords us far greater help and support than that which (i) Jacob ever found in leaning on 'the top of his staff', Heb. 11. 21, (ii) the hypocrite found in leaning 'upon his house', Job 8. 15, or (iii) the Assyrian wrongly assumed Hezekiah hoped to obtain by leaning on Egypt and its king, 2 Kgs. 18. 21. It is not for us to 'lean' on our 'own understanding', Prov. 3. 6, but rather to say with HORATIUS BONAR, 'I have no help but Thine; nor do I need another arm save Thine to lean upon; it is enough, my Lord, enough indeed'. Amen, Lord!

April 21st

Isaiah 6. 1-13

WHOM SHALL I SEND, AND WHO WILL GO FOR US?

Isaiah chapter 6 records the prophet's vision of the heavenly temple, with its throne and its altar. In English, the section contains three rhyming monosyllables: 'Woe', 'Lo', and 'Go'. The 'Woe' introduces Isaiah's *confession*, v. 5; the 'Lo' introduces Isaiah's *cleansing*, v. 7; and the 'Go' introduces Isaiah's *commission*, v. 9. The Lord's word to him ('Go') followed Isaiah's ready response to His two-part question, 'Whom shall I send, and who will go for us?' The two parts of the Lord's question view the prophet's mission from both God's own standpoint and from Isaiah's. The prophet is spoken of, not only as one who is 'sent' by God, but as one who agrees to go. The two parts of God's question, with the change from 'I' to 'us', may also suggest something of the mystery of the Holy Trinity.

It was no easy mission to which God called Isaiah. With the death of King Uzziah, the political situation facing the nation of Judah appeared ominous in the extreme. But the most serious threat came not from without but from within. For, as the first five chapters have shown, the people were morally and spiritually corrupt. And the Lord therefore warned Isaiah that, on account of His people's stubbornness, the prophet's message would serve only to 'make their ears heavy, and shut their eyes; lest they see with their eyes, and hear with their ears, and understand with their heart, and convert, and be healed', v. 10.

We know that Isaiah heard and recorded these words 'when he saw His glory (the glory of the Lord Jesus), and spake of him', John 12. 40-41. Our Lord Jesus Christ, that is, was none other than 'the Lord of hosts' whom Isaiah saw and heard. We can only bow in worship when we realize that: (i) the One who *sent* Isaiah would Himself be *'sent'* about 735 years later, though not, as the prophet, only to preach, but 'to be the Saviour of the world', 1 John 4. 14, (ii) the One *'lifted up'*, high on His heavenly throne, would one day be *'lifted up'* on a cross. John 12. 32-33, and (iii) the One before whom seraphim *hid their faces* in reverence on account of His transcendent glory would one day experience men *hiding their faces* from Him in disgust at His features then so brutally disfigured, Isa. 53. 3.

April 22nd

Isaiah 7. 1-13

WILL YE WEARY MY GOD?

Pekah, the king of Israel, and Rezin, the king of Syria (Israel's northern neighbour), had joined forces to oppose the rising power of Assyria. But Ahaz, king of Judah, had refused to join them, and, in consequence, Pekah and Rezin were now poised to attack the kingdom of Judah and to replace Ahaz with a 'puppet-king' who would co-operate with them. Fearing their attack, Ahaz intended to send to the king of Assyria for help.

At this point the Lord sent Isaiah to confront Ahaz. The prophet's message was simple. There was no need for Ahaz to panic; the alliance would come to nothing. True, earlier in his reign, as a chastisement on him for his idolatry, the Lord had permitted both Rezin and Pekah to defeat Ahaz in battle, 2 Chr. 28. 5-8. But now these kings, who had then been 'fire-brands', were now only smoking embers. Ahaz had no need therefore of aid from Assyria. He had only to trust calmly in God. But, Isaiah warned Ahaz, everything was down to how the king responded to God's message through him. If Ahaz and his people refused to believe God, they would not 'be established'. To strengthen their faith, God instructed the king to ask for a sign as confirmation that He would deliver Judah from its foes.

Later, Ahaz's son (Hezekiah) would gladly accept a confirming sign from the Lord that, in response to his prayer, he would recover from his otherwise terminal illness, 2 Kgs. 20. 1-11. But Ahaz had already made up his mind. He much preferred the tangible help of Assyria to the promised help of God. And so, hypocritically hiding his lack of faith behind a mask of unwillingness to put God to the test, he refused to request any sign. But, as Isaiah made clear, for Ahaz to refuse to ask for a sign when God Himself commanded him to do so was to do just what he insisted he would not; namely, to test God and His patience. For the king's lack of trust in God 'wearied' Him, just as did the people's empty and merely outward observances of worship, Isa. 1. 14. We do well to take heed. For clearly the One who is never wearied by any amount of His own activity or exertion, 40. 28, *is* wearied, not only by our insincere and merely formal service, but by our lack of confidence in Him.

April 23rd

Isaiah 10. 1-4

TO WHOM WILL YE FLEE FOR HELP?

The first four verses of chapter 10 comprise the final stanza of a poem which begins in chapter 9 verse 8. Each of these stanzas ends with the same solemn refrain, 'For all this his anger is not turned away, but his hand is stretched out still'. The first stanza, Isa. 9. 8-12, focuses on Israel's pride and defiance; the second, vv. 13-17, on Israel's corrupt and deceitful leadership; the third, vv. 18-21, on Israel's selfishness and internal strife; and this, the fourth, on the heartless oppression of the poor by Israel's unrighteous judges and government officials.

These ungodly men preyed on the most vulnerable classes, the poor, the widows and the orphans. They abused their power and their office by passing iniquitous laws and decrees, which the poor were in no position to challenge. Their purpose in thus manipulating the legal system was that they might feather their own nests at the expense of those unable to protect themselves. And so, in the very place where widows and orphans should have been defended, they were defrauded.

But Isaiah declared that a day of reckoning was to come, when it would be 'woe' indeed to such men. For then, when the nation was taken into captivity, all their property and wealth would be irretrievably lost. 'Where', he asked them, 'will ye leave your glory?' Where, that is, will you deposit your ill-gotten riches so as to reclaim them again? The answer of course was 'nowhere'. For when the righteous Judge 'visited' the nation in judgement, these corrupt judges would be stripped of all the valuable possessions they had unfairly acquired, and would either be led off as captives or lie among the slain.

'To whom', Isaiah asked, 'will ye flee for help?' Certainly not to Him who is 'a strength to the poor, a strength to the needy in his distress, a refuge from the storm', 25. 4. For their very desolation would represent the outpouring of the wrath of Him who is the only true Refuge and Help of the afflicted – and whose anger they had provoked. Truly, 'it is a fearful thing to fall into the hands of the living God', Heb. 10. 31. But, thank God, it is a blessed thing to be held secure in those very hands, assured that none can snatch us from them, John 10. 28-29.

April 24th

Isaiah 28. 1-13

WHOM SHALL HE TEACH KNOWLEDGE?

In all likelihood, the questions, 'Whom shall he teach knowledge? . . . whom shall he make to understand doctrine?' came from Judah's priests and false prophets. These ungodly men shared the addiction of many in the northern kingdom of Israel to wine and strong drink, Isa. 28. 1-8. It was an indication of their deplorable spiritual and moral state that priests (who, in the course of their official duties, were forbidden by God's law to imbibe any intoxicating drink, Lev. 10. 8-11) should be seen staggering and reeling from the effects of over-indulgence!

These profane and evil rulers not only rejected Isaiah's message; they poured scorn on it as undeserving of their attention. 'Who', they said in effect, 'does this man think he is, presuming to instruct *us*, the spiritual masters of the nation, as if we were a group of mere infants? All we ever hear from him is religious baby-talk, a stream of unending petty rules and regulations'.

Isaiah responded by proclaiming God's judgement upon them. Because they had consistently rejected the 'rest' and 'refreshment' which the Lord had offered them on condition that they trusted in Him rather than in their political schemes, He would deliver them into the hands of the foreign invader. Isaiah turned their mocking words back on them. They had derided him for the simplicity of his messages, regarding what he said as mere babbling and childish nonsense. Therefore, the Lord, Isaiah declared, would speak to them through utterances which they would regard as even less refined and acceptable – through the language of a foreign conqueror! It was not so much that Israel would understand the meaning of the words, but the very fact that they were forced to hear the language of the foreigner would be the Lord's 'word' to them, both pronouncing judgement on their apostasy and calling them to repentance.

The question, 'Whom shall he teach knowledge?' was originally asked in mockery. But, as our Lord, we can praise God that, although He hides His glorious truths 'from the wise and prudent' of this world (from those who are 'wise in their own eyes', Isa. 5. 21), He reveals 'them unto babes' (to those who embrace His message with childlike faith), Matt. 11. 25.

April 25th

Isaiah 33. 13-22

WHO SHALL DWELL WITH . . . DEVOURING FIRE?

The historical setting of this passage is the city of Jerusalem immediately following the spectacular defeat of the army of the king of Assyria in the days of Hezekiah. Shortly before, Sennacherib had accepted a large sum of money sent by Hezekiah to dissuade him from besieging Jerusalem, 2 Kgs. 18. 13-16. Sennacherib had then entered into a covenant of peace with Hezekiah. But he treacherously broke the covenant and proceeded to besiege the city, 2 Kgs. 18. 17; Isa. 33. 1, 8, causing both Judah's brave warriors and the 'ambassadors' who had returned from peace talks with Sennacherib to weep publicly in its streets, Isa. 33. 7. But the Lord intervened dramatically to defend Jerusalem. In one night, the angel of the Lord struck down 185,000 Assyrian troops, as a result of which Sennacherib withdrew and returned to Assyria, 2 Kgs. 19. 35-36.

This wonderful demonstration of God's power and holiness struck terror into the hearts of the ungodly and unrepentant inhabitants of Jerusalem. For many of these, hypocritically, while professing to serve the Lord, had secretly looked to Egypt for their deliverance.

Many years before, Moses had spoken of the Lord Himself as 'a consuming fire', Deut. 4. 24; 9. 3; cp. Heb. 12. 29. Now, awed by God's judgement on the Assyrians and fearing that His holy wrath would fall next on them, the 'sinners in Zion' shuddered and cried out, 'Who among us shall dwell with the consuming ('devouring', KJV) fire?' JND. Who, that is, can abide in the holy presence of God?

In words reminiscent of Psalms 15 and 24, Isaiah replied that the Holy One of Israel chooses to dwell 'on high', cp. Isa. 33. 5 and 16, with the person whose *feet* continually tread the paths of righteousness, whose *lips* speak only that which is pure, whose *heart* abhors any gain obtained by extortion, whose *hands* reject any proffered bribes, whose *ears* are closed to suggestions of violence or murder, and whose *eyes* are shut to that which is evil and defiling. To such, God graciously extends, not only His *presence*, but His *protection* ('his place of defence') and His *provision* ('his bread' and 'his water'), v. 16 RV.

April 26th

Isaiah 40. 12-31

HAST THOU NOT HEARD, THAT THE EVERLASTING GOD . . . FAINTETH NOT, NEITHER IS WEARY?

The people of God were discouraged. Under the pressure of adverse circumstances, they felt that the Lord had overlooked both their *course* and their *cause*. 'My way is hid from the Lord', they sighed, 'and my judgment is passed over from my God'. Alas, such despondent feelings are by no means dead. How many of us, faced with gruelling trials and troubles, have been tempted to doubt the Lord's concern and care?

In response, the prophet pointed the people of God then – and us today – to the greatness and majesty of God. Already, Isaiah had invited believers to lift their eyes and consider both the heavens and who it was that had created the starry host there, v. 26. Only omnipotence can 'create' stars, and only omniscience can 'number' and 'name' them. How, Isaiah implied, could One with infinite knowledge fail to remember His people, and One with infinite power lack the ability to help them?

But, to reinforce the fact that the interests of God's people rest safe in His hands, Isaiah adds more. Surely they had proved in their own experience ('Hast thou not *known*?') and had been taught by others ('Hast thou not *heard*?') that the Lord, 'the everlasting God' (not limited by time) and 'the Creator of the ends of the earth' (not limited by space), neither fainted nor grew weary. And this each of them had known and heard personally and individually; contrast the double *'thou'* (singular), v. 28, with the double *'ye'* (plural), v. 21. Thank God, He is *not* too great to care about His people; He is too great *not* to care!

The Lord never 'faints', as would a man through lack of nourishment, nor does He grow 'weary', as would a man through lack of rest. The dependable Lord is never fatigued or exhausted through over-exertion. Indeed, far from being faint Himself, He gives power to those who otherwise would become so, and, far from being weary Himself, He increases the strength of those who otherwise would become so, v. 29. Those who wait on Him for His help and for the fulfilment of His promises – who put their trust and confidence in Him – shall themselves 'run, and not be weary' and 'walk, and not faint'.

April 27th

Isaiah 52. 13 – 53. 6

WHO HATH BELIEVED OUR REPORT?

In the closing section of chapter 52, Isaiah spoke of the exaltation of the Servant of Jehovah, our Lord Jesus Christ, in His manifested kingdom. Then, in contrast to the time when many had been dumb with astonishment at His features so cruelly disfigured by the violence of wicked men, the very kings of the earth will be mute in awe of His majesty. The first six verses of chapter 53 detail the response of repentant Israel when they witness the glory of the Messiah's second advent. Then, recognizing Him as the One they had once 'pierced', they shall 'mourn for him', Zech. 12. 10, confessing that previously they had despised and rejected both Him and all they had heard concerning Him. 'Who', they shall then ask (literally translated), 'has believed that which is heard?' By which, in all probability, they mean, 'Who *of us* has believed that which *we* heard?', inviting the unspoken and tragic answer, 'Very few, if any'. For, although the Gentile kings will then understand 'that which they *had not heard*', Isa. 52. 15, the nation of Israel shall then confess that they had failed to believe that which they *had heard*.

For when, at His first advent, our Lord 'came to his own', they had not 'received' Him, John 1. 11. John further explains that 'though he (the Lord Jesus) had done so many miracles before them, yet they believed not on him: that the saying of Esaias the prophet might be fulfilled, which he spake, Lord, who hath believed our report?' 12. 37-38. Later, following the Saviour's glorification, His nation rejected the message of the cross. Paul observed that, although many had preached 'the gospel of peace' to them, the majority of Jews had refused to believe their preaching; 'they have not all obeyed the gospel', he wrote, 'for Esaias saith, Lord, who hath believed our report?' Rom. 10. 15-16. Certainly, it was not that the Jews had 'not heard', for the gospel had been sent throughout the whole known world, v. 18. The nation had therefore been without excuse. This they shall confess at our Lord's manifestation in glory, acknowledging that, largely on account of His humble appearance, they had failed to recognize Him and had therefore rejected Him. But today, we can, with unqualified *gladness*, adopt the words which, tingled with *sadness*, Israel will utter then, 'He was wounded for *our* transgressions, he was bruised for *our* iniquities'.

April 28th

Isaiah 55. 1-13

WHEREFORE DO YE SPEND MONEY FOR THAT WHICH IS NOT BREAD?

Although, in its context, the chapter is addressed in the first instance to Israel, it is worded in such a way as opens up to all (both Jew and Gentile) the offer of God's free grace and salvation. Verses 1-5 speak of God's *proffered blessings*, verses 6-9 of His *pardoning mercy*, verses 10-11 of His *powerful word*, and verses 12-13 of His *promised liberation*, Rom. 8. 19-22.

Jehovah's opening words, 'Ho, every one that thirsteth, come ye to the waters', are later echoed by both our Lord Jesus, 'If any man thirst, let him come unto me, and drink', John 7. 37, and the Holy Spirit, 'Let him that is athirst come . . . whosoever will, let him take the water of life freely', Rev. 22. 17. And to those who are willing to listen to His voice, the Triune God extends the invitation to come and to receive from Him, not only spiritual *refreshment* (symbolized by 'waters'), but spiritual joy (symbolized by 'wine', Ps. 104. 15) and spiritual *nourishment* (symbolized by 'milk', Judg. 5. 25).

All this superabundant provision is made freely available; '*without money* and without price'. 'Wherefore', the Lord therefore asks, 'do ye *spend money* for that which is not bread? And your labour for that which satisfieth not?' For, although God graciously invited everyone to *receive* 'for nothing' (freely), the majority in their self-will continued to *labour* 'for nothing' (fruitlessly), finding, to their cost, that the things of earth could never fully satisfy the human heart. Men expended their silver and their toil for that which was 'not bread'. By way of contrast, He who is 'the true bread', John 6. 32, satisfies completely. We thank God that, whereas the world always falls short of our expectations, our Lord Jesus always exceeds them.

'Do not labour for the food which perishes', He said, 'but for the food which endures to everlasting life', speaking of men's need to appropriate both Himself and the saving benefits of His death, John 6. 27, 33, 51-58. For, although our spiritual blessings were truly 'without price' to us, they were anything but 'without price' to Him! We enjoy them freely only because He first paid for them in full. Praise Him!

April 29th

Isaiah 66. 1-4

WHERE IS THE HOUSE THAT YE BUILD UNTO ME? AND WHERE IS THE PLACE OF MY REST?

Through the prophet Isaiah, the Lord had earlier foretold that His people would go into exile and would subsequently return to their land. In the last chapter of Isaiah's prophecy, God comforts and encourages the godly remnant of His people with the promise of future glory, vv. 5-24. But, before He does so, He reproves the hypocrites among them for their unfounded ideas in connection with their temple and worship.

At the outset, the Lord corrects the impression entertained by such that, in common with the so-called gods of the heathen, He could be enclosed in any man-made temple. He draws attention to His heavenly kingship and majesty, 'The heaven is my throne, and the earth is my footstool'. And so, because (in the words of Solomon), 'the heaven and heaven of heavens cannot contain' God, 'how much less' could any 'house' built by man either contain Him or adequately set forth His glory? 1 Kgs. 8. 27. Many centuries later, the apostle Paul reasoned with the Athenian philosophers, 'God that *made* the world and all things therein, seeing that he is Lord of heaven and earth, dwelleth not in temples *made* with hands', Acts 17. 24. It is inconceivable, Paul was saying, that the One who *'made'* all things should Himself be confined in a dwelling-place *'made'* by human hands. But the Lord has a second question, 'What place shall be my rest?' Isa. 66. 1 RV. Because, that is, the earth itself is no more than a *resting-place* for God's feet (His 'footstool'), no structure erected on that earth could function in any semi-physical sense as the *'place'* of His *'rest'*.

Nevertheless, in His grace, God does condescend to manifest His presence in a special way in and among His people. In the *past*, He dwelt among His people in both the tabernacle, Exod. 25. 8, and the temple at Jerusalem, 2 Chr. 6. 2. In the *present*, He dwells (a) in the local church as His house, 1 Tim. 3. 15, and His temple, 1 Cor. 3. 16-17; 2 Cor. 6. 16, and (b) in the individual believer, 1 Cor. 6. 19. And, in the *future*, He will dwell in both the millennial and the eternal city, Ezek. 48. 35; Rev. 21. 2-3. What an immense privilege His people enjoy!

April 30th

Jeremiah 8. 4-22

IS THERE NO BALM IN GILEAD; IS THERE NO PHYSICIAN THERE?

When Jeremiah posed these questions, the nation of Judah lay under the shadow of the imminent Babylonian invasion. The prophet could already hear, as it were, the snorting of the advancing war horses coming from Dan on the northern frontier of Israel, v. 16. The prospect of the forthcoming devastation and subsequent exile overwhelmed Jeremiah with sorrow and dismay. In his grief, Jeremiah poured out three questions, v. 22.

The only reasonable answer to the first two questions was, 'Of course there is'. For in the Lord there certainly was both 'balm' and 'physician' available for the healing of the spiritual, moral and political ailments of the nation. Indeed, immediately following Israel's exodus from Egypt, had not God claimed for Himself the name, 'Jehovah-Ropheka' – 'I am the Lord that healeth thee', Exod. 15. 26?

Yet this very answer compelled Jeremiah to ask a third question, 'Why then has the health of the daughter of my people not been restored?' ESV. But the Lord had already answered this last question when responding to the bitter complaints which, prophetically, Jeremiah had heard the people voice from their captivity. God had then made it clear that the only reason He, their King, would not intervene to save them was that they had provoked Him to anger by their idolatry and had steadfastly refused to return to Him in repentance, Jer. 8. 5-6, 19.

So much for the contextual interpretation of the questions. But there is no reason that we cannot employ the expression 'Balm in Gilead' as a beautiful picture of our Lord Jesus, and so answer Jeremiah's first question with the words of the African-American spiritual song,

> 'There is a balm in Gilead
> To make the wounded whole;
> There is a balm in Gilead
> To heal the sin-sick soul'.

And the Great Physician can heal, not only 'sin-sick' souls, but troubled hearts. Truly, 'He healeth the broken in heart, and bindeth up their wounds', Ps. 147. 3. Trust Him today.

May 1st

Jeremiah 18. 1-17

O HOUSE OF ISRAEL, CANNOT I DO WITH YOU AS THIS POTTER?

The prophet was commanded to pay a visit to the potter's house to watch him at work. What was particularly noticeable was the failure to make the intended vessel, which was marred, (literally 'disfigured'), whereupon the wet clay was reworked into another vessel, 'as seemed good to the potter to make it', v. 4.

The significant truth is the perseverance of the potter to re-make the clay into another vessel. The parable is a vivid picture of God's sovereignty over humanity, and specifically Israel. He has complete mastery over the clay, v. 6. Yet, the following verses qualify the meaning. Nations and individuals are not insensible lumps of clay. Prophecies both of doom and blessing are contingent upon the response of human hearts, vv. 8-11; Jonah 3. 10. On the other hand, there is no escaping the stark message of these chapters that the nation is going to be radically reshaped by the Potter using the exile in Babylon. That this is inevitable is seen from the stubborn resistance and sarcasm of the 'clay', v. 12. Verses 13-15 indicate that the apostasy of Judah is unnatural, irrational, and tragic. The entreaty of verse 11 being scornfully rejected, the sentence becomes inescapable; God will forsake them, v. 17.

The thought of clay in the potter's hands reminds us of the humble origin of man, Gen. 2. 7. Later in Isaiah, the word 'formed' occurs over twenty times to indicate the care of the Potter in moulding the nation, e.g. Isa. 44. 21, 64. 8. There is thus a gracious and purposeful design in the heart of our Maker for each of our lives. Yet, as our passage shows, it is possible for us to resist God's plan; the design may not take shape as originally planned and has to be reformed. How encouraging to know that whilst that process may be costly, the Potter will persist until a worthy vessel is formed, Heb. 12. 6; Phil 1. 6!

Have thine own way, Lord! Have thine own way!
Thou art the potter, I am the clay.
Mould me and make me after thy will,
While I am waiting, yielded and still.

[ADELAIDE A. POLLARD]

May 2nd

Jeremiah 32. 16-35

BEHOLD, I AM THE LORD, THE GOD OF ALL FLESH: IS THERE ANY THING TOO HARD FOR ME?

The events of this chapter take place during the tenth year of Zedekiah, a short time before the fall of Jerusalem, 2 Kgs. 25. 1-3. The city had been besieged by the enemy and faithful Jeremiah was considered too pro-Babylonian to be kept at liberty. God commands Jeremiah to purchase a field in Anathoth in Judah, even though it was already in enemy hands! This extraordinary directive, vv. 1-15, leads to Jeremiah questioning God's ways, vv. 16-25. God's response is clear, vv. 26-35, yet coupled with a merciful commitment to bring the exiles home again, vv. 36-44. Broadly speaking, if the first half of chapter 32 deals with the 'prophet of God', the second half focuses on the 'God of the prophet'.

Faced with contradictory implications of his purchase, compared with the consistent prophecies of Jerusalem's doom, and notwithstanding his own words in verse 16, Jeremiah turns to prayer. As with Daniel, the prayers of God's servants are often full of strivings veiled by their fearless public pronouncements.

He recalls the nature of God, omnipotent and omniscient, vv. 17, 19, the Lord of history. He has intervened in the past despite His people's faithlessness, vv. 21-23. In answer to today's question, 'nothing is too hard' for God to do, vv. 17, 27. The words echo the indignant question of God Himself in response to Sarah's incredulous laugh when told that she would bear a son in her old age, Gen. 18. 14. 'Hard' can be literally rendered 'wonderful', and understood as 'exceptional' or 'difficult'. Thus Jeremiah is challenged to exercise faith in God's ultimate purposes, in the face of misgivings about the validity of his purchase, cp. Heb. 11. 1, 6.

What a God is ours! He will act both in judgement and restoration, for His ways are 'past finding out'. The dreaded Babylonian is but an instrument in the accomplishment of His sovereign purposes, Jer. 25. 9. Paul assures us that He is 'able to do exceeding abundantly above all that we ask or think, according to the power that worketh in us', Eph. 3. 20. So why not trust Him today in every aspect of life?

May 3rd

Jeremiah 45. 1-5

SEEKEST THOU GREAT THINGS FOR THYSELF?

With this chapter, the narrative of the book returns to the fourth year of Jehoiakim, 604 BC, to the time when Baruch wrote down by dictation the prophecies of Jeremiah, which the king then burned, as recorded in chapter 36. Baruch was Jeremiah's companion in all his experiences in Egypt. He belonged to an influential Judaean family and his brother Seraiah had been a chamberlain in attendance on King Zedekiah, Jer. 51. 59.

Verse 3 reveals Baruch's distress as he realises the personal and national implications of the predictions he has been recording. God's answer through Jeremiah highlights His profound sorrow at having to destroy the kingdom and testimony, which He had sought so long to preserve. Baruch had aspired to a successful career, but must now in fellowship with God abandon such ambitions, for he will see the prophecies of judgement that he recorded amply fulfilled. So catastrophic will be the judgements that he will count himself fortunate to survive: to escape with one's life is as good as it gets for the vanquished, v. 5; 21. 9.

One obvious lesson from such tragic days is that all our plans need to be subject to God's will, 'for that ye ought to say, If the Lord will, we shall live, and do this, or that', Jas. 4. 15. But what about the validity of ambition, as expressed in today's question? The answer will largely depend on our motives. The ungodly world is full of damaging selfish ambition, and sadly it infects the church, as in the case of Diotrephes, 3 John 9. A safe preservative is to don the apron of humility, 1 Pet. 5. 5-6, and God will use us in His own good time.

Our Lord taught, 'Seek ye first the kingdom of God, and his righteousness; and all these things shall be added unto you', Matt. 6. 33. God wants us to be faithful stewards in developing both our natural talents and spiritual endowments, Matt. 25. 14ff.; 2 Tim. 1. 6. Spiritual gift is not to be thought of as a static thing, for we read, 'Therefore let him who speaks in a tongue pray that he may interpret', 1 Cor. 14. 13 NKJV. Yet love must be the vital controlling motive, always seeking the building up of one's fellow-believers, 1 Cor. 13; 14. 12, 26.

May 4th

Lamentations 1. 1-13

IS IT NOTHING TO YOU, ALL YE THAT PASS BY?

Lamentations is a poetic book consisting of five laments arranged in acrostic form. The book highlights the devastating sense of loss associated with the destruction of Jerusalem, its temple and rituals, and the transportation of the cream of its populace to exile in Babylon. The Hebrew title of the book is 'How . . . !' the opening word of three chapters, 1. 1; 2. 1; 4. 1, expressive of shock and despair.

The opening verses of chapter 1 lament the fate which the city is now experiencing, vv. 1-11. In the remainder of the chapter, the city itself speaks. Jeremiah has often been regarded as 'the weeping prophet' and like him, the city weeps throughout the night, with the despair of a desolate widow. The approaches to the city are empty of their customary bands of pilgrims and her celebrated gates are desolate, v. 4. Proud adversaries are in the ascendant, and allies have proven treacherous, vv. 2, 5, 9. Predatory pagan conquerors have entered the hallowed sanctuary and carried off the spoil. Now in the ruined city survival is a daily challenge for the remaining inhabitants, v. 11. Most crushing of all is the overwhelming sense that the *Lord Himself* has brought this about because of the enormity of Judah's transgressions, vv. 5, 12, cp. Deut. 32. 30. At length, v. 12, Jerusalem speaks. As heaven is silent, she appeals to those who 'pass by', just as she had appealed to God, vv. 9, 11. Fire is a biblical metaphor of judgement and recalls the doom of Sodom and Gomorrah, Gen. 19. 23-29.

The 'weeping prophet' surely points forward to the Man of sorrows, Isa. 53. 3. How comprehensive were the sorrows He bore as He made His way to the cross! Luke 19. 41; John 13. 18. Yet there in His utter abandonment 'the Lord . . . laid on him the iniquity of us all', Isa. 53. 6. May we experience the drawing power of His vicarious sufferings ever more deeply!

All ye that pass by, to Jesus draw nigh;
To you is it nothing that Jesus should die?
Your ransom and peace, your surety He is,
Come, see if there ever was sorrow like His.

[Charles Wesley]

May 5th

Ezekiel 18. 1-32

HAVE I ANY PLEASURE AT ALL THAT THE WICKED SHOULD DIE?

Today's chapter must be read in the context of the exiles in Babylon. They had a saying, 'The fathers have eaten sour grapes, and the children's teeth are set on edge', v. 2. This proverb meant that the sufferings of a generation were due to the sins of their forebears. There is no doubt that the Old Testament stresses corporate responsibility and the exile is seen as God's climactic judgement on the nation after generations of accumulated guilt, 2 Chr. 36. 15-16. The danger was, however, that the exiles would succumb to cynicism and fatalism, feeling that their situation was hopeless, and even denying their individual responsibility. Moreover, they could be tempted to accuse God of injustice, vv. 19, 25.

The chapter therefore stresses individual responsibility before God and thus acts as a necessary balance to the indiscriminate judgement that overtook the nation. Righteous Israelites might well suffer alongside the wicked in unclean Babylon, but they would not share their ultimate fate. Every human being matters to God, for He says, 'All souls are mine', v. 4. The answer to today's question is an emphatic negative, 'I have no pleasure in the death of him that dieth, saith the Lord God: wherefore turn yourselves, and live ye', v. 32.

Again, we must avoid the hasty conclusion that the chapter is teaching salvation by works. As is common in scripture the contrast is between the 'righteous' and the 'wicked'. The 'righteous' sought to live up to God's standard, so very conscious that his best efforts were as filthy rags, Isa. 64. 6, and was cast upon the mercy of God. The 'wicked' was one who rejected the claims of God's law either in whole or in part. His actions betrayed his true heart-attitude to God. Positively, the chapter stresses God's longing for genuine repentance, vv. 21, 27, 28, 30, something He will mark with the promise of 'life'.

Let us beware of blaming our spiritual circumstances on the faithlessness of previous generations! Grace meets us in our present need and God rewards personal responsibility and piety, however discouraging our lot at times may seem, Rev. 3. 20.

May 6th

Ezekiel 34. 1-10; Acts 20. 28

SHOULD NOT THE SHEPHERDS FEED THE FLOCKS?

Throughout the Old Testament, the role of an ideal king is likened to that of a shepherd, a true reflection of God's tender care over His purchased people, Isa. 40. 11. Sadly, and fully in line with Samuel's prediction in 1 Samuel chapter 8 verses 11 to 18, successive kings exacted heavy levies on the people; note particularly the recurring phrase 'he will take'.

Three accusations are levelled against these kings. Firstly, they cruelly exploited the people under their care, vv. 2, 3. Secondly, they showed themselves devoid of the pastoral qualities required to care for the weak and defenceless, v. 4. Thirdly, instead of maintaining the unity of the flock, they allowed the people to be scattered – a term pointing to dispersion in exile. Thus God solemnly reminds the leaders of His people that they must give account for the treatment of those who are consistently referred to throughout the chapter as 'my flock', v. 10. The passage reads like a job description for pastoral leadership, and on every criterion, the rulers had failed comprehensively.

The New Testament is equally insistent on the priority of the pastoral care of the dearly-purchased flock of God. Paul reminds the Ephesian elders that the Holy Spirit had placed them as overseers in the flock to 'shepherd the church of God', Acts 20. 28 NKJV. 'Shepherding' is a much more comprehensive term than feeding or even overseeing, and points to all the activities highlighted by God in Ezekiel chapter 34. Peter, referring to himself as a fellow-elder, directs, 'Shepherd the flock of God which is among you, serving as overseers, not by compulsion but willingly, not for dishonest gain but eagerly; nor as being lords over those entrusted to you, but being examples to the flock', 1 Pet. 5. 2, 3 NKJV.

Happy the church of God whose leaders are sacrificial in their labours, preserving unity, on the watch for danger, and above all providing food in abundance – thus 'tethering the flock by their teeth'! Just as Israel was promised the coming of the messianic shepherd Prince among them, we await the appearing of the 'chief Shepherd', Ezek. 34. 23, 1 Pet. 5. 4. All shepherds will then be called to render account, Heb. 13. 17.

May 7th

Ezekiel 37. 1-14

SON OF MAN, CAN THESE BONES LIVE?

Today's reading is arguably the most famous passage of the book and has been put to good use by preachers. It must be remembered however that it is a prophecy of Israel's spiritual resurrection, a glorious event which may come to pass sooner than many think, Rom. 11. 15, 26.

The scene depicted is that of an ambushed army, with the added indignity of the bones of the fallen strewn unburied on the battlefield. The bones are 'very dry', ruling out the return from exile in Babylon as a possible fulfilment of the prophecy. The imagery points rather to the hardened spiritual state of Israel during the present age. The question of verse 3 self-evidently suggests a negative answer – apart, that is, from the supernatural regenerating power of God.

The miracle proceeds in two stages. First, the action of prophesying the word of the Lord is attended by an earthquake, v. 7 RV. Bodies are reconstituted but as yet are lifeless, v. 8. The wind is then invoked to breathe life into these helpless bodies. The same Hebrew word can be variously translated 'wind', 'breath', 'spirit' in verses 5, 6, 8, 9, 10, and 14. It recalls God's creative gift of life to man, Gen. 2. 7. This transformation from death to life points to a mighty miracle of divine power and grace: the new transformed Israel will have no living link with the past; national election and blood descent cannot of themselves provide a people fit for God's own possession, John 1. 13. We note that the return to the land of Israel will be accomplished by the hand of God, vv. 12, 14.

Perhaps as we survey our personal lives and church lives at times we resemble the dry bones. What was once like a mighty army is now hopeless and undone. The ruin is apparent for all to see. We fear there is no way back, at least from a human standpoint, v. 3. Yet the passage points to the limitless life-imparting power of the word of God and the Spirit of God. 'Man's extremity is God's opportunity', and it pleases Him to take up the weak things to confound the mighty. The prophet's responsibility amidst the conscious frailty implied in his designation 'son of man' was to be fully obedient to God's direction, vv. 3, 7, 10.

May 8th

Daniel 3. 19-30, Isaiah 43. 1-2

DID NOT WE CAST THREE MEN BOUND INTO THE MIDST OF THE FIRE?

Three Hebrew youths determined that 'our God whom we serve is able to deliver us from the burning fiery furnace, and he will deliver us out of thine hand, O king', Dan. 3. 17. Far from home and kindred, they recognized that they could not acquiesce with a blatant act of idolatry: they must 'obey God rather than men', Acts 5. 29. Proud Nebuchadnezzar in his fury ordered the furnace to be superheated, yet almost immediately God began to speak to the despot through the loss of his chosen soldiers, v. 22, Gen. 12. 3. Shadrach, Meshach, and Abednego fell bound into the midst of the fiery furnace, a picture on the one hand of abject human weakness, but at the same time absolute dependence on the vindicating power of God.

Faith did not have long to wait, Heb. 11. 34, for presently they found themselves free and blessed with a mysterious Companion, in the words of the king, 'one like a son of the gods' RV. In this extreme environment, this is likely to be the Angel of the Lord – God Himself manifested for the comfort and support of His faithful servants. The fire that consumed the king's men was powerless against them, cp. Exod. 11. 7. Note the wonderful gradation implied in the description of verse 27, culminating in not even the smell of fire upon their persons!

Those who in all ages determine to be godly face persecution, Luke 21. 16-18; 2 Tim. 3. 12; Rev. 13. 15. Yet what glorious consolations are extended to those called to undergo such ordeals! When traversing the harsh road to exile in Babylon, God promised, 'When thou passest through the waters, I will be with thee; and through the rivers, they shall not overflow thee: when thou walkest through the fire, thou shalt not be burned; neither shall the flame kindle upon thee', Isa. 43. 2. Note carefully that what is promised is not exemption *from* trial, but God's gracious, sustaining presence *throughout* the trial.

Perhaps God will call us to experience our own fiery trial, 1 Pet. 4. 12. We may feel like Luther that we are all alone. Yet, assuredly, we can count on the support of One who has pledged, 'I will never leave thee nor forsake thee', Heb. 13. 5, 6.

May 9th

Daniel 4. 19-37

NONE CAN STAY HIS HAND, OR SAY UNTO HIM, WHAT DOEST THOU?

This chapter supplies the remarkable account of Nebuchadnezzar's dream, its interpretation, his subsequent pride and humiliation and his restoration under the gracious hand of God. It required considerable courage and faithfulness on the part of Daniel to convey the weighty interpretation of the dream to the despotic world-emperor, 4. 19, 25. We too must not flinch from declaring the whole counsel of God, Acts 20. 27. Daniel acts fearlessly, yet with all due respect because he fears a higher Monarch, v. 26, Rom. 13. 1.

Alas, after a full year of God's longsuffering during which he resisted Daniel's call to repentance, the heart of the proud autocrat is lifted up with pride, v. 30, cp. Acts 12. 21-23. In that very moment the dread sentence is pronounced from heaven. He is to be reduced to a bestial existence, the seven periods of time signifying the comprehensive and emphatic nature of the divine judgement.

At the end of the days of his humiliation, prodigal-like, he turns his eyes heavenward. Immediately, he is blessed with a return to reason, v. 34. How merciful is our God and how quick to receive the penitent! In chastened language he wisely acknowledges the Most High, the true universal Sovereign, vv. 34, 35. It is vital for us too to be assured that 'the most High ruleth in the kingdom of men, and giveth it to whomsoever he will', v. 25. The assurance that God is on the throne, has been the comfort and refuge of the godly throughout the generations, Ps. 46.

Let us also learn well from this Gentile emperor that 'God resisteth the proud, and giveth grace to the humble', 1 Pet. 5. 5. If we fail to humble ourselves, God may well bring us low. If His people fail to heed the summons to repent they invite Christ's sovereign disciplinary dealings, Rev. 2. 5, 16, 21, 22.

How remarkable are the statements of Nebuchadnezzar as he finally acknowledges the justice of God's ways! What an incentive for us to emulate the faith of Daniel and to pray earnestly 'for kings, and for all that are in authority', 1 Tim. 2. 2.

May 10th

Daniel 6. 11 -28

O DANIEL . . . IS THY GOD . . . ABLE TO DELIVER THEE FROM THE LIONS?

Daniel's name means 'God is my Judge', and the story of his preservation in the den of lions is a stirring example of committing oneself to Him that 'judgeth righteously', 1 Pet. 2. 23. The promotion of Daniel, due no doubt to his extraordinary ability to govern, coupled with complete personal integrity, made him the target of the bitter envy and intrigues of his subordinates, Dan. 6. 3. As believers we should be aware that transparency of character and godly behaviour may carry a cost both in the workplace and in society generally. It is part of the inescapable tension involved in living out the principles of the kingdom of God in a corrupt culture.

No royal decree could deter Daniel from his habitual practice of intercessory prayer, 1 Kgs. 8. 46-50; he must obey God rather than men, compare Acts 5. 29. At the same time King Darius is cunningly manipulated to the point at which he must consign Daniel to the den. Out of love to Daniel, the king expresses the faint hope, 'Thy God whom thou servest continually, he will deliver thee', Dan. 6. 16, yet spends an anguished night in the palace. Where man is helpless God intervenes and preserves Daniel whose faith 'stopped the mouths of lions', Heb. 11. 33. Like the Lord, he was with the wild beasts, Mark 1. 13, yet their ravenous appetites were subdued.

Paul reminds us that in his lonely hour of need he 'was delivered out of the mouth of the lion (Emperor Nero)', 2 Tim. 4. 17. There are metaphorical lions as well as literal ones – cruel opponents of God and His people. Perhaps we question whether God can deliver us from 'the lions' in our lives?

In answer to our question, the chapter shows that God was indeed able to preserve His faithful servant not simply through the extremity of one night, but throughout the totality of his personal exile in Babylon. Not only so, but Daniel was enabled to be a powerful testimony at the highest levels of world empire, personally modelling the ideal of what God always intended Israel to be, see Gen. 22. 18. May we follow such a faithful example!

May 11th

Hosea 11. 1-12

HOW SHALL I GIVE THEE UP, EPHRAIM?

Hosea's prophetic ministry occupied the latter half of the eighth century BC, during which time the threat from the Assyrian empire was all too apparent. His focus is on the unfaithfulness of Israel variously and vividly portrayed as a promiscuous wife, an indifferent mother, an illegitimate child, and in chapter 11, an ungrateful son. Nevertheless, despite the nation's persistent idolatry and obstinacy, God's invincible yet unrequited love is described in a manner unsurpassed in the Old Testament.

The Lord's covenant love for Israel is introduced in this chapter in a most touching way. He calls His son out of Egypt and coaxes him to walk as a toddler with a parent, vv. 1, 3. In verse 4 the imagery appears to change to that of a considerate farmer easing the yoke on his working animals and ensuring that they are fed. Sadly, God's tender love was repeatedly spurned, v. 2. Thus a harsher tone is introduced with the threat of exile to Assyria and, ironically, Egypt – two nations with whom Israel had played politics, vv. 5-7.

Under the law a stubborn son was to be sentenced to stoning, Deut. 21. 18-21, but God's irrepressible love and compassion cannot allow Him to abandon His wayward people to the fate they so richly deserve. In a plaintive rhetorical question God pours out His emotions, 'How shall I give thee up, Ephraim?' v. 8. His loyalty to this faithless people is no formality! By contrast, the cities of Admah and Zeboiim were totally destroyed along with Sodom, Gen. 14. 2, 8; Deut. 29. 23. However, the steadfast love of the Lord towards Israel means that He can never make a full end; a remnant must be spared, Jer. 30. 11; Rom. 11. 5.

What a revelation of the heart of God Hosea presents! As Paul could declare, 'the gifts and the calling of God are irrevocable', Rom. 11. 29 NKJV. One glad day the merciful ways of God with Israel will be fully vindicated, Rom. 11. 26-32. Whilst we dare not provoke God as Israel did, it is good to know that God will perfect His purposes concerning us, Ps. 138. 8. May we seek grace to maintain that same resilient love towards others that God showed to His wayward people!

May 12th

Amos 5. 18-27

WOE UNTO YOU THAT DESIRE THE DAY OF THE LORD! TO WHAT END IS IT FOR YOU?

Verse 18 is the earliest use of the term 'the day of the Lord', a key concept that occurs widely in the later prophets. In Old Testament times, the godly were acutely aware that the world did not reflect the perfection of God's rule, nor did they reap the expected rewards of righteousness. Accordingly they yearned for the day when God would intervene and His perfect will be done on earth as it is in heaven. This intervention is called the day of the Lord; however, the term is not reserved exclusively for God's final intervention, but includes earlier visitations of divine judgement.

In the popular mind there was a clear and simple expectation that Israel would be vindicated and exalted as God's people, Deut. 32. 35-37; Isa. 2. 1-4. By contrast, Amos delivers a solemn and startling rebuke. There are those who are arrogantly confident of their coming vindication, pinning their hopes on the splendour of their religious observances, v. 21. Yet they have fundamentally mistaken the principles upon which God operates. When the day of the Lord comes, ritual observances will not avail to protect them; He will consign them to exile for their neglect of basic justice and morality, cp. Matt. 23. 23. Verses 21 to 23 present the chilling spectacle of well-executed but formal religion. The repetition of the adjective 'your' suggests that there is little in it for God; in fact their worship is positively burdensome to Him, v. 23, Isa. 1. 14.

The only remedy is to unblock the course of the river of justice, which has been so frequently thwarted by the nation. Righteousness needs to flow on like a perennial stream, v. 24. Otherwise, the Lord will indeed intervene, but it will be for their judgement, not vindication, vv. 18-20.

How dangerous to presume that the judgement seat of Christ will always result in the accolade, 'Well done!' Matt. 25. 21. Not so, say both Paul and James, 2 Cor. 5. 10; Jas. 2. 12-13. Perhaps we would do well to examine our ways and return to the Lord? He desires above all the fervent devotion of His people, Rev. 2. 4. Reformation now will pay eternal dividends.

May 13th

Jonah 1. 1-16

WHAT IS THINE OCCUPATION?

The city of Nineveh to which Jonah was sent was the magnificent capital of the Assyrian empire. At the time of his ministry, 2 Kgs. 14. 23-28, the Assyrians threatened the entire ancient Near East and their barbaric cruelties in warfare are a matter of historical record. Nevertheless, the major theme of this book is God's boundless compassion not simply for Israel but for all nations, even the Ninevites, Jonah 4. 11. Unable to accept this, when commissioned by God to go to Nineveh and cry against it, 1. 1-2, Jonah decided to go as far as possible in the opposite direction. The very possibility of Ninevites experiencing the mercy and loving-kindness of God was too much for him to bear, 4. 2. As Christians, we must beware of regarding certain classes of sinners as beyond the matchless mercy and redemptive power of God, 1 Cor. 6. 11.

With His disobedient prophet asleep in the boat, the sovereign Lord unleashed a mighty tempest. It is sadly ironic that Jonah had to be roused to pray by a pagan captain who would be grateful for the help of any god, 1. 6. The ancients had a deep sense of causality in events and sought to ascertain the reason for the sudden storm, v. 7; Prov. 16. 33.

As soon as Jonah was identified as the offender, he faced a barrage of questions from a desperate crew. He stated, 'I am an Hebrew; and I fear the Lord, the God of heaven, who made the sea and the dry land'. But his actions belied his profession, and his admission intensified the foreboding of the sailors, v. 10. They also recognized that Jonah's fate was pivotal to their own preservation, v. 11.

How sad that this information had to be dragged out of God's disobedient servant by pagans in a dire extremity! When we are disobedient to God's commandments we can become a liability to those around us. Yet God in His invincible mercy used the ordeal to bring the mariners to fear Him.

God has commissioned us to go to seek the lost, Matt. 28. 19-20. Do our colleagues, friends, and neighbours understand that we are servants of God? Are we ashamed to confess Christ, or are we ready to give an answer, Rom. 1. 16; 1 Pet. 3. 15?

May 14th

Jonah 4. 1-11

AND SHOULD NOT I SPARE NINEVEH?

Chapter 3 verse 1 records that 'the word of the Lord came unto Jonah the second time'. Thank God, He is patient and merciful to His servants, cp. John 21. 15-17. The result of Jonah's obedience is an outstanding example of thoroughgoing national repentance, resulting in God's relenting from threatened judgement, Jonah 3. 6-10; 2 Pet. 3. 9.

God in His sovereignty used Jonah's simple preaching in a mighty way, yet the prophet is still far from the mind of God. God's merciful way with the Ninevites is a vexation to his mind. Thus he prays his *angry* prayer, Jonah 4. 1-4. In chapter 2 by contrast we have his *grateful* prayer of thanksgiving, celebrating the Lord's faithfulness and mercy. Sadly however, he could not contemplate the possibility that grace could reach out to 'them' as well as to 'us'.

To teach his peevish servant a salutary lesson, God prepares a gourd, a worm, and a hot desert wind, vv. 6-8. Our faithful God has much work to do *in* us as well as through us, compare Acts 10. 9-16; Phil. 1. 6. The plant afforded Jonah vital but short-lived relief from the sun. Soon, however, a scorching east wind of God's appointment reduced him to faintness, and in the absence of the gourd he repeated his request to die, v. 8. As God had questioned the basis of Jonah's anger over the salvation of the Ninevites, now He questions his anger over the destruction of the plant, vv. 4, 9. The sad reality is that Jonah for selfish reasons is far more concerned about a plant that lasted a day than over the 120,000 persons 'that cannot discern between their right hand and their left hand'. This description points to the fact that the populace is morally and spiritually unaware.

Could it be that we are more concerned about present comfort than the plight of the lost? At several points in the book Nineveh is described as 'great', 1. 2; 3. 2; 4. 11. The city was great in God's eyes, not because of its imperial pomp, but because of the multitude of lost souls dwelling therein. And if Jonah could not allow God's concern for beings created in His image, might he not at least care about the animals? May we share the yearnings of our God over a lost world!

May 15th

Micah 6. 1-8

WHAT DOTH THE LORD REQUIRE OF THEE?

The theme of Micah's prophecy is judgement and forgiveness. A contemporary of Isaiah, his message reflects conditions in Israel prior to the reforms under King Hezekiah, and alternates between messages of doom and hope.

Chapter 6 introduces the Lord's indictment against Israel. Creation is summoned as a witness for the prosecution, vv. 1-2. The following verses spell out God's redeeming and saving power put forth on behalf of His covenant people, vv. 3-5. God desires to bless and not to curse His people as His allusion to Balaam and Balak shows. Verses 6 to 8 supply a contrite people's response and the prophetic comment.

Israel unlike any other nation enjoyed a sacrificial system permitting approach to the transcendent God in worship. These verses present an ascending scale of sacrifice. Only the rich could afford valuable calves a year old, v. 6. Thousands of rams might be offered on state occasions, 1 Kgs. 8. 63, but would be wholly unaffordable for the individual. Rivers of oil would imply meal offerings on an unimaginable scale. Can the mere multiplication of ritual offerings really secure the favour of God and atone for past failures? The danger for Israel was in coming to think of the endless Levitical sacrifices as mechanical transactions, as mere penalty fees, and thereby tantamount to licences to sin.

But God looks beyond ritual to the heart. The use of the term 'O man' in verse 8 conveys a personal urgency. God's ultimate desire has been made clear in the law, Deut. 6. 5; Lev. 19. 18. To 'act justly' is to act with integrity in the full round of human relationships – all of life being brought to the test of scripture. To love 'mercy', literally 'steadfast love', is to reflect the covenant loyalty and love of God Himself. To 'walk humbly with thy God' is to be cast upon Him for all the resources to lead a godly life, devoid of any sense of merit or pride.

These celebrated verses describe the essence of true piety and are directly applicable today, Jas. 1. 27. The Lord preserve us from the ever-present danger of externalism and enable us to cultivate that obedience and heart devotion which He treasures!

May 16th

Habakkuk 1. 1-11

O LORD, HOW LONG SHALL I CRY AND THOU WILT NOT HEAR?

Habakkuk was by no means the first person to feel that his prayers were not being heeded. All who pray to God need to remember that seeming silence from heaven does not mean God has not heard, nor does it mean that He has not answered, Dan. 10. 2-13. Paul prayed three times before he received an answer, 2 Cor. 12. 8-9. In fact, the response Habakkuk receives is, 'I am doing a work in your days that you would not believe if told', Hab. 1. 5 ESV. God had already begun to put into effect His plans. God's timing is always right: ours seldom is.

Habakkuk was troubled not just because He thought God was indifferent to the prayers of His believing people, but also because he thought God was indifferent to the ways of the wicked, 'Why dost thou show me iniquity and cause me to behold grievance?' v. 3. 'Wherefore lookest thou upon them that deal treacherously and holdest thy tongue when the wicked devoureth the man more righteous than he?' v. 13. This time, however, he waits patiently for the answer, 'I will . . . set me upon the tower and will watch to see what he will say unto me', 2. 1. The answer about the vision comes back, 'Though it tarry, wait for it; because it will surely come', vv. 2-3.

God's response to Habakkuk was clear; the Chaldeans will come to bring God's judgement on His rebellious people. Yet He would not be indifferent to the sins of the Chaldeans either, and several woes are pronounced upon them in chapter 3. God can raise up even the wicked to fulfil His purposes, but they will not thereby be exempt from His judgement. He is 'of purer eyes than to behold evil', and cannot look upon iniquity in an excusing way, no matter who does it.

The thought of the wicked getting away with things was too much for Asaph, too, 'My feet were almost gone; my steps had well-nigh slipped', Ps. 73. 2. From the sanctuary, however, things looked different and his response was, 'It is good for me to draw near to God', v. 28. And Habakkuk's? 'He will make my feet like hinds' feet . . . upon mine high places', 3. 19. No stumbling, then, while we patiently await God's timing.

May 17th

Haggai 2. 1-9

WHO IS LEFT AMONG YOU THAT SAW THIS HOUSE IN HER FIRST GLORY?

As a result of an edict from King Cyrus, the people of God had returned to the land to rebuild the temple of God in Jerusalem, Ezra 1. 1-4. Yet, opposition from their enemies resulted in another edict, this time from King Artaxerxes, which meant that the work of rebuilding the temple came to an untimely end, 4. 23-24. Sixteen years later, God sent two prophets, Haggai and Zechariah, to His people to stir them up to resume the work. Haggai bursts on the scene with the message, 'Is it time for you to dwell in your ceiled houses, and this house lie waste?' Hag. 1. 4. So stirring was his challenge to them to consider their ways, that they resumed work almost immediately and the temple was finished in less than a month.

No matter how well they had done the work, there was no way in which the re-built temple could compare to Solomon's, who had lavished his vast wealth by bringing in timber from Lebanon and spreading gold everywhere. Even the Lord, and those who had remembered the temple before it had been sacked, acknowledged this when He said, 'Is it not in your eyes in comparison of it as nothing?' 2. 4. Yet, the important thing was not the physical beauty of the building but the fact that it was in use once again. For to 'this house' (and God saw it as *one* house, not a succession of houses) God would bring greater glory in a day to come, 'I will fill this house with glory', v. 7.

When did, or when will, this prophecy come true? In the first place, 'this house', even in its further re-incarnation as Herod's temple, had greater glory in it when God's own Son walked its courts, and prayed and taught within its walls. Spiritual glory is always more important to God than outward beauty and show. But secondly, in a millennial day, when the temple is rebuilt in Jerusalem, and when 'the desire of all nations' has come, it will be a fabulous building, for God has said that in that day, 'The latter glory of this house shall be greater than the former', 2. 9 ESV. God's message to the people in Haggai's day was, as it still is now, 'Be strong and work; for I am with you'. Greater glory lies ahead yet, in the will and purposes of God.

May 18th

Haggai 2. 10-23

IF ONE BEAR HOLY FLESH IN THE SKIRT OF HIS GARMENT AND WITH HIS SKIRT DO TOUCH BREAD . . . SHALL IT BE HOLY?

Haggai's first message had been directed to the people as a whole, and his second and fourth were directed to Zerubbabel. His third message, however, was addressed to the priests. It consisted of two points relating to temple procedure. If a priest with an un-dedicated cloth picked up an offering that had been dedicated and made holy to the Lord, would the holiness of the offering be transferred to anything the cloth touched? The answer of the priests, in accordance with the teaching of Leviticus chapter 6 and verse 27, was, 'No; whatever touches the offering shall become holy (the cloth itself, in this case) but the cloth could not pass on holiness'. Back came the second question, 'If someone who has become ceremonially unclean by touching a dead body touches something else, will the uncleanness of the man be transferred to anything he touches?' The answer is, 'Yes', Lev. 11. 27-28. The uncleanness of the dead body, is transferred to the man and his clothes.

What was God trying to teach the priests? Uncleanness is more easily transferred than holiness. The cloth which touches a holy offering becomes holy, but that holiness is not then passed on by touching the cloth; on the other hand, the uncleanness of a dead body is transferred to the one who touches it and anything he touches becomes unclean too, 'So is this people and so is every work of their hands; and that which they offer there is unclean', Hag. 2. 14. Whatever they did for God was unacceptable to Him because heart and attitude were wrong. Samuel had it right. 'To obey is better than sacrifice, and to hearken than the fat of rams', 1 Sam. 15. 22. 'Bring no more vain oblations', says God, Isa. 1. 13. If the heart is wrong so is everything else.

Believers today need to remember that the influence we have on others can be huge, but it is easier to do damage to the people of God by wrong attitudes than it is to influence them for good by our lives. And nothing we offer to God is acceptable if we are not right in the first place. Clean hands and a pure heart are still essential for our worship to be acceptable to God.

May 19th

Zechariah 1. 7-17

O LORD OF HOSTS, HOW LONG WILT THOU NOT HAVE MERCY ON JERUSALEM?

The prophet Zechariah had delivered his first warning to the people of God in Jerusalem some two months after Haggai's first message. God's first message to Zechariah had been oral; His next messages would be visual. The younger of the two prophets was given a succession of visions which he communicates to the people.

In the first vision Zechariah sees a man sitting on a red horse, which in turn is standing in a valley full of myrtle trees. Behind him, also on different-coloured horses, sit three other riders. The rider on the red horse appears to be the Angel of the Lord, Zech. 1. 11. The Angel of the Lord is more than a mere angel, as He receives worship from men. He is a Christophany – an appearance of Christ in visible form before the incarnation. Zechariah, therefore, saw Christ sitting upon a horse with His hosts behind him, who have themselves returned from walking to and fro through the earth, v. 11. They are at His command.

Christ sits upon the horse as though He were waiting for something. The valley shows He waits with His people in a place of humiliation, of weakness. He sits among the myrtle, the leaves of which bush were often used for healing. But again, the myrtle is an insignificant bush. It is no strong, majestic cedar. It is a lowly bush seen in a lowly place. Yet, in this lowly place stands the Son of God, taking His place with His people in their weakness. And He is the One who cries out to the Father on the throne, 'How long wilt thou not have mercy on Jerusalem?'

It is no New Testament truth alone that tells us God stands with, and for, His people, 'When thou passest through the waters I will be with thee', He had said. The Father answers with a word of encouragement to His beleaguered people, 'My house shall be built' in Jerusalem, 'and the Lord shall yet comfort Zion', vv. 16-17. What an encouragement this must have been! Our High Priest still stands for us, His spiritual people, today, and represents us before His Father's throne. His work of atonement is once and forever done; His work of intercession will not stop till the myrtle bushes are exchanged for glory.

May 20th

Zechariah 4. 1-14

WHAT SEEST THOU? . . . BEHOLD, A CANDLESTICK

Zechariah has had four visions delivered to him in one night, and he is exhausted. There are more still to come, however, and the first is a vision of a magnificent golden, seven-branched candlestick, reminiscent of the candlestick that once stood in the temple of God. However this candlestick is different. The one in the temple had to be fed and maintained with olive oil by a constant watch of priests, whose task it was not to allow the light to go out. Yet this one had a constant supply of olive oil provided by two living olive trees standing on each side, and which seemed to grow the olives, crush them and feed the oil directly into the bowls through seven (some say forty-nine) pipes. Zechariah is puzzled. He would have understood what the original candlestick represented, but what is this?

Once again an angel comes to interpret the vision for him. The point of the vision is summed up before the details are given. This is a word of encouragement to Zerubbabel himself, 'Not by might, nor by power, but by my spirit saith the Lord'. Zerubbabel, you may be getting weary in the work of leading the re-building, but learn this: you cannot do it in your own strength. However, as your hands have begun the work, so shall they finish it', Zech. 4. 9.

But, says Zechariah, what about those two olive branches? 'These are the two anointed ones (lit. 'sons of oil') that stand by the Lord', replies the angel. In the immediate context, the two olive trees feeding the candlestick represent both Zerubbabel, the royal prince, head of government in Israel, and Joshua, the high priest, who was the religious head. These two had been appointed by God to feed the work of re-building the temple, and would be sustained by God to do just that. The work could not fail, therefore; God would see to that.

Light is often a picture of testimony in a dark place. The temple must be re-built to establish once again the worship of Jehovah in a pagan world. In a millennial day to come Messiah Himself will combine both offices of priest and king and will one day reign supreme in this earth. In the meantime, all work done for Him will receive power and supply through His Spirit.

May 21st

Zechariah 8. 1-15

IF IT BE MARVELLOUS IN THE EYES OF THE REMNANT OF THIS PEOPLE IN THOSE DAYS, SHOULD IT ALSO BE MARVELLOUS IN MINE EYES?

Zechariah receives yet more words from the Lord which he is to pass on to the people. God tells them of His immense love for 'Zion', Jerusalem itself. He was immensely jealous to guard her as His own, Zech. 8. 2. Ezekiel the prophet had the grim task of recording the grievous sight of the Shekinah glory of the Lord lifting itself from the temple and disappearing back into heaven, a symbolic gesture of the fact that God had left His earthly seat, Ezek. 10. 4, 18. There will come a day, however, when the glory of the Lord will return as, 'I am returned unto Zion and will dwell in the midst of Jerusalem', and Jerusalem shall be a faithful city, Zech. 8. 3. In that day, says the Lord, there will be such peace in My holy mountain that even the elderly will be able to sit outside in the streets and pass away their days in peace, while the boys and girls will play safely in the streets once more. And though only a remnant of the fit and strong had returned, yet the time will come when all generations shall rejoice in the peace of that city, and God will bring His people from the land of the setting sun and the rising sun.

When would this take place? Is it possible that a city that still lay in ruins and was comparatively empty would one day thrill to the sound of the voices of wisdom and fun, of peace and play? Is this not something so unlikely that when the day comes they will consider it an incredible, a marvellous thing, something hitherto thought impossible? Well, says God, if you think it so impossible as to be marvellous when it happens, why should I think it so marvellous that I cannot bring it about? Has this day ever been fulfilled in its entirety yet? No, though there was no doubt a partial fulfilment as the generations of people lived in Jerusalem and children played in the streets in the time of our Lord. But there will come a time when Messiah will reign in this earth and in that millennial day, peace will fill the earth and Jerusalem. Yet, before that day comes, Zerubbabel, 'Let your hands be strong'. The future will come when the duties of the present are fulfilled.

May 22nd

Malachi 1. 1-14

I HAVE LOVED YOU, SAITH THE LORD. YET YE SAY, WHEREIN HAST THOU LOVED US?

In a succession of eight statements from God, followed by the rebuttals of His people, we see the dire spiritual state of the nation in the days when Malachi prophesied. His was the last voice of a long line of prophets whom God had sent to His people. After Malachi's voice is silent, no more word is heard from God for 400 years.

Malachi's prophecy begins with God's heartening words to His erring people the Israelites, 'I have loved you'. But instead of exulting in that fact, their riposte is, 'How have you loved us?' The question is phrased in terms of denial, rather than request. It could be paraphrased in today's language as, 'As if!' How impertinent of God's people to question His love for them! It is true they had gone into exile, but they were back in the land, and the temple had been re-built as a result of God's encouragement.

God answered by showing them how, when, and why His love for them had begun. Isaac had two sons, He said. Yet I loved your father, Jacob, more than I loved his brother Esau. God's love for Jacob had been a sovereign love, totally unconditional, for His choice of Jacob for spiritual blessing as an individual had been made even before the twins were born, and had nothing to do with anything they would do, Rom. 9. 11-13. God's sovereign choice of Jacob's children to be His people was also unconditional, 'The Lord did not set his love upon you, nor choose you, because ye were more in number than any other people . . . but because the Lord loved you', Deut. 7. 7-8.

It would have been more pertinent for the people in Malachi's day to question their love for God rather than His love for them. As believers, we too have been chosen in Christ 'before the foundation of the world', Eph. 1. 4. His sovereign choice of us to spiritual blessing was also an unconditional one for He has said, 'I will have mercy upon whom I will have mercy', Exod. 33. 19; Rom. 9. 15. Is it not passing strange if we doubt God's unfailing, prevenient love for us, and base our appreciation of such love upon our feeble, failing, love for Him?

May 23rd

Malachi 2. 10-16

HAVE WE NOT ALL ONE FATHER? HATH NOT ONE GOD CREATED US?

The fact that every man, woman and child, is made 'in the image of God' is a truth that should remind us of the dignity of the human race. We are all, no matter what class, tribe, caste, or creed, equal before Him. This truth brought with it a responsibility to preserve the life of a fellow human being. Because mankind is made in the image of God, the taking of a human life is equivalent to raising a hand against God Himself. Such dignity of life is to be preserved, by God's command, by invoking the death penalty on all who deliberately murder a human being, Gen. 9. 6; Exod. 21. 12. The apostle Paul also alludes to this common bond all of mankind has when he said God 'hath made of one blood all nations of men', for 'we are his offspring', Acts 17. 26, 28.

The prophet Malachi goes one step further. He pleads with God's people to recognize that having one Father means they should not only preserve human life, they should also *respect* it. This common bond of having the same father, God, means that they are brothers, not just fellow creatures. This bond of being brothers means that there should be mutual respect in their dealings with one another. Can it be right that brother defrauds brother? The basis of your relationships with fellow Israelites, he urges, should not be according to importance or class, but according to nationhood. Otherwise, they are guilty of having respect of persons, Mal. 2. 9, which is an attitude that God does not have, for He is no respecter of persons.

As believers today, we also should 'love as brethren', 1 Pet. 3. 8. It is true that we are to do good unto all men, but 'especially unto them who are of the household of faith', Gal. 6. 10. Our common humanity is a strong bond; our common faith, and the one Father we share in the faith, should bring us together all the more. This bond should prevent believers from going to court against one another, it should prevent us from defrauding one another, and from speaking evil about one another, 1 Cor. 6. 1-8; Jas. 4. 11. The spiritual bond of brothers in Christ is one that we should hold in great affection and esteem.

May 24th

Malachi 3. 1-5

BUT WHO MAY ABIDE THE DAY OF HIS COMING?

God answers yet another less-than-respectful response from His people – 'Where is the God of [justice]?' Mal. 3. 17 – with a promise, 'I will send Him. But before He comes, I will send my messenger to prepare the way'. Our Lord indicates that John Baptist was the very messenger to whom God alludes in this passage, 'This is he of whom it is written, Behold, I send my messenger', Matt. 11. 10. This means, of course, that our Lord indicates that He Himself is 'the Lord whom ye seek', Mal. 3. 1. The first coming of our Lord as a man to this earth is, therefore, a fulfilment of this prophecy. John came to prepare the way before Him, and He came to His temple. Now we know that the primary purpose of His first coming was 'to seek and to save', not to judge. Yet there were those who were condemned by Him during His lifetime down here, those whom He called 'a generation of vipers', those who were driven out of the temple, those who felt they were without sin. In a very real sense, the unrepentant, the self-righteous, the proud, and the hypocrites whom He encountered could not endure the day of His coming.

But the first coming of our Lord to earth was only a partial fulfilment of this prophecy. In a day to come, when His feet will once again touch the Mount of Olives, He will come, not with the express purpose of bringing spiritual salvation to the repentant, but of bringing the fiery judgement of God upon the unrepentant. When such a divine Judge appears then, no one will be able to stand proudly and defiantly before Him. He will bring the fire of judgement to purge away the dross that lessens the purity of the silver, and the strong soap needed to wash away impurities from cloth, and none will be able to withstand Him.

But there is a sting in the tail. Israel must take no comfort from this coming, for He will not come to purify and judge the heathen, the enemies of His people. Their judgement will come on another day. He will come to purify Israel, His own people, the ones who in Malachi's day, and in that day to come, despise and reject Him and His ways. Judgement must begin at the house of God. His earthly people, and we His spiritual people, need to take care, for 'our God is a consuming fire', Heb. 12. 29.

May 25th

Malachi 3. 6-15

WILL A MAN ROB GOD?

Despite the frequent impertinence His people had shown Him in their sarcastic, challenging answers to His statements, which showed their hearts and spirits were far from Him, were proud and self-righteous, God lovingly holds out His hands to them and says, 'Return unto me, and I will return unto you', Mal. 3. 7. We could paraphrase their response by saying, 'What do you mean, return? We've never been away from You! How, why, should we return?' 'You have robbed Me', is God's response. 'And it isn't just you. Each generation of you, since the very beginning of your status as My people, has robbed Me'.

Was the response of the people one of grief and repentance? Not a bit of it! 'How have we robbed you?', they reply arrogantly. 'We have never taken anything from You'. Perhaps not, but they failed to realize that when they withheld from God the things that were rightly His, that in itself was robbery. They defrauded Him, they spoiled His goods, they kept back from Him His entitlement to the tithes that they should have given Him and His servants. And in keeping back from Him what was rightfully His, they showed that they despised Him and held Him in low regard.

As believers, we today do not need to tithe our goods. We are not under Old Testament law and the giving of a tenth of our possessions is not essential. Yet, should we who know so much more of God's forgiveness, peace, and love as individuals, give Him less than a tithe? We ought to be giving Him as *much* as we can, not as little as we can. The widow who put in her two mites in the temple was commended, not for the amount she put in, but for the amount she withheld – nothing. She gave all she possessed. We, too, should not rob God by depriving Him of time, talent, resources, energy. The old Puritan was right when he confessed before God his sin in 'the neglect of Thy word, in prayer irreverently offered and coldly withheld, in time misspent and of substance unduly hoarded, improvidently squandered and not consecrated to the Great Giver'. Could our God reprove us for robbing Him? If He could, would our response be more penitent than His people's in Malachi's day?

May 26th

Matthew 2. 1-12

WHERE IS HE THAT IS BORN KING OF THE JEWS?

A considerable amount of unbiblical legend has grown up around the visit of the Magi to see the new-born King of the Jews. Legend has it that there were three men, that they were kings and even gives us their names. Scripture is silent on the number, merely telling us that three gifts were given. It would appear that the Magi were astronomers of some sort, if not astrologers, who saw great significance in the appearance of a new star in the east. They may have been familiar with the hopes of the Jewish Diaspora in their area, and therefore saw this new star as the herald of the birth of the long-anticipated Messiah. Bearing in mind that it took Ezra several months to travel from Babylon to Jerusalem, their journey would have been equally long and arduous.

Why did they go to Jerusalem and not Bethlehem? There is no evidence that the star took them to Jerusalem, and it may be that their own expectations led them to Herod's palace. Human assumption will frequently lead us astray if we are not careful. Did the wise men do wrong in alerting Herod? No. The scripture about Rachel weeping for her children had to be fulfilled, as did the scripture that said, 'Out of Egypt have I called my son'. Yet it is undoubtedly true that, had they sought God's guidance more fully, they would never have had to ask a cruel king the question, 'Where is he?'

Upon leaving Herod, the star led them away from Jerusalem to the house, not the stable, in Bethlehem where the young child was and actually 'stood over' where He lay. When they came into the house, and saw the young Child with Mary His mother, their immediate response was to worship Him and to give to Him. Perhaps, as they listened to Mary's story and heard the prophecies given about Him at His birth, they were led to see that, in this Child, all the treasures of Godhead were to be found, Col. 2. 3. As a result they opened up their treasures and gave Him gifts corresponding to what they had heard of Him, a divine Being, yet One who was to be a suffering and rejected King. It may be, too, that, as a result of seeing 'the face of Jesus Christ', they received treasure in earthen vessels, 2 Cor. 4. 7.

May 27th

Matthew 3. 1-12

O GENERATION OF VIPERS, WHO HATH WARNED YOU TO FLEE FROM THE WRATH TO COME?

When the Lord commended John the Baptist in saying that he was 'more than a prophet', Matt. 11. 8-9, He did not only have John's huge privilege of being the forerunner of the Messiah in mind. Like many of the prophets God had sent to His people of old, John was fearless in His preaching. He was no 'reed shaken by the wind'. His message was an uncompromising one, 'Repent, for the kingdom of heaven is at hand'. He pulled no punches when he spoke to tax collectors ('Exact no more than that which is appointed you', 3. 13), to soldiers ('Do violence to no man, neither accuse any falsely; and be content with your wages', v. 14), or even to a king ('It is not lawful for thee to have thy brother's wife', Mark 6. 18). Neither was he afraid of the rulers of the Jews, the Pharisees and Sadducees. Doubtless he knew the purpose of their visit – not to repent, as others did, nor yet to be baptized into a baptism of repentance for the remission of sins, seeing as they saw themselves as being unlike other sinners, Luke 18. 11-14. He saw their hypocrisy, and addressed it fearlessly. An 'offspring of vipers', he called them, Matt. 3. 7 RV, as did our Lord, 12. 34.

But why had they come anyway? As with our Lord, John had not come to call the righteous but sinners to repentance. John's call had been a warning to the repentant to flee from God's wrath. In their response to the Lord, as to John, these Pharisees and Sadducees rested in their privileged birth as children of Abraham and of the promise, 3. 8; John 8. 39. Yet John would have none of that. God could raise up more responsive children of Abraham from the hard stones round about them than from their hard hearts.

There would not have been many who did not fear the power these men could wield. Yet, his response was to tell them that judgement upon the unrepentant had already begun; the axe was already laid at the root of the trees and the trees that did not bring forth the fruit of repentance were to be cast down and thrown into the fire, regardless of what sap flowed through them. Neither God, nor John, would be respecters of persons!

May 28th

Matthew 3. 13-16

I HAVE NEED TO BE BAPTIZED OF THEE AND COMEST THOU TO ME?

We ought not to forget that, though John the Baptist awaited a sign from God which would identify to him the true Messiah, Jesus of Nazareth was no stranger to him. He was related to our Lord, as John's mother Elisabeth was a 'cousin' (KJV) to Mary, the mother of our Lord. They had visited and prayed with each other before either of the boys were born and it is highly probable that John would have known from his mother's knee that Jesus was to be called 'the Son of the Highest', Luke 1. 32, that 'the Lord God shall give unto him the throne of his father David', v. 32, and that 'of his kingdom there shall be no end', v. 33. No doubt he had also been told that he had leaped for joy in his mother's womb at the visit of Mary and that his mother called Mary 'the mother of my Lord', Luke 1. 43.

It is hardly surprising, then, that when he saw Jesus coming to him, expressing His readiness to be baptized 'unto John's baptism', Acts 19. 3, John would have demurred. In the first place, John would have felt that the greater should not be baptized by the lesser. Secondly, his baptism was 'a baptism of repentance for the remission of sins' and John would surely have known that the Lord was utterly and completely different to all those who came to be baptized by him, having no sin of which He needed to repent. His consternation and question to the Lord, then, is perfectly understandable.

Our Lord wished to be baptized by John. The sign that John had been given, 'upon whom thou shalt see the Spirit descending, and remaining on him, the same is he which baptizeth with the Holy Ghost', John 1. 33, would be shown him at His baptism. As our Lord descended into the water He took His place with sinners and so identified Himself with them. He humbled Himself yet again, submitting to a baptism of which He was unworthy, in the company of sinners of whom He was unworthy and in waters of a river which even a Syrian general had once despised, 2 Kgs. 5. 10-12. Obedience to the will of the Father led our Lord into humbling experiences, and took John where he did not want to go. Are we too proud to submit?

May 29th

Matthew 5. 13-16

IF THE SALT HAVE LOST HIS SAVOUR, WHEREWITH SHALL IT BE SALTED?

Those of us who like to add salt to our meals are happy to quote our Lord to those who condemn its use. 'Salt is bad for you', they say. 'Ah!' is the reply, 'But didn't the Lord say, "Salt is good"', Mark 9. 50?

But for what is salt good? It may not be good for blood pressure, but it is good for adding flavour to food. As long ago as patriarchal times, Job asked the question, 'Can that which is unsavoury (tasteless ESV) be eaten without salt?' Job 6. 6. Salt is also good as a preservative. It prevents decay in food where there is no ice to slow down decay. Even today, fish and meat are often brushed or rubbed with salt to preserve them.

It is presumably with the latter use in mind that the Lord says of believers, 'Ye are the salt of the earth'. The Lord would not think believers would add flavour to this world, for there can never be anything wholesome about sin; but we can, by our godly and God-fearing ways, prevent the world from being as rotten as it could be. In the same way as light dispels the darkness with which it comes into contact, salt preserves the food with which it comes into contact. Believers are to counteract the influence of evil by counteracting spiritual darkness in a world ignorant of God, and spiritual rottenness in a world at odds with Him. To do this, of course, the light must be allowed to shine in the darkness and the salt must come into contact with the world. Light that is hidden under a bushel is useless; salt that is kept in a jar is pointless. Living lives in seclusion may help us to be holy; it does not help the world to be less rotten. Though believers are not 'of the world' we are still 'in' it. We should promote Christian values, speak out against sin, and live holy lives. Then we will have some wholesome influence in the world.

Un-salty salt is 'good for nothing' and cannot regain its saltiness. How often has a lost testimony led to rejection by men ('Who are you to preach?') and therefore to rejection by God as useful service. We need to keep close to the Lord to ensure our 'saltiness' is not compromised. When men have reason to think we do not practise what we preach we have become useless.

May 30th

Matthew 6. 25-34

IS NOT THE LIFE MORE THAN MEAT AND THE BODY MORE THAN RAIMENT?

'Eat, drink and be merry' is the motto of the man who has 'much goods laid up for many years' but has no fear of God, Luke 12. 19. Yet, our Lord has stressed, 'A man's life consisteth not in the abundance of the things which he possesseth', v. 15. Paul's instruction to 'young' Timothy is one all believers should take to heart, 'Godliness with contentment is great gain. For we brought nothing into this world and it is certain we can carry nothing out. And having food and raiment let us therewith be content', 1 Tim. 6. 6-7. Job knew this fundamental truth, too. 'Naked came I out of my mother's womb, and naked shall I return', Job 1. 21. Paul goes on to stress, 'But they that will be rich fall into temptation and a snare and into many foolish and hurtful lusts, which drown men in destruction and perdition. For the love of money is the root of all evil', 1 Tim. 6. 6-10. 'Better is a little with righteousness than great revenues without right', Prov. 16. 8, and, 'Better is a dinner of herbs where love is, than a stalled ox and hatred therewith', 15. 17. The fear of God, a good conscience, righteousness, and love are the most important things for the people of God to possess.

Yet, we should not seek contentment with having the basics of life only. The thrust of what the Lord is teaching here is that the basics of life should neither be a priority with us, nor should they be a pre-occupation. 'Take no thought' means, 'Do not be anxious' about these things. We should ask for them to be provided – after all, our Lord did teach His disciples to pray, 'Give us this day our daily bread', Matt. 6. 11, and it is essential that a man 'provide for his own', 1 Tim. 5. 8. To do otherwise would be to be worse than an unbeliever. But the believer does all these things looking to God for help and provision, knowing that He who can care for the fowls of the air and the lilies of the field can, and will, look after His own. To those who put God and His interests first comes the promise, 'All these things shall be added unto you', Matt. 6. 33. And to the 'rich in this world' comes the exhortation not to 'trust in uncertain riches', 1 Tim. 6. 17. Only God is reliable in the end.

May 31st

Matthew 7. 1-5

OR HOW WILT THOU SAY TO THY BROTHER, LET ME PULL OUT THE MOTE OUT OF THINE EYE?

It is a universal characteristic of the sinful nature that we are harder on others than we are on ourselves. When admonished by God in paradise, the response of the man was evidence of the way sinners would respond to God from then on, 'It wasn't me, Lord', but 'the woman whom thou gavest to be with me, she gave me of the tree and I did eat', Gen. 3. 12. And how did Eve respond, in turn? 'The serpent beguiled me, and I did eat', v. 13. So we are all inclined to see more wrong in others than we ever are in ourselves. Our Lord tells us here that we are inclined to notice other people's faults before we notice our own. 'Why *beholdest* thou the mote that is in thy brother's eye; but considerest not the beam that is in thine own?' Matt. 7. 3. I am not inclined to notice the log of wood in my own eye because I am too pre-occupied with the speck in yours.

Not only is the sinful nature more inclined to see the small speck in others' eyes and ignore the larger one in its own, it is also more inclined to want to give others advice than to take it. Our Lord adds the second thing here, 'How wilt thou say to thy brother, *let me pull out* the mote out of thine eye, and behold, the beam is in thine own?' v. 4. We would rather tell others how to sort themselves out than to sort out ourselves. But our Lord sees this not just as unwarranted intrusion into the lives of others; He sees it as hypocrisy, 'Thou hypocrite, first cast out the beam out of thine own eye; and then shalt thou see clearly to cast out the mote out of thy brother's eye', v. 5.

How can we avoid this sort of hypocrisy? If we could esteem each other better than ourselves we would go a long way to being harder on ourselves than on others, Phil. 2. 3. If we would compare ourselves with God we would always be humble in our self-assessment. Our Lord also says, 'Judge not that ye be not judged', Matt. 7. 1. Does that mean we should never exercise our judgement about anyone? No. It means that I should not be harsh on others and easy on myself, for 'with what measure ye mete, it shall be measured to you again', v. 2. Being harsh on others means God will be harsh on us!

June 1st

Matthew 8. 28-34

WHAT HAVE WE TO DO WITH THEE, JESUS?

In chapters 5 to 7 the King has been setting out the policies of His kingdom – His manifesto. What follows in chapters 8 to 9 is a demonstration of the King's power, a power that proves His ability to carry out those policies. Already, in chapter 8 He has exhibited His power over various sicknesses and a storm; in the verses before us He will display His power over demons.

An examination of the various Gospel records of this incident will reveal a number of significant differences, but differences are not discrepancies. Matthew informs us that there were two men, Mark and Luke focus on just one of them and tell us his name was Legion. Mark and Luke emphasize his deplorable condition and the transformation that took place after he met Christ; Matthew leaves out much of this detail, choosing to concentrate on the attitude of the people of the city.

This event, which occurred in the country of the Gadarenes, supplies several contrasts. However, none is comparable to the contrast between the demons that dwelt within Legion and the Lord that stood before him. One was marked by malignity, the other by meekness. The demons were unclean, Mark 5. 2, Christ was undefiled, Heb. 7. 26. The 'light of the world' would meet and overcome the power of darkness.

These contrasts are highlighted in the question we are considering today. Seeing Jesus, the demons cried out, 'What have we to do with thee, Jesus, thou Son of God? art thou come hither to torment us before the time?' These evil spirits had greater intelligence than the religious hierarchy of Israel, for they recognized that Jesus was the Son of God. They also acknowledged His absolute power over them, accepting that one day they would be subjected to eternal judgement.

In addition, the demons knew that there was nothing in common between them and the Son of God and so they ask, 'What have we to do with thee?' Light has no communion with darkness; there is no concord between Christ and Belial, 2 Cor. 6. 14-16. Leaving the man, the demons are allowed by Christ to enter into the swine – eternal salvation being of greater import than the temporary preservation of unclean animals.

June 2nd

Matthew 9. 14-17

WHY DO WE AND THE PHARISEES FAST OFT, BUT THY DISCIPLES FAST NOT?

Although unaware of it when they posed this question, John's disciples embraced two distinct companies of believers from two separate dispensations in this one sentence. In addition to their comment about the Pharisees, they referred to themselves and to the Lord's disciples. John and his followers belonged to an age that was drawing to a close and which would be replaced by something entirely different. We can see this transition presented illustratively in the incident recorded by John in his Gospel, chapter 1 verses 35 to 37.

In contrast to the ignorance that characterized the questioners, the Lord's response indicates His absolute knowledge of all that was going to ensue. John's disciples belonged to an era that was ending but His disciples were going to be the inaugural members of an age that was soon to commence. One set of disciples belonged to that which was 'old' whilst the other set of disciples pertained to that which was 'new'.

The law, and all that it represents, is portrayed by the Lord as being an 'old garment', v. 16, and 'old bottles', v. 17. The message of the law, as seen in the 'old garment', was going to be replaced by the 'new cloth' of the gospel. These two messages cannot be joined together; they are mutually exclusive. In addition, the descent and indwelling of the Holy Spirit, as seen in the 'new wine', could be received only by the 'new bottles', i.e., those who were under the new covenant and who, through salvation, were a 'new creation', 2 Cor. 5. 17.

Before the Lord gives this illustrative response, He deals with the issue that was perplexing the questioners. His disciples didn't fast like the Pharisees and John's disciples because He, the Bridegroom, was with them. As such, it would be inappropriate to fast, it was correct that they should enjoy a time of joy and feasting. However, the time would come when His disciples would fast and that would be when He – the Bridegroom – should 'be taken from them', v. 15. Quite clearly the Lord is making a veiled reference to His impending death, a death that would be the basis for the 'new' dispensation that was to come.

June 3rd

Matthew 9. 27-31

BELIEVE YE THAT I AM ABLE TO DO THIS?

It is only Matthew who records this incident, and the one that follows, concerning the demon-possessed mute. This is not surprising for no Gospel writer recorded all that the Lord did, and had he attempted to do so probably 'the world itself could not contain the books that should be written', John 21. 25. Throughout His public ministry the Lord healed many that were blind but on a number of occasions detailed information is given. Such is the case here.

There were times when the Lord acted without delay and the afflicted were cured instantly, but on this particular day He chose to postpone things for a time. These two unnamed men first accosted the Lord as He moved along the road to the house but it seemed as if He was ignoring them. Undaunted by this apparent setback, the men pursued Him into the house and there poured out their earnest appeal, 'Thou Son of David, have mercy on us', Matt. 9. 27.

Maybe you have known what it is to struggle with burdens and even though you have sought the Lord to make an immediate intervention He chooses to keep you waiting, just as He did to these two men. How interminable those delays feel and perhaps you've even felt like asking the question posed by the disciples, 'Master, carest thou not that we perish', Mark 4. 8.

The Lord was not indifferent to the plight of these blind men. His delay was not the consequence of apathy but derived from a far nobler motive. His initial response indicates that He was fully aware of what they needed. However, He wanted to test the reality of their faith and hence He asks, 'Believe ye that I am able to do this?' v. 28. Unwaveringly, they responded, 'Yea, Lord', and immediately the Lord touched their eyes, adding, 'According to your faith be it unto you', v. 29.

The Lord has the ability, should He so wish, to grant whatever we require in an instant. However, even though it is hard to appreciate it at the time, how much more blessed we are when we, with childlike faith, wait upon Him. The spirit of the age in which we live is 'I want it yesterday', but sometimes the Lord keeps us waiting until tomorrow in order to increase our faith.

June 4th

Matthew 10. 26-33

ARE NOT TWO SPARROWS SOLD FOR A FARTHING?

Matthew chapter 10 brings into focus our Lord's dealings with His disciples and it centres on three significant matters. The chapter opens in verses 1 to 4 with the **call** of this band of men. This was not their original call to become His disciples, nor was it the initial call to serve Him. This was a specific call to a particular sphere of service, and, for the first time in the New Testament, they are called 'apostles', v. 2.

Having received and responded to the call, verses 5 to 15 present the **commission** the Lord gave the apostles. That commission included instruction concerning the content of the message and the conduct of the messengers. Those preachers were told where to go, what to preach, and how to react to the various circumstances that would confront them.

Finally, in verses 16 to 42, the Lord gives **counsel** to the twelve, counsel that gave clear warning that persecution and opposition were to be expected. They would have to endure scourging, interrogation before governors and kings, and suffer even martyrdom. However, blended with those warnings were words of reassurance and encouragement.

A sparrow was a very insignificant bird, possessing none of the beauty of a peacock or the majesty of an eagle. In size and value it was inconsequential and, as such, two sparrows could be purchased for a farthing. In Luke's Gospel these birds are further devalued in financial terms for there the Lord says, 'Are not five sparrows sold for two farthings', Luke 12. 6. A single sparrow therefore was worth just a few mites – a miniscule amount of money. Despite being of limited value in the eyes of men, these birds were the object of divine providence, and not one of them was outside the scope of God's care.

If sparrows were so watched over by God how much more would His eye rest upon those who engage in His service? The relationship between the sparrow and God was that of creature to Creator; however, the relationship between the disciples and God was far more intimate, for they could call God their Father, Matt. 10. 29. Furthermore, the disciples were of 'more value than **many** sparrows' – their value to God was unquantifiable.

June 5th

Matthew 11. 1-19

ART THOU HE THAT SHOULD COME, OR DO WE LOOK FOR ANOTHER?

John was no ordinary man; he was second cousin to Jesus and a descendant of Aaron. Being a Levite he could have served as a priest but his reputation as a prophet outshone the honour of his priesthood. Such was his status as a prophet the Lord said, 'Among those that are born of women there is not a greater prophet than John the Baptist', Luke 7. 28.

This exceptional man was given a unique task. He was to be the forerunner of the Messiah, 'For this is he, of whom it is written, Behold, I send my messenger before thy face, which shall prepare thy way before thee', Matt. 11. 10.

Our chapter opens with John in prison, and it was there that his short life ended. Although only in his early thirties, John was executed by Herod and his decapitated body was buried by his disciples. Whilst in prison, John heard about the works of Christ and, sending two of his disciples to Jesus, he asks, 'Art thou he that should come, or do we look for another?' v. 3.

As John contemplated his own difficult circumstances and reflected on the general condition of the nation, seeds of doubt began to rise in his mind. Yes, Jesus was doing some amazing things but He was not achieving all that the Old Testament had promised. Why was He not overthrowing the tyranny of Rome and establishing His own kingdom? Why was evil abounding? Maybe Jesus was not the one 'that was to come'; perhaps the people should be looking for someone else.

The Lord knew that John would have been aware of Isaiah's writings foretelling that the promised Messiah would heal the sick, cure the blind, and enable the deaf to hear, etc. So the Lord told John's disciples to report back that they had seen these very things taking place. These credentials would prove conclusively to John that Jesus was the promised Messiah, and thus strengthen his faith.

Despite John's doubts, it is touching to observe that the Lord does not criticize him but speaks in glowing terms of His illustrious forerunner, vv. 7-15.

June 6th

Matthew 12. 9-14

IS IT LAWFUL TO HEAL ON THE SABBATH DAYS?

For the second time in this chapter there is a confrontation between the Pharisees and Christ, and both are in relation to the sabbath day. The first altercation resulted from the disciples plucking ears of corn as they walked through the field, prompting the Pharisees to remark, 'Behold, thy disciples do that which is not lawful to do upon the sabbath day', Matt. 12. 2.

This second incident relates to a man with a withered hand being present in the synagogue on the sabbath, and this time the Pharisees ask, 'Is it lawful to heal on the sabbath days?' v. 10. Sadly, these religious bigots had no concern for the incapacitated man. Instead of having mercy on the sufferer they were driven by malice towards Christ and were looking for any pretext to accuse Him before the Sanhedrin.

The Lord's initial reaction to this challenge was to ask two questions in response. The first was, 'What man shall there be among you, that shall have one sheep, and if it fall into a pit on the sabbath day, will he not lay hold on it, and lift it out?' v. 11. His second question was, 'How much then is a man better than a sheep?' As we consider the first question we need to note that the Lord was implying that the sheep was owned by the man – and because he owned it he would lift it out, even if it was on the sabbath day. That sheep was of value to the owner and for that reason he would rescue it.

The point the Lord was making was obvious. The debilitated man that stood in the synagogue was of value to Christ. If the Jews would rescue a suffering sheep on the sabbath, how much more should He, the Lord of the sabbath day, meet the need of a suffering man, given that men are of greater value than sheep?

Anyone with a withered hand would be restricted in his service for God and in some respects the condition of the man typified the condition of the nation of Israel, and the Pharisees in particular. The significant difference between the man and those that posed the initial question was that he responded to the words of Christ and by his obedience and faith he was blessed, his hand was healed. In contrast, the Pharisees went out and 'held a council against him, how they might destroy him', v. 14.

June 7th

Matthew 12. 22-32

OR ELSE HOW CAN ONE ENTER INTO A STRONG MAN'S HOUSE, AND SPOIL HIS GOODS?

These verses, and the remainder of chapter 12, bring us to a seminal point in Matthew's Gospel and in the ministry of the Lord Jesus. Twice already in chapter 12 the Pharisees have assailed the Saviour, but now they are about to launch a third attack that would far outweigh those that preceded it for its malignity.

A most pitiful spectacle is presented to us, Matt. 12. 22. We are introduced to a man who was demon-possessed, and the consequence of this thraldom was that he was both dumb and blind. On being brought to the Lord, the man was instantly healed, resulting in him being able to speak and see. In spite of this, the miracle invoked an immediate retort from the Pharisees that was wicked in the extreme.

What they could not refute was that an amazing phenomenon had occurred, nor could they deny that something supernatural had transpired. What had just taken place before their very eyes was a display of divine power, but instead of attributing what had happened to the power of the Spirit of God they said, 'This fellow doth not cast out devils, but by Beelzebub the prince of the devils', v. 24.

Not only was this verdict inaccurate, it was also illogical, and the Lord highlights that irrationality in his response saying, 'If Satan cast out Satan, he is divided against himself; how shall then his kingdom stand?' v. 26. However, the judgement of the Pharisees was far more serious than just being inaccurate or illogical, it was *blasphemy* of a unique kind. To ascribe to Satan what had clearly been the product of the Holy Spirit's power was a sin of such magnitude that it could not be forgiven.

The question in today's title was used illustratively by the Lord to explain what had taken place in this incident. Satan is the strong man, but, by delivering the demon-possessed mute, the Lord demonstrated that He is stronger than Satan and had overpowered him. Because He is stronger, He was able to spoil Satan's house, He had plundered Satan's domain and released the poor man from satanic control.

June 8th

Matthew 12. 33-37

O GENERATION OF VIPERS, HOW CAN YE, BEING EVIL, SPEAK GOOD THINGS?

It was noted in yesterday's meditation that the conclusion reached by the Pharisees, when they witnessed the deliverance of the blind and dumb man, was both inaccurate and illogical. The Lord exposes the absurdity of their reasoning by giving an illustration from nature, Matt. 12. 33. Fruit produced by a tree is governed by what kind of tree it is, a good tree can produce only good fruit and, similarly, a corrupt tree can yield only corrupt fruit. In healing the man the Lord had done something that was obviously good, yet the Pharisees accused Him of doing it by an evil power, their rationale was ridiculously inconsistent.

In verse 34 the Lord changes the metaphor from a tree to the heart, but the point being emphasized in both is the same. A tree can produce only its own kind of fruit; similarly, what a person is at heart will determine how he speaks, 'for out of the abundance of the heart the mouth speaketh'. In the following verse the Lord reinforces the principle He has just articulated, saying, 'A good man out of the good treasure of the heart bringeth forth good things: and an evil man out of the evil treasure bringeth forth evil things', v. 35.

Having established His point the Lord then applies it directly to His challengers, saying, 'O generation of vipers, how can ye, being evil, speak good things?' The problem with these insincere leaders did not derive from what they said but from what they were. By adhering to a rigid external ritualism, the Pharisees loved to give the impression that they were holy and spiritual, but in reality the converse was true. Later in this Gospel, the Lord castigates them saying, 'Woe unto you, scribes and Pharisees, hypocrites! for ye are like unto whited sepulchres, which indeed appear beautiful outward, but are within full of dead men's bones, and of all uncleanness', 23. 27.

The Pharisees were morally responsible for their attitude towards Christ because they had deliberately attributed what He had done to the power of Beelzebub. Therefore, just as a bad tree yields only a harvest of corrupt fruit so these men could speak only ill of the Saviour because of what they were within.

June 9th

Matthew 13. 10-17

WHY SPEAKEST THOU UNTO THEM IN PARABLES?

In a recent meditation (June 7th) it was noted that the latter section of chapter 12 is a pivotal point in Matthew's Gospel, and in the ministry of the Lord Jesus. The Pharisees had already challenged the Lord as to the legality of His disciples plucking ears of corn on the sabbath day, Matt. 12. 2. Subsequently, they confronted Him about His healing a man with a withered hand on the sabbath day. Instead of rejoicing in the man's restoration, the Pharisees went out and plotted how they might kill the Lord.

The final and most serious issue arose when the Lord healed the demon-possessed man. Although the miracle was obviously a work of the Holy Spirit, the Pharisees credited the healing power to Beelzebub the prince of the devils, v. 24. At that moment they reached a point of no return; they had finally and irrevocably rejected their Messiah. The consequence of their rejection of Him was that He rejected them, and, from verse 38 to the end of the chapter, the Lord foretells of impending judgement and of His severing of natural links with Israel.

It is against this backdrop that chapter 13 opens with these poignant words, 'The same day went Jesus out of the house, and sat by the sea side. And great multitudes were gathered together unto him . . . And he spake many things unto them in parables', 13. 1-3. For the first time in this Gospel the Lord spoke to the people in parables, and being unaccustomed to hearing this mode of teaching the surprised disciples asked, 'Why speakest thou unto them in parables?' v. 10.

In His response the Lord said, 'For whosoever hath, to him shall be given, and he shall have more abundance: but whosoever hath not, from him shall be taken away even that he hath', v. 12. The Pharisees were those who 'had not' because they had intentionally rejected the truth. Therefore, because they wilfully closed their eyes and ears to what was true, the Lord spoke in parables to conceal from them His teaching. In quoting from Isaiah's prophecy in verses 14-15, the Lord was providing further evidence that the nation had rejected its King, and consequently He spoke to them in parables so that their self-inflicted state of blindness would remain.

June 10th

Matthew 13. 24-30, 36-43

SIR, DIDST NOT THOU SOW GOOD SEED IN THY FIELD?

At the start of chapter 11, Matthew states, 'And it came to pass, when Jesus had made an end of commanding his twelve disciples, he departed thence', Matt. 11. 1. Then, towards the end of chapter 13, he writes, 'And it came to pass, that when Jesus had finished these parables, he departed thence', 13. 53. These two phrases bind together chapters 11-13 into one section, and that point is integral to a right understanding of the subject matter in today's question.

During his ministry, John the Baptist had sounded out a clear warning to the Jews that there was one soon to come who would baptize with the Holy Spirit, and with fire. He then added, 'Whose fan is in his hand, and he will throughly purge his floor, and gather his wheat into the garner; but he will burn up the chaff with unquenchable fire', 3. 12. John fully expected Christ to establish His kingdom, put down all opposition, and remove all evil. However, that did not happen and instead John ended up in prison facing execution.

This apparent failure of Christ to rectify things perplexed John and he queried whether Jesus was the promised Messiah. John's problem was one of timing. He had anticipated that the kingdom age would be inaugurated by the Lord at that time, and that He would do it by judging evil-doers. In the first parable of Matthew 13, the Lord indicated that the preparation for His kingdom would not begin by the judgement of evil people, but by preaching the word of the kingdom to them. The point to note in this parable is that there is only one sower and he sows good seed; it is the soil that is the problem.

Today's question is found in the second parable in which we learn that there are **two** sowers and **two** kinds of seed. There is the 'good seed' sown by the Son of man and there are 'tares', something counterfeit, sown by the devil. The devil constantly tries to corrupt God's testimony on earth by introducing false profession. However, one day there will be a judgement to segregate the good from the evil. Those who are false will be judged and the genuine will go into the kingdom.

June 11th

Matthew 13. 53-58

WHENCE HATH THIS MAN THIS WISDOM, AND THESE MIGHTY WORKS?

From before the remote ages of antiquity He had dwelt in the unsullied glory of heaven. In that uncreated abode of the Godhead, He had been loved by His Father and revered by seraphim. Now, the Eternal had stepped into time and, for a while, He was made a little lower than the angels. The One who thought it not robbery to be equal with God made Himself of no reputation and exchanged the opulence of heaven for the obscurity of Nazareth. His association with that despised city was such that He became known as 'Jesus of Nazareth', an epitaph that hung above Him as He was nailed to the cross.

While He was here there was very little that He owned, for He had voluntarily become poor. However, there are a few references in the Gospel records to things which are called 'His own'. One of those was Nazareth, called 'his own city', Matt. 9. 1, and in today's reading it is called 'his own country', 13. 54. Sadly, His experience at Nazareth can be summarized in the words of John, 'He came unto his own, and his own received him not', John 1. 11.

How obtuse His fellow countrymen were as they posed the question that heads today's meditation, 'Whence hath this man this wisdom, and these mighty works?'! They failed to appreciate that the One that lived amongst them for almost thirty years was wisdom incarnate, for in Him 'are hid all the treasures of wisdom and knowledge', Col. 2. 3. Little did they know that the One who they called 'the carpenter's son' had once spoken and by the word of His power 'the earth brought forth grass . . . and the tree yielding fruit', Gen. 1. 12. Not only did He make furniture and wooden implements at the carpenter's bench, but He was the source of the trees from which the wood was hewn!

The Son who had been the centre of heaven's adoration stood lonely and unwanted in His own city and regrettably had to say to His fellow citizens, 'A prophet is not without honour, save in his own country, and in his own house', Matt. 13. 57. The sad consequence of this was that 'he did not many mighty works there because of their unbelief', v. 58.

June 12th

Matthew 14. 22-33

O THOU OF LITTLE FAITH, WHEREFORE DIDST THOU DOUBT?

This is not the first time the disciples had been embroiled in a storm on the Sea of Galilee; a similar incident is recorded by Matthew in chapter 8. However, there are a couple of differences between the two episodes. In chapter 8, the Lord was physically present in the boat with the disciples, albeit fast asleep. In today's reading, the Lord was not with the disciples on the sea, but was up a mountain praying.

On both occasions the Lord delivers a rebuke because of a deficiency of faith. In chapter 8 it is addressed to all the disciples; this time the rebuke is addressed solely to Peter. Catching the sinking fisherman, the Lord said to him, 'O thou of little faith, wherefore didst thou doubt?' Matt. 14. 31. Despite these variations, one feature common to both events is that the disciples were right in the centre of the Lord's will when the storm burst around them. In chapter 8, they followed the Lord into the ship and here in chapter 14 He 'constrained his disciples to get into a ship, and to go before him unto the other side', v. 22.

Many lessons and applications can be drawn from these nautical ordeals, but just two will be considered now. Firstly, compliance with the will of God does not necessarily result in His servants being exempt from difficulties. Throughout the Bible there are numerous examples of servants of God enduring opposition, rejection or hardship, even though they were doing what God had requested them to do.

Secondly, it is vital to observe that the Lord was not indifferent to the needs of the Twelve. Although they were toiling on the sea and He was invisible to them, they were not hidden from Him for Mark says, 'And he saw them toiling in rowing', Mark 6. 48. The waves that were creating such fear in the hearts of the disciples became the pathway by which He drew near to them.

One thing was certain, those disciples would reach the other shore and when they did, the Lord would be there too. Soon the tempests of life will be stilled for all who are Christ's, and as they step onto the heavenly shore He will be there with them – for He will have met them already 'in the air', 1 Thess. 4. 17.

June 13th

Matthew 15. 1-9

WHY DO THY DISCIPLES TRANSGRESS THE TRADITION OF THE ELDERS?

One thing is certain, no one has ever loved and fulfilled the law of God to the degree that the Son of God did. His moral excellence was attested by Heaven, by humans and by hell. His betrayer, His judge and His executioner all acknowledged His innocence and righteousness. David wrote prophetically of Christ, 'Then said I, Lo, I come: in the volume of the book it is written of me, I delight to do thy will, O my God: yea, thy law is within my heart', Ps. 40. 7-8.

Despite His unimpeachability, the Pharisees were relentless in their hatred of Christ, their ire being directed against Him because of His non-compliance with their traditions. Over many centuries a stringent set of oral regulations had been compiled which, although well intentioned, were not part of God's law. These policies were excessively severe and imposed great burdens upon the people, causing the Lord to say of the religious leaders, 'They bind heavy burdens and grievous to be borne, and lay them on men's shoulders', Matt. 23. 4.

As so often happens, these man-made policies became so ingrained they were deemed to be as authoritative as the word of God and were known as the oral law or the tradition of the elders. One regulation they had devised related to a rigorous washing of the hands prior to eating bread, and when the disciples did not conform to this imposition the Pharisees were ready to challenge the Lord about it.

Jesus exposes the hypocrisy of these bigots, for although they were uncompromising in the defence of their traditions, they were negligent of laws that were ordained by God. He does the same again in chapter 23 saying, 'Woe unto you, scribes and Pharisees, hypocrites! for ye pay tithe of mint and anise and cummin, and have omitted the weightier matters of the law, judgment, mercy, and faith', v. 23.

How imperative it is to ensure that the failures of the scribes and Pharisees are not perpetuated today! The word of God is non-negotiable, but any human instruction, however well intentioned, must **never** be given equal status with the scriptures.

June 14th

Matthew 15. 32-39

WHENCE SHOULD WE HAVE SO MUCH BREAD IN THE WILDERNESS, AS TO FILL SO GREAT A MULTITUDE?

For the second time, Matthew records the miraculous feeding of thousands of people with food that was probably sufficient only for one person. Despite certain similarities, there are several differences to be noted. In chapter 14, there was less bread, five loaves were used instead of seven, but more people were fed, five thousand instead of four thousand. In the first miracle there were two fishes, but in today's account the number is not stated, Matthew just notes there were 'a few little fishes', Matt. 15. 34.

The amount of food left over when the five thousand were fed was significantly less than when the four thousand had eaten. Although the number of baskets was greater, twelve compared to seven, the baskets were different. Those in chapter 14 were small, whereas these baskets were similar to the one in which Paul was let down by the wall, Acts 9. 25.

Although they had witnessed the Lord feeding more people with less bread on a previous occasion, the disciples' lack of trust surfaced again. When He informed them that He would not send the people away hungry, they assessed the situation through the eye of reason rather than faith and said, 'Whence should we have so much bread in the wilderness, as to fill so great a multitude?', Matt. 15. 33. Sadly, how often we may be guilty of repeating that same mistake today!

Just as the transfiguration of the Son of God in chapter 17 is a prefiguring of the glorious kingdom age, so this miracle is a foretaste of what life will be like in the millennial kingdom. Isaiah had prophesied that the time would come when Jehovah would 'make unto all people a feast of fat things, a feast of wines on the lees', Isa. 25. 6.

The apostle Peter describes this kingdom as 'the times of restitution of all things', Acts 3. 21. Such will be the abundance of food in that day that 'the plowman shall overtake the reaper, and the treader of grapes him that soweth seed; and the mountains shall drop sweet wine, and all the hills shall melt', Amos 9. 13. At long last, creation will be liberated from its curse.

June 15th

Matthew 16. 5-12

WHY REASON YE AMONG YOURSELVES, BECAUSE YE HAVE BROUGHT NO BREAD?

In yesterday's meditation it was noted that on two occasions the Lord Jesus had fed thousands of people with a meal that was adequate for only one person. Despite the pitiful resources, and the inadequacy of the disciples, the Saviour demonstrated His omnipotence by transforming this meagre fare into meals sufficient to meet the needs of multitudes.

In Matthew chapter 16 the Lord brings these two events together to challenge His disciples. Firstly, He issued a warning to them saying, 'Take heed and beware of the leaven of the Pharisees and of the Sadducees', Matt. 16. 6. However, the disciples missed the significance of the Lord's admonition and jumped to a wrong conclusion. They assumed that because they had forgotten to get bread for the journey the Lord was referring to that oversight.

Not only did they make an incorrect assumption, but their reasoning showed that they failed to appreciate Christ's ability to supply all their need. Twice over, He had proved His sufficiency in such contingencies, and yet they had overlooked these miracles. Whether they had brought no bread or only a little bread was irrelevant, He was able to minister to their physical needs. Therefore, before progressing with His point concerning the leaven of the Pharisees and Sadducees, He challenges the disciples about their lack of faith, vv. 8-10. When the Lord repeated His initial warning the disciples grasped the point that He was referring to 'the doctrine of the Pharisees and of the Sadducees', v. 12.

Leaven always typifies that which is corrupting and evil, and various forms of leaven are mentioned. Here it is the leaven of the Pharisees and of the Sadducees. The doctrine of the Sadducees denied the existence of angels and of resurrection whereas the doctrine of the Pharisees elevated their rules almost to the status of scripture. The one group took away from the word of God and the other added to it. How vital it is that we heed the Lord's warning and avoid both of these twin evils. Legality and liberalism are to be shunned with equal vigour.

June 16th

Matthew 16. 13-20

WHOM DO MEN SAY THAT I THE SON OF MAN AM?

The Lord Jesus asked this question, not because He was ignorant of what others thought of Him, but to evoke a response from His disciples. Note that He uses the title 'Son of Man', which identifies with His humanity, and He wants to hear what the popular world view is concerning Him as man. The disciples said that some thought He was the reincarnation of John Baptist, or Elijah, or Jeremiah. The common people had been impressed enough with the Lord to identify Him with these illustrious men of God from the past. But the Lord then asked the critical question, 'But whom say **ye** that I am?' This provoked Peter to make that great confession, **'Thou art the Christ, the Son of the living God'**.

Peter had seen beyond the 'Son of Man,' to 'Son of the living God.' He had recognized that behind the veil of His flesh, absolute deity was enshrined in all its fullness. The ark of the covenant was wrapped in the veil when in transit through the wilderness, but beneath that veil, it was the same ark that had been bathed in the scintillating light of the Shekinah glory in the holy of holies. So also was the Christ.

Others had wondered at the wonderful works that the Lord had done, and Nicodemus was prepared to go as far as to say, 'No man can do these miracles that thou doest, except God be with him', John 3. 2. But Peter goes further. It is not just that God is with Him, but that He Himself *is* God.

Many today in the religious realm would be prepared to acknowledge the greatness of Christ as an historical figure, but would stop short of acknowledging Him as 'Son of the living God'. But anything short of acknowledged deity will not suffice. Our salvation depends on Him being, not only 'Son of Man,' but 'Son of the living God'. It is only as such that He could be our Saviour.

Verily God, yet become truly human,
Lower than angels to die in our stead;
How hast Thou, long promised Seed of the woman,
Trod on the serpent and bruisèd his head!

[HENRY D'ARCY CHAMPNEY]

June 17th

Matthew 17. 14-21

WHY COULD WE NOT CAST HIM OUT?

The Lord's disciples had experienced an embarrassing public failure in their inability to heal a sick child. Surprisingly, the father of the child does not give up hope at this point, but he turns to the Lord, evidently feeling that He has greater powers than that of the disciples. Without any hesitation, the Lord rebukes the demon, and the child is cured.

This situation troubled the disciples, and afterwards they ask the Lord, 'Why could we not cast him out?' v. 19. The Lord then explains that it was because of their unbelief, and that where faith is present, great things can happen. The Lord also knew that this failure had shaken the disciples' confidence, and lest they should feel that they were now impotent in His service, He holds out hope for their future, and says, 'Nothing shall be impossible to you', v. 21. But the Lord now brings another factor into the equation. Having stressed the importance of faith, He goes on to say, 'Howbeit, this kind goeth not out, but by prayer and fasting', v. 21. Here is another practical prerequisite for success in their service.

There are lessons that we can learn from this incident that relate to our service for the Lord today. At times, we may have known the embarrassment of failure, and our confidence may have been undermined. Also, we might have questioned as to why this should be. First, we learn that the element of unbelief must be absent. Regarding our asking from God, James reminds us, 'But let him ask in faith, nothing wavering. For he that wavereth is like a wave of the sea driven with the wind and tossed. For let not that man think that he shall receive any thing of the Lord', Jas. 1. 6-7.

Our minds turn to the healing of the paralytic in Luke chapter 5, where we read, 'And when he [the Lord] saw their [the man's friends'] faith, he said unto him, Man, thy sins are forgiven thee', v. 20. It is evident that the faith of these men who carried the paralytic went hand in hand with the practicalities of bringing him before the Lord, and making heroic efforts to do so. May the Lord enable us to have similar faith, labouring both in prayer and in practical actions!

June 18th

Matthew 17. 24-27

DOTH NOT YOUR MASTER PAY TRIBUTE?

The temple tax was a half-shekel, which was collected to cover temple expenses, and Peter confirmed that his Master paid the temple tax. When Peter returned to the house, the Lord posed a question. He asked Peter who it was that paid taxes, a king and his family, or strangers? Peter answered correctly, that it was strangers who paid taxes. The Lord responded, 'Then are the children free', v. 26. The Lord had come as the King of Israel, and as such He and His were exempt from such duties that were exacted from others. However, the Lord does not insist on claiming this exemption, and, lest it would cause offence, he instructs Peter to go to the sea and find the required tax in the mouth of the first fish that he hooked, sufficient to pay for Himself and for Peter.

In this incident the Lord is teaching us that we must not give offence to others needlessly, whether governments or persons, where the matter involves only our 'rights', and where there is no compromise of principle. The apostle Paul echoed this truth as he wrote to the Corinthians, saying, 'Give none offence, neither to the Jews, nor to the Gentiles, nor to the church of God', 1 Cor. 10. 32.

Perhaps a broader application could be made of this incident in a redemptive sense. The Lord, because of His sinless perfection, was exempt from the common lot of humanity, where the penalty of death is exacted because of sin. But, praise God, He who was exempt and free, voluntarily paid the price of our sin in order that we who were in bondage to sin, death, hell and the grave, might also be free. It is worthy of note that Peter took the coin from a fish in the sea, the sea being indicative of the Gentile nations who would soon come under the blessing of salvation through Christ. The children's chorus rightly says:

He paid a debt He did not owe,
I owed a debt I could not pay.
I needed someone to wash my sins away,
And now I sing a brand new song,
Amazing grace the whole day long,
For Jesus paid a debt that I could never pay.

June 19th

Matthew 18. 21-35

LORD, HOW OFTEN SHALL MY BROTHER SIN AGAINST ME, AND I FORGIVE HIM?

Having directed this question to the Lord, Peter offered a tentative response saying, 'Till seven times?', v. 21. The Lord responded by saying 'Until seventy times seven', v. 22. The Lord was not indicating that when the number of offences against us by any one brother reaches four hundred and ninety, we are no longer obliged to forgive. No! The Lord was demonstrating the principle of forgiveness as it applies in the age of grace, compared with the unrelenting demand for vengeance that is characteristic of fallen man, Gen. 4. 24. Concerning forgiveness, J. N. DARBY, *Synopsis* 3.139, wrote, 'We must pardon to the end, or rather, there must be no end; even as God has forgiven us all things'.

However, forgiveness can be exercised only where the offender repents of his offence. This is a principle that runs throughout the canon of scripture. Joseph is a good example of this principle in operation. We remember when his guilty brethren arrived in Egypt, Joseph put them through test after test, to find evidence of repentance, and it was only after he had heard them say, 'We are verily guilty concerning our brother', Gen. 42. 21, and after demonstrating their love for his brother Benjamin, that he extended his beneficent grace and pardon to them. Luke, dealing with the same question of forgiveness, records, 'If thy brother trespass against thee, rebuke him; and **if he repent**, forgive him. And if he trespass against thee seven times in a day, and seven times in a day turn again to thee, saying, **I repent**; thou shalt forgive him', Luke 17. 3-4. The apostle Paul stressed this in his preaching of the gospel. We read, 'Testifying both to the Jew and also to the Greeks, **repentance toward God**, and faith toward our Lord Jesus Christ', Acts 20. 21. Repentance precedes faith in Christ.

So it is in matters of offence between brethren. We must always carry the spirit of forgiveness, but the exercise of that forgiveness must await evidence of repentance on the part of the offender. Then, we must offer pardon in the same lavish measure as we ourselves have received of God.

June 20th

Matthew 19. 16-30

BEHOLD WE HAVE . . . FOLLOWED THEE, WHAT SHALL WE HAVE THEREFORE?

The section of scripture under consideration begins with a man enquiring how he might have eternal life. The Lord tests this man by quoting the law, and the man claims, 'All these have I kept from my youth up: What lack I yet?' The Lord then tests his profession by asking him to dispossess himself of all worldly goods, and to come and follow Him. We read that this man went away sorrowful, for he had great possessions. The Lord proved that the man had failed to keep the very first commandment – 'And thou shalt love the Lord thy God with all thine heart, and with all thy soul, and with all thy might', Deut. 6. 5. Another god occupied the throne of his heart – his wealth.

It is against such a background that Peter asks the subject question. Unlike the man referred to above, the disciples had forsaken all, and followed Him, and Peter wished to know what reward the future would hold for those who had fulfilled the conditions demanded. The Lord made it very clear that those who are prepared to live sacrificially for Him will be amply compensated in the coming kingdom. The Lord said to His disciples, 'If any *man* will come after me, let him deny himself, and take up his cross, and follow me', Matt. 16. 24, and He followed this by saying, 'For when the Son of man shall come . . . then he shall reward every man according to his works', v. 27.

Similarly, the believer in this age is asked to live sacrificially for Christ. At the end of his days the apostle Paul wrote, 'I have fought a good fight, I have finished *my* course, I have kept the faith: henceforth there is laid up for me a crown of righteousness, which the Lord, the righteous judge, shall give me at that day: and not to me only, but unto all them also that love his appearing', 2 Tim. 4. 7-8. He also said, 'If so be that we suffer with *him*, that we may be also glorified together', Rom. 8. 17.

Let us determine to live our lives in the light of the judgement seat of Christ; being assured that we shall receive a glorious reward.

June 21st

Matthew 20. 1-16

IS IT NOT LAWFUL FOR ME TO DO WHAT I WILL WITH MINE OWN?

In this parable, a householder went out early in the morning and hired labourers to work in his vineyard. At the eleventh hour, he went out again, and hired others who were still unemployed in the market place. At the end of the day, he gave one penny to those who had worked all day, and also to those who had worked only part of the day. The early workers complained that since they had worked longer, and under much more arduous conditions, they should receive more. In response, the householder reminded them that they had agreed to work for a penny, and that he had honoured his word. Also, because no one had hired the second group earlier, through no fault of their own, they did not have the same opportunity to work as long as the others. In these circumstances, he had opened his heart to them and paid them for the whole day.

This parable, being a kingdom parable, primarily relates to the Lord's second advent, when he will come to the earth, and judge Israel and the nations, but the principles involved can be applied to the coming day of reckoning, when the saints will stand before the judgment seat of Christ. We learn here that the Lord in His sovereignty chooses to use us in His service. Many dear saints have borne the heat of the day, and laboured for a lifetime. Others have served well, but for a shorter time due to ill-health, premature death, martyrdom, or the Lord's predetermined tenure for their service, for example, John Baptist. Also, the rapture of the church will mean that the service of younger servants will be cut short. In such circumstances, the criteria for reward will not be the length of service given, but the willingness to serve when opportunity was available to serve, and the faithfulness with which that service was exercised.

In light of these facts, how important it is that we do not compare our service with the service of others, or assume entitlement to greater glory. We must humbly accept that the Lord, who could have done His work without us poor earthen vessels, has chosen to use us, and to give us reward according to His sovereign grace. To Him be all the glory!

June 22nd

Matthew 20. 20-28

WHAT WILT THOU?

In these verses, the mother of Zebedee's children, James and John, came to the Lord to ask for a special favour for herself and for her sons. She asked that her two sons, James and John, should have a place of prominence in the kingdom – that one should sit on the Lord's right hand and the other on the left, and it appears from the text that James and John were with her when she made this request. Perhaps she felt that she was entitled to make this request. After all, Jesus had called her sons into His service and they had immediately left the fishing business in which they were partners with their father, and they had followed Christ. Undoubtedly, the departure of James and John, had resulted in domestic sacrifices, and disruption of the business, and perhaps their mother thought that it was time to claim some reward.

The Lord challenges them whether they are willing to tread the same path of suffering that He, the King, was about to tread. He speaks about the cup that the Father had given Him to drink, and the baptism that He was soon to be baptized with – referring to the cross – and they said, 'We are able', v. 22. The Lord said that indeed they would take part in these sufferings, but that it was the Father's prerogative to determine prominence and power in the kingdom. The Lord then showed them that the terms for promotion in the world of men, are opposite to the terms for reward in the kingdom. In the world of men, those who scramble to the top are those who receive rewards, but in His kingdom, it is those who are humble, and who have the 'servant spirit' who will be rewarded. He had already taught them, 'Blessed are the meek: for they shall inherit the earth', Matt. 5. 5.

From this incident we learn that the criterion for reward is not how far we have climbed, but how far we have stooped. Not how much we have suffered or sacrificed, but how we have served. The Lord reminded them, 'The Son of Man came not to be ministered unto, but to minister', Matt. 20. 28. May God give us that spirit of service and sacrifice that characterized our Lord, and leave the question of reward with Him.

June 23rd

Matthew 20. 29-34

WHAT WILL YE THAT I SHALL DO UNTO YOU?

The incident in these verses took place as the Lord was leaving Jericho. He would never return there again, as He was on His way to the cross. Two blind men sitting by the wayside seemed to grasp the urgency of the moment, and were anxious to meet Christ, and to receive their sight. They began to call insistently, 'Have mercy on us, O Lord, thou son of David'. The crowd tried to silence them, but they would not be quietened. It was then that the Lord stood still and asked them, 'What will ye that I shall do unto you?' The men replied, 'Lord that our eyes may be opened'. We read, 'So, Jesus had compassion on them, and touched their eyes: and immediately they received their sight, and they followed him', v. 34. There are practical lessons that we can glean from this incident.

At the commencement of His public ministry, the Lord, as the Messiah, Son of David, had announced he would give 'recovering of sight to the blind', Luke 4. 18. So these men had a sound basis upon which they made their request, and the Lord recognized the legitimacy of their claim, and healed them.

So also, if we expect to have our prayers answered, we must have a sound basis for making our requests. For example, when Daniel prayed for the release of Judah from Babylon, it was because 'he understood by books', Dan. 9. 2, that the time had come. Again, we read, 'If we ask any thing according to his will, he heareth us', 1 John 5. 14.

There is nothing more powerful than praying in the will of God, as revealed in His word, and knowing an answer is assured. Also, knowledge of the will of the Lord must not hinder our earnest prayers for fulfilment.

It should also be noted that the Lord was undoubtedly aware of these men and their need before they called, but He awaited their call, before responding. Joel wrote, 'Whosoever shall call upon the name of the Lord shall be delivered', Joel 2. 32, and Peter echoed this on the day of Pentecost, Acts 2. 21. So it is today, whether to receive salvation as sinners, or answers to prayer as saints, He awaits our call. May we know His will, and call upon His name, to be blessed!

June 24th

Matthew 21. 1-11

WHO IS THIS?

In this passage, the Lord has come to Jerusalem, and He comes, as King, riding upon an ass, in fulfilment of the prophecy of Zechariah concerning His coming, Zech. 9. 9. Great multitudes attend Him, and cast their garments and branches of trees in His way, as befits the entry of a king, 2 Kgs. 9. 13. The city rings with the acclaim of the crowds, crying, 'Hosanna to the Son of David: Blessed is he that cometh in the name of the Lord; Hosanna in the highest', Matt. 21. 9. But strangely enough the city dwellers were asking, 'Who is this?' v. 10. They did not know Him, and the city was troubled at His entry. Indeed, it would not be very long before the fickle crowd would cry, 'Let him be crucified', 27. 22.

When Matthew writes his Gospel, he begins thus, 'The book of the genealogy of Jesus Christ, the son of David, the son of Abraham', 1. 1. The multitude knew Him only as 'Son of David', and as such the Lord had legal right to the throne of Israel, but as 'Son of Abraham' He must go to the altar. This the Jews could not conceive. When they cried, 'Hosanna', meaning 'save now', they had only political aspirations in mind – that the King would save them from the Roman oppressor. But the true significance of Hosanna, 'save now', would, in the purposes of God, go far beyond the borders of Israel, to embrace the entire world. This would mean that the Lord, as 'Son of Abraham', must go to Calvary's altar. In their ignorance, those surrounding the cross cried, 'Save thyself. If thou be the Son of God, come down from the cross', 27. 40. Little did they know that apart from His sacrifice on the cross, there would be no salvation for them, or a doomed world. We thank God that, 'He endured the cross, despising the shame', Heb. 12. 2.

Zechariah describes the future return of the King to this world, 'They shall look upon me whom they have pierced, and they shall mourn for him', Zech. 12. 10. It is then they will realize that the cross was in the 'determinate counsels and foreknowledge of God', Acts 2. 23, to make salvation available to a lost and perishing world. Who is this? He is both 'Son of David,' and 'Son of Abraham'.

June 25th

Matthew 21. 23-27

BY WHAT AUTHORITY DOEST THOU THESE THINGS?

When the Lord commissioned His disciples, He said to them, 'Behold, I send you forth as sheep in the midst of wolves: be ye therefore wise as serpents, and harmless as doves', Matt. 10. 16. In the subject verses, the Lord was, in a very real sense, among the wolves – the chief priests and elders of the people. They had been educated in the schools of men and they felt that this had given them authority, so they came challenging the authority of this unschooled Prophet from Nazareth. It mattered not to them that the Lord had demonstrated the powers of heaven. Under such hostile conditions, the Lord demonstrated how His instruction to His disciples was to be carried out.

In response to their question, the Lord posed another question. He asked them to tell Him from whom the unschooled John the Baptist had received his authority, from heaven or from men? This placed these scheming men in a dilemma. John was exceedingly popular with the people, who believed that he was a prophet sent by God, and that his authority came from heaven. Also, the Pharisees had tried to join the crowds to be baptized by John, giving credence to his authority, 3. 7?

As a result, the priests and elders feared that the people would turn against them if they said that John's authority was from men. However, if they said that it was from heaven, they would be admitting that God does give authority to unschooled men like John, and, by inference, to the Lord, whose authority they were challenging. So they lied and said, 'We cannot tell', 21. 27. Jesus then said, 'Neither tell I you by what authority I do these things', v. 27.

In this incident, the Lord demonstrated in practical terms how His instruction to the disciples should be carried out. Faced with hostile antagonists with ulterior motives, the Lord unmasked their dishonesty, and refused to entertain further debate. Truly, 'There is a time to keep silence, and a time to speak', Eccles. 3. 7.

May the Lord grant us the same wisdom to be 'as wise as serpents, and harmless as doves'!

June 26th

Matthew 21. 28-32

WHETHER OF THEM TWAIN DID THE WILL OF HIS FATHER?

This parable tells of two sons, each of whom was asked to work in his father's vineyard. The first said that he would not go, but afterwards repented and went. The second said that he would go, but did not. The Lord asked His religious antagonists to say which had done the will of their father, and they rightly answered that the first had done so. The Lord then showed that they were like the second son, in that they had been invited to respond to the ministry of John Baptist, who came 'in the way of righteousness,' but they had refused to believe him, therefore others, who were unrighteous but repented, would enter the kingdom of God before them. The Pharisees had also come to John to be baptized, but John saw their hypocrisy and said to them, 'O generation of vipers, who hath warned you to flee from the wrath to come? Bring forth therefore fruits meet for repentance', Matt. 3. 7-8.

This parable demonstrates that repentance, and not self-righteousness is the only basis of acceptance by God, and this truth is fundamental to the doctrine of salvation. Time and again scripture stresses that repentance is an essential prerequisite to salvation. The Lord Jesus said to the self-righteous Pharisees, 'I came not to call the righteous, but sinners to *repentance*', Luke 5. 32. The apostle Paul summarized the essence of the gospel saying that it involved, 'Testifying both to the Jews, and also to the Greeks, *repentance* toward God, and faith toward our Lord Jesus Christ', Acts 20. 21. Unfortunately, in much modern gospel preaching, the call to repentance has been displaced by an 'easy believeism' which fosters false professions, since the question of sin has never been addressed. Let us return to the example of the Lord and the apostles, and ensure that the need for repentance is included in every presentation of the gospel.

When free grace awoke me by light from on high,
Then legal fears shook me, I trembled to die;
No safety, no refuge in self could I see,
Jehovah Tsidkenu my Saviour must be.

[R. M. Mc Cheyne]

June 27th

Matthew 21. 33-46

WHAT WILL HE DO UNTO THESE HUSBANDMEN?

In this parable, the Lord tells how that a householder had a vineyard. When the time of harvest came, he sent his servants to receive the fruit of the vineyard, but the husbandmen beat one and murdered another. The owner then sent another deputation, and they were similarly treated. He then sent his son, but they cast him out of the vineyard and slew him, intending to take the inheritance.

Isaiah chapter 5 likens Israel to Jehovah's vineyard but He was disappointed in them. Isaiah wrote, 'For the vineyard of the Lord of hosts *is* the house of Israel . . . and he looked for judgment, but behold oppression; for righteousness, but behold a cry', Isa. 5. 7.

The martyr Stephen echoed the words of Isaiah saying, 'Which of the prophets have not your fathers persecuted? and they have slain them which shewed before of the coming of the Just One; of whom ye have been now the betrayers and murderers', Acts 7. 52. It was this that provoked them to kill yet another servant that God had sent to them.

The Lord closes the parable by asking his hearers what should be done to these wicked men and they responded, 'He will miserably destroy those wicked men, and will let out *his* vineyard unto other husbandmen, which shall render him the fruits in their seasons', Matt. 21. 41. This was fulfilled shortly after the Lord was crucified and had ascended. God temporarily set Israel aside, and the church (the other husbandmen) was introduced, Acts 2. The Romans pillaged Jerusalem in 70 AD.

Today, we are the branches of the vine, and God has expectations that we will bear much fruit. We can only do so if we abide in Him, John 15. 4-5. May we rise to the Father's expectations and bear much fruit for Him!

Ours are peace and joy divine,
Who are one with Christ,
When like branches in the vine,
We abide in Christ.

[W. Reid]

June 28th

Matthew 22. 1-14

FRIEND, HOW CAMEST THOU IN HITHER WITHOUT A WEDDING GARMENT?

In this parable, a king prepared a wedding feast for his son, and he sent out his servants to bid the invited guests to come, but they refused to attend. Another deputation was sent, but they treated them despitefully, and slew them. The king in his anger sent his armies to destroy these wicked men, then he sent his messengers out again to the highways and byways, inviting all who would to come, and the house was filled.

This parable has deep dispensational undertones, and can be understood only in that context. The invited guests relate to privileged Israel, but they refused to come, and slew the messengers God sent, including His Son. Then, in the early chapters of the Acts, God made further advances to Israel, but again, they refused the invitation, and slew the messenger, Stephen. Subsequently, the gospel took on a universal aspect, and the unprivileged came into blessing. In due course, Israel was overtaken by the war with Rome and Jerusalem was decimated by the Roman legions in 70 AD.

Now what shall we say about the man without a wedding garment? We understand that it was customary for the host to provide a garment for each of the guests to wear. Evidently, this man refused the garment, and chose to wear his own. He was cast into outer darkness, where there is weeping and gnashing of teeth.

In the kingdom of God, as distinct from the church, there is both true and false, wise and foolish, wheat and tares etc. – representing the believer and the mere professor. In this case, the intruder to the feast was not a true believer, but one who depended on his own garment to be acceptable. The message is clear: all who would enter must lay aside every attempt at self-righteousness and accept the garment of salvation, provided at vast cost by God, through the sacrifice of Christ at Calvary.

The parable closes with the statement, 'For many are called but few are chosen'. Yes, the gospel must go out to every creature. Sadly, most will choose not to believe. But those who make the choice to believe will be among the chosen.

June 29th

Matthew 22. 41-46

WHAT THINK YE OF CHRIST?

In this narrative, the Lord asked the Pharisees the question, 'What think ye of Christ? Whose son is he?' Matt. 22. 42. The Pharisees responded by saying that He was the Son of David. Having received this admission, the Lord pressed the question further by asking how then it was that David called Him 'Lord', Ps. 110. 1? This question placed the Pharisees on the horns of a dilemma.

The Pharisees were prepared to admit that Christ was David's son, but if they admitted that Christ was also David's Lord, they would be obliged to confess that He was the eternal Son of the eternal God. Confounded by the Lord's wisdom, they remained silent, and refrained from asking Him any more questions.

The genealogy given in Matthew's Gospel clearly identifies Christ as 'son of David, son of Abraham', Matt. 1. 1, and this links him with humanity, royalty and Calvary. However, in the Epistle to the Romans the apostle wrote, 'Concerning his [God's] Son Jesus Christ our Lord, which was made of the seed of David according to the flesh; And declared *to be* the Son of God with power, according to the spirit of holiness', Rom. 1. 3-4. Here, we are reminded that although of the seed of David as regards His humanity, He is also the Son of God, possessed of full deity. We are also reminded in these verses that the Holy Spirit had witnessed to this fact.

At the baptism of the Lord, the heavens were opened and the Father was heard to say, 'This is my beloved Son in whom I am well pleased', Luke 3. 22, and the Spirit, in endorsement of that declaration, descended upon Him in the form of a dove, thus clearly identifying the Lord for who He was.

In our day, He is acknowledged as Lord in the midst of the church, but the apostle Paul, anticipating a future day of glory when the entire universe will acknowledge Him as Lord, wrote, 'That at the name of Jesus every knee should bow, of things in heaven, and things in earth, and things under the earth; And that every tongue should confess that Jesus Christ is Lord, to the glory of God the Father', Phil. 2. 10-11.

June 30th

Matthew 24. 3-14

TELL US, WHEN SHALL THESE THINGS BE?

In the previous chapter, the Lord had wept over Jerusalem, sorrowing, that for all His tender entreaties, they had spurned Him. It is with genuine sorrow that the Lord said, 'And ye would not'. The Lord then declared, 'Behold your house is left unto you desolate', Matt. 23. 38. Following this, in a symbolic act of departure, the Lord left the temple precincts, telling the disciples that it would be completely destroyed. Upon arriving at the Mount of Olives, the disciples asked the Lord, 'Tell us, when shall these things be? and what shall be the sign of thy coming, and of the end of the world (lit., 'age')?' Matt. 24. 3.

In answering the disciples' question, the Lord gave them a preview of events far beyond their day, and even ours, when the time of 'Jacob's trouble' would arrive, otherwise known as the 'Great Tribulation', or 'Daniel's Seventieth Week'. The Lord identifies the features that will emerge during this time:

1. False Christs, and false prophets will arise deceiving many;
2. Wars and rumours of war;
3. International conflict, famines, pestilences and earthquakes;
4. The gospel of the kingdom will be preached to all nations;
5. The Man of sin will sit in the temple as God;
6. Israel threatened with extinction, but delivered by the second advent of the Lord;
7. The Son of Man will appear in power and glory, and all the tribes of the earth shall mourn.

Such are the unspeakable horrors that await our world, and in particular the nation of Israel, prior to the appearing of the Lord to establish His kingdom here in this world, Rev. 11. 15-18.

As believers in the church age, we are thankful that we will not be part of these events. The apostle wrote, 'For God hath not appointed us to wrath [the wrath of the day of the Lord] but to obtain salvation by our Lord Jesus Christ', 1 Thess. 5. 9. Unlike Israel, we do not look for signs, but we listen for sounds – the voice of the archangel and the trump of God – when we shall be raptured from this world, and 'so shall we ever be with the Lord', 1 Thess. 4. 17. What a blessed hope we have!

July 1st

Matthew 24. 38-51

WHO THEN IS A FAITHFUL AND WISE SERVANT?

When you were young can you remember playing hide and seek with friends, and the person who was 'IT' would count to 100 and then shout, 'Ready or not, here I come'? That expression just about sums up the teaching of the Lord Jesus in verses dealing with His sudden and unexpected return as the conquering Messiah. Continuing to use parables, which He commenced in chapter 24 verse 32, He explains the signs which will introduce the messianic kingdom, and in doing so emphasizes attitudes that should characterize the godly as they await His return. These can surely be applied to the believer today as we await the rapture, firstly with alertness, secondly with readiness, and thirdly with faithfulness.

The unexpectedness of Christ's return calls for alertness and readiness. In the days of Noah, Matt. 24. 36-44, people went on normally with the daily routines of life. The natural concerns of family, society, and business can lull us into a dangerous attitude of complacency. Despite the preaching of Noah and the evidence of an ark, people were taken completely by surprise. The contrast is highlighted in verse 42 where we have the present imperative, 'be continually alert', a cry for constant vigilance.

We must also 'be ready'. I don't know if my house will ever be burgled but as a house owner I take precautions which hopefully prepare me for that possibility. With the Lord's coming there is no uncertainty: it will happen, and maybe sooner than anticipated.

But it is not all about watching and waiting. There is the encouragement to be *working*, with the responsibility to be faithful, 1 Cor. 4. 2. The word translated 'faithful' comes from the Greek word *peitho*, 'worthy of belief, trust, or confidence'. It is used here of a person who is trustworthy and consistent in the performance of his duty to God and to others. On His return the Lord will recompense the faithful with responsibilities in the kingdom, but the unfaithful will lose their reward, 3. 13-15. How tragic is the fate of the ungodly, assigned 'a portion with the hypocrites . . . [where] there shall be weeping and gnashing of teeth'!

July 2nd

Matthew 25. 31-46

WHEN SAW WE THEE AN HUNGRED, AND FED THEE?

I do not have much knowledge of animal husbandry, but I am reliably informed that there are significant differences in nature between sheep and goats! Apparently, goats operate entirely with a selfish nature, to the point that they stop at nothing to get their own way, and care only for their own needs.

'The Old Testament indicated that Gentiles would enter the kingdom, Ps. 72. 8-11; Isa. 14. 1-2; 60. 3, 5, 12; 62. 2. This parable explains the criteria for their entrance and in view of God's original promises to Abraham, "I will bless them that bless thee, and curse him that curseth thee", Gen. 12. 3; it will be an appropriate measure', J. GIBSON. The nations are being judged on how they treated the Lord's people. Those who responded to a persecuted remnant with acts of kindness are told they belong in His kingdom because, in ministering to the saints, they ministered to Him, Matt. 10. 40; 18. 5. They demonstrated a genuine faith in God; hence, they are called righteous, and, at peril of their lives, were prepared to feed the hungry.

The humility of those blessed is something to learn from. They do not have a plaque on the wall declaring that they have been voted humanitarian of the year! They don't seem even to know what the Lord is talking about and ask, 'When saw we?' It is lovely to see that in His answer the Lord identifies Himself with the least of His brethren. 'The least, the most insignificant, the most inconsequential life is intimately integrated with the life of the Lord Jesus Christ', JOHN MACARTHUR. The reward is great, 'Come, ye blessed of my Father, inherit the kingdom prepared for you from the foundation of the world'.

In applying this to our lives today, it can be said truly that 'how we treat the Lord's people is an indication of our heart's attitude towards the Lord', *Bible Reading Notes, Ballingry.* Service rendered to another believer is the mark of a genuine Christian, 1 John 3. 16. James continues in that vein by making it clear that an evident sign of the reality of faith is showing the same care and kindness to brethren and sisters in need, Jas. 2. 14-25.

July 3rd

Matthew 26. 14-16

WHAT WILL YOU GIVE ME?

Judas is in many ways a tragic figure. He was called to be one of the disciples and named an apostle along with the others, Mark 3. 13-19, and, as such, received the power to heal and all of the other benefits associated with that holy privilege. Yet, despite this affiliation and his association with Christ, he was not a true believer. He was with them but not of them, and that serves as a salutary lesson even today!

By inserting a flashback to describe the feast at Bethany, only John gives us a chronological account of events at this time; Matthew highlights the contrast between the action of Mary and that of Judas. As the Lord gathered with His friends in the house of Simon, a few miles away the religious leaders were conspiring against Him. Out of love and appreciation, Mary breaks a very costly box of ointment, which some have valued at around £20,000 in today's market, and, by doing so, shows her devotion. Judas, being the spokesman who criticized Mary's action by voicing the question 'Why this waste?', goes off and makes a deal with the priests to deliver Jesus to them for a paltry thirty pieces of silver, the price of a common slave, Exod. 21. 32.

Whatever motivated Judas, be it jealousy, greed, or disappointment, the scriptures make it very clear that Satan had entered his heart, John 13. 2, 27. In contrast to what the devil had intended, he became a solemn fulfilment of Old Testament prophecy. The poignant words of the psalmist come to mind, 'Even my own familiar friend in whom I trusted, who ate my bread, has lifted up his heel against me', Ps. 41. 9 NKJV; 55. 12-14.

Warren Wiersbe notes, 'We can never understand the heart and mind of Judas but he was given many opportunities to be a true disciple. He had great privileges not least having his feet washed by the Saviour and had often been warned as he listened to His teaching'. The question Judas asked in relation to Mary could in the end be asked of him, 'Why this waste?' May that question never have to be asked of us in our life of service for Christ!

July 4th

Matthew 26. 17-25

LORD, IS IT I?

The detailed accounts of the final Passover feast by the four Gospel writers underline its significance to the Lord Jesus. From Luke's narrative it is apparent that the Lord had a great and intense desire to have this meal with His disciples, and as the evening developed it became apparent that it was going to be more than just the usual Passover meal!

As the meal was under way the Lord made a startling statement that one of them was going to betray Him. It is hard to imagine the shock this must have given the disciples. In those days the meal was a symbol of friendship, and His words obviously upset them deeply. As HINDSON and BORLAND note, 'In the original language, the question "Surely not I, Lord?" suggests that a negative answer was cautiously expected by each one – "It is not I, is it?"' A buzz went round the table, 'they began to ask each other who it was', Luke 22. 23. And yet, in what HENDRIKSEN describes as 'a wholesome self-distrust', they were not too proud to acknowledge that, very aware of their own weaknesses, they were all capable of such an act.

Is it not amazing that even now they do not recognize Judas as the traitor? They had seen no difference in the way that Jesus had treated him, that in itself was a remarkable testimony to the Lord's grace and patience. In fact, even at this late hour, He had done what He could to keep Judas close, by sitting him on His left-hand side, which was a place of great honour. It was to him that Jesus dipped and gave the sop. The others had not detected anything in Judas' behaviour to indicate that he was the obvious culprit! They had no reason to doubt his integrity as they had chosen him to be the treasurer of whatever meagre resources they had.

Before Judas goes out to do his worst, the Lord cuts through their shock and dismay to show them that his betrayal is no tragic mistake. He is not a victim of man's treachery or of a plan which has gone very wrong. Everything that is happening and will continue to unfold through the remarkable night ahead is the fulfilment of 'the determinate counsel and foreknowledge of God'.

July 5th

Matthew 26. 47-56

THINKEST THOU THAT I CANNOT NOW PRAY TO MY FATHER?

Is it not truly remarkable that right up to the last minute before Judas is revealed as the betrayer of Jesus he is referred to as 'one of the twelve'? It brings with it a sense of incredulity that someone could spend three years with Christ as one of this select group and yet do what he did. A. T. ROBERTSON points out, 'The very horror of the thing is thus emphasized, that one of the chosen twelve apostles should do this dastardly deed'. How sad that the garden which the Lord and the disciples had no doubt visited for peace and quiet on many occasions should be the place chosen for His shameful arrest.

Judas demonstrated his lack of understanding and appreciation of the character of the Lord by the small army he brings with him to arrest Him. Christ surprises them all by immediately submitting to the indignity and shame of the betrayer's kiss by calling him 'friend'.

At this point some of the disciples ask, 'Lord, shall we smite with the sword?', Luke 22. 49. It is no surprise that before any answer is forthcoming Peter acts first: the fisherman becomes a swordsman with predictable results! Interestingly, it is not until much later when John as an old man writes his Gospel that Peter is identified as the swordsman. The other Gospel writers protect him against any possible repercussions in drawing a sword, after the Lord takes the lead in shielding him by healing Malchus' ear.

The Lord then teaches the folly of violent resistance by drawing attention to the resources that are immediately available to Him. An angelic task force of more than 72,000 angels were only a prayer away. Jewish history has already recorded, 2 Kgs. 19. 35, that the angel of the Lord slew 185,000 Assyrians all by himself! What a contrast to the force who had come to arrest Him! What an encouragement to all believers who are recipients of the power of God, 1 Cor. 1. 18, and are kept by it, 1 Pet. 1. 5!

Why did it have to be this way? The answer is, 'That the scriptures of the prophets might be fulfilled', Matt. 26. 56.

July 6th

Matthew 26. 57-68

ANSWEREST THOU NOTHING?

Someone has said, 'Silence is one of the hardest arguments to refute'. Having been exposed to the unrelenting ruthlessness of men, the Lord Jesus stands in dignified silence. For Caiaphas, speed is now of the essence to get the conviction of Jesus signed, sealed, and delivered quickly, before dawn and before any awkward questions could be asked. They have had a parade of false witnesses concocting lies about Christ, and not one of them has been successful. The high priest, in sheer frustration, rises out of his seat and almost pleads with the Lord, 'Aren't you going to say anything?' The Lord Jesus simply stands there with a gaze which is steadfast and never says a word. He said nothing because there was nothing to say! What a contrast there is between the calmness of Christ and the fury of Caiaphas!

If the religious leaders were not going to uphold the law, then the Lord Jesus was. He was also going to fulfil the prophecy of Isaiah, 'As a sheep before her shearers is dumb, so he openeth not his mouth', Isa. 53. 7. No need for retaliation, vindication or self-defence! He stands resolute, having 'stedfastly set his face to go to Jerusalem', Luke 9. 51.

Then, as a last resort, Caiaphas calls for a solemn oath. Indeed, this was probably the most sacred oath a Jew could ever call for – a vow before the living God, Num. 30. 2, which compelled an answer, 'Tell us whether thou be the Christ, the Son of God', Matt. 26. 63. In our world where perjury and a careless attitude to truth are an acceptable part of public life this might seem insignificant, but Caiaphas sought an admission that could be the foundation of a blasphemy charge. The Lord Jesus did not disappoint him. He gave the answer by applying Messianic prophecies to Himself, Dan. 7. 13; Ps. 110. 1. In these two quotations 'Jesus predicted His resurrection and ascension and return in glory. This would mean salvation to those who trust Him, but for Caiaphas it would mean condemnation', WIERSBE.

The time for caution was over. By His own words He condemned Himself in the eyes of the religious leaders, and the inexorable journey to the cross gathered pace.

July 7th

Matthew 27. 3-10

WHAT IS THAT TO US?

After the brief early morning meeting of the Sanhedrin, Matt. 27. 1; Mark 15. 1; Luke 22. 66-71, where the verdict against Jesus is made official, Judas learns that the Saviour has been condemned to death. This discovery causes Judas to change his mind about his treachery, for he starts to regret what he has done. As he has done before, Matthew gives us a contrast as he recounts the sorrow and suicide of Judas only a few verses after the godly contrition of Peter. He thus underlines the difference between biblical repentance and selfish remorse. The Greek word *metanoeo* is used to describe the behaviour of Peter and subsequently every person who comes to God for salvation, whereas the more emotional and worldly term *metamelomai* is used to describe the remorseful change of mind of Judas. It is also important to note the behaviour of Christ towards the two disciples; He prayed for Peter that his faith would not fail, Luke 22. 32, whereas in respect of Judas He simply says, 'Woe unto that man by whom he is betrayed', v. 22. Furthermore, immediately after his fall Jesus looked upon Peter with such love and concern that Peter went out and 'wept bitterly', yet there was nothing for Judas who was already a 'vessel of wrath prepared for destruction', Rom. 9. 22.

To salve his guilt and deliver himself from a life of despair and a tortured conscience, Judas tries to undo what he had done. Seized with remorse he tries to hand back the money he has been paid for carrying out the betrayal, confessing that Jesus is completely innocent. If anyone could have discovered in Christ sinful words or actions it was Judas, who had spent three years in His company, and betrayed Him with evil motives. His confession is mocked and dismissed by the chief priests who could not care less about his predicament. They had used him to get the Messiah, and now 'the chief priests and elders had no more pity for Judas [than] they had for Jesus; no remorse troubled them, they had secured the Saviour, and they cared nothing for any of the consequences of their action. As for the traitor, he had made his bargain, and he must abide by it', C. H. SPURGEON, *The Gospel of Matthew*.

July 8th

Matthew 27. 15-23

WHAT SHALL I DO THEN WITH JESUS?

Pilate asks what is possibly the most important question anyone could ever ask, 'What shall I do then with Jesus which is called Christ?' The eternal destiny of every human being is determined by their answer to the question. According to the Lord Jesus, to answer it wrongly is to perish forever, 'Unless you believe that I am He, you will die in your sins', John 8. 24 NASB. Moreover, no one can escape giving an answer of some sort. To make no decision for Jesus Christ is to already decide against Him. To refuse to acknowledge the truth of His claims is to automatically heap upon Him the greatest of insults.

This passage brings us closer to the cross and to the climax for which Jesus came into the world. The events of the night in which He was betrayed have moved rapidly. The narrative takes us swiftly from the upper room to the garden of Gethsemane, from where we visit the house of Annas and then Caiaphas, following which we are rushed to Pilate's judgement hall, over to Herod, and finally back again to Pilate. Despite the accusations cast at the Lord Jesus on five separate occasions, His innocence is clearly attested, while He remains silent. As Peter later wrote, 'While being reviled, He did not revile in return; while suffering, He uttered no threats, but kept entrusting Himself to Him who judges righteously', 1 Pet. 2. 23 NASB. What a lesson! In the midst of such trial the Saviour is absolutely content to entrust the whole matter to God.

Desperate to extricate himself from a potentially explosive situation, Pilate seizes on a plan in the assurance that the people would respond as he wanted. He uses the equivalent of a 'get out of jail free card', a pardon to celebrate the feast, and asks the leaders which of two victims he should release, Jesus or Barabbas. The plan backfires. Rather than let Christ go, men prefer a convicted terrorist. Pilate capitulates to the mob, an action all the more astounding considering his three formal declarations of the Lord's innocence. Yet, even in his cowardly acquiescence, Pilate was unconsciously fulfilling God's eternal purposes, Acts 2. 23. As C. S. Lewis has said, 'Those who will not be God's sons become His tools'.

July 9th

Mark 2. 1-12

WHETHER IS IT EASIER TO SAY THY SINS BE FORGIVEN THEE?

This passage, the first detailed miracle in Mark's Gospel, provides the key to all gospel miracles. Now was the time for the Lord Jesus to demonstrate what His ministry was all about. We see the determination of the perfect Servant as He deliberately went back into Capernaum despite the difficulties of unwanted publicity created by the leper in the previous chapter. He was persistent in His duty of preaching the word, always His priority despite the clamour of crowds interested only in the miracles He performed, Mark 2. 12. The people needed to understand the spiritual lessons behind the miracles.

It has been said that 'all gospel miracles are gospel messages'. This one is no exception. The man's lameness pictures the human race's total inability to walk in the way that God would have us to do, Ps. 1. 1, while the cure demonstrates the unfailing power of the Lord to save. The determination of the four friends demonstrates a faith acknowledged by the Lord, Mark 2. 5, as undaunted they carried a burden upon their heart as well as in their hands. What a practical lesson in true friendship for us! Today, we can obey the command, 'Bear ye one another's burdens, and so fulfill the law of Christ', Gal. 6. 2.

His friends thought that the paralysis was his biggest difficulty, but the Lord, who knows the heart, dealt with his greatest problem first. The word translated 'son' conveys the idea of tenderness. The word 'forgiven' implies that the man's guilt, shame, and sin had been taken away! The first word brought him into the *family*; the second brought him into *fellowship*!

The Lord had created a huge problem for the watching scribes and Pharisees when He forgave the man's sin, as they rightly knew that only God can forgive sins, Exod. 34. 7; Ps. 130. 4. They were confronted with a stupendous claim which they could not accept. Therefore, the Lord answered their objections with a miracle: not only did He pronounce the man's sin forgiven, He also visibly cured his paralysis. He used the outward and physical to demonstrate the inward and spiritual and in so doing proved who He was – Israel's Messiah and God.

July 10th

Mark 2. 18-22

CAN THE CHILDREN OF THE BRIDECHAMBER FAST, WHILE THE BRIDEGROOM IS WITH THEM?

It is apparent that a large part of the Pharisaic lifestyle included periods of fasting, of which they were very proud, Luke 18. 12. The intention was good: a time of self-denial, serving to focus the mind and heart on seeking the face of God. Fasting was never directly commanded in the law, although it may have been inferred from the regulations concerning the Day of Atonement, when God told His people to 'afflict your souls', Lev. 16. 29. However, by the time of the Lord's earthly ministry it had become an accepted part of the Jewish religion.

The problem with what the Pharisees were doing was highlighted by the Lord, Matt. 6. 16-18. There He exposed their hypocrisy in wanting everyone to see their piety while simultaneously attempting to burden others. They had elevated a human tradition to the same authority as God's law, and this is what prompted their criticism of the Lord and His disciples.

In responding to the original question, the Lord does not belittle the action of fasting as such. Indeed, it could be a genuine tool for believers today who seek a closer walk with God. However, He goes on by contrast to use a joyful event as a wonderful illustration of His presence in Israel. It is not a time for mourning, asceticism, and sadness, but for celebration and gladness. He further reveals that one day the Bridegroom would be taken away and then would come a time of sadness. But for now, with Him present, His own people can acknowledge Him with joy as of a wedding feast. Note that the absence of any suggestion of a bride at the feast implies that the church is still in the future. Caught up with their rituals and traditions, the Jews had missed the blessed reality of the Messiah in their midst. Is it possible that sometimes we can be equally guilty, acting merely out of habit or tradition and failing to recognize the Saviour's constant presence with us?

Two further illustrations from everyday life emphasize that He had not come to patch up worn-out religion or preach a new and improved Judaism, but rather to accomplish something new – to redeem sinners and give them new life in Himself.

July 11th

Mark 3. 22-30

HOW CAN SATAN CAST OUT SATAN?

Have you ever been misunderstood? Have you ever been misrepresented? Has anyone ever taken your words and motives and twisted them against you? Mark chapter 3 continues to chart the growth of opposition to the Lord Jesus Christ, describing the Pharisees' murder plot, Mark 3. 6, the misunderstanding of the Lord's own earthly family, v. 21, and the malicious slanders of the scribes, v. 22. It demonstrates that 'all true service for God will meet with stiff opposition, sometimes from the most unexpected quarters and yet nothing hindered this perfect Servant's ministry', D. J. NEWELL.

In considering His words and work the scribes attribute His miracles to the power of a Canaanite deity whose name literally means 'Lord of the flies', or 'Lord of filth'. How cruel was this attack on the perfect Servant of Jehovah in order to undermine His teaching and reputation! By making a few wild accusations, how easy it is to destroy a life, reputation, or ministry! But the Lord totally destroys their arguments in a wonderful way by using three illustrations, vv. 24-26, which demonstrate their foolish logic and theology. If He were using the power of Satan, then Satan was fighting against himself, which meant that his house and kingdom were on the verge of collapse. The fact that the Lord had power over demons proves that He was the stronger force; 'A stronger than he shall come upon him', Luke 11. 22, and anticipates His great work on the cross where He finally 'through death [destroyed] him that had the power of death, that is, the devil', Heb. 2. 14.

In response to their accusations, the Lord issues a very serious warning about the danger of 'crossing the line' with God. Although His words can be a comfort, in that all sins can be forgiven because of the cross, one sin remains unpardonable. Many believers have lived in dread of this for many years. But verse 30 is crucial, proving that this sin cannot be committed today, because it relates uniquely to the period of the Messiah's earthly ministry. This sin could be committed only by people who looked into His eyes, saw His miracles, heard His words, experienced His love in action, and yet said He was of the devil.

July 12th

Mark 3. 31-35

WHO IS MY MOTHER, OR MY BRETHREN?

I must admit I am not a great fan of 'self-help' books. However, the title of one, co-authored in 1983 by the psychiatrist Robin Skynner and the comedian John Cleese, does strike a chord. Of *Families and How to Survive Them*, the authors themselves have said that the aim of the book was 'to make intelligible and accessible the psychological aspects of how families behave and function, what makes some work and others fail'. While wonderful in many aspects, family life can bring with it stresses and difficulties. It must have been particularly so in the carpenter's home in Nazareth. Mary, the mother, was a spiritually sensitive woman who alone knew the full and wondrous story of the birth of Christ. On the other hand, there was also a group of brothers who were not necessarily bad men but simply did not understand their older sibling, and maybe responded to His sinless life in much the same way Joseph's brothers reacted against him.

In our passage the Lord's family have come to try to bring Him home, being, it seems, genuinely concerned for His mental health, thinking Him 'beside himself', Mark 3. 21, Gk. *existemi*, 'to be out of one's mind'. On the surface, His response appears shocking, as He poses the question of our title. His mother must have been devastated – she was on that occasion conspicuously unable to reach the Lord Jesus – and His brothers very angry. It created a tension, yet was designed to teach at least two very important truths. Firstly, it emphasizes that *spiritual business takes priority over earthly business.* The Lord's family had their attention focused on earthly, albeit legitimate concerns, whereas His attention was focused on doing the Father's business. Nothing was more important to Him than the Father's will, John 4. 32. Secondly, *spiritual relationships take priority over human relationships*. This was 'not a denial of earthly relationships and their attendant responsibilities, Mark 7. 9-13; John 19. 25-27; 1 Tim. 5. 8, but a rightful emphasis upon the priority of spiritual claims, Luke 14. 25-27. For the believer, the Saviour, the word, and the things of God must come first and govern all other relationships and activities', D. J. Newell.

July 13th

Mark 4. 35-41

MASTER, CAREST THOU NOT THAT WE PERISH?

It had been a long and difficult day for the Lord Jesus. The events of this day began in Mark chapter 3 verse 20. He had a confrontation with the Pharisees, vv. 22-30. His friends and family thought He had gone crazy and wanted Him back home with them, vv. 21, 31-35. And when the day was over, He called His disciples to set sail for the other side of the lake.

While they guided the boat, Jesus lay fast asleep in the rear of the vessel. He was weary from the business of the day and this is one of the clearest portraits of our Lord's humanity in the Gospels, helping us understand that He knows our weakness, Ps. 103. 14. Very soon a fierce storm arose, and the disciples, including the seasoned fishermen, were frightened by the severity of it. We can all understand their anxiety: the storms of life are often severe, causing anguish and pain. Regardless of the source of the storm (whether from God, from Satan, or a natural phenomenon), the disciples were going to discover that there is no storm on earth that heaven cannot calm! No problem is too great for the Lord to solve.

The disciples' doubt that night is so often shared by us that we are in no position to be judgemental. Firstly, they doubted the Lord's *goodness* by accusing Him of not caring about their peril. Why this doubt? After all, they had already seen His compassion and goodness in action. He does care for His people, as Hebrews makes clear, Heb. 4. 15-16! Secondly, they doubted His *grace*, 'we perish', for it was the Lord who had sent them out onto the sea and into an impossibly dangerous situation in the first place. They were afraid that He was just going to let them all die. The Lord did not save us to abandon us when the going gets a little tough. He is absolutely committed to our welfare and will never forsake us, 13. 5. Thirdly, they doubted His *guarantee*, as the Saviour had already told them before the journey started that they were headed to the other side of the lake. Had they believed His words, they could have smiled in the face of the storm. If we could learn to simply take Him at His word, then we too could face the storms of life without fear, Rom. 8. 28.

July 14th
Mark 6. 1-6

IS NOT THIS THE CARPENTER?

The American author THOMAS WOLFE wrote a novel entitled *You Can't Go Home Again*. It is about a man named George Webber, the author of a successful book about his home town. When he returns home, he expects to receive a hero's welcome. Instead, he is driven out of town by his own friends and family. They feel betrayed by what he has written about them and, shaken by their reaction to his work, he abandons his childhood home to go and find himself. He discovered that those who know you best tend to respect you the least.

In our passage Jesus returns home to Nazareth. You may think that, after word of His preaching, teaching, and miracles had spread to His home town, His reception would have been very different from the first visit, Luke 4. 16-29, when they tried to kill Him by throwing Him over a cliff! Not so. Admittedly, on this occasion they do not attempt murder, but they appear to be seriously offended, first of all by His *preaching*, Mark 6. 2, 'From whence hath this man these things?' He spoke with divine authority and left no doubt that His words were filled with truth, John 7. 46. Secondly, they were offended by His *power*, 'How are such mighty works done by his hands?', Mark 6. 3 ESV. As a result, as on His first visit, because of their unbelief Jesus was unable to perform many miracles, and only a few folk were healed.

Thirdly, they were offended at His *Person*. On His first visit they called Him the son of Joseph; now He's the son of Mary. Behind the declaration, 'We were not born of sexual immorality', John 8. 41 ESV, lurks a barely-veiled slur on His character; they disdainfully view Him as the illegitimate child of Mary. Because they failed to understand Him they resorted to ridicule and were 'offended at him', Mark 6. 3. They could not explain Him so they rejected Him. They 'failed to recognize the infinite grace and condescension of Him who saw fit to be born of a virgin, and to hide His eternal majesty under the guise of lowly humanity', VAN RYN. He marvelled at their unbelief, in striking contrast to when He marvelled at great faith, Luke 7. 9. The despised Messiah left Nazareth never to return.

July 15th

Mark 8. 31-38

FOR WHAT SHALL IT PROFIT A MAN . . . ?

The passage commences with the Lord Jesus confiding a secret to His disciples: He was going to Jerusalem to die on a cross! This they could not understand as it went against everything they had been taught about Israel's Messiah. True to his character, Peter is the one who voices the general concern and has to be rebuked by the Lord for something of which we are all so frequently guilty – seeing things from the human, not the divine perspective. Despite his deep love for the Lord, Peter displayed an ignorance of God's will.

The Lord Jesus goes on to underline a very practical issue: His followers had to understand that 'if there was a cross in His future there would be one in their future as well', WIERSBE. There could be no crown without the cross, and no glory without suffering. That Peter eventually learned this lesson is proved by his First Epistle, 1 Pet. 1. 10-12. There is a price to pay for true discipleship! Paul, writing to the Philippians, also refers to the profit and loss account of Christian service, concluding, 'What things were gain to me, these I have counted loss for Christ', Phil. 3. 7-8 NKJV.

In about 1000 AD the tomb of Charlemagne, the King of the Franks, was opened. By then this great king had been dead for about 180 years. Those who unsealed his tomb not only found great treasure, but also encountered an amazing sight. They discovered the skeleton of Charlemagne seated on a throne, a crown still resting on his skull. In the bony hands of the skeleton was a copy of the Gospels. A finger was pointing to this text, 'For what shall it profit a man, if he shall gain the whole world, and lose his own soul? Or what shall a man give in exchange for his soul?' When it came time for Charlemagne to die, he had left robes, riches, and royalty behind and went out into eternity to meet God. The story may, of course, be the stuff of legend. However, when we reach the end of our earthly journey, nothing we have achieved or accumulated in this life will matter save our relationship with the Lord Jesus Christ. The only thing that will count is to have willingly lost our lives to His will, so that He might live through us.

July 16th

Mark 9. 2-13; Matthew 11. 4; Malachi 3. 1; 4. 4-6

WHY SAY THE SCRIBES . . . ELIAS MUST FIRST COME?

This question is asked by the disciples following the transfiguration. Like many of us one of their lowest moments follows one of their greatest. They had just witnessed the glorious manifestation of the Saviour accompanied by Moses and Elijah. This was a vision of a future day when He will be manifested as the Messiah with those who like Moses have died and those like Elijah who have been taken without dying.

The Lord has mentioned His resurrection and this has led to some confusion among them, mainly because of their continued inability or reluctance to accept that He must die and that His glory would be preceded by humiliation. But perhaps also the idea of a resurrection *from among* the dead rather than of all the dead was not previously known to them, even after witnessing two of the dead being raised already. The question regarding Elijah seems to change the subject but the Lord uses it to teach them, and us, the principle of suffering preceding glory.

In the discourse recorded at the end of chapter 8, Peter had been rebuked for failing to accept the need for Christ to die, and they had then been told that each of them would be required to 'deny himself, and take up his cross, and follow me', before they could share in His glory. Now as predicted, three of them had seen His glory without yet having tasted death. However, lest they still should seek the glory without the cross, the Lord uses this question to make matters clearer. Firstly, the scriptures regarding Elijah must be fulfilled, just as those concerning His suffering and rejection must be, and, secondly, 'Elijah' had come and was none other than John the Baptist. This can be seen in the similarities as to their appearance, dress, message, royal opposition, and outspokenness, but is also explicitly confirmed in Matthew's account of this incident. But, further, this second Elijah had been put to death, he had not experienced the glory without the suffering, and neither would the Christ and neither would they or us! Let each of us take up our cross daily and follow Him, remembering that any sufferings are not comparable to the glory that follows, Rom. 8. 18.

July 17th

Mark 10. 1-12; Matthew 19. 1-9; Deuteronomy 24. 1-4

IS IT LAWFUL FOR A MAN TO PUT AWAY HIS WIFE?

In yesterday's study we concluded by considering the death of John the Baptist as a result of his faithful opposition to the sinful matrimonial practice of Herod the king. Now, as the Saviour nears Herod's jurisdiction, the Pharisees seek to trap Him on the same issue. Matthew's account has a more comprehensive question and answer, including the so called 'exception clause'. Much has been made of the fact that Mark does not include this exception but it is not uncommon for Mark, which is a far shorter Gospel, to give less detail than Matthew and we have no scriptural ground to read too much into this. Other examples include the omission of an explicit reference to John the Baptist in our previous meditation and the omission of the 'exception' of Jonah in answering the request for a sign, compare Matt. 12. 38-24, with Mark 8. 11-12.

The controversy over these differences, which cannot be adequately covered in this brief format, has sadly obscured the real point of the Lord's answer. Had the Lord given a one-word answer it could only have been, 'Yes, it is lawful', as His referral to Moses would prove. However, the real question which needed answered is, 'Is it sinful?'

The Lord does not in any way devalue Moses or scripture, Deut. 24; it is undoubtedly the word of God, not merely of Moses, and part of the inspired canon of scripture. However, He does *qualify* it. God had introduced divorce because of their hard hearted rejection of their wives, with no just cause. This would leave the woman unprotected and destitute so the bill of divorce was introduced to protect these women, another example of how God protects women and gives them real freedom, not the false liberation of modern society. But what of those who have initiated this hardhearted divorce? What they have done is lawful, but contrary to God's intention from creation of one man and one woman in a lifelong union. If they subsequently remarry they are committing the sin of adultery. Likewise in our society, divorce is lawful by the law of the land, but unjustified divorce and remarriage is still sinful. However, as with all sin, forgiveness is available if there is true repentance.

July 18th

Mark 10. 17-31

GOOD MASTER, WHAT SHALL I DO THAT I MAY INHERIT ETERNAL LIFE?

Following the question about divorce the Lord Jesus carefully moves on to the related matter of children in Mark chapter 10. Despite the disciples' objections, He demonstrates His great love and concern for these little ones by embracing them and blessing them. He thus illustrates the great truth of the need for child like faith to 'enter' the kingdom of God. Sadly, the one who asks today's question failed to grasp the lesson.

Mark's account tells us he was rich, while Matthew and Luke further reveal that he was 'young' and 'a ruler'. Humanly speaking, he seemed to have everything, yet he clearly appreciates that he lacks the most vital thing of all, eternal life. How like so many in our current affluent society! They have everything, yet without Christ they have nothing. This man made the same two mistaken assumptions that many still make: that eternal life is either merited by what 'I do', or that we simply 'inherit' it by circumstances of birth, family, or national, or religious affiliation. Perhaps it was by such means that the young man had become rich and a ruler, but the Saviour would teach him that these things can never achieve salvation.

In John chapter 3, speaking to a similar individual, Nicodemus, the Lord had made it clear that flesh and blood cannot inherit eternal life, but that 'ye must be born again'. Here, He confirms that it cannot be inherited and that it cannot be earned either. In answer to the Lord's questioning, it is clear that the young man was doing well in observing the man-ward commandments of God, but what about the God-ward? Could he forsake the riches he held most dear to 'love the Lord thy God with all thy heart' and rely on Christ only? Sadly, he could not. Despite his privileged position, good living, respect for the Saviour, and the Lord Jesus' love for him, Mark 10. 31, the man left sad and still in his sins, without eternal life, unable to rest on faith in Christ alone.

Surely, we all who in simple faith have accepted this great gift should bow our hearts in thankfulness, and as our Master did, show love and compassion to those who have not.

July 19th

Mark 10. 35-45

CAN YE DRINK OF THE CUP THAT I DRINK OF?

This question is asked by the Lord of James and John the sons of Zebedee. These two brothers were already greatly privileged to be among His followers, indeed they were part of the chosen Twelve. Beyond this, along with Peter, they had already been marked out to share in the most intimate of experiences, such as the raising of Jairus' daughter and the transfiguration. Yet, the human heart is never satisfied and they seek further exaltation.

All the disciples had already been reproved by the Lord for discussing who would be the greatest. Yet these two brothers, led by their mother, are still seeking position, according to Matthew. Though no doubt desiring what was best for her children, they needed to be shown further the need for service before reward, and suffering before glory. The Lord is now a matter of weeks away from the cross, where John and his mother would witness His crucifixion. One wonders whether they would desire to be on either side of Him then? He urges His disciples not to follow the world's drive for position, rank, and authority, but to follow His path of service and sacrifice resulting in true exaltation and glory – incomparable to even our greatest sufferings, Rom. 8. 18.

Thankfully, these outstanding brothers learned the lesson. The 'sons of thunder', who on occasions had been sectarian, judgemental, and ambitious, were transformed by Christ. They indeed would go on to 'drink' of His 'cup' of sufferings and His 'baptism' of death. James would be the first of the little band to be martyred while John would become the 'apostle of love', caring for God's people even in exile, to a great old age. He would rebuke those who 'love to have the pre-eminence', 3 John 9, and tenderly comfort those who suffer.

Oh that we too would learn the same lessons! There seems to be such a clamour for recognition today, whether by occupying the platform or seeking the 'position' of elder. Before he ever reigned as king, David risked his life for 'a few sheep' in the wilderness. Moses also meekly endured similar service. How we need those who would serve God's people and shepherd His flock in humility, like Moses, David, and indeed John!

July 20th

Mark 12. 13-17

IS IT LAWFUL TO GIVE TRIBUTE TO CAESAR?

This question is one of a series designed by the religious leaders of the day to entrap the Lord Jesus. Though not sincere questions, the Lord's answers provide tremendous help for us on several issues we still face in our day.

In chapter 10, as the Lord approached Judea, He is questioned about divorce, seeking to cause Him problems with Herod who had already murdered John the Baptist over this issue. In chapter 11, they questioned His authority in the temple, thus seeking to catch Him out on religious grounds. Now, in Jerusalem, they seek to cause Him problems with the Roman authorities by asking about paying tax to Caesar. On each occasion, the Master gives a clear and instructive answer which they cannot contest.

Tiberius Caesar was not the desired ruler of the Jewish people but rather a Gentile Roman dictator whose armies had invaded their land. Though perhaps not as debauched as his predecessor Augustus Caesar, also known as Octavian, he was nonetheless a heathen godless man. Yet, it is notable that neither here or at any other point did the Lord Jesus make any attempt to displace him, undermine his authority, or get involved in any civil protest of any kind. The Saviour leaves us the supreme example to observe: no matter how objectionable they may be, 'the powers that be are ordained of God', Rom. 13. 1.

The Lord also gives us the example of paying taxes, or 'tribute' as they are called in scripture. Whether the temple tax, Matt. 17. 24, or tribute to Caesar, as here, the Lord makes it clear that His people must cause no offence and fulfil their responsibilities. This is confirmed in Romans chapter 13, where not only has tribute, equivalent to income tax, to be paid, but also 'custom', the equivalent of duty. After all, we must remember that He provides for all our needs, as seen with Peter in the first reference above. As God's people we should be exemplary in this matter. We must not only obey the letter of the law but be morally irreproachable, paying our way in society and being 'no man's debtor'. Above all, we have a higher responsibility towards God, Acts 4. 19.

July 21st

Mark 12. 28-34

WHICH IS THE FIRST COMMANDMENT OF ALL?

Mark's Gospel ascribes this question to one of the scribes. Matthew tells us the man was also a Pharisee and a lawyer. Though still testing the Lord, as Matthew further reveals, he is also seemingly impressed by His answers to a series of questions, in particular to the Sadducees, on resurrection.

As a lawyer, this man asks the Lord a question regarding the Ten Commandments. His question relates not to first in order, but in pre-eminence. The Lord confirms, as we concluded yesterday, that man's primary responsibility must always be towards God. He quotes the summary of the God-ward commandments confirmed as the greatest in Deuteronomy chapter 6. But He then further reveals that the words, 'Thou shalt love thy neighbour as thyself', Lev. 19. 18, form the second greatest. As the first summarizes the God-ward commandments, this summarizes the man-ward. God's requirements for man are contained in these simple statements.

Sadly, we live in a day when the commandments are unknown, ignored, or wilfully broken. Some prominent rebellious men have even suggested an alternative set, based on doing as we please and enjoying sin. Yet, if they would only stop to think and consider this summary and the commandments as a whole, they would discover that, if observed, they benefit all mankind. Imagine, for a moment, a world with no false religion enslaving millions, no religious wars, or atrocities. There would be no murders, robberies, or burglaries to fill our news media. No need for vast expense on defence, crime prevention, and security, but instead these resources could be used to relieve suffering, poverty and hunger. There would be no broken families leaving children insecure, without role models, feeling abandoned or worthless, causing them to turn to crime, addictions, and self-harm. What a transformed society that would be! May we, the people of God, live in accordance with this summary, serving God and loving our fellow men, thus showing them a better way and perhaps bringing them, like this man, nearer to salvation. His response, as confirmed by the Lord, tells us that God requires this above extensive religious observance.

July 22nd

Mark 14. 32-42

COULDEST NOT THOU WATCH ONE HOUR?

Having instituted the Lord's Supper in the upper room, the Lord now leads His disciples out to the Mount of Olives. Again, He reminds them of His impending death and forewarns them that they will forsake Him. As usual, Peter speaks up to protest his loyalty and, even after the Lord predicting his denial, goes on to proclaim his willingness to 'die with thee'.

Peter, along with James and John who had earlier declared their willingness to share in the Saviour's 'cup' of suffering and 'baptism' of death, are afforded the privilege of accompanying the Lord further than the rest of the group. These three have enjoyed such experiences before as they had accompanied Him to witness miracles and His transfiguration. But now the principle of privilege bringing responsibility is to be seen. The Lord is not entering into glory but agony. Now He is contemplating the 'cup' of suffering, which will be His as He is 'made sin' for us at Calvary. They are not being asked to share in this, but simply to support Him in watching and praying.

Sadly, as the Lord's agony increases, He returns to find them sleeping and asks Peter the searching question, 'Couldest thou not watch one hour?' How small a request He had made of them, in contrast to the great demand upon Him! Before we become over-critical, we must remind ourselves how like these weak disciples we are. We declare great intentions, in prayer or in song, but so often fail even to come close to them. What is required of us in service is only reasonable compared to His great sacrifice, Rom. 12. 1-2, yet repeatedly we fall short. Similarly, these three, though given two further opportunities to 'watch and pray', still fail by falling asleep.

No doubt their tiredness and sorrow contributed to their failure, but the Lord makes them aware of the major reason, 'the flesh is weak'. Fortunately, He knows our frame and that we are but dust. But we, unlike the disciples at that time, have the permanent indwelling Spirit. Still 'the flesh lusts against the Spirit' and the flesh finds prayer irksome. So we must strive to pray, lest we also enter into temptation and failure. May the weakness of our flesh be overcome by the power of the Spirit!

July 23rd

Mark 15. 21-40, Psalm 22. 1

MY GOD, MY GOD, WHY HAST THOU FORSAKEN ME?

These words of the Lord Jesus are the central cry of the seven sayings of the cross. Uniquely they are recorded in two Gospels, Matthew and Mark. These Gospels record none of the others, three of which are found in each of Luke and John. It is the only saying directly quoted from the Old Testament, and the only words spoken during the three hours of darkness.

When approaching this question we must realize we are on holy ground and much is beyond both our experience and comprehension. The darkness covered these events from men's gaze and, similarly, much is hidden from our understanding. Nevertheless, there are some truths and lessons we can learn. In Gethsemane, the Lord had contemplated Calvary, but now, in the darkness, its awfulness bears in upon Him. The prophetic word sheds light on this abandonment as we are reminded, 'But thou art holy, O thou that inhabitest the praises of Israel', Ps. 22. 3. Further, 'Thou art of purer eyes than to behold evil, and canst not look on iniquity', Hab. 1. 13. When we hear these words our heads should bow in shame and our hearts in thankfulness. Consider what it cost this holy, sinless, spotless One to be made sin for us. He who knew, did, and in whom was, no sin, experiences separation from His God because of our sin!

Consider His *selflessness* who had spoken three times to address the needs of others; asking forgiveness for His tormentors, granting salvation to the dying thief and providing for His mother. Only after this He cries regarding His own circumstances. What an example for us to follow, Phil. 2. 4-5!

Consider further the *sympathy* of One who cries, 'Why?' Whatever experience of life we are called to go through, He alone can understand our anguished cry for explanation for He has experienced far more than we can, Heb. 2. 17.

Before we leave this study let us remember that the hours of darkness have passed. The Sin-bearer, who knew separation from His God, starts and finishes His seven sayings as the Son who addresses His Father. His final sayings confirm that every detail is 'finished' and He has now been received into heaven.

July 24th

Luke 1. 5-25

WHEREBY SHALL I KNOW THIS?

As a result of this question, Zacharias, the father to be of John the Baptist, was struck dumb until his son was born. It is clearly a question of doubt and disbelief. Before we become too critical of Zacharias we should consider his circumstances.

Several centuries have passed since God last spoke through the inspired word in the Book of Malachi. The nation of Israel had stumbled from one oppressor to another and was now occupied by the Romans. Despite this, Zacharias had maintained his tribal purity, married a fellow member of the priestly family and continued to exercise his priestly duties in the temple. His personal circumstances were also not ideal, because his wife Elisabeth was barren and childless. Perhaps these conditions left him doubting that God could still act as He had in the past and still fulfil His promises. Maybe sometimes we feel the same way.

As a priest Zacharias should have been familiar with the scriptures and aware that God had dealt with barren women before, including such well-known ones as Sarah, Rebekah, Rachel, Hannah, and Manoah's wife. From Daniel's prophecy he should have known that various empires would rise to occupy the Holy Land. Surely an angel appearing beside the altar of incense should have been enough for him to accept that God was able to perform the messenger's words? Yet, the angel has to make himself known as Gabriel – the very one who had revealed the succession of empires to Daniel nearly five centuries earlier, which had now culminated in the Roman empire. Further, Gabriel quotes from the last prophet, Malachi, the promise of another prophet as great as Elijah in character. God could, and indeed would, fulfil the promise and Zacharias would praise Him for it once the child was born. What a lesson for us today! We seem to constantly hear that this is a day of small things and all is decline and departure. But God has not changed! In many parts of the world He is blessing in remarkable ways as He did in the days of the early church. Thousands are being reached daily, and His people built up and blessed. Could such things happen here? Surely, we too should hold our tongues and wait in faith for God to move in power!

July 25th

Luke 1. 26-38, 46-56

HOW SHALL THIS BE, SEEING I KNOW NOT A MAN?

Unlike Zacharias' question to the angel Gabriel, Mary's is not met by censure or rebuke. In contrast to the elderly priest in the temple at Jerusalem, this was a young woman in the humble surroundings of her home in Nazareth. She was not being told of something God had done many times before, opening the womb of the barren, she was being told of the unique event of a virgin conception. Quite reasonably, she asks how, as although betrothed, or engaged, to Joseph she had never been physically intimate with him or any other man.

As with Zacharias and Elisabeth her relative, Mary had maintained her tribal identity and also her personal purity. She was in the circumstances and condition where God could use her. She is visited by the heavenly messenger on his final great revelation. Nearly half a millennium earlier Gabriel had appeared twice to Daniel revealing a prophetic schedule which would culminate in the Messiah Himself first being 'cut off' and then ruling universally over all the world kingdoms and empires. Now, having recently appeared to Zacharias to reveal the birth of the Messiah's forerunner John the Baptist, he reveals to Mary the birth of Messiah Himself.

The revelation takes place in the unlikely surroundings of Nazareth, the disreputable town in which the Messiah would spend the bulk of His life here on earth, although His birth would be in Bethlehem in accordance with scripture. How encouraging for us to know, as Mary's song declares, that the Lord regards the lowly, visits, and exalts them. Yes, she needed a saviour like every one of us, but, by faith, she had laid hold on God, lived for His glory in humility, purity, and faithfulness and was now to be blessed and exalted in association with Christ.

God used neither man nor woman to create Adam, a man only to form Eve, men and women to reproduce every other member of the human race, but now would use this blessed woman alone to bring His beloved Son into the world. His holiness would be preserved but His manhood would be real as He would be 'born of a woman'. Let each bow in worship and proclaim, 'Great is the mystery of godliness', 1 Tim. 3. 16.

July 26th

Luke 2. 41-52

WIST YE NOT THAT I MUST BE ABOUT MY FATHER'S BUSINESS?

This question forms part of the first recorded words of the incarnate Christ in scripture. How appropriate for the One 'which is in the bosom of the Father'! His first and last words on the cross would be addressed to His Father, as were His final words in the upper room. Today's words are spoken to His mother, who, as we considered yesterday, was indeed the most blessed of all women, was not sinless, immaculate, or perfect. Wondrous though her relationship to Him was, it was transitory, earthly, and natural. In contrast, the relationship of Father and Son in the Godhead is eternal, heavenly, and spiritual.

The setting is that while He 'tarried' in the temple, His 'parents' supposed He was with them 'in the company'. Upon finding Him, His mother expresses her understandable concern, referring to 'thy father and I'. The Holy Spirit refers to Joseph as His 'supposed' father and here refers to them as parents, not father and mother. The Lord gently reminds Mary that His Father is the one in whose house, or temple, they had found Him.

This incident should not be taken to imply that the Lord was in any way acting inappropriately or beyond His years; this would be impossible for the perfect One. Immediately prior to the incident, scripture reminds us of His perfect development as an infant moving into childhood, Luke 2. 39-40. As a twelve-year-old, those in the temple were 'astonished' at Him, not concerned or perturbed. Following these events, the text reveals that even in the normally difficult transition of adolescence the perfect One was always 'in favour with God and man'.

Verse 51 also tells us that the Creator of the universe returned to Nazareth and was subject to the lowly carpenter and his wife. That carpenter would subsequently die, and, as a result, the One whose guardian he had been would succeed him as the Heir to the throne of David. Yet, in humility, Jesus would take on the role of breadwinner and provide for the family. When His word now calls us to be in subjection to Him, our spiritual leaders, employers, husbands, parents, or each other, He has left us the perfect example of submission to follow.

July 27th

Luke 6. 1-11

HAVE YE NOT READ SO MUCH AS THIS, WHAT DAVID DID?

This question was asked by the Lord following one of the occasions on which He was criticised regarding observance of the sabbath. It was often healing that brought on such criticism but here it is His disciples plucking, rubbing, and eating corn. The critics were the Pharisees who prided themselves on strict observance of the scriptures and, in particular, the law of Moses.

Yet they had a misunderstanding of the purpose of the sabbath, which, as the Lord makes clear, was made for man's benefit. Indeed, though the commandment regarding the sabbath is the only one not repeated in the New Testament, it is still beneficial to have a day set aside, like the Lord's Day, but we must stress this is not the same as the sabbath. The Lord also points out elsewhere that He is Lord of the sabbath and it is right to do good when the opportunity arises, even on a sabbath.

Now He turns them to the very scriptures they were so keen to uphold. They needed, as we do, to learn the lesson that scripture must be applied as a whole, not in isolation. God requires scripture to be observed in detail and no one made this clearer than the Lord Jesus. However, real human need, suffering, or hunger, must take precedence over ceremonial observance. In 1 Samuel chapter 21, David and his men were experiencing hunger, largely because God's rightful king was being rejected. Likewise, the disciples were perhaps experiencing hunger for similar reasons. The bread David took had already been replaced on the table by fresh shewbread and they were simply taking the priests' portion because their need was greater.

The disciples had done no wrong; indeed, they had not deceived as David did. They were not harvesting, threshing or reaping, which would have been contrary to the law, but simply enjoying the provision made for travellers, Deut. 23. 25. Under Old Testament law, scripture shows that even the Passover could be moved by a month, if it was to meet genuine need, Num. 9; 2 Chr. 30. God has never required legal observance to take precedence over genuine need, compassion, or mercy, and neither should we, Mic. 6. 6-8.

July 28th

Luke 6. 27-36

FOR IF YE LOVE THEM WHICH LOVE YOU, WHAT THANK HAVE YE?

Today's reading comes from Luke's abbreviated account of the Sermon on the Mount, recorded more fully in Matthew chapters 5-7. Some would try to limit the applicability of this teaching to future kingdom conditions. However, while it is true the Lord Jesus Christ is currently a King rejected by the world, His supremacy is already acknowledged by us, His people. As such, we have a responsibility to seek to live as He lived and to display the conditions that His teaching demands now.

The whole tenor of this record of the life of 'Jesus of Nazareth' can be summarized in the words of Peter, 'Who went about doing good', Acts 10. 38. Indeed, in the opening verse of the Acts of the Apostles, Luke reminds us that his Gospel records 'all that Jesus began both **to do** and teach'. Surely, this is the pattern we must follow today as the early church did? Yet we often hear such comments as, 'We are not here to present a social gospel'. Now, while it is true that man's greatest need is spiritual and we must present the gospel and its claims, the clear evidence of the New Testament is that the preaching is often preceded and enhanced by good works. Maybe we need to repeat the Lord's question from yesterday's study, 'Have ye not read so much as this?' Christ's first miracle was a material one. Further, the only miracle recorded in every Gospel is the feeding of the 5000. Though He knew that many only thronged to Him because of material benefits, it did not stop Him bestowing these benefits. He continually advocated providing for the poor, loving our neighbour as ourselves, and, as in today's reading, even loving our enemies by doing them good. His parables and illustrations, such as that of the Good Samaritan, further emphasize this and His, and His Father's, example confirm it.

Many of us have become *isolated*, rather than separated, from our fellow men and only display love to those who reciprocate our love and fellowship. Christ warns there is no credit for this but only for true charitable love which expects nothing in return, and indeed may receive only antagonism from the recipients – but will be recognized by Him.

July 29th

Luke 7. 18-28

WHAT WENT YE OUT INTO THE WILDERNESS FOR TO SEE?

John the Baptist is languishing in Herod's prison, but still hearing of Christ's miracles. Doubts arise in his mind and maybe in others also. If Jesus is the Christ, why is John still imprisoned? Do his circumstances reflect some failure on John's part?

Even the greatest of God's servants, as confirmed here, can be subject to discouragement and dismay, especially when weakened by suffering. Yet, though the Lord may need to encourage them to greater faith, He will also openly recognize their faithfulness. In John's case this is done by a series of questions which teach us much about service for God.

Firstly, God's servants must be *consistent*. Like John, they do not bend with the wind of popularity. He was not a 'reed shaken with the wind'; he stood against the prevailing conditions of the day, including the sin of the king in taking his brother's wife. It is an easy thing to present truth when all in the audience agree and 'Amens' abound, but faithfulness requires us to be 'instant in season and out of season', 2 Tim. 4. 2. This may, of course, result in a heavy price being paid, as with John.

Secondly, God's service is *not* always *comfortable*. John was not clothed with the luxurious clothes of those recognized by men as of great authority and renown. He wore rough camel's hair and leather, rather than fine cloth. Maybe this reflected his message; it was not smooth and comfortable but demanded repentance and a change of life. Faithful servants often carry an uncomfortable message. John's message found him not in the king's palace but in the king's prison.

Finally, God's servant is *commended*. The third question is answered by the Lord. John indeed was a prophet and 'more than a prophet'. He is the greatest of the prophets because of his message and his timing in God's calendar. He is the one spoken of by Malachi when the Old Testament ended and he now fulfils that, the forerunner of the Christ. His message, like ours, is greater than all who went before in the old economy. Its subject, Christ, is the greatest there could ever be, and to be in His kingdom is the greatest position of all.

July 30th

Luke 7. 36-50

TELL ME THEREFORE WHICH OF THEM WILL LOVE HIM MOST?

This incident, recorded only by Luke, once again finds the Saviour questioning the Pharisees. It follows the washing and anointing of His feet by a woman in the house of Simon the Pharisee. In seeming contrast to the self-righteous Pharisee, the woman was a known sinner, as confirmed by Simon and the Lord. The details of her sins are not revealed to us; they seem to be a matter between her and the Lord alone! The Lord indicates that her actions reflect the greatness of her sin and He grants her forgiveness on the basis of faith alone. It is worth noting that she is one of a number of notable women the Lord encounters and frees from the awfulness of sin, including the woman of John chapter 4; the woman taken in adultery, John 8; and Mary Magdalene.

The Lord uses the incident to show that the greater our awareness of what we have been forgiven, the greater our love and devotion will be. Many of us are the children of believing parents, perhaps saved in childhood. By God's grace we were saved before becoming involved in sin to the same extent as others from less privileged backgrounds. Sadly, this may result in a lack of appreciation of the wonder of our salvation and a reduced devotion to the Lord. In addition, perhaps like Simon, we look down on others and consider them as greater sinners, unworthy of the closeness to the Lord we believe we have.

We must realize that *all* sinners are trophies of grace. The cost of salvation is equal for all of us; the blood of Christ and His blood alone can cleanse each of us 'from all sin'. Maybe we should consider ourselves even greater debtors to grace, if early salvation has preserved us from certain depths of sin?

In contrast to this woman, and those mentioned above, there are many others close to Him, with less obviously sinful backgrounds. Among them is one who enjoyed His fellowship in a special way in the home of another Simon at Bethany. Yet like this woman, Mary also demonstrated her gratitude by anointing Him at great cost. May each of us follow the example of both these women and appreciate the great debt to grace we all owe!

July 31st

Luke 9. 37-45

HOW LONG SHALL I BE WITH YOU AND SUFFER YOU?

Coming down from the heights of the Mount of Transfiguration with Peter, James, and John, the Lord enters a sad scene below. The rest of the disciples had been unable to deliver a young boy from the power of demon possession and now his desperate father, accompanied by a multitude of onlookers, brings him to the Lord. The incident takes place at the end of the Lord's Galilean ministry. He then sets His face to go to Jerusalem, is rejected in a Samaritan village, and carries out His Judean-Perean ministry in the months leading up to the cross. Up to this point, most of His ministry for over two years had been in Galilee. This is probably the last recorded miracle there and His words are some of His final ones to its people.

The most comprehensive account is found in Mark's Gospel, that of the perfect Servant. After over two years of dedicated, faithful and flawless service, the Lord must have been saddened by this situation. The disciples lacked the prayer and self-denial required to meet the need. The desperate father confesses his own lack of faith, and the boy lies convulsed by the last desperate throws of the demon. But it is the crowd who appear to disappoint Him most. He had performed many miracles in their region, including the first in Cana, a raising of the dead in Nain, and feeding the 5000 near Bethsaida. Yet, they still fail to appreciate who He really is, and He describes them as a 'faithless and perverse generation'. In Luke's next chapter, He sends His disciples into Judea; He laments the rejection of the cities of Galilee and warns of their judgement.

Here, His question is, 'How long?' The answer is clear: their day of opportunity was finishing, His service there was closing, and, indeed, He now tells the disciples again that His life on earth would soon end. However, He would 'suffer them' a little longer and would bless with healing once more. What an example He sets for us! We too are called to serve in a faithless, perverse, and wicked world. For two thousand years now they have largely rejected Christ and the gospel preached by His people. But we must, like Him, carry on till the day of service is past.

August 1st

Luke 10. 25-37

AND WHO IS MY NEIGHBOUR?

A certain lawyer stood up to tempt our Lord with a question about how to obtain eternal life. The Master directed the expert in the law of Moses to the law itself. In response to the Saviour's question, 'How readest thou?' the lawyer recited the two most important commandments. The Lord commended him on his right answer regarding one's relationship to God and man.

But he, willing to justify himself, asked, 'And who is my neighbour?' His desire to justify himself betrayed a deep sense of guilt. But who was accusing him? Obviously, his own conscience was accusing him, because he was resisting the law and trying to find an excuse for not keeping the commandment, Rom. 2. 15.

The Lord did not answer his question by defining who his neighbour was. Instead, He demonstrated to him through a story how, by asking such a question, he, the lawyer, did not have a neighbourly attitude. On the other hand He showed him how the Samaritan, whom he despised, made himself a neighbour to the man in need. By contrast, the priest and the Levite passed the man by.

In marvellous divine wisdom the Lord would have the lawyer himself give the answer to the last question in the story. 'Which, now, of those three, thinkest thou, was neighbour unto him that fell among the thieves?' The lawyer had no choice but to answer, 'He that showed mercy on him'. As a result, the command, 'Go and do thou likewise' came out loud and clear from the mouth of the blessed Saviour.

What a lesson that man, who rested in the law and made his boast in God, had learned that day! The greatest of teachers showed him beyond any doubt that the issue was not, 'Who is my neighbour?' but, 'Are you a neighbour to whoever comes into your neighbourhood in need?'

And for us we also learn from the case of the lawyer that knowledge of the law or ability to memorize it, cannot impart life. Even engaging in the performance of its ordinances, as in the case of the priest and the Levite, cannot justify sinners, but faith in the redemption that is in Christ Jesus can, 3. 24.

August 2nd

Luke 11. 1-13

IF A SON SHALL ASK BREAD . . . GIVE HIM A STONE?

Our Lord is portrayed in Luke's Gospel as the Man of prayer. So many are the occasions on which He is seen praying that we cannot but mention the fact. In the days of His flesh, Heb. 5. 7, He has left us an example of His total dependence on God as the lowly Son of man. At the request of the disciples, who saw Him praying, and asked to be taught how to pray, the Master gave them a pattern prayer. He then went on to teach His hearers about the necessity of persistence in prayer, see Luke 18. 1.

The parable of the importune friend was given to illustrate this point. The importunity, or shamelessness, of the friend is mentioned as the means by which he had his request granted. Yet it is obvious that the motive for the giver in meeting his friend's need was only his desire for a restful night. The giver in the parable was a mere mortal man with limited affection for his friend, and limited resources too.

The parable was then followed by a clear promise from the Saviour that asking, seeking, and knocking will be rewarded by God, vv. 9-11. In praying to Him, however, we will not be asking of a mortal human with limited resources and inadequate love. We will be asking of One whose love is limitless and who is the Possessor of heaven and earth, Gen. 14. 19.

The Lord went on to remind them how the love, kindness, and mercy of their heavenly Father are far greater than the parental ties of natural earthly fathers. He, the Creator, has planted such affection in the hearts of His creatures towards their children. Under normal circumstances, all should enjoy such loving and giving relationships with their natural fathers. How much greater is divine love and care which the Father of spirits has towards us? It is inconceivable that an earthly father, who is evil by nature, would give a useless stone or harmful serpent or scorpion to his son in response to a request for a good food item. 'How much more' shall our heavenly Father be pleased to grant the great blessing of the Holy Spirit to those who ask Him by faith and who have received the word of the gospel, believed on His Son and been born again of Him?

August 3rd

Luke 12. 13-21

WHOSE SHALL THOSE THINGS BE?

How often we see our Lord turn what seems to be an ordinary question into a great moral lesson! Here is an example of one who asked the Lord to interfere in a family dispute over the division of inheritance. The Master used the occasion to denounce covetousness and to promote a sound perspective on earthly possessions. First, the Lord refuses to accept the position of judge or arbitrator between the two feuding brothers. After all, He was sent by the Father to be the Saviour of the world, 1 John 4. 14. Doubtless, there is a coming day when He will judge both the living and the dead, Acts 10. 42, but that day has not yet come.

The Lord then gave a clear warning about covetousness, a known ailment of the human heart. Scripture equates it with idolatry, Eph. 5. 5. A covetous person allows his strong desire for more acquisitions to replace God in his heart, thus he becomes a worshipper of self and its lusts. The Saviour went on to say that the essence of life and the purpose for which God gave it to man is not to amass more material goods, Luke 12. 15.

The Lord again uses parabolic teaching to illustrate this truth. A certain man who was already rich had a year of great blessing from God, in that his ground produced a plentiful harvest. The produce was obviously far beyond his needs, even greater than his capacity to store it. What was he to do with such plenty? Did he recognize that it was God who had bestowed such blessing on him? Did he think of sharing some with the poor, or of giving some to the cause of his Creator? No! That poor, self-centred man called God's bounty 'my' crops and 'my' goods, see 1 Sam. 25. 11. He even dared to call God's gift of life 'my' soul, forgetting that all of these blessings, including life itself, were lent to him by God for a certain time. And under the false impression that he still had many years to live he thought he could set out for a life of rest and pleasure. How sad to know that the night in which he had these thoughts within himself was his last on earth! The Lord's final verdict on him and all those like him was, 'So is he that layeth up treasure for himself, and is not rich toward God', Luke 12. 21.

August 4th

Luke 15. 1-7, Matthew 18. 12-14

WHAT MAN OF YOU HAVING AN HUNDRED SHEEP?

During His earthly ministry our blessed Lord endured such contradiction of sinners against Himself, Heb. 12. 3. Our chapter here gives us a clear example of that. Of all the classes of society at the time, the publicans and sinners were the ones that drew near to hear Him, Luke 15. 1. By contrast, the respectable Pharisees and learned scribes made it their business to murmur against Him for receiving sinners and eating with them. They could not comprehend what attracted those sinners to Christ. Nor could they understand why He was interested in seeking after them and finding them. We sinners, saved by His grace, find their criticism of Him to be rather an approbation, for, praise His Name, He received us when we came to Him.

Therefore, the Lord spoke to them a parable that illustrates His love, care and mercy for sinners. And though the parable has three different components, the message is one. It speaks of His willingness to save sinners, of the value of one single, sinning soul in His sight and of the joy He has when a repentant sinner turns to Him in faith.

The Saviour used the familiar picture of the shepherd and the sheep. He spoke of Himself in John chapter 10 as the Good Shepherd. Isaiah aptly described us as 'sheep that have gone astray', Isa. 53. 6. Sheep by nature are notorious for wandering and getting lost; this is usually born out of folly and ignorance. The love of the shepherd takes him out searching for one single lost sheep having left the other ninety-nine in the wilderness. No difficulty is too great and no distance too long for him to go. Such love speaks, though faintly, of the love of the Good Shepherd who gave His life for the sheep. Having found the lost one he carefully carries it on his shoulders rejoicing. This points us to the careful shepherding that Christ exercises towards those who believe on Him. Christ's delight in the saving of souls is seen in the joy and rejoicing of the shepherd, his friends and neighbours. Applying the parable, the Lord said that 'joy shall be in heaven over one sinner that repenteth' more than over ninety-nine self-righteous persons who deceive themselves in thinking they need no repentance, Luke 15. 7.

August 5th

Luke 18. 1-8.

WHEN THE SON OF MAN COMETH SHALL HE FIND FAITH ON THE EARTH?

This question was asked by our Lord at the end of a parable directed to His disciples, Luke 17. 37. The parable was given to stress the importance of persevering in prayer. It immediately followed a fearful account given by the Lord of the times of the great tribulation that will befall the world at large, but especially Israel, just before His appearing in glory, vv. 22-36.

That 'men ought always to pray, and not to faint' is wise counsel which is profitable to all believers in all ages and at all times. Prayer is the only resource for a child of God, Phil. 4. 6. Even when an answer appears to be delayed we need not faint. The widow in the parable got her desire through her importunity. But unlike the unjust judge, our God in due time will avenge His elect speedily, though He bear long with them. To the believer in New Testament times asking to be avenged of his enemies seems to be a strange request, because it seems to contradict the exhortation 'not to avenge ourselves' since vengeance belongs to the Lord, Rom. 12. 19. It is rather a language more fitting for Old Testament saints, Ps. 18. 47.

Therefore, in light of the context, applying it specifically to the cries of the faithful remnant of Israel between the rapture and the appearing seems to be particularly appropriate, Rev. 6. 10. In those times they will have no other resource but to cry to God for deliverance from their enemies, and persevering in prayer then, as it is now, will surely grant them God's merciful response. For He will shorten the days for the elect's sake, Matt. 24. 21, 22.

Our Lord's question at the end of the parable gives us His prediction that at the time of His second advent there will be only a comparatively small number of true believers who will be exercising their faith in God. This is very much in keeping with what He said about the days of Noah and Lot in the previous chapter. Only eight people were saved in the ark. Likewise in the days of Lot only four people left Sodom. In the Lord's own words, 'Even thus shall it be in the day when the Son of man shall be revealed', Luke 17. 30.

August 6th

Luke 18. 18-30

WHO THEN CAN BE SAVED?

A rich young ruler in Israel came to Christ asking Him how to obtain eternal life. And though he received from the Lord a clear answer he did not, as far as we can tell, follow the Master's advice. He went away sorrowing because of his great wealth with which he was not willing to part, Luke 18. 23. He became an example of how great riches can be a reason why people err from the way of salvation. Many people in our time would rather keep their wealth than come to Christ for salvation. The mammon of unrighteousness becomes their idol in preference to the true God.

The Lord saw how very sorrowful that man was, and since He knows what is in man, John 2. 25, He perceived how his wealth stood between him and eternal life. The Saviour said, 'How hardly shall they that have riches enter into the kingdom of God!' Luke 18. 24. He likened it to the passage of a camel, the largest common animal, through the eye of the needle, v. 25. To the Jewish mind at the time being rich was a sign of God's favour. Therefore, those words of the Lord drew from His audience the reaction, 'Who then can be saved?' v. 26. If there was so much difficulty for the favoured rich to be saved, how can anyone else be saved?

The Lord, however, has spoken of it as a difficulty, not an impossibility. His answer to their question pointed them to the truth that 'with God nothing is impossible', Gen. 18. 14. Our God is able to save both poor and rich. 'The things which are impossible with men are possible with God', Luke 18. 27.

We see God's almighty power both in creation, Heb. 1. 3, and in providence, Acts 17. 28. But when it came to providing salvation for mankind it took more than His power! It took the incarnation, death, and resurrection of His blessed Son, Heb. 1. 3. Thus, He made purification for sin by the sacrifice of Himself. How remarkable to see Him on the way to the cross, talking about the value of His sacrifice in the sight of God! Hence He could assure the crowd that day that 'he is able also to save them to the uttermost that come to God by him', 7. 25, regardless of whether they are materially rich or poor.

August 7th

Luke 20. 27-40

IN RESURRECTION WHOSE WIFE OF THEM IS SHE?

The Sadducees, the heretics of the time, approached the Lord with a difficult question they felt was based on the word of God. Their aim, however, was to justify their false doctrine rather than to learn the truth. Like the devil when trying the Saviour in the wilderness, they resorted to quoting scripture, choosing a passage that deals with levirate marriage, Deut. 25. 5, 6. They thought they could debase the doctrine of the resurrection of the dead. It was obvious that the case they put before the Lord was factious, yet they felt they could silence Him.

Their hopes, however, were soon dashed when they heard the Master's reply. He told them that the root of their opposition to the truth was simply their ignorance; firstly, their ignorance of the status of human beings in the other world, beyond death; secondly, their sheer ignorance of the scriptures.

The Lord in His answer explained how there is a clear distinction between the situation here on earth and that which exists in heaven. 'The children of this world' are married and given in marriage so as to maintain the perpetuity of the race, since they are all subject to death. On the other hand, those who are accounted worthy of resurrection life cannot die any more. Therefore, there is no need for marriage in the heavenly realms. They are all equal unto the angels and are children of resurrection. Thus, the Saviour exposed the thought of any similarity between the status on earth and in heaven as a misconception.

Furthermore, the Lord went on to show how the truth of the resurrection of the dead was a clear scriptural doctrine. Hundreds of years after the death of Abraham, Isaac and Jacob, Jehovah appeared to Moses in the burning bush, Exod. 3. 3. There He describes Himself as the God of Abraham, Isaac, and Jacob. He was speaking about men of whom He is not ashamed to be called their God, Heb. 11. 16. Is it conceivable that those dead patriarchs did not continue to exist? Is He the God of the dead? God forbid; they all live unto Him, Luke 20. 38. He is indeed the God of the living. Well did Christ say of them, 'Ye do err, not knowing the scriptures, nor the power of God', Matt. 22. 29.

August 8th

Luke 22. 63-65

PROPHESY, WHO IT IS THAT SMOTE THEE?

This question was asked by wicked men who held the Saviour in the hour of the power of darkness, Luke 22. 53. So far, during His ministry they could not stretch forth a hand against Him. But now, having been falsely accused and condemned to death by their leaders, those wretched minions thought to physically man-handle Him. They mocked His claims by spitting in His face, smiting and buffeting Him. Then, they thought of further humiliating Him by blindfolding Him, striking Him, then asking Him to tell who it was that had carried out the mean action. Did they really want to test His prophesying ability? Or were they just putting Him to an open shame, Heb. 6. 6?

Were they really interested in learning the truth about His Person? Did they have a genuine desire to know if He was indeed a prophet? Certainly not! This was simply a clear demonstration that 'the carnal mind is enmity against God', Rom. 8. 7. Every proof that Jesus of Nazareth was the Prophet they were waiting for was given to that nation. When earlier that night He was asked by Annas about His doctrine, Christ's answer was simple and straightforward, 'I spoke openly to the world; I ever taught in the synagogue, and in the temple, where the Jews always resort; and in secret have I said nothing', John 18. 20.

As to His Messiahship, He was approved of God among them by miracles and wonders and signs which God did by Him in their midst, Acts 2. 22. Their leaders were quite cognizant of all His miracles, including those where He raised the dead. Yet they chose to ignore all of those infallible proofs of His claims and plotted His demise, John 11. 46-50.

But why would the incarnate God accept such humiliation from His creatures? He could have easily willed them out of His presence and they would have vanished from before His face. His calm submission to insults shows His commitment to finish the work given to Him by His Father, John 17. 4. Therefore, He endured the cross despising the shame. How brightly does His moral glory shine here! 'Who, when he was reviled, reviled not again; when he suffered, he threatened not; but committed himself to him that judgeth righteously', 1 Pet. 2. 23.

August 9th

Luke 23. 26-31

FOR IF THEY DO THESE THINGS IN A GREEN TREE, WHAT SHALL BE DONE IN THE DRY?

What a sad procession was seen in Jerusalem on that fateful morning when the Lord of glory was led by His captors in shame! He, bearing His cross with help from Simon the Cyrenian, was taken across the city streets to a place called Calvary to be crucified. This city had, over the centuries, become known as the killer of the prophets and the stoner of those who were sent unto her, Matt. 23. 37. This time, however, the Victim was no ordinary prophet nor was His innocence in doubt. Why was He condemned to death in exchange for a murderer? Did that great company of people that followed recall His deeds and His words? Had they not witnessed how He went about doing good and healing all that were oppressed of the devil? Was the wailing and lamenting of the women among them a sign of repentance or even remorse? Or was that a mere psychological reaction to the tragic scene enacted before their eyes?

His words to them were prophetic and eerily ominous, 'Daughters of Jerusalem, weep not for me, but weep for yourselves and for your children. For, behold, the days are coming, in which they shall say, Blessed are the barren, and the wombs that never bore, and the paps which never gave suck. Then shall they begin to say to the mountains, Fall on us and to the hills, Cover us', Luke 23. 28-30. Earlier in His discourse to the disciples He had predicted the doom of the city, 21. 20-24.

Here the Lord spoke of Himself as the green tree and of how they had dealt with Him. The citizens of Jerusalem, where a measure of law and order should have prevailed, had overruled the governor who was intent on letting Him go. And the priests, who should have obeyed the divine law which they taught, had set aside all their religious qualms and condemned an innocent Man. If they had done so with the green tree, what will the Romans do to that dried up nation from whom the moral sap was completely drained? She will have to pay for the sin of crucifying her Messiah. The Owner of the vineyard will not pass over this sin, 'He shall come and destroy these husbandmen, and shall give the vineyard to others', 20. 16.

August 10th

Luke 23. 39-43

DOST NOT THOU FEAR GOD, SEEING THOU ART IN THE SAME CONDEMNATION?

The two malefactors, who were crucified, one on each side of the Saviour, were the epitome of the two categories to which humanity could be divided. One of them represents those who reject Christ's offer of forgiveness and end up perishing. The other represents those who ask for it and are saved. Both these opposite attitudes towards the crucified One exist today. Both men were wrong-doers and were receiving their due temporal punishment from the earthly justice system of the time. Likewise, all humanity can be said to 'have gone astray, we have turned every one to his own way', Isa. 53. 6.

The first malefactor, though suffering pain, did not seem to recognize his guilt before God. His words to Christ did not contain any confession of his own sins nor did they reflect any sense of repentance. He never asked for divine forgiveness. Instead, he railed on the Lord, challenging Him to prove His Messiahship by saving Himself and the two malefactors from temporal punishment only. There was no response from the Lord to such a request. How many people today refuse to acknowledge that their sin is against God Himself, Luke 15. 21!

The second malefactor, on the other hand, confessed his guilt and accepted that they were justly receiving the due reward of their deeds. He then openly and plainly declared Christ's innocence. Did he do so as he witnessed how Christ prayed for forgiveness for His executioners? Was the Holy Spirit dealing with him, convicting him of his need of divine forgiveness? Did the Spirit also convict him of the eternal punishment awaiting him after his imminent death? He seemed to have been convicted that the innocent One crucified by his side was none other than the Messiah of Israel, the coming King. 'Remember me when thou comest into thy kingdom' was his clear request of the Saviour. In His marvellous grace our blessed Lord, knowing that the thief's repentance was true indeed, answered him, 'Verily I say unto thee, *Today* shalt thou be with me in paradise'. What a contrast between the two malefactors' attitudes!

August 11th

Luke 24. 1-12

WHY SEEK YE THE LIVING AMONG THE DEAD?

'Resurrection of the dead in the last day' was a commonly held belief among pious Jews in the days of our Lord, John 11. 24. But that someone should rise *from among* the dead would have been totally foreign to their thinking. Nevertheless, the Saviour had repeatedly taught that about Himself on numerous occasions. But it seems that His followers, both the disciples and the women that followed Him from Galilee, never understood or grasped this truth, 'For as yet they knew not the scripture, that he must rise again from the dead', John 20. 9.

Luke records the names of three of the women who went with others to the tomb very early in the morning. They were Mary Magdalene, Joanna, and Mary the mother of James, Luke 24. 10. They had prepared spices and ointments which they brought with them intending to embalm the dead body. To their surprise and perplexity they found the stone rolled away and the tomb empty. Just two nights previously they had witnessed how Joseph and Nicodemus had laid the body of the Saviour in Joseph's tomb, 23. 55. But now the body is gone. Had they really believed His words that He must rise from the dead the third day, there would have been no need for preparation of spices and ointments. Nor would there have been any reason for their perplexity!

The perplexity soon gives way to fear as they see the angels and hear their words, 'Why seek ye the living among the dead? He is not here, but is risen', is the angels' gentle rebuke to them. The angels then remind them of the Lord's words spoken in Galilee where they came from, 24. 6-7. Their mission to inform the disciples causes Peter to go to the tomb where he verifies their report, yet he departs wondering!

Remarkably, however, we do not see Mary of Bethany with the other women at the sepulchre. Her absence reminds us that she anointed Christ before His death, John 12. 1-8. This may indicate that she understood the truth of His resurrection better than the others. Therefore, she sees no need to go to the tomb, for she believes He will rise again, 'I am he that liveth, and was dead; and behold, I am alive for evermore, Amen', Rev. 1. 18.

August 12th

Luke 24. 13-35

OUGHT NOT CHRIST TO HAVE SUFFERED THESE THINGS, AND TO ENTER INTO HIS GLORY?

'But we trusted that it had been he who should have redeemed Israel', Luke 24. 21. These sad words expressed the deep disillusionment the two disciples felt in light of what had happened in Jerusalem earlier that week. Their idea of a redeemer of Israel was that of one who would deliver them from bondage to Rome. They had followed Him because they trusted that He was King Messiah. But now their hopes lie buried in a grave, hewn in a rock. In following Him, listening to His words and observing His deeds, they were convinced of His Messiahship. When He steadfastly set His face to go to Jerusalem, 9. 51, they followed Him on the way. There was a sense of keen anticipation as He approached the city that His kingdom would soon appear, 19. 11. And when they joined in singing His hosannas as He entered His capital city, they were almost assured of His ascending the throne of David there and then.

But none of this happened and the chief priests and the rulers condemned Him to death, and the Romans crucified Him. News of His resurrection confirmed by angels and carried to them by the women failed to dispel that awful sight of Calvary, where the King hung on a cross between two thieves. And, furthermore, they have yet to see Him alive, 24. 24. The conflict in their minds was reinforced by their selective reading of the scriptures. They preferred, like all their fellow Jews, to remember the passages that spoke of Messiah coming in power and glory and opted to ignore the ones that spoke of His sufferings. The Stranger that approached them had to correct their thinking.

This He did by first laying down the foundational truth of Messiah's suffering at His first advent before going back to heaven, v. 26. What a unique lesson this was when the Living Word took up the written word and expounded to them from all the scriptures, 'things concerning himself'! Their hearts were burning with the glow of His enlightening them. Could there be any doubt left in their minds after that truthful explanation of the scriptures? All they needed now was for Him to reveal Himself to them, as He did in the 'breaking of the bread', v. 35.

August 13th

Luke 24. 36-49

WHY ARE YE TROUBLED? AND WHY DO THOUGHTS ARISE IN YOUR HEARTS?

The passage before us here is one of many occasions in which the risen Lord showed Himself alive to the apostles after His passion by many infallible proofs, Acts 1. 3. We should realize that the Lord's appearances after His resurrection were true revelations because He allowed people to recognize Him only at His will. Even the most intimate of His acquaintances could not recognize Him immediately. Mary Magdalene had to hear His voice calling her by name. The eyes of the two on the way to Emmaus were held until He broke the bread before them. The seven disciples in the boat could not recognize the Stranger on the shore of Gennesaret until they saw the miracle of the draught of fish.

The glorified body of our Lord after His resurrection was not subject to physical laws. He would appear suddenly in their midst and would vanish from their sight just as suddenly. He would appoint a place to meet with them, but did not accompany them on the way as He used to do in the days of His flesh. On this occasion, this must have been one reason why they were terrified when they saw Him. The doors were securely locked for fear of the Jews. How could He have come in? Or were they seeing an apparition? It is one thing for us to hear of someone coming back from the dead: it is another thing for him to appear before our eyes. Was this another reason for their fear?

The loving Lord would not leave them in doubt for long. He wanted to prove that He was the same Jesus who loved them and cared for them. So He first offers Himself to their sight, 'Behold my hands and my feet', Luke 24. 39. These were now bearing the nail prints. Then, He invites them to handle Him, 'It is I myself', He asserts. He was not just a spirit but He had a body of flesh and bones. Their joy was so overwhelming, though it was mixed with unbelief, therefore, He asked for some food to consume before them. They gave Him broiled fish and honeycomb which He promptly ate before their eyes. These were the very same men who then went preaching repentance and remission of sins in His name among all nations, v. 47.

August 14th

John 1. 19-28

WHAT SAYEST THOU OF THYSELF?

As God was preparing the world for the first advent of His blessed Son, one could recognize two categories of people in the Jewish nation. The overwhelming majority cared very little for the coming of Messiah, yet among them there was a pious minority that were in keen anticipation of that event. At the time of the Saviour's birth we meet with men and women like Simeon the aged, and Anna. Those were described as 'waiting for the consolation of Israel', and they 'looked for the redemption of Jerusalem'. To the Jew at the time that translated into 'the coming of Messiah'. Did those saints of God, like Daniel of old, 'understand by books the number of years' and therefore were in such state of anticipation of His coming?

Thirty years later that sense of anticipation has been heightened even more. For there appeared on the scene a man whose descent was from Levi; he was indeed the son of a priest. He was in the wilderness preaching the baptism of repentance for the remission of sins. People from every social and religious class were flocking to him asking to be baptized. But who was he? Even the leadership in Jerusalem were at a loss about his identity. It was possible that they may have recognized in him some similarities to the character and message of Elijah. But it was also obvious that those 'learned' men could not differentiate between Elijah and Messiah. Worse still, they did not know that Messiah and the Prophet of Deuteronomy chapter 18 were one and the same Person. This was reflected in their questions to the Baptist when they had sent a delegation to him.

Of John, the angel Gabriel said, 'He will go before the Lord in the spirit and power of Elijah', Luke 1. 17. The Lord Himself described him as Elijah whom the leadership knew not, Matt. 17. 12-13. But John would not take that honour to himself. He went back to Isaiah's prophecy of him, describing himself as the mere voice of 'one crying in the wilderness', John 1. 23. He then carefully pointed his questioners to the truth of One greater than him who was already standing among them. Thus, this faithful servant of Christ was content with taking his place at the feet of his Master, v. 27.

August 15th

John 1. 35-42

RABBI, WHERE DWELLEST THOU?

The young men who surrounded the Baptist, and became his disciples, most certainly belonged to that minority of Jews who were awaiting the coming of Messiah. They attached themselves to John because, unlike their religious leaders, they recognized that his baptism was from heaven, Matt. 21. 25. But when John declared that he was not the Christ, and pointed out Jesus as 'the Lamb of God', John 1. 29, and 'the Son of God' v. 34, later confirming the same truth, v. 36, two of his disciples followed Jesus. When our Lord saw them following, He asked a most searching question, 'What seek ye?' Their answer came in the form of another question, 'Rabbi, where dwellest thou?'

They were obviously seeking to know Him, but what a question to ask God incarnate where He dwelt! Where could He have possibly lived here on earth? His earthly abode must have been so simple and undistinguished from other homes. It was certainly not to be compared with the 'ivory palaces' where He dwelt for all eternity. Our Saviour must have been still living in Nazareth at the time, for John was not yet cast into prison, Matt. 4. 12-13. But why lowly Galilee, and why despised Nazareth? Why not Rome, or Alexandria, or even Jerusalem? We may find the answer in the prophecy of Isaiah, 'For thus saith the high and lofty One who inhabits eternity, whose name is Holy: I dwell in the high and holy place, with him also who is of a contrite and humble spirit', Isa. 57. 15.

'Come and see' was the gracious invitation. They came and saw and abode with Him that day. The apostle John, who was certainly one of the two, left us no record of what they saw, what conversation they had with Him, or whether they had shared a meal with Him. But we know the deep and lasting impression they had of their time with the Master. They had found in Him the answer to all their questions, the fulfilment of all their aspirations, the embodiment of all their hearts had so longed for. Now they have to go out and share their great find with others. Andrew first found his own brother Simon and his clear testimony was, 'We have found Messiah', John 1. 41. And to show him what he meant, he brought him to Jesus, v. 42.

August 16th

John 1. 43-51

CAN ANY GOOD THING COME OUT OF NAZARETH?

Because of the words of Nathaniel, we have often come to think of the city of Nazareth as the epitome of hopelessness and wretchedness, as if he were conveying the sheer impossibility of anything of worth gracing its murky streets. He may not actually have in mind such dire conditions but rather that this place did not feature in the prophetic programme that would usher in the Messiah to our world. Whatever his intention, the unlikelihood of finding 'him, of whom Moses . . . and the prophets, did write' in lowly Nazareth is clear from his words.

It is strange though, that God has on several occasions brought His Son to our attention from unlikely places:

Out of **Bethlehem** – Matt. 2. 6 – tells of His **Government**;
Out of **Egypt** – Matt. 2. 15 – tells of Him **Guarded**;
Out of **Nazareth** – John 1. 46 – tells of His **Growth**;
Out of the **Ivory Palaces** – Ps. 45. 8 – tells of His **Grace**;

Though no mention is made of this city in the Old Testament, the prophecy of His coming from Nazareth is sometimes linked with His appearance as the Branch, Zech. 3. 8, in the tender plant, and as the root out of the dry ground, Isa. 53. 2-3. How precious that we read concerning this special place, 'He came to Nazareth, where he had been brought up', Luke 4. 16. How much is contained in that short phrase!

The years of **Silent Seclusion** – no record save the desire to be about His Father's business, during which time no cause is given for accusation of any kind;

The years of **Sanctified Separation** – the true Nazarite who walked apart from all that would contaminate, while being in Himself incapable of sinning;

The years of **Supreme Satisfaction** – the tender plant growing up amid the wilderness of earth's weeds and thorns, of whom the Father speaks as He steps into public life, 'In whom I am well pleased', Mark 1. 11.

Peter testified how Jesus of Nazareth was anointed, appreciated, accompanied, announced and appointed, Acts 10. 38-39.

August 17th

John 2. 1-11

WOMAN, WHAT HAVE I TO DO WITH THEE?

These words at first reading seem almost a rebuff, or at best a refusal to become involved. How easy to have been offended at such an answer to a legitimate concern and yet this remarkable woman rises to what was certainly a challenge to faith. She recognizes that the patient thirty years of waiting and keeping 'sayings in her heart', Luke 2. 19, 51, are soon to end and the 'hour' of which He spoke is about to dawn. Though she is called 'the mother of Jesus' twice in the passage, yet she must learn that in His public ministry He enters now a new sphere where the all-consuming passion of 'my Father's business' becomes pre-eminent and her former relationship with Him is thus eclipsed. Her reaction to His words display a calm understanding of a greater work to be done, previewing, no doubt, a millennial scene linked with another sabbath, another wedding celebration, and a fuller display of His glory. May we, like Mary, recognize that His presence with us is ever an opportunity for Him to display His power. Mary is not rebuffed by His answer but responds instead with a significant charge to His disciples to obey His every word. How many of us would have gone off in a huff at an apparent snub and thus would have lost the vital communication to the servants.

How often an apparent reticence on the part of the Lord preceded a wonderful revelation of Himself:

'He was asleep on a pillow', Mark 4. 38;
'He would have passed them by', Mark 6. 48;
'He made as though he would have gone further',
Luke 24. 28.

Obedience to His word is the best recourse even when circumstances are not easily understood by us. When His word seems to cut across our ideas or plans we can be sure that the Lord has His own agenda.

Blind unbelief is sure to err,
And scan His work in vain;
God is His own interpreter,
And He will make it plain.

[WILLIAM COWPER]

August 18th

John 2. 12-22

WHAT SIGN SHEWEST THOU UNTO US, SEEING THAT THOU DOEST THESE THINGS?

This episode at the commencement of the Lord's ministry differs slightly from those recorded in the synoptic Gospels in both the accusation to the offenders in the temple and the answer to the Jews requiring a sign. It is interesting that it is only in John's gospel that He refers to 'my Father's house' as distinct from 'my house' in the others. Here, He also gives as an answer the reference to His own resurrection and not to John the Baptist's ministry. This is in keeping with His presentation as the Son in John, both in His claim of God as Father and in the ultimate sign of authority given to Him 'to execute judgment' as demonstrated in His resurrection. How strange that they should seek a further sign from one who had so recently performed the miracle at Cana and who had single-handedly cleansed of the temple. Their seeking of a sign was a further demonstration of the unbelief of a wicked generation, cf. Matt. 12. 39; 16. 4; Luke 11. 27. The absence of any sense of wrongdoing or anger towards those who had violated the temple is in keeping with their failure to appreciate the true character of Him who was the representation of God dwelling with men, John 1. 14. They could see no further than an earthly building, while in their midst was One who would take 'temple worship' to new heights, John 4. 24, and would one day be the central figure in a scene where there was no temple, Rev. 21. 22. His resurrection power would be that which established His own right to rule and would empower His disciples in their service for Him in His absence, Matt. 28. 1-19.

In their ultimate rejection of Him who could have effected the return of the glory lost to the temple? What was spoken of as 'my house' became merely 'your house, left desolate', Matt. 23. 38. At the beginning of His ministry, the emptying of the temple of all sacrificial livestock symbolized what would be effected at its close – the one sacrifice for sin for ever.

Faithful amidst unfaithfulness, midst darkness only light,
Thou didst Thy Father's name confess and in His will delight.

[James G. Deck]

August 19th

John 3. 1-17

HOW CAN A MAN BE BORN WHEN HE IS OLD?

Childbirth is one of the most amazing experiences and yet, unlike other landmarks in our history, the baby plays no active part. From the implanted seed and the conception, through the period of growth that followed, to the point of eventual delivery, it contributes nothing; life comes from God the Giver. There will, however, come a day when we will be held accountable for our actions in this life, the introduction to it was not of our own making. To this point, we are all in agreement, as was Nicodemus. It is interesting that the Lord should use the illustration of 'birth' to show us the principles through which a man is introduced into spiritual life, cp. 1 Pet. 1. 23. Natural birth gave us a fitness to enjoy life on earth with the capacity to breathe in earth's atmosphere, eat its food, speak its languages, hear its melodies, reach out and touch the wonders we can see and appreciate. This same amazing transformation takes place at the new birth. Like Nicodemus, we need to learn to look in and see our helplessness to effect such a change, for no matter if we could be born a number of times, which is impossible, this would link us only with flesh and earth. We need a divinely operated change to fit us for heaven, so that we can have a life that will enjoy God even presently and adjust to spiritual values. Hence, to be 'born again' is to be 'born from above'. Such a life is imparted, not by contact with religion, but by faith in Christ. The Old Testament story of an uplifted serpent, Numbers chapter 21, which speaks of a look that brought instant life and healing, is compared to an uplifted Saviour whose death on a cross has made available a greater healing, this time from the 'sting' of sin, and brings with it the guarantee of life eternal. Though it may not have been physically possible for all to have actually seen the serpent on the pole given their distance from it, yet every individual would have known exactly where it was situated so they could turn in faith to look and to claim the promise.

The serpent 'lifted up' could life and healing give,
So Jesus on the cross bids me to look and live.

[Arthur T. Pierson]

August 20th

John 4. 4-24

FROM WHENCE THEN HAST THOU THAT LIVING WATER?

With two thirds of the earth's surface covered by water and the human body consisting of 75 per cent of it, it is clear that water is one of the prime elements responsible for life on earth. Our drinking water today, far from being pure, contains some two hundred deadly commercial chemicals. Add to that bacteria, viruses and inorganic minerals and you have a chemical cocktail that could be positively dangerous. It is in such conditions that 'living water', speaking of spiritual blessings and the Spirit-filled life, should be of interest to us today, as to this woman of Samaria. Consider:

1. The Source of the living water

Not Jacob but Christ. He is the source of all that is eternal in quality. As with the new wine, ch. 2, and the new birth, ch. 3, so with the new water and the new worship, ch. 4. It is the great 'I AM' who is the supreme supplier, v. 26.

2. The Satisfaction of the living water

We live in a thirsty world seeking to quench that thirst in the pleasures of sin. This woman's lifestyle reflects a thirst for satisfaction, which to date she had not found, but she admits that and the offer of living water becomes appealing. Like Israel, many hew out broken cisterns that cannot hold water, Jer. 2. 13.

3. The Search for the living water

'Give me this water', is her plea for help. While perhaps failing to appreciate the full import of His teaching yet she is anxious, nonetheless, to have it. Not for the everlasting life it brings, as yet, but to end the fruitless, beaten path to earthly satisfaction. Nevertheless, it is the start on the road to blessing.

4. The Sharing of the living water

The drink becomes both a well and a spring, a reservoir and a refreshment, the benefits of which are soon shared – 'come see a man', v. 29, 'and many of the Samaritans . . . believed on him for the saying of the woman', v. 39. The leaving of her water-pot is emblematic of the new refreshment now carried within her. Now none but Christ can satisfy!

August 21st

John 5. 1-15

WILT THOU BE MADE WHOLE?

The man's future hangs in the balance as his answer is awaited. There has been nothing else before his mind for all of thirty-eight years and yet the challenge is fresh on this occasion. He has had to pass a number of milestones on the road to this point.

a. The Fact of his Own Shortcomings

His own inherent weakness has become more obvious with the passing years. His pathetic admission, 'Sir I have no man' strikes a chord in every heart that has longed for blessing, and in all who recognize their own helplessness to obtain salvation.

b. The Frustration at Others' Success

Add to that the frustration of seeing others receiving what he so desires, to the point of overtaking him on the way to the pool, and we have a man who could so easily have given up in despair. Many have tried so many times to be saved, watching others enjoy what they begin to feel will never be theirs to enjoy. Still he has waited refusing to abandon hope.

c. The Force needed to Overcome the Situation

'Rise, take up thy bed and walk' was not the expected prescription! Perhaps he expected (in our terms) an injection, a lotion, a tablet, a prayer, a restorative miracle upon the bed or even a lift to the pool – any one of which could open the door to possibility. Had he waited thirty-eight years for what seemed, though simple, an impossible demand?

d. The Faith required to Obey the Saviour

As in every case where blessing is to be found, here too there is an appeal for faith. In his case he would never feel the waters of the pool, never see an angel touch them nor experience a method of healing similar to others but he must seize the moment and respond believing that He who had spoken the word would give the necessary strength to perform it. Thus is salvation still obtainable. To any reader longing to find peace I ask, 'Wilt thou be made whole?' Is it the first priority in life and are you prepared to accept it on God's terms?

How simple God's way of salvation, not 'trying' or
'doing one's best'
But simply believing on Jesus, the weary and sinful find rest.

August 22nd

John 5. 21-47

HOW CAN YE BELIEVE WHICH RECEIVE HONOUR ONE OF ANOTHER?

Every blessing received from God is on the basis of humility and the acceptance of our true state. It is impossible to receive anything from Him when we are marked by pride and the love of honour or the approval of men. The passage is teaching that men can be the hindrance to their own blessing in their love of praise and position. Some examples of this are found in the Bible.

a. Balaam – He wished to die the death of the righteous yet ran greedily after the offer of Balak for reward, Num. 23. 10

b. Nebuchadnezzar – In his pride he boasted of the great Babylon that he had built until he learned that the Most High ruled in the kingdoms of men, Dan. 4. 25.

c. Saul – He had disobeyed and rejected the word of the Lord and had been in turn rejected by Him, yet he appeals to Samuel, 'Honour me now before the elders', 1 Sam. 15. 30. God had said 'them that honour ME I will honour', 1 Sam. 2. 30.

d. Herod – Though sympathetic to the case of John the Baptist, he was not prepared to lose face before the company and we read he could not 'for his oath's sake', Mark 6. 26.

e. Rich young ruler – who went away grieved, having great possessions when within sight of the blessing of eternal life, Mark 10. 22.

f. The Pharisees – They refused to confess Christ for they loved the praise of men more than the praise of God, John 12. 43.

g. Pilate must be one of the clearest illustrations of our text as when faced with the challenge that if he let this man go he would not be Caesar's friend, hands Him over to be crucified, Mark 15. 15.

It is not that these people could *not* have believed, but that in their search for place, and in their existing status, each effectively blocked the flow of blessing. It is rather like a child sitting upon a trunk and trying to open it, to no avail, since it is his own weight that is keeping it closed. The ability to open it is not in question, but he must climb down to do so.

August 23rd

John 6. 25-40

WHAT SHALL WE DO THAT WE MIGHT WORK THE WORKS OF GOD?

It has been well said that in the plans of man relating to God and eternity the prominent word is 'do', while in the plans of God, the emphasis is rather on the word 'done'. These people who had come from the other side to Capernaum, had misunderstood the Lord's words in relation to 'labouring for that meat that endureth', and perhaps genuinely sought what they could do. Many in their early contact with the Lord and with the apostles talked in this way, such as the rich young ruler, the Philippian jailer and others, asking. 'What must I do?' The answer then was, and still is, that the only response God requires is **faith**. This teaching is emphasized in the Epistle to the Ephesians where a man who was 'afar off' is 'made nigh' on the principles on which God has always operated – namely **grace** and **faith**, Eph. 2. 13. It was true in the days of Naaman the leper when the same difficulties and barriers to faith were seen, 2 Kgs. 5. Like him, today:

Many are **unacquainted** with the **provision**. They are ignorant that there is a work that has been done by Another that makes salvation available. Thank God for every 'little maid' such as was in Naaman's house to tell of One who can meet the need!

Others are **uncertain** about the **place**, even though they have heard of the possibility of blessing. They refuse to see the unique value of the 'place, which is called Calvary', judging the preaching of the cross to be foolishness.

Few admit to the **uncleanness** of the **plague** of sin, happy enough to have their need described in other terms but baulking at the reference to uncleanness. It seems to be this that caused Naaman's wrath. Such prohibits the possibility of our works participating in salvation, Isa. 64. 6.

Most feel the **unlikelihood** of the **prescription** as being too simple. Thus the servants of Naaman confront him, 'If the prophet had bid thee do some great thing, wouldest thou not have done it?' 2 Kgs. 5. 13. Working the works of God is essentially **believing God**.

August 24th

John 7. 25-44

WHEN CHRIST COMETH, WILL HE DO MORE MIRACLES THAN THESE WHICH THIS MAN HATH DONE?

a. The Incomparable Person

The chapter is full of mixed reactions as regards the Lord's Person and His claims. It is clear that His own brethren in the flesh did not appreciate Him, John 7. 5, while in others there was a conflict of opinion as regards the validity of His claims, v. 12. Some had doubts about His city of origin, while at times open antagonism was declared by His hearers, v. 44. Indeed, verse 43 seems to sum up our chapter as we read, 'There was a division among the people because of Him'. To all those who saw Him through the eye of faith there was, however, something unique in the Man before them and even some opponents were forced to acknowledge, 'Never man spake like this man', v. 46.

b. The Indisputable Proof

Not only was He distinct in His words but also in His works. Those who did believe in Him testified to His power. This had been witnessed not only by the meeting of individual needs as in Nicodemus and the woman of Samaria, John chapters 3 and 4, but also in the case of a man in his helplessness and of the multitude in their hunger, chapters 5 and 6

c. The Indescribable Provision

The full provision for need chapter 7 verse 45, extends beyond the boundary either of personal or local needs and expands to an international capacity when we read those precious words, 'if any man . . .' To feed and satisfy a hungry and thirsty world is the full programme of His purpose.

d. The Inescapable Promise

'Where I am ye cannot come'. How sad then are the words of chapter 7 verse 34, set against the background of such a full provision and such wondrous grace! That His blessing can, and will, be missed by some is a sobering thought. We have the same unbreakable promises, each with their own certainties – 'He that believeth' and 'He that believeth not', John 3. 36. The alternative to Unquestioning Faith is Unquenchable Fire.

August 25th

John 8. 1-11

WOMAN, WHERE ARE THOSE THINE ACCUSERS?

The way in which the woman's accusers withdrew seems to indicate an awareness of their guilt though no condemning word is actually spoken by the Lord. The mystery as to what was actually written has given rise to much speculation with no definite answer possible. It is interesting to note that each time a divine hand is seen to write on earth, the words were not always appreciated, but the exercise was effective.

1. Exod. 31. 18 Finger of Communication

And he gave unto Moses, when he had made an end of communing with him upon Mount Sinai, two tables of testimony, tables of stone, written with the *finger* of God'. One wonders, did the act in John 8 conjure up in their mind any picture of the giving of the law as he wrote on the 'pavement' of the temple. He is not siding with them, or with the woman, or even with Moses, but lets the force of the word speak for itself.

2. Dan 5. 5 Finger of Condemnation

'In the same hour came forth *fingers* of a man's hand, and wrote over against the candlestick upon the plaister of the wall of the king's palace: and the king saw the part of the hand that wrote'. Again God's standards would be impressed upon a man with serious consequences. The message told of:

a. a divine Announcement
b. a divine Assessment
c. a divine Appointment

3. John 8. 6 Finger of Conviction

'This they said, tempting him, that they might have to accuse him. But Jesus stooped down, and with his *finger* wrote on the ground, as though he heard them not'. In each case the stark contrast between the darkness of the people and the holiness of the light of God's presence is evident. John in his writings has a great deal to say on this subject and the Lord follows immediately after this passage into His teaching about the Light of the world.

August 26th

John 8. 31- 41

HOW SAYEST THOU, YE SHALL BE MADE FREE?

The words of the Lord Jesus are indeed precious, 'The truth shall make you free'. It is interesting to note that the Lord in His public ministry neither condoned nor condemned slavery as a practice. He did, however, concede that it existed and used it as an illustration of the kind of service he expected from His own. The freedom envisaged brought about a number of things:

Deliverance. Salvation brings an end to the tyranny in which sin held us, and our enslavement to the devil. The hymn says, 'the bonds of sin are broken and I am free'. We sometimes limit the thought of our freedom to this aspect but the truth is that the 'service' into which we are thus brought is a 'bond service', that of a slave in fact! A slave was not only freed but he was bought, and as such was expected to show a new

Devotion to his master. His every interest was sacrificed and he had now no rights of his own. His interests were completely in harmony with those of the One who had bought him. So it ought to be with us. Paul and others of the apostles could speak of themselves as the 'bondservants' of Jesus Christ. Paul could say that to him, to live was Christ and to die was gain. Furthermore, the slave would be in complete and utter

Dependence upon his master for his every need. His welfare was in the master's hand and for his protection and provision he counted on him. All could be safely left in the master's hands. It is interesting that the Lord addresses his disciples with these words concerning freedom, contrasting the service of sin in which they once were held with the willing slavery of the new relationship.

R. C. CHAPMAN of Barnstaple once said, 'To be a slave of men is the most horrendous of all things, but to be a slave of Jesus Christ, is heaven begun on earth'.

Though I am free, I am not my own.
Jesus my soul to Himself hath won
Mine now to serve Him, and Him alone
Glory to His Name!

August 27th

John 8. 42- 59

WHICH OF YOU CONVINCETH ME OF SIN?

We live in a world that has relegated the position of the Person of Christ to that of a mere man, or at best in their films – a superstar. We, as Christians, deplore the profanity of these suggestions into which creep the insinuations that as man, He knew the carnal passions of fallen humanity. If He is to be our Saviour, and this was the great purpose of His coming, He must be the sinless One who could bear away the sin of the world. His perfections extend not only to His not having sinned, but further to the *impossibility* of such ever taking place, being as He was, the eternal Son of the eternal God. In His life as at the time of His death there are voices raised to attest to His perfections.

a. The Father declares Him to be the one in whom He is well pleased, Matt. 3. 17; Mark 1. 11.
b. The writers of the Bible say that He was holy (in Him is no sin), harmless (He did no sin), undefiled (He knew no sin), and in His every movement, separate from sinners, Heb. 7. 26; 2 Cor. 5. 21; 1 Pet. 2. 22; 1 John 3. 5.
c. The devil was forced to abandon every attempt to sully His character, 'The prince of this world cometh and hath nothing in me', John 14. 30.
d. The absence of any concrete witness to the accusations made against Him at His trial led Pilate to say, 'I find in him no fault at all', John 18. 38

The temptation in the wilderness was enacted not to see if He would sin or not, but to show that He was incapable of sinning. We stand firm on the solid ground of His impeccability. He is the Lamb, without blemish and without spot, both untainted and untaintable. As such, and only as such, is He the perfect Substitute for the sinner.

Without a trace of Adam's sin,
A man unique in origin.
All fair without, all pure within,
Our glorious Lord.

[ISAAC EWAN]

August 28th

John 9. 1- 12

MASTER, WHO DID SIN, THIS MAN, OR HIS PARENTS,THAT HE WAS BORN BLIND?

The Lord's claims in John's Gospel are often accompanied by signs that show the validity of such. It is the occasion of the hungry multitude in chapter 6 that leads up to His being presented as the Bread of Life. Similarly, in chapter 11, the crisis at Bethany comes just before His teaching concerning Himself as the Resurrection and the Life. In this chapter it is significant that He brings light to a darkened life just after His being seen as the Light of the world. While men can rightly trace every heartache, pain and sorrow to the entry of sin into the world, the Lord is quick to disassociate such speculation here. The case is but a further opportunity for Him to display His glory and power in circumstances of great need. Note:

a. The Impossible case . . . Blind from his Birth
b. The Improbable Cure . . . Clay on his eyes
c. The Imperative Command . . . Go and wash
d. The Impressive Change . . . Came seeing
e. The Impregnable Claim . . . One thing I know

The chapter is also of interest to all who serve Him still as we witness not only the **manifestation** of His power but the **material** He is pleased to use. It is truly wonderful what the Lord can do with clay! We are reminded that He has put the treasure of the gospel in the earthen vessel that the excellency of the power may be of God, and not of us, 2 Cor. 4. 7. That He should be pleased to use clay in the exhibition of His power to save, will ever be a mystery to us. We learn the lesson of the humility of the product and the importance of the Hand that has the anointing power. Had another hand mixed and made the clay it is certain no blessing would have accrued, just as no other hand could have effected the change to the loaves and fishes in chapter 6.

Channels only, blessed Master,
But with all Thy wondrous power,
Flowing through us, Thou canst use us
Every day and every hour.

[Mary E. Maxwell]

August 29th

John 11. 17-44

BELIEVEST THOU THIS?

We are about to witness one of the greatest miracles which the Lord performed during the years of His public ministry. Prior to its enactment He is giving teaching both in relation to the physical impartation of life by His power and also spiritual life. We have already seen this duality of purpose in John chapter 5 verses 25 and 28. In that chapter the criterion for blessing is also seen as faith, as in 'he that heareth my word and believeth'. Here, too, Martha's answer rings out, 'I believe'.

Note the three cases of resurrection in the Gospels each with its own lesson and indication of the Lord's power:

1. Jairus' daughter, Luke 8. The case is of a child at home. Most of us have, or have had them. Sheltered and protected, yet not immune to the ravages of disease and indeed the effects of sin. We recognize that only the power of Christ can bring life. No amount of privilege or prayer in itself can bring the spiritual life we so desire for our children. We long that they meet Him while they are young. He is able to save!

2. Widow of Nain's son, Luke 7. The home sphere is past. The tender treatment is gone. She witnesses her only son borne along by others to the great sepulchre of the world. With breaking heart she must have longed for the days at home to have been lengthened but such is not to be. Many a parent reading this may identify with her despair. Can the youth still be rescued, though out of our reach? The same hand that grasps the child is outstretched to the young man. We long to see the procession stopped that bears our young ones away. He is able!

3. Lazarus, John 11. 'By this time he stinketh' is the sorry tale. He is so long dead as to seem a hopeless case. If only Christ had met him when he was at home or even on the way to the tomb but now the worst is to be faced. Is all hope gone? No indeed, for we see the God of the impossible at work. He calls: the dead lives! Pray on, dear friend, for He who imparts life can do it at any stage of the journey. He is able still!

Sing it softly through the gloom, when the heart for mercy craves; Sing in triumph o'er the tomb, Jesus saves! Jesus saves!

[Priscilla J. Owens]

August 30th

John 12. 1-8

WHY WAS NOT THIS OINTMENT SOLD FOR THREE HUNDRED PENCE, AND GIVEN TO THE POOR?

Economic issues play a great part in the decision making of our times. The world's economy has been plunged into chaos largely through greed and corruption on the part of those who manage our finances. The stock markets fall and the once apparently solid pillars of financial institutions crumble to dust. Mistakes were also made in Bible times on the ground of economic considerations with potentially devastating outcomes.

1 Sam. 15. 14-22. There was a day when Saul would spare that which God had destined for destruction claiming economic grounds but He had to hear the words of the prophet in verse 22, 'Hath the Lord as great delight in burnt offerings as in obeying the voice of the Lord? Behold to obey is better than sacrifice'. At times we too, to justify our disobedience, claim that we are doing something big for God. There was logic in Saul's theory, but not obedience. This should be pre-eminent in our path of service. Unscriptural practices and methods can never be justified. Better by far to simply obey His word!

John 12. 1-8. On the other hand we have the case of a man who would deprive God of His portion on the altar, on the grounds of economy. Judas saw as a 'waste' that which would be spent on the Lord. So, while Saul put **on** the altar that which God did not appreciate, Judas would have kept **off** the altar what was precious to Him. It is interesting that both men did it in view of economic considerations.

Our estimate of values needs to be brought into accord with the currency of heaven. We often find in travelling around the world that currency values can be different. Rates of exchange in currency vary and we are encouraged to 'shop around'. Heaven, by contrast, knows only one set of values and that entails obedience to God's word. This 'market' will never fall. No devaluation on earth ever threatens it, for it is monitored by One who as in days of old sits 'over against the treasury, Mark 12. 41. Mary seized the opportunity to do something that day which was denied to others who had waited until His burial. How vital to embrace present opportunities to honour Him!

August 31st

John 12. 20-23

NOW IS MY SOUL TROUBLED; AND WHAT SHALL I SAY?

The world's greatest hour is shortly about to dawn, that hour toward which every clock marking earthly time has relentlessly marched. Trouble has marked some of its dark hours throughout its history but never has such a shadow fallen upon its page as on this occasion. The cross, drawing near, weighs heavy upon His mind and heart, and doubtless the recent visit to a tomb, served to remind Him of a day to come in His own life.

With unswerving devotion He follows the pathway determined by the Father, whose voice from heaven answers His call with a reassurance of glory still to come. The words of this chapter preview Gethsemane with its sore amazement and heaviness. We are reminded of a night that was cold enough for men to need a fire to warm at, yet upon the ground a man sweats, 'as it were great drops of blood falling down to the ground'. The loneliness of the cross is anticipated, foretold in some measure by the experience of another faithful servant, Uriah the Hittite, in the days of David. A man goes out to die for another's sin carrying his own death warrant, coldly penned by the hand of a king from whom we would have expected better things. Picture him in the battle's heat, in the place where valiant men are, and watch as he turns around in the hour of his deepest need, in which he expects full support from those who share the struggle. Imagine then his horror as he finds himself alone, for another has decreed, 'Retire ye from him that he may be smitten and die'. His is the experience of the psalmist, 'I looked for some to take pity and there was none and for comforters and found none', Ps. 69. 20. Uriah has invested in a kingdom, the full glory of which he may never see, but all is not to be forgotten. We see another pen lifted and the name of one so cruelly maltreated, adorns the page of recognized greatness and forms perhaps the apex of the roll of honour as the final name of David's mighty men.

In like manner, He whose soul was troubled shall yet 'see of the travail of his soul and shall be satisfied', Isa. 53. 11 . . . 'That at the name of Jesus, every knee should bow', Phil. 2. 9.

September 1st

John 14. 1-14

HOW CAN WE KNOW THE WAY?

The discourse between the Lord and His disciples continues here whilst they are still in the upper room. They were troubled no doubt by His words, 'Where I am going, you cannot come', John 13. 33 NKJV. Peter asks the question, 'Lord, where are you going?' Not only Peter but all of them were no doubt deeply upset that He had said He would be leaving them.

So the Lord comforts them, 'Let not your heart be troubled: ye believe in God, believe also in me', 14. 1. As they believed in the invisible God, so they must now believe in Him, even as He too, would soon become invisible. He continues to comfort them by telling them that He is to go and prepare a place for them in the Father's house and that He will come again to take them there to be with Him. He further pronounces, 'You know the way to where I am going', see v. 4.

Thomas is confused and maybe thought the Lord was talking of some journey on earth, 'Lord, we know not whither thou goest; and how can we know the way?', v. 5. Jesus answers with one of His seven great 'I Am' statements, 'I am the way, the truth and the life', v. 6. The Lord confirms that there is no other way of access to heaven and the Father, 'No man cometh unto the Father, but by me', v. 6b; it is by faith in Christ alone that entrance into heaven can be gained. There is certainly no access by way of so-called good works, for all mankind has failed because of sin, 'Therefore by the deeds of the law shall no flesh be justified in his (God's) sight: for by the law is the knowledge of sin', Rom. 3. 20.

The Lord will not merely show them the way but He is **the Way**. There is perhaps an echo here of chapter 10 verse 11, 'I am the door'; access through the Door and the ensuing Way was facilitated only by His going to the cross and enduring unutterable sufferings for our sin. He is **the Truth** – every moral beauty dwells in Him and each in fullest manifestation. He is **the Life** – life in abundance for those who will trust in Him, not just for physical life on earth, but for eternity in heaven.

Thomas' question had been answered, **the way** is now manifestly clear to all who will sincerely accept Christ.

September 2nd

John 14. 15-24

HOW IS IT THAT THOU WILT MANIFEST THYSELF?

Judas, not Iscariot, asks, 'Lord, how is it that thou wilt manifest thyself unto us, and not unto the world?', John 14. 22.

This question was asked by Judas because of what the Lord had said, 'Yet a little while, and the world seeth me no more; but ye see me: because I live, ye shall live also', v. 19. Judas may well have been thinking of the Lord manifesting Himself at the setting up of His kingdom. This was common thinking amongst the disciples; right up to the cross they assumed He, as Messiah, would take up His kingdom and throw off the Roman yoke from Israel. They could not understand that He was on His way to betrayal and the cross. 'For he taught his disciples, and said unto them, The Son of man is delivered into the hands of men, and they shall kill him; and after that he is killed, he shall rise the third day. But they understood not that saying, and were afraid to ask him', Mark 9. 31-32. Bearing in mind this expectation, Judas may well have asked this question because he anticipated the Lord would, on the setting up of His kingdom, reveal Himself in glory to the whole world and not just His followers. The Lord indicates 'a little while', and shortly it did indeed come to pass for having gone by way of the cross He then rose again. It was after that 'little while' that He manifested Himself to them secretly on numerous occasions during the forty days prior to His ascension. The world at large did not get even one glimpse of Him!

Later still, He would continue manifesting Himself to the early believers by the Spirit and so with us today. What a joy it is to be the subjects of His fellowship and abiding presence as He promised, 'If a man love me, he will keep my words: and my Father will love him, and we will come unto him, and make our abode with him', John 14. 23!

His manifesting Himself to us is, as this verse confirms, conditional. We will know nothing of His presence and revelation unless we love Him and that love is worked out practically in obedience to His word. But what a privilege is ours, far beyond anything this world has to offer! The Lord Himself, manifesting Himself personally to every believer.

September 3rd

John 18. 28-40

WHAT ACCUSATION BRING YE?

Try as they might, the chief priests and elders could not find any witnesses against the Lord, even though they sought for those who would give a lying testimony. When two came forward there was still disagreement between them, Mark 14. 59.

Having trumped up the charge of blasphemy, the Jewish leaders delivered Him to Pilate who threw out the challenge, 'What accusation bring ye against this man?', John 18. 29. The charge of blasphemy would not stand under Roman law and so they modified their accusation, 'Whosoever maketh himself a king speaketh against Caesar', 19. 13. Their sheer hypocrisy was accentuated by their refraining from ceremonial defilement in refusing to enter Pilate's judgement hall, 18. 28, even though in their hearts they were intent on murder; utter darkness!

But what accusation could ever be brought against the blessed Lord? Of His enemies Judas confessed, 'I have betrayed the innocent blood', Matt. 27. 4. Pilate said three times, 'I find no fault', John 18. 38; 19. 4, 6. Even Herod came to the same conclusion, Luke 23. 15. The thief on the cross said, 'This man hath done nothing amiss', v. 41. Pilate's wife sent a warning to her husband, 'Have thou nothing to do with that just man: for I have suffered many things this day in a dream because of him', Matt. 27. 19.

Later the disciples would confirm the absolute sinlessness and impeccability of Christ. Peter, the man of action, wrote, 'Who did no sin', 1 Pet. 2. 22. Paul who was knowledgeable wrote, 'Who knew no sin', 2 Cor. 5. 21 and John who was so closely acquainted with Him, wrote, 'In Him is no sin', 1 John 3. 5. When addressing the Jews He challenges them 'Which of you convinceth me of sin?' John 8. 46. No doubt many who were unfavourably disposed towards Him were constantly watching to see if He erred in any way. None of them could recall one single instance of failure or weakness.

Surpassing all of this testimony was that of the Father's whose voice was heard from heaven on two occasions, 'This is my beloved son, in whom I am well pleased', Matt. 3. 27; 17. 5.

Not only did Christ not sin, He could not sin.

September 4th

John 21. 15-19

LOVEST THOU ME?

This question was asked of Peter on the occasion of the Lord's third appearance to the disciples as a group, John 21. 14. This time there were seven of them. Peter had already met the Lord privately, Luke 24. 34, and had been restored, but here the Lord gives him the opportunity to confess his love publicly.

Three times Peter had denied the Lord and it is significant that the Lord asks him three times, 'Lovest thou me?'. On the first and second occasions the Greek word *'agapao'* is used which means love embracing the deliberate assent of the will as a matter of principle and duty, whereas the third time the word *'phileo'* is used, which means to be a friend, to fondly love – to have affection as a matter of sentiment or emotion. The former word is used chiefly of the head and the latter of the heart. Peter answered twice, 'Thou knowest that I love (*phileo*) thee', and so the third time the Lord uses Peter's word. Normally the word *agapao* would be stronger as it is used for God's love towards us, however in this context, it would appear that *phileo* is the stronger word. The Lord with the third question is really saying to Peter, 'Do you *really* fondly love (*phileo*) Me?'

Peter, along with all the others, now surely did love the Lord with all his heart and would have made any sacrifice however large. Subsequently, he would lay down his life, as did most of the others. Though John was not martyred there is no doubt he would have been prepared to be.

All of this is a tremendous challenge to us today. The same question rings in our ears, 'Do you really love Me?'. The test of true love for Him is obedience to His word, 'If ye love me, keep my commandments', 14. 15. We must not be as some so-called 'Menu-picking Christians' i.e. picking out from God's word that which happens to please us and neglecting the rest because it does not suit us. Nor must we be 'spectator Christians', i.e. those who turn up when it pleases us, but do not wish to be closely involved and contribute in the local church, lest we have to become committed. May the Lord preserve us from spiritual lethargy and may we with Peter whole-heartedly say, 'Yea, Lord; thou knowest that I love thee'.

September 5th

John 21. 20-23

WHAT SHALL THIS MAN DO?

The Lord confirms to Peter that he would be martyred, but not until he is old, John 21. 18. When Peter was taken by Herod, no doubt he was assured that as he was still a young man, the Lord would keep him from the evil intent of the king and therefore he was able to sleep peacefully through the night, Acts 12. 6.

Peter may have thought his service was over after his denials. He probably thought that the Lord was finished with him forever. If we should fail the Lord in some way and feel that our days of serving Him are over forever, remember that He is the great Restorer! He restored Moses after he misguidedly killed a man. He used David after he had committed the serious sins of adultery and murder by proxy, and now he will use Peter who had vehemently denied Him three times. So the Lord tells him what the future holds for himself and that even though he had failed so recently, he would be given courage to bring glory and honour to Christ to the very last.

Having received this insight from the Lord into his future, Peter then wonders what will happen to John, 'Lord, and what shall this man do?' John 21. 21. What, he thought, would the future hold for John who had not denied the Lord? The Lord answers by telling Peter that He alone is the One who has every saint in His hands, and indeed the end of all men, and that he should not be so concerned with John's service and circumstances, but should undistractedly continue in following the Lord, v. 22.

From the Lord's answer we learn, firstly, that our main business is to follow the Lord. Secondly, Jesus will take care of all His true disciples, and that we should trust the Lord who will only ever deal with them for their very best and for His own honour and glory. Thirdly, we should go forward to whatever and wherever He calls us, whether it be a long life, persecution or to be cut off by a martyr's death, not envying the lot of any other man, and desiring only to do the will of God.

It is a great comfort to know that we as His believing children are in His hands. It is His will that determines what is best for us, v. 22, to His own glory.

September 6th

Acts 1. 1-11

LORD, WILT THOU AT THIS TIME RESTORE AGAIN THE KINGDOM TO ISRAEL?

The disciples were gathered together with the Lord at Jerusalem, Acts 1. 4, shortly before His ascension. They seem still to cherish the expectation that He as Messiah will shortly take up His reign over Israel and through the nation rule the whole earth as promised in Daniel chapter 7 verse 27, 'And the kingdom and dominion . . . shall be given to the people of the saints of the most High, whose kingdom is an everlasting kingdom, and all dominions shall serve and obey him'.

They had had expectations all the way through His earthly public ministry that He would relieve them of the Roman yoke and set up His kingdom, and this in spite of His numerous efforts to explain the true nature of that kingdom. This expectation was almost destroyed by His death on the cross, but now He had risen, they supposed that He could easily carry through all His purposes and take up His kingdom. The disciples had perhaps been thinking about His promise of the Holy Spirit. They may have remembered that the prophet Joel spoke of the outpouring of the Spirit in connection with the Messiah's glorious reign, Joel 2. 28, 'And it shall come to pass afterward, that I will pour out my spirit upon all flesh', and shortly following the Spirit's outpouring there would also follow a fulfilment of verse 32 of that same chapter, 'For in mount Zion and in Jerusalem shall be deliverance, as the Lord hath said, and in the remnant whom the Lord shall call'.

The Lord did not reprove them for expecting His literal reign on earth, for this hope was and is justified by the scriptures. However, He informs them they could not know the timing as to when His kingdom would be set up. The date has been fixed by the Father's sole prerogative, and He has chosen not to reveal it. It is information that belongs exclusively to Himself.

So the Lord directs their attention to what was more immediate and important, the nature and sphere of their service for Him. They were to be witnesses throughout the world, starting at Jerusalem, then in all Judea and Samaria, and finally to the ends of the earth, Acts 1. 8.

September 7th

Acts 2. 1-12; 1 Cor. 14. 22-28

HOW HEAR WE EVERY MAN IN OUR OWN TONGUE?

The disciples being 'filled with the Holy Ghost, began to speak with other tongues, as the Spirit gave them utterance', Acts 2. 4. From the ensuing verses, it is clear they were miraculously given power to speak foreign languages, which they had never learned.

It was not the gibberish or self-induced ecstatic utterances of modern times, but other definite languages, then spoken by visitors to Jerusalem from foreign parts, vv. 9-11. This was the first instance of the gift of tongues and was one of the signs which God used to bear witness to the truth of the message which the apostles preached. Other occurrences of the gift of tongues in Acts are at the conversion of the Gentiles in the house of Cornelius, 10. 46, and at the re-baptism of John's disciples in Ephesus, 19. 6.

The scriptures had not yet been completed, the New Testament not yet having been written, but now that the complete word of God is available, the need for the sign gifts has passed. The gift of tongues on the Day of Pentecost should not be used to substantiate that the gift is invariably the accompaniment of the gift of the Spirit, for if that were the case, why is there no mention of tongues in connection with the conversion of the 3,000, 2. 41, the conversion of the 5,000, 4. 4, and the reception of the Holy Spirit by the Samaritans, 8. 17?

When writing to Corinth the apostle Paul reproaches the assembly for misusing this gift in their gatherings, the gift still being extant at the time. To correct this he lays down some conditions for its use: there must be only two or three by course, not all at the same time, 1 Cor. 14. 27; there should be an interpreter (confirming again that real languages were being spoken), v. 27; the gift is a sign to unbelievers and therefore only to be used if non-believers are present, vv. 21-22.

On the Day of Pentecost the Jews among the audience were given a clear sign that if they did not repent and trust Christ as Saviour, judgement would befall them as in the captivity of Babylon, 'With men of other tongues and other lips will I speak unto this people, v. 21; cp. Isa. 28. 11.

September 8th

Acts 2. 22-41

MEN AND BRETHREN, WHAT SHALL WE DO?

Those who heard Peter's first sermon were 'pricked in their heart', Acts 2. 37. The word 'pricked' means to be 'pierced through'. What they heard that day caused them to be deeply troubled in their hearts, which is what conviction by the Holy Spirit is all about.

They were convinced by the fact that God had kept His word, vv. 14-21, and convinced too by God's work, vv. 22-36. Even as Peter preached Christ and Him crucified, people all over Jerusalem were talking of the One who had risen from the dead! After all, there were over 500 who had seen Him after His resurrection, 1 Cor. 15. 6. Now these followers of Jesus were filled with the Spirit and telling the multitudes that He had indeed risen from the dead.

The Day of Pentecost was exactly fifty days from the day Jesus rose from the dead and only ten days from His ascension back into heaven. Peter finally brings home the fact to the Jews that the blame for the death of Christ, their Messiah, rested squarely upon their shoulders, v. 36, and so they became convicted of their guilt. True conviction is a necessary precursor to salvation. God brings people under conviction so that they might be aware of their utter sinfulness before Him, 'And when he (the Holy Spirit) is come, he will reprove the world of sin, and of righteousness, and of judgment', John 16. 8. No one can ever be saved, until God opens their eyes to what they are.

Like the Philippian jailor the Lord must bring us to the place where we cry out, 'What must I do to be saved?', Acts 16. 31. The day a person becomes convicted of sin can be the day their life begins to change for the better; the day they take the first steps toward Christ and His salvation.

When the word of God comes to us in our sins and brings conviction, it will hurt deeply, 'For the word of God is quick, and powerful, and sharper than any twoedged sword, piercing even to the dividing asunder of soul and spirit, and of the joints and marrow, and is a discerner of the thoughts and intents of the heart', Heb. 4. 12. After conviction should come repentance towards God and faith in the Lord Jesus, Acts 20. 21.

September 9th

Acts 3. 11-26

YE MEN OF ISRAEL, WHY MARVEL YE AT THIS?

When Peter saw the people running into the porch and wondering at the miracle, he asks them a question 'Ye men of Israel, why marvel ye at this? or why look ye so earnestly on us, as though by our own power or holiness we had made this man to walk?', Acts 3. 12.

The people were looking on Peter and John as if they had performed the miracle of the healing of the lame man by their own power, but Peter is quick to divert their attention away from themselves to the Lord; something that every servant of Christ should be quick and very ready to do, for any spiritual gift that we have is totally of Him, *'Every virtue we possess, and every victory won, and every thought of holiness, are His and His alone'*. Peter and John now knew and were working out practically the truth of that which the Lord had told them, 'The branch cannot bear fruit of itself, except it abide in the vine; no more can ye, except ye abide in me . . . without me ye can do nothing', John 15. 4, 5. But the Jews should have understood what had happened. They were surely acquainted with miracles, to know where they came from, and they ought not therefore, to have ascribed them to men, but rather to enquire why the Lord was working in this new way.

Having in humility disclaimed any honour that might have been directed towards himself and John, Peter then quickly brings them to the true Author of the miracle. This was the whole point of the miracles in the early days of the New Testament. To show the people that God was introducing a new thing and, from the prepared ground of their amazed hearts, Peter now preaches the Christ: the One whom they had rejected and had crucified, God had raised from the dead and had now glorified Him in heaven.

Now, says Peter, through faith in Him, this man has been cured and through faith in Christ salvation is available to all who will repent and trust Him as Saviour, 'Repent ye therefore, and be converted, that your sins may be blotted out', Acts 3. 19. This was an appeal to the nation of Israel at that time, but it applies equally to individuals today.

September 10th

Acts 5. 1-11

WHY . . . LIE TO THE HOLY GHOST?

Great blessing had been poured out upon the early church and many had been saved and added to it, but wherever the Lord is working the enemy is busy as well. It was so in the day when Christ walked on earth and now Satan seeks to curb the work of His followers.

In subtlety, Satan seeks to smash the sanctity of the early church through the love of money and the deceitfulness of hypocrisy. In the case of the rich young man faced with giving up his possessions for Christ, at least he was marked by honesty, Matt. 19. 22. But now Ananias and Sapphira seek to deceive the apostles. However, they had left the Lord out of the equation and Peter, being divinely informed of the deception, pronounces judgement upon them. It was important that the sanctity of the church, God's new creation, should be preserved and so judgement was immediate and severe.

It would have been absolutely above board if they had kept back part of the price and been honest about it, but they lied and said that part of the proceeds was the whole. This was play-acting – seeking to appear better and more sacrificial than was the case. The Lord Jesus above all others condemned the Pharisees for hypocrisy or acting out a part, which was false in the eyes of God. He could see through them and in condemnation describes them as 'whited sepulchres', i.e. on the outside seemingly respectable but inside 'full of dead men's bones and of all uncleanness', Matt. 23. 27.

All of this is a salutary lesson to us as believers that we cannot deceive the Lord. We must live in transparent honesty before Him, ensuring that there is no unconfessed sin within. We do well to remember that 'neither is there any creature that is not manifest in his sight: but all things are naked and opened unto the eyes of him with whom we have to do', Heb. 4. 13.

Ananias and Sapphira sought to deceive the apostles but their sin was more deeply described by Peter as 'lying to the Holy Ghost', Acts 5. 3. The Lord sees our motives; may our prayer be as David's, 'Search me, O God, and know my heart: try me, and know my thoughts', Ps. 139. 23.

September 11th

Acts 8. 26-35; Romans 10. 14

UNDERSTANDEST THOU WHAT THOU READEST?

It is wonderful how the Lord can directly overrule to cause people's paths to cross; in this case directing that Philip should go down to Gaza to meet the Ethiopian. Philip might well have wondered what on earth the Lord intended, for he was conducting a successful campaign in Samaria; why should he go down to a seemingly empty desert place? But God was ahead of him and knew well the seeking heart of the Ethiopian.

All of this reminds us that the Lord not only prepares His children, but also He works in the hearts of all who truly seek Him. The pertinent question is, are we willing as Philip was to obey His voice? Sadly, too often we let opportunities slip from our grasp. Peter exhorts us, 'But sanctify the Lord God in your hearts: and be ready always to give an answer to every man that asketh you a reason of the hope that is in you with meekness and fear', 1 Pet. 3. 15. Philip was in the right place spiritually, for he was busy in the Lord's work, the Lord could trust him, he was close enough to the Lord to hear His voice and discern His will, and finally he was quick to obey, Acts 8. 30.

But how will anyone ever understand the Bible? Those who have not yet believed and have not the indwelling Spirit cannot discern or even begin to understand for 'the natural man receiveth not the things of the Spirit of God: for they are foolishness unto him: neither can he know them, because they are spiritually discerned', 1 Cor. 2. 14. Many times we have come across people who have read their Bible, even become familiar with the words of scripture, but have not come to a true understanding of God's way of salvation. Unless a person takes the vital steps of 'repentance toward God, and faith toward our Lord Jesus Christ', Acts 20. 21, they are without the Spirit of God and cannot truly understand. So, today, many trust in their own good works to earn favour before God, but the Bible says, 'By the deeds of the law there shall no flesh be justified in his sight', Rom. 3. 20.

Philip joins the eunuch and finds him reading Isaiah chapter 53 aloud! He helps him to understand, preaches the gospel of Christ to him, the Ethiopian believes and is saved, Acts 8. 37.

September 12th

Acts 8. 36-40; Matthew 28. 18-20

WHAT DOTH HINDER ME TO BE BAPTIZED?

The Lord commanded that after a person becomes a Christian they should obey two simple ordinances. The first is baptism; this serves in figure to identify the believer with the Lord's own death – going down into the water; burial – under the water; and resurrection – rising up out of the water. By these the believer publicly confesses identification with the Lord in all three respects. The second command was that we remember Him in the breaking of bread regularly, as was the apostles' practice, on the first day of the week.

The Ethiopian upon believing asks the question, 'See, here is water; what doth hinder me to be baptized?' Acts 8. 36. Philip having been deceived by Simon in Samaria, vv. 13-23, makes it clear to him, that he must first truly believe and accept Christ as the Son of God. The Ethiopian assures him that he has trusted in the Lord, upon which confession Philip baptizes him, v. 37.

In the early church believers were baptized at the outset of their Christian experience, for in that day, to make a profession and be publicly identified with Christ in baptism, would probably have meant opposition and persecution. Only those who were sincerely saved would therefore want to go through with such a thing and generally there was no need to wait to see if the profession of a person was genuine. Today, however, in many countries, particularly in the Western world, it is a day of easy profession and elders may need to wait a while to see if a person has been changed by the indwelling presence of the Spirit of Christ, 2 Cor. 5. 17.

But what of hindrances to baptism? Surely there are some who upon being saved, unnecessarily delay being baptized? Is it maybe because they do not want to become too committed? This is lack of obedience to the Lord and will result in stunted spiritual progress, Heb. 5. 12.

The only thing that might have hindered the Ethiopian was lack of water, but in his case the Lord provided, 'They came unto a certain water: and the eunuch said, See, here is water; what doth hinder me to be baptized?' v. 36. Clearly, baptism as taught in the Bible was by full immersion, vv. 38-39.

September 13th

Acts 9. 1-9

LORD, WHAT WILT THOU HAVE ME TO DO?

Of all the responses that a believer might make to the Lord to please Him, this must surely rank first! It shows a subdued humbled spirit. A few moments previously Saul had been following the dictates of his own will, under the commission and authority of the Jewish Sanhedrin, but now he will renounce all and under authority of the risen Christ will seek only His will.

Paul was a model Christian because:

1. He was baptized as soon as he possibly could be, Acts 9. 18. Is there a reason why you have not obeyed the Lord's command to be baptized? 'Go ye therefore, and teach all nations, baptizing them in the name of the Father, and of the Son, and of the Holy Ghost', Matt. 28. 19. If there is undue delay does this not amount to disobedience to His direct command?
2. He had full and regular fellowship with other Christians, Acts 9. 19, 28. This is very necessary, for if we neglect it we will not be able to encourage other believers, nor will they be able to encourage us. The assembly is a divinely instituted community and without it we would very soon grow cold, 'Not forsaking the assembling of ourselves together, as the manner of some is; but exhorting one another: and so much the more, as ye see the day approaching', Heb. 10. 25.
3. He witnessed to others, Acts 9. 20, 29. Again, this is a direct command of the Lord, 'Go ye into all the world, and preach the gospel to every creature', Mark 16. 15.
4. He grew in spiritual knowledge and strength, Acts 9. 22. How necessary it is to move forward in the Christian life! There can be no standing still, 'But grow in grace, and in the knowledge of our Lord and Saviour Jesus Christ', 1 Pet. 3. 18.
5. He continued faithful, in spite of fierce opposition, Acts 9. 29. It would have been easy to have given up!

Complete submission should be the aim of every believer, if we are to live lives well pleasing to the Lord. What other purpose or reason is there for the Christian to exist, but to constantly fulfil the Lord's will and bring pleasure to Him? Consider Enoch who 'before his translation . . . had this testimony, that he pleased God', Heb. 11. 5.

September 14th

Acts 9. 19-30

IS NOT THIS HE THAT DESTROYED?

Saul, later known as Paul, was completely changed by the Lord. It was true of him as with other believers by the empowering of the Holy Spirit, that the old life had been completely finished with. So Paul could later write, 'Therefore if any man be in Christ, he is a new creature: old things are passed away; behold, all things are become new', 2 Cor. 5. 17.

Paul was from the tribe of Benjamin, and Jacob in his final address to his sons, speaks of that tribe as it were in its unregenerate state saying, 'Benjamin shall ravin as a wolf: in the morning he shall devour the prey, and at night he shall divide the spoil', Gen. 49. 27. This was indeed the character of Paul prior to his conversion. But later, Moses too pronounces by the Lord, blessings on each tribe and his word concerning the tribe of Benjamin was then completely different, 'And of Benjamin he said, the beloved of the Lord shall dwell in safety by him; and the Lord shall cover him all the day long, and he shall dwell between his shoulders', Deut. 33. 12. How true this was now in the experience of this son of Benjamin! Those that heard him said, 'Is not this he that destroyed them which called on this name in Jerusalem, and came hither for that intent, that he might bring them bound unto the chief priests?', Acts 9. 21.

Sometimes, today, people will make a profession of faith in Christ but unfortunately this profession is not backed up by a change in their manner of living. Instead of the old things passing away, they continue practising their former sins and, furthermore, do not have a conscience. Elders, in these cases, would be quite entitled to doubt the person's profession of faith.

In each believer's life there are times when failure is present and sins are committed, but true believers will become unhappy and convicted about this and seek to confess the wrong to the Lord, for they will know they are out of fellowship with Him. John writes, 'If we say that we have no sin, we deceive ourselves, and the truth is not in us. If we confess our sins, he is faithful and just to forgive us our sins, and to cleanse us from all unrighteousness', 1 John 1. 8-9. May we, like Paul, show that a clear and unmistakable change has taken place!

September 15th

Acts 10. 1-8

WHAT IS IT, LORD?

Cornelius was a man who was sincerely seeking God and because of this the Lord revealed Himself to him, as He will to everyone who truly seeks, 'And ye shall seek me, and find me, when ye shall search for me with all your heart', Jer. 29. 13.

Cornelius was a devout man: he feared the one true God, he gave to charity, he consistently prayed and he influenced others so that his whole household followed him in his piety, Acts 10. 2. At the very moment of the appearance of the angel he was fasting, v. 30. He is an example of a man who lived up to the light which God gave him and while this was not sufficient to save him, God would ensure that he was given the additional light of the gospel of Christ. Before Peter's visit, he did not have the assurance of salvation, though he reverenced and sought to worship the one true God.

To be justified before God and to receive His salvation, all that Cornelius was and all that he practised was not enough. God would need to move in order for him to be saved, for good works in themselves will never save us: 'Not by works of righteousness which we have done, but according to his mercy he saved us', Titus 3. 5.

Cornelius shows his readiness to receive God's word, for with humility he asks the question, 'What is it, Lord?' Acts 10. 4. The angel tells him what to do and with unquestioning obedience he immediately sends his servants to bring God's messenger. Upon hearing the message of the gospel from Peter, he and those with him were ready to believe and receive Christ as Saviour. Only then did they receive God's salvation, this being evidenced by the indwelling Holy Spirit, vv. 43-44.

There are some today who say that it is enough to live a good life, as did Cornelius, to gain favour before the Lord, v. 4. Even today there may be people like him who have never heard the gospel, but are truly seeking God. We are sure that God will reveal to them the way of salvation. But many who shelter under this argument have heard the gospel and have either neglected or rejected it. This is entirely different for, 'How shall we escape, if we neglect so great salvation?', Heb. 2. 3.

September 16th

Acts 10. 24-48

CAN ANY MAN FORBID WATER . . . ?

Peter's question was framed in such a way that its answer was self-evident.

There was no national or **racial** reason that these should not be baptized. Acts chapter 10 marks the first practical out-working of our Lord's great commission. To that gathered group of Jewish disciples came the command, 'Go ye therefore, and teach all nations, baptizing them in the name of the Father, and of the Son, and of the Holy Ghost', Matt. 28. 19. The Jews were not primarily evangelistic. They were exclusive. In fact they were positively warned against mixing with the other nations. Although they welcomed those willing to submit to God, they did not actively seek converts. The gospel, however, was not limited to one nation but was for the whole world. This account in Acts 10 is the first significant movement of the Spirit of God in the conversion of Gentiles. We too should have a worldwide view of the spread of the gospel. Racial prejudice or national pride should never be part of a Christian.

There was no **spiritual** reason that these should not be baptized. The Holy Spirit was poured out on the gathered company as evidence they had believed the message that was preached. GRIFFITH THOMAS called it 'the Pentecost of the Gentiles'. This confirmation of the genuine faith was the basis upon which they should be baptized. Faith always precedes baptism. Christendom baptizes people, even teaching that such baptism secures their soul's salvation. Even infants are baptized. But the New Testament is clear that baptism is not the basis of salvation but the *evidence* of it. It is a witness to the reality of one's faith in Christ. No one can be saved by being baptized. But every believer should be baptized. What about you?

There was no **practical** reason that these should not be baptized, 'Can any man forbid water?' was the question. The primary elements of both baptism and the Lord's Supper are based on simple things readily obtainable. For over twenty centuries, Christian believers have practised these two ordinances. This simple emblem, like bread and wine, would not become an idol or icon. How wise our God is!

September 17th

Acts 11. 1-18

WHAT WAS I THAT I COULD WITHSTAND GOD?

This was a rhetorical question as Peter brought his case before his Jewish brethren answering the charge, 'Thou wentest in to men uncircumcised, and didst eat with them', Acts 11. 3. The early church were mostly Jews and, as such, the full implication of the new dispensation of grace was unclear to them. Much of what was legitimate under the law was now no longer applicable and the practical effects were being brought to bear.

Verse 2 of the chapter states, 'They that were of the circumcision contended with him'. Such contention could have ignited an explosive reaction from Peter. The flesh in any of us would easily react that way.

But Peter took the high road and responded calmly with the facts surrounding the incident. While this particular issue is settled and should never be a point of conflict for the believer today, other conflicts do arise. Disagreements come to play among Christians. We can learn from Peter on how to react when we are challenged as to some course of action with which our brothers and sisters in Christ may disagree.

We notice, firstly, Peter simply reported the facts, without embellishment, together with his own understanding of what they meant. Secondly, he confirmed his understanding by citing the word of the Lord and its application to the situation, v. 16.

In any matter of controversy over spiritual things it is always wise to bring scripture to bear. Experience may be relevant, but without the confirming authority of scripture it is not binding on other believers.

Peter's question, 'What (or who) was I . . . ?', was a powerful conclusion to his argument. This demonstrates the maturing of Peter. There was a time when he attempted to withstand God, Matt. 16. 22; 26. 31, 33. But, now, a more mature spiritual man discerned the movements of the Lord and yielded to Him. Jew and Gentile were now one body in the church. Defilement is not the result of food, clean or unclean, but the condition of the heart, Mark 7. 19b. Imposing food restrictions is described as a departure from the faith, 1 Tim. 4. 3, and is to be completely avoided.

September 18th

Acts 13. 4-12

WILT THOU NOT CEASE TO PERVERT THE RIGHT WAYS OF THE LORD?

Acts 13 is the divine history of the beginning of the worldwide missionary movement that continues to the present day.

Today's question was asked, in a tremendous story of fierce opposition to the gospel, but also one of a great triumph in gospel work.

The question was spoken by Paul to a man who was far away from God. Elymas not only turned from the truth – he was a Jew – but turned to darkness: he was a sorcerer. Not only that, but he endeavoured to turn others away from the truth. This was not the last time men of this character would arise. Paul warned that in these last days of the church as men turn from the truth there will be false teachers who readily advance darkness, 2 Tim. 4. 3, 4.

Paul's courage in confronting Elymas was a result of the fact that he was filled with the Holy Spirit, Acts 13. 9. This was entirely consistent with the basis of the entire missionary endeavour, as both Barnabas and Paul were sent forth by the Holy Spirit, v. 4, and it had been the Holy Spirit who spoke to the assembly at Antioch about this special call to missionary service.

This work of the Holy Spirit confirmed by a commending assembly is a safeguard to prevent would-be missionaries going out into missionary service on the basis of an imagined call rather than a genuine call from God. Missionary work is sure to meet hostile opposition and only those called and filled by the Holy Spirit will be capable of fulfilling the task.

We, equally, need to be men and women filled by the Holy Spirit, which by definition means being empty of self. The Holy Spirit can use such believers with power. There are many like Sergius Paulus around us and many like Elymas too.

How fitting that the opponent of the gospel was struck with blindness! The man who offered his dark occultic practice as light, was himself struck with a temporary blindness.

Happily, the account concludes with the sound conversion of Sergius Paulus. Gospel light overcame spiritual darkness!

September 19th

Acts 15. 1-21

NOW THEREFORE WHY TEMPT YE GOD?

The book of Acts chronicles certain historical events of great importance in connection with the gospel going out to the whole world. Each controversy settled an important question and brought increasing clarity for the message of the gospel. Today's question is another advance in understanding the world's greatest message.

It had already been settled that the gospel invitation was to be extended to Gentiles. Not only Jews, but Gentiles could be saved as well. However, controversy arose regarding the grounds or basis on which Gentiles could be saved. Was the gospel one and the same for the whole world or were there different gospels for Jew and Gentile? Was it a universal message?

The advance of a false message by certain professing believers invited compromise. However, in matters of truth there is no room for compromise and these early brethren stood firm and left us in no doubt about the true nature of the gospel.

Some Jewish believers were promoting, without authority, another 'gospel', which, to borrow Paul's phrase from Galatians, was not another at all, Gal. 1. 6-7. This 'new gospel' took the gospel of grace and added to it the rite of circumcision. Whenever something of works is added to the gospel as the basis of salvation, the true gospel is lost. This was an attack on salvation by grace.

To many of us in our day, this might seem rather obvious. Who could ever preach that salvation must be accompanied by circumcision? Yet church history proves that the gospel has been corrupted by adding rites, such as baptism, as a means of salvation. Acts chapter 15 sets the record straight for us.

The question was put by Peter to the 'Pharisees which believed'. To 'tempt' or 'test' the Lord is to refuse to follow His guidance and direction. It is provoking God to intervene in something where He has already spoken. They were resisting this movement of the Holy Spirit and His communication to the apostles. This serves as a reminder to all lest we fall into the subtle trap of testing the Lord by our own resistance to His word. His word is the final word!

September 20th

Acts 16. 16-34

SIRS, WHAT MUST I DO TO BE SAVED?

This is without doubt the most important question any man or woman could ever ask. Salvation is vital and without it nothing else matters. This question was asked by the Philippian jailer who was charged with keeping Paul and Silas in the inner prison. They were falsely charged with civil disobedience as verses 35-40 confirm. But God's ways are not the same as ours, and He sent His courageous servants into a difficult set of circumstances which resulted in the salvation of this man and his family.

An earthquake struck. Prison doors opened and prisoners had opportunity to escape. Foundations were broken up. In many ways the foundations of the jailer's life were broken up too. This meant certain death for him, as indicated by his frantic attempt at suicide. Sometimes it takes the foundations of our life to be hit by an earthquake before we pay attention to God!

In addition to the false charges of civil disobedience, Paul and Silas evidently had developed a reputation as messengers of salvation, Acts 16. 17. It was this salvation the jailer asked about, 'What must I do to be saved?' How simple is the answer to such a profound question, 'Believe on the Lord Jesus Christ, and thou shalt be saved', v. 31! What does it mean to be saved? The Bible's message of salvation means we are saved from the penalty of sin. It means we are saved from the destructive power of sin in our lives. Ultimately, the prospect for the Christian is to know an eternal salvation even after physical death.

Such a salvation is necessary because of our sin. It is sin that incurs guilt and ultimately final judgement. It is sin that has a corrosive power in lives. And sin, without salvation, will send us to an eternal loss.

It is for this reason that the jailer was pointed to Christ for salvation. It is through Christ's death at the cross that the penalty of our sin is fully met. It is His resurrection life that secures us from sin's rule, and ultimately guarantees us eternity in heaven. His death cleanses us from sin and gives us salvation.

To believe on Him is to cease depending on anything else. Are you saved? Believe on the Lord Jesus Christ today!

September 21st

Acts 16. 35-40

AND NOW DO THEY THRUST US OUT PRIVILY?

Each account of the spread of the gospel in the Acts provides an enduring lesson for the work of the gospel in every period of history. Release from prison had been ordered by the magistrates. What good news! But it was not to end so easily. Many of us likely would have been glad of the release and hastily made a trip out. However, the great missionary knew there was something more at stake.

It was vital for the sake of the gospel that the charges of civil disobedience be overturned. As far as the general public knew, these missionaries were troublemakers. This would have been the reputation and association for the future work of the local assembly. Here Paul seizes on his rights as a Roman citizen to secure a complete public vindication.

We notice that this was not done for merely personal interest. Paul could have invoked his citizenship when the charges were first brought. But that was not the issue then. And it was in the purpose of God that Paul and Silas be sent to prison. The intrepid missionaries took the beating and imprisonment and kept on singing. What a lesson for us all!

It was in that prison that the jailer was saved. It was in that prison that his household was saved. It was because of that prison that countless have come to Christ through the clear witness to the jailer, 'Believe on the Lord Jesus Christ, and thou shalt be saved', Acts 16. 31.

We also learn from this demand from Paul that civil authority is a legitimate right of the Christian. Government is of God, Rom. 13. 1. The Christian is not only called to obey such authority but also is entitled to its protective benefits. Here Paul boldly challenges the magistrates to accompany him and Silas, so that all could see that the charges against them were false.

This wisdom of Paul's enabled him to leave the city without condemnation. He visited the believers again. What an encouragement all of this must have been for them! The Epistle to the Philippians tells us of the sound and thriving work that resulted in Philippi. Europe had now been 'infected' with the gospel.

September 22nd

Acts 17. 16-31

MAY WE KNOW WHAT THIS NEW DOCTRINE . . . IS?

Paul was given a tremendous opportunity to preach the gospel in Athens. Unlike many of the Jews of Thessalonica who rejected the gospel on the basis of their own religious ideas, these philosophically-minded Athenians were prepared to listen to this message.

Part of the motive to hear the gospel was the nature of these people, in that they simply liked to hear new ideas, 'For all the Athenians and strangers which were there spent their time in nothing else, but either to tell, or hear some new thing', Acts 17. 21. It was evident that Paul's preaching of the gospel was unlike anything they had heard before. It was 'some new thing'. The gospel is unique. Although often categorized by people as just one of many religions, it is not so. It is different! Christians should never forget that.

But there was something else that explained the Athenians' desire to hear Paul. And Paul captured that and prefaced his message with this truth that applied not only to the Athenians, but to all men. That is, their interest in worship and ideas about men were actually God-given. In every man or woman there is a sense and desire for God. Despite man's denial of this, he cannot get away from the fact of God. The Athenians' worship demonstrated that. Even though their religious and philosophical notions were badly misdirected, it at least demonstrated their yearning after God.

What caught their attention was Paul's witness to the resurrection, v. 18. It is the resurrection that makes the gospel unique. No other religion or philosophy, whether of eastern or western origin, can point to a resurrection. Nothing can deal with the matter of death and life after death in such clear and unmistakable terms as the gospel of Christ. This is because no other system of belief has, as its central Person, One who walked into death, turned around, and walked back out of death. No human priest, or prophet, or philosopher has done that. On this basis, the Lord Jesus Christ invites me to trust Him for eternal life. And the undeniable proof of the dependability of His offer is that He has been raised from the dead.

September 23rd

Acts 19. 1-7

HAVE YE RECEIVED THE HOLY GHOST?

Today's question was put by Paul to a group of twelve disciples at Ephesus. They teach us an important historical lesson in that they were men who lived in two different dispensations. That is, they lived when God dealt with men through the law, and they lived in the new and present dispensation of grace. By dispensation we mean God's method of dealing with men, and man's responsibility to God. When John the Baptist appeared, he came as the forerunner of the Messiah of Israel, the Lord Jesus Christ. John's message was one of repentance to a nation that was externally observing a law without regard to the moral intent of that law. They found ways of giving lip service to God and observing religious ceremonies, but they had no heart obedience to the Lord. When John came, he called Israel to repentance in light of the coming Messiah who would demand a true righteousness, not a false one. Many in Israel responded to John's preaching and came forward and were baptized in repentance, acknowledging their sin and expressing their desire for the true righteousness Messiah would bring. These men in Acts chapter 19 were among those who were baptized unto John's baptism.

But John's baptism did not have the accompanying promise of receiving the Holy Spirit. The Lord Jesus told His disciples in the upper room that the Holy Spirit would come after His ascension. Evidently, Paul recognized that these disciples had not received the Holy Spirit. They had never seen the full picture of who Christ was as the Saviour. They could not see the new dispensation they were now living in, that the gospel of the grace of God was now going out into the whole world. That the risen Christ was building His church and that baptism was the act of obedience which gave evidence to faith in Christ.

The response of these disciples indicated their ignorance of these facts. DARBY'S translation puts their question to Paul this way, 'We did not even hear if the Holy Spirit was come', Acts 19. 2. But the Holy Spirit had come! Their baptism as believers resulted in Paul's identification of the coming of the Holy Spirit. Today, every believer in Christ has the Holy Spirit within.

September 24th

Acts 19. 11-20

JESUS I KNOW . . . PAUL I KNOW; BUT WHO ARE YE?

Ephesus was a hotbed of spiritism. Sadly, it was many of the Jews who were involved in this evil. Today's account confirms not only the reality of an evil spiritual world, but also the triumphant power of true spiritual realities found in the Lord Jesus Christ.

False spirituality is an imitation of the true. These professional exorcists attempted to identify themselves with the true power of the Lord as was seen in Paul's ministry. Disease and evil spirits departed from those who had contact with handkerchiefs or aprons that came from Paul. Does this happen today? No. Firstly, we notice that Luke points out, 'And God wrought special miracles by the hands of Paul', Acts 19. 11. These were 'special' or extraordinary miracles suited to the particular situation, not something that could be duplicated for any occasion of gospel witness. Secondly, we are told in Hebrews chapter 2 and verses 3 and 4 that God wrought special confirmation of His truth spoken by the apostles to 'them that heard Him'. Further, we notice it was unscrupulous men who attempted this imitation. Any similar practice today should be rejected as false.

The reality of evil spirits is not questioned in Luke's account. They were real. Their true character is revealed by the way they refer to the Lord Jesus Christ, 'Jesus I know', v. 15. Did they? They would not bow to His Lordship and address Him as such. They did not really know Him. Demonic sources may refer to Christ, but they will not yield to Him.

This incident demonstrated how dangerous involvement with the occult really is. The men who attempted to control the evil spirits were themselves controlled, and these beings turned violently on the exorcists. And it proved to be a powerful witness to the truth when the true nature of a false spirituality was exposed, in contrast to the true witness of the gospel. Spiritual blessing resulted in believers coming forward and making a clean break with their own association with these evil practices. Burning their resources, regardless of the cost, spoke loudly to the Ephesians, 'So mightily grew the word of God and prevailed', v. 20.

September 25th

Acts 21. 37-40; Romans 10. 1

MAY I SPEAK UNTO THEE? . . . CANST THOU SPEAK GREEK?

Paul's life was one of both privilege and pain. The Lord Himself said of Paul, 'He is a chosen vessel unto me, to bear my name before the Gentiles, and kings, and the children of Israel: For I will shew him how great things he must suffer for my name's sake', Acts 9. 15-16. The privilege of being God's chosen servant included suffering for Christ. This has not changed.

The realization of this was seen in today's account of the fierce opposition in Jerusalem. Jerusalem, the city that 'kills the prophets', was true to its history. Like the circumstances of Philippi, Paul found himself falsely accused and almost suffered death. It was the intervention of the Romans that spared his life. But it was the Lord who was in it all. It may surprise us that the Lord allowed Paul to suffer. True witness in the gospel is not an easy one. God's ways are not our ways.

Paul was a true evangelist. Quickly he realized this life-threatening circumstance would give him an opportunity to preach the gospel to his beloved countrymen. His heart cry recorded in Romans chapter 10 and verse 1 shows us much about Paul, 'Brethren, my heart's desire and prayer to God for Israel is, that they might be saved'. This was the real motivation in Paul's life. Even his life itself was secondary to the advancement of the gospel.

Paul seized on the situation at hand and courageously asked the chief captain for an opportunity to speak. We notice Paul's courtesy in the situation. Most men would have acted quite differently. The captain likely noticed this and saw that the potentially explosive situation could be settled. There is a lesson for us all here in Christian deportment. Few believers today face what Paul faced. Yet, we too can find ourselves in situations where Christ-like behaviour will open doors. Even the world recognizes an injustice. The chief captain saw this and gave Paul an opportunity.

Paul's discretion gave added weight to his message. Not only was Paul able to address the Jews in that company, but the rulers in the temple as well. The Lord was in control.

September 26th

Acts 22. 1-21

AND NOW WHY TARRIEST THOU?

Paul was giving his personal testimony to a hostile crowd of fellow Jews. One might wonder what the point was. They seemed intent on killing him. This was not merely a difference of opinion on some fine point of religion. No, they were violent. But Paul had a great love for his people and knew that the gospel was the answer for them. May the Lord give each of us that same care and concern for the lost, and look beyond their apparent apathy or even anger towards us!

His testimony is not just a restatement of Luke's record in chapter 9. Paul is carefully telling the story to a Jewish audience, giving a reasoned explanation for his behaviour. He had sympathy with them at one time, but a miraculous event occurred that could not be denied. He had been as zealous for God as they were. He was a persecutor of the gospel, as they were.

But something happened that dramatically changed everything: he met Jesus of Nazareth. Here was the central issue. Paul, and the mob, were not just persecuting Christians, they were persecuting *Christ*. This likely began to stir the crowd that had become somewhat settled in listening to Paul. But Paul was not going to water down the message. Jesus was Lord, *the* Lord. And this fact could not be ignored. It was central to the gospel.

Paul's miraculous conversion touched on something that would have resonated with the Jews. Today's question came from Ananias, a man respected by the Jews. He urged Paul to obey promptly the command to be baptized. Why wait? Why delay? Baptism expressed Paul's death to all that had gone before in his life, and the new resurrection life that was his. Verse 16 appears to link this baptism with the washing away of sins. But the grammar of the sentence actually links 'wash away thy sins' with 'calling on the name of the Lord'. In other words sin was cleansed when Paul believed on the Lord. Baptism was the outward expression of the inward reality of faith. Baptism alone accomplished nothing if there was no accompanying faith. It is not part of salvation.

So, today, men need cleansing, but it will come only through faith in Christ. Have you put your faith in Him?

September 27th

Acts 23. 12-24; Romans 8. 28

WHAT IS THAT THOU HAST TO TELL ME?

The events surrounding today's question are one of many in the Bible that teach us a Christian should never live in anxious worry. Paul was the object of a hostile Jewish conspiracy. The objective was to murder Paul. It was driven by a religious fanaticism whereby men believed they were doing God's service. This, incidentally, was anticipated by the Lord Himself. And while it was misplaced it was nonetheless evil, and these were men who wilfully did not know the Father, cp. John 16. 2, 3.

However, these enemies of the gospel unwittingly became its servants. These events were the first in a series of circumstances that took Paul from Jerusalem to Rome, a place where the Lord wanted Paul to go with the gospel. We should not panic whenever the enemy seems to get an advantage. Paul's enemies had not anticipated the Lord in their schemes.

We know little of Paul's natural family. Here an unnamed nephew appears at a critical moment. Whether he was a believer or was simply acting out of natural family sympathy, he courageously rose to the occasion to provide Paul, and later, the Roman guard, vital information that rescued Paul. May we be men and women of courage to always do what is right. Who knows what can happen from such actions?

Further, we notice that while the Lord was working things, Paul too did what he thought wise. He directed his nephew to the centurion. Likewise, in life's circumstances we need to do what we can, and leave the Lord to do what we cannot. This is not a matter of trying to take things into our own hands but prayerfully considering when to act. Likely, Paul saw his nephew's report as an answer to prayer and so acted on it. This is quite different from acting impetuously and anxiously when trouble is near.

The civil authorities reacted quickly. Wisdom demanded that Paul be removed from the religious conflict and brought to civil authorities. Paul later wrote to Timothy exhorting us all to pray 'for kings, and for all that are in authority; that we may lead a quiet and peaceable life in all godliness and honesty', 1 Tim. 2. 2.

September 28th

Acts 26. 1-18

WHY SHOULD IT BE THOUGHT . . . INCREDIBLE . . . THAT GOD SHOULD RAISE THE DEAD?

Paul's case was now firmly in the hand of civil authorities. The Jews' charges were only relevant to the Romans to the extent it could be proven if Paul and the gospel were promoting civil disobedience and treason. In this turn of events Paul is permitted to give a defence of the crucial components of the gospel message. And while it is firmly rooted in Israel, its application is seen to be much wider in scope. It truly is the message of hope for the whole world.

The gospel calls men and women to faith in the risen and divine Christ. The Jews did not reject the promise of the Messiah. What they vehemently opposed was Paul's message that Jesus of Nazareth was that Messiah and that Gentiles as well as Jews could be saved. For many Jews, their view of Messiah was merely in the realm of political power. Even the disciples themselves were not entirely without this opinion.

But the compelling element of the witness of Paul and other Christians was that the saving power of Jesus Christ was confirmed by God Himself when He raised Christ from the dead. It was this insistence on resurrection that set the gospel apart.

Was it true? Paul proceeds to give his own personal eyewitness account of the reality of the resurrection. If anyone wanted to reject the resurrection it was Paul. The early witness did not persuade him and so he set about to destroy the Christians. It was on one of those very missions that Paul was confronted with indisputable evidence. He met Christ Himself. Now everything was changed forever. No longer could an honest man like Paul continue this mad career of persecution. It was true! Jesus was the Messiah of Israel and hope of the world.

Why should it be thought incredible that God should raise the dead? Are there matters of evidence that put this to the test? Have remains of Christ been found? Was the tomb empty or not? Are there logical reasons to reject resurrection? Is it reasonable to assume that the God of creation and life could not raise the dead? Of course not! The hope for all mankind is found in the saving of power of Christ, a message not incredible.

September 29th

Acts 26. 19-32

KING AGRIPPA, BELIEVEST THOU THE PROPHETS?

The prophets were God's chief channel of communication to men, 'God, who at sundry times and in divers manners spake in time past unto the fathers by the prophets', Heb. 1. 1. Peter tells us, 'Holy men of God spake as they were moved by the Holy Ghost', 2 Pet. 1. 21. This divine method has effectively communicated the mind of God to men. No other ancient book has been capable of commanding the attention of men and women around the world. Here we are in the 21st century still talking about the Bible. True, it has always had, and still does have its critics. But it cannot easily be dismissed.

The Lord Jesus Christ Himself pointed out that man's response to the prophets is primarily moral, not intellectual. In the account of the rich man and the beggar Lazarus it was concluded that the rich man's brothers would reject a miraculous visitor from the dead, if they would reject the prophets, 'If they hear not Moses and the prophets, neither will they be persuaded, though one rose from the dead', Luke 16. 31. That is to say, their refusal to hear and believe the prophets was not an honest intellectual conclusion, but a moral decision not to believe.

The prophets are believable. Their design lends itself to human comprehension. There is nothing in the prophets that is contradictory or inconsistent. It is this that commends them to our belief. Men write several centuries apart and yet they produce one coherent message that miraculously points to Christ. There is no rational explanation for their existence apart from the fact their writings are the product of a divine revelation.

Paul's appeal to the prophets before Agrippa was a powerful argument. Agrippa knew that the prophets could not simply be set aside. The matter of Paul had now taken on proportions beyond a squabble among religious Jews, or even administration of Roman law. The gospel appeal was unassailable. Paul hit the conscience of this earthly ruler. Agrippa attempted to dismiss Paul's message in the public forum, but he could not deny the power of the message. Men are born again by the word of God, 1 Pet. 1. 23. We too should have confidence in this living word to do its own work in bringing men and women to Christ.

September 30th

Romans 2. 17-29

SHALL NOT HIS UNCIRCUMCISION BE COUNTED FOR CIRCUMCISION?

Today's question seems strange when read out of its context. But, like much of the book of Romans, this is part of a logical development of thought. This question read in its context makes perfect sense.

Paul has been showing why the wrath of God has been righteously revealed from heaven. In proving the guilt of man Paul demonstrates that such guilt is real and has been fairly and honestly assessed. Man is guilty in his own right and not as the result of his environment, or because God is impulsive. In chapter 1, Paul shows how the pagan is guilty by wilfully turning from the evidence of God. In chapter 2, he shows how the moralist is also guilty by professing one standard of right and yet not practising what he preaches. In the latter part of chapter 2 Paul takes up the special case of the Jew whose claim to being righteous was based on his privilege, as one to whom God gave His law. However, the guilt of the Jew was that he failed to live out the righteous requirements of the law. Publicly, the Jew engaged in an impressive ritual of worship attended to in meticulous detail. The Jew condemned the Gentile nations for their sin. The Jew, with a smug sense of self-righteousness, condemned the Gentiles as being 'uncircumcised'.

Circumcision was a special sign which God gave to Abraham. It was the cutting off of the male flesh indicating that it was not in man's flesh that salvation and life was found, but God. However, it lost that significance to the Jew and became a mere ritual, and Paul proves that circumcision alone cannot save. Gentiles, he argues, while not circumcised did, in many cases, live moral lives, showing their awareness of a moral law. God's righteousness was not to be trivialized. An uncircumcised Gentile who lived morally was as good (or bad) as a circumcised Jew who lived immorally. Hence the question, 'Shall not his uncircumcision be counted for circumcision?'

The conclusion of Paul's argument is that both Jew and Gentile alike are guilty. Salvation comes by grace through faith in Christ alone.

October 1st

Romans 3. 1-8

WHAT ADVANTAGE THEN HATH THE JEW? OR WHAT PROFIT IS THERE OF CIRCUMCISION?

At the religious and civil trials prior to Calvary our Lord was condemned because He claimed to be the Son of God and the King of Israel. The Epistle to the Romans upholds these claims and shows the relationship of Jew and Gentile to the 'seed of David according to the flesh' and the 'Son of God with power, according to the spirit', Rom. 1. 3-4.

The Jew trusted in three things: his descent from Abraham, the law, and circumcision. He was 'confident' that he had a racial and ceremonial advantage over other men, 3. 19. Paul had been a Pharisee and well understood the objections that the Jew would raise to being included in the universal condemnation preached in the gospel.

There are four arguments raised by the Jew in verses 1, 2, 5 and 7, which the apostle answers in verses 2, 4, 6 and 8.

The main argument is found in verse 1 and the others are supplementary objections to Paul's teaching. The Jew is asking Paul what was the point of having the ancestral advantage of a Jew, or the religious advantage of circumcision? Paul answers this question, in verse 2, by reminding them that they had been entrusted with the Old Testament, the oracles of God, which was to them a prophetic voice foretelling the coming Messiah. The Jew was the first of all men to read such glorious passages as Exodus chapter 12, Psalm 22, and Isaiah chapter 53. He had the opportunity to believe in Christ before other nations.

But the audacious counter arguments in verses 3 and 5 caused the apostle to exclaim, 'God forbid'. For the Jew admitted that he had read the scriptures that spoke of Christ but did not believe them, and trusted that the faithfulness of God to the nation would cancel out his unbelief! He even went on to argue that his unrighteousness and lies only commended and glorified God!

Let all who trust in their nationality, religion and privilege heed the warning of this section. God will never excuse a person who does not believe in His Son. God 'taketh vengeance' on all such – 'whose damnation is just', v. 8.

October 2nd

Romans 3. 9-20

WHAT THEN? ARE WE BETTER THAN THEY?

Paul now shows the important difference between the privilege and the standing of the Jew. There was advantage 'much every way' in being a Jew with regards to privilege. However, when he thinks of their standing before God, he declares, 'No, in no wise', as all men are under sin and not one is righteous. The condemnation includes all men and excludes none.

The evidence against all men had been gathered. The pagan took pleasure in sin while knowing that 'they which commit such things are worthy of death', Rom. 1. 32. The moralist who judged others but did the same things treasured up 'wrath against the day of wrath', 2. 5. And the Jew who 'sinned in the law shall be judged by the law', v. 12.

Paul now makes the formal charge 'that they are all under sin', 3. 9, and to support the charge he gives evidence from fourteen Old Testament quotations. As the Jew had made the strongest objection to the charge, the Jewish scriptures are used to indict them. Even Gentile nations could not excuse themselves on the ground of having no relationship to the law, for the quotations are taken from the Psalms and Isaiah. They proved that men have sinned in their conduct, their speech, their walk – their depravity is total.

Normally, men would offer a defence against charges made against them in a court of law. The whole world stands before the supreme court of heaven and there is absolute silence – 'every mouth is stopped', v. 19.

As no defence is made, the final verdict is given – the entire world is 'guilty before God', v. 19. Paul then explains in verse 20 the two important principles behind the verdict. Man has first of all misused the law by seeking to be justified in the sight of God through his deeds. Justification can never come by this path. Man has also failed to understand that the standards revealed in the law were impossible to achieve and were intended to produce 'the knowledge of sin'.

God can do nothing for a man who prays, 'I am not as other men are'. But the man who exclaims, 'God be merciful to me a sinner' can go to his house justified, Luke 18. 10-14.

October 3rd

Romans 3. 21-31

WHERE IS BOASTING THEN?

Having established universal guilt and condemnation, Paul announces the great change in God's dealings with mankind. God is offering righteousness to men apart from the law. In the past, this righteousness was 'witnessed by the law and the prophets'. Moses and Elijah were able to speak of the death of Christ on the mount of transfiguration. Now that righteousness 'is manifested', it is available through faith and not only to the Jew but is 'unto all and upon all them that believe', Rom. 3. 22.

In the past, God in His forbearance 'passed over' but did not put away the sins of those who believed. He credited them with the death of Christ which had not yet taken place. 'At this time' God is declared to be 'just and the justifier of him which believeth in Jesus', v. 26. He is seen to be just in relation to His past and future dealings with all sinners who believe.

God had declared that He will 'by no means clear the guilty', Exod. 34. 7. What has brought about this remarkable change? The mercy seat of old was hidden behind the veil. Cherubim gazed at the throne of gold. On the Day of Atonement, the blood was brought in and sprinkled on the mercy seat. The cherubim then saw blood on the gold, which declared that God's righteous standards had been met for another year. Now God has set Christ forth, not just to Israel but to the whole world, as a 'propitiation'. He is the mercy seat. His death has met God's righteous standards and through Him there is freely offered justification and redemption.

If righteousness is offered by God on the basis of the death of Christ, 'where is boasting then?' God has introduced a new law that supersedes the old – 'the law of faith'. In the past God commanded men to work, now He commands men to place their faith in Christ. The ground of justification is the same for Jew and Gentile. If it is established that there 'is no difference' with regard to sin, then it is also true with regard to salvation.

Faith in Christ does not 'make void' or cancel out the righteous standards of God revealed in the law. The person who believes is accepting God's verdict. The law proved that man is guilty and Calvary established that the law was correct.

October 4th

Romans 4. 1-12

WHAT SHALL WE SAY THEN THAT ABRAHAM . . . AS PERTAINING TO THE FLESH, HATH FOUND?

If chapter 3 explains how justification is 'unto all', chapter 4 shows how justification comes 'upon all' who believe. Abraham believed in divine promise. David believed in divine mercy. Both were reckoned as righteous by God apart from their works.

The simple answer to the opening question is, 'Nothing'! Yet, every Jew knew that Abraham had been given three things by God. He received righteousness, v. 3. He received an inheritance as 'heir of the world', v. 13. He received posterity as the 'father of many nations', v. 17. Paul shows that each of these gifts was on the basis of faith alone. Abraham could not boast before God, even though men might admire all that he received.

Abraham's faith was not meritorious. His faith, while recognized by God, was 'counted for righteousness'. It should be noted that the same Greek word is variously translated throughout the chapter as *count*, *impute,* and *reckon*, KJV. The term should be understood throughout the chapter in the sense of 'putting to account'. Faith does not introduce us into a religious process that will eventually result in justification, as Roman Catholicism teaches. Immediately Abraham believed, righteousness was put to his account.

David is then introduced to provide a contrast to Abraham. Both men had righteousness put to their account but in very different circumstances. Abraham was justified when he was uncircumcised, prior to the giving of the law, and as a man who was living a good life. David was justified as a circumcised man, living under the law, while condemned as an adulterer and murderer.

The great hope for mankind in the stories of these two men is that God has reckoned both an uncircumcised and a circumcised man to be righteous. If this was true prior to Calvary, it is certainly true in our dispensation. Righteousness can now be imputed, not to the circumcision only, but to all who 'walk in the steps of that faith of our father Abraham, which he had being yet uncircumcised', v. 12.

October 5th

Romans 6. 1-14

WHAT SHALL WE SAY THEN? SHALL WE CONTINUE IN SIN, THAT GRACE MAY ABOUND?

It is important to notice the change of subject that commences at chapter 5 verse 12. Up to this point Paul has been considering the sinner and his sins. Now he takes up the theme of the saint and his sin. The answer to the problem of sins is the truth of justification. The answer to the problem of sin is the truth of deliverance. The sinner needs to understand that Christ died for me. The saint needs to understand that I died with Christ. 'For he that is dead is freed from sin', Rom. 6. 7. To continue in sin would deny the truth of our death with Christ.

Paul presents three aspects of the believer's death to sin: *Godward* – I died to sin from God's standpoint at Calvary when Christ died; *Inward* – I accepted my death to sin on the day of my conversion; *Outward* – I publicly declared my death to sin when I was baptized.

Paul presents a seeming paradox in these verses. Naturally speaking, a man would be crucified, and as a result would die and then be buried. In Romans chapter 6, the believer is seen to die, v. 2, be buried, v. 4, and then be crucified, v. 6.

We must observe a moral sequence in this chapter, if we are to be delivered from sin: *'Knowing'* – truth about the past, vv. 3, 6, 9; *'Believing'* – truth about the future, v. 8; *'Reckoning'* – applying truth to the present, v. 11. Recognizing that we have died to sin automatically forbids the thought that we can live any longer therein. A new life awaits the believer. He walks in newness of life, involving the negative aspect of being 'buried with him by baptism into death', but the positive aspect of being 'freed from sin', vv. 4, 7.

Furthermore, the believer is to remain dead to sin until the day of resurrection when 'so also we shall be of [his] resurrection', v. 5 JND. We are to morally anticipate our future life with Christ by living here and now as 'dead indeed unto sin but alive unto God', v. 11. Christ is held up as our great Example in all this, for He has already done what we are exhorted to do, 'For in that he died, he died unto sin once: but in that he liveth, he liveth unto God', v. 10.

October 6th

Romans 6. 15-23

WHAT THEN? SHALL WE SIN, BECAUSE WE ARE NOT UNDER THE LAW, BUT UNDER GRACE?

Many people wrongly assert that to be under grace involves a lower standard of living than that required by law. Often this question is quoted as a statement – 'we are not under law, but under grace' – to support lower standards of behaviour amongst believers. But the previous verse sets the tone for the standard for the believer – 'sin shall not have dominion over you'. If sin does not have dominion over us, we will automatically meet and even exceed the standards of the law. Paul's ultimate conclusion is that 'the righteousness of the law might be fulfilled in us, who walk not after the flesh, but after the Spirit', Rom. 8. 4.

Paul's premise in this section of the chapter is that the believer, who *knows*, *believes* and *reckons* his identification with Christ in death to be true, is now in a position to *yield* himself to God as an obedient servant to acts of righteousness. The Lord had made it clear in the Sermon on the Mount that 'no man can serve two masters', Matt. 6. 24. The person who has 'obeyed from the heart' the message of the gospel has left the service of sin and begins a new life as a servant of righteousness.

This argument raises the question; does the believer merely exchange one life of service for another? Paul explains that he is using the metaphor of service, speaking in the manner of men, to show what a complete change the gospel brings to a believer's motives and actions. If the believer reflects upon his past life, he will come to the solemn conclusion that he was 'free from righteousness', v. 20. Now he is in the happy position of being free from sin and able to live a righteous life. 'If the Son therefore shall make you free, ye shall be free indeed', John 8. 36.

It is possible for us to say we have believed the gospel, but the test of having new life in Christ is the fruit we produce. The hallmark of salvation is to be ashamed of our past lives of sin. Grace has broken our link with that way of life, but those who continue in it face death at the end. The true believer is viewed as moving on from the shame of the past life, to serving God, bearing the fruit of holiness and enjoying everlasting life.

October 7th

Romans 7. 1-6

KNOW YE NOT . . . THAT THE LAW HATH DOMINION OVER A MAN AS LONG AS HE LIVETH?

Many suggestions have been made as to the identity of the man who is presented in Romans chapter 7. Some think that Paul discusses a hypothetical man; others that he is remembering his own experience as an unregenerate man. Some have seen the conflict between the Spirit and the flesh in these verses, even though Paul does not mention the Spirit in this chapter.

It is suggested that Paul is relating his personal experience, as one who clearly understood at the time of writing that law-keeping could not bring justification to the sinner, nor could it bring sanctification to the saint.

In verses 1-6, he describes his understanding of the Christian life at the time he wrote the Epistle to the Romans. He reminds the readers of three facts relating to marriage. Only death can break a marriage bond. If a woman is married to two husbands at the same time she is publicly called an adulteress. But if her husband dies, she is free from the law. In applying the illustration, Paul cannot go on to say that the law has died but he can state that we have died to the law through our identification with Christ.

Sanctification therefore comes from a realization that we are freed from the law through the death of Christ, and we are empowered to live for God by our union with Christ in resurrection. We are 'married to another', which introduces the thought of our affections.

The man who wrote the Epistle to the Romans was not a 'wretched man'. No one should think that this chapter is presenting normal Christian experience. He fully understood that it was impossible to be married to the law and at the same time be married to Christ. He lived in the good of this truth and had long since learned that power for Christian living was to be found in the enjoyment of the support and love of Christ and not through law-keeping. He lived in 'newness of spirit and not in oldness of the letter', Rom. 7. 6. He found that love could triumph where the law had failed – 'I live by the faith of the Son of God who loved me and gave himself for me', Gal. 2. 20.

October 8th

Romans 7. 7-13

WHAT SHALL WE SAY THEN? IS THE LAW SIN?

Freedom from the law had not always been his experience. And so, in verses 7-13, he recalls the time when he was a sinner and was married to the law. He had found that his sinful nature rebelled against the law and promoted desires to do evil that once he had been unaware of existing within him. He found also that his sinful nature always took sides with sin against the law, until he became aware that this terrible condition would lead only to death.

The question in verse 7 follows on from the statement in verse 5, 'the motions of sins, which were by the law, did work in our members to bring forth fruit unto death'. If the motions (passions) of sin were by the law, surely the law itself must be sinful? This thought is dismissed – 'God forbid'. The purpose of the law is now examined by Paul and he reaches two important conclusions.

The law *reveals* sin that is within us. The sinful nature within was exposed when the law said, 'Thou shalt not covet'. Instead of seeing this as a prohibition from God, sin took this as a suggestion. His sinful nature then moved him down a pathway that he had not considered before. The law also *provokes* us to sin. In verse 9, he pictures sin as lying dormant but reviving, or stirring within him, when the law came along.

There was a time when 'he was alive without the law'. Could this be describing his boyhood? If so, when he came to the age of responsibility, the full extent and demands of the law were impressed upon him. He thought at one time that he was equal to these demands; 'from my youth . . . that after the most straitest sect of our religion I lived a Pharisee', Acts 26. 4.

But sin deceived him and one day he found himself on the road to Damascus, blinded by the glory of the risen Christ, and learning that in persecuting the church, he had become the 'chief of sinners', Acts 9; 1 Tim. 1. Truly, by the commandments sin had been revealed as 'exceeding sinful', as it took a man 'who touching the righteousness which is in the law' was blameless and turned him into a 'blasphemer, and a persecutor, and injurious', Phil. 3. 6; 1 Tim. 1. 13.

October 9th

Romans 7. 14-25

O WRETCHED MAN THAT I AM! WHO SHALL DELIVER ME FROM THE BODY OF THIS DEATH?

In verses 14-25, he remembers a time after his conversion when he tried to become a better person, a holier person by keeping the law. Perhaps he reasoned that the law being 'holy, just and good' would come to his assistance as a saint, where once it had failed him as a sinner. He, therefore, for a time in his Christian life sought sanctification through keeping the law, but found that while the law was spiritual he was not. The law did not support him in his desire for holiness and only revealed his shortcomings as a saint, as it had done when he was a sinner.

The real problem is revealed by his repeated use of personal pronouns. He uses the pronoun 'I' thirty times; the personal pronoun 'me' twelve times; the personal pronoun 'my' four times and 'myself' once. Clearly, when a believer is taken up with himself – forty-seven times in nineteen verses – the outcome can only be disappointment and a feeling of total wretchedness. Being a 'wretched man' is not Christian experience but has been the experience of many a Christian.

Law-keeping is about what I can do for God. Grace is about what God does for me. He found that as long as he sought sanctification on the principle of law, he excluded God and focused on himself. He found himself powerless to cease what he did not want to do, or to perform what he did want to do. Twice over he concluded, 'Sin dwelleth in me', Rom. 7. 17, 20.

And so, he came to see that he not only needed to be delivered from the law but also from himself. If he was to know deliverance, it would come from outside of himself – 'Who shall deliver me from the body of this death?' v. 24. He had turned from the 'what' of law to the 'who' of Christ. By the time he wrote Galatians he clearly had passed through these experiences. He had learned that the secret of Christian living was 'not *I*, but *Christ*'. Christ could do what he had utterly failed to do. In fact, he learned that the only person who can successfully live the Christian life is Christ!

'I am crucified with Christ: nevertheless I live; yet not I, but Christ liveth in me', Gal. 2. 20.

October 10th

Romans 8. 28-34

WHO SHALL LAY ANY THING TO THE CHARGE OF GOD'S ELECT?

Once we are clear about the need to be delivered from Adam, sin and law keeping, and that our only resources are to be found in Christ Jesus, we are free to enjoy the leading of the Spirit and the help of the Spirit, v. 14, 26.

Throughout this epistle, Paul has stressed the guilt and responsibility of the sinner. Now, he turns to the standing and security of the believer. The believer's standing in Christ is based entirely on the purpose of God. God does not allow the will of man to decide the outcome of His purpose. There are five links in the chain of divine purpose for us:

Foreknown, Predestinated, Called, Justified, Glorified.

Each of these stages from God's viewpoint is in the past tense. We are not yet glorified but as far as God is concerned we are as sure of heaven now as when we finally stand in His presence. God is not content to rescue sinners from hell, or even to save them to become His servants. God's eternal purpose is that those who once lived on earth as sinners will live in heaven 'conformed to the image of His Son', v. 29.

Should any doubt their standing in Christ, the emphatic declaration is made, 'If God be for us, who can be against us?' v. 31. Calvary is the constant proof to the believer that God intends only our highest good. The God who saved the sons of other men like Noah and Abraham has 'spared not his own Son, but delivered him up for us all', v. 32.

Paul began the doctrinal section of this epistle by showing that Barbarian, Greek, and Jew had been brought before the court of God. The verdict – 'all the world' is 'guilty before God', 3. 19. Now, in chapter 8, he returns to the same court and finds it is empty. No one stands to accuse the saints, and since it is 'God that justifieth', there is no court of appeal, v. 33.

Furthermore, the only Man who could condemn, because He lived a sinless life in the same world in which we live, makes intercession for us, v. 34! Therefore, the believer has an Intercessor on earth and One in heaven – how fully our present circumstances are known and met by God!

October 11th

Romans 8. 35-39

WHO SHALL SEPARATE US FROM THE LOVE OF CHRIST?

Two historical events give character to the present dispensation: A Man has gone to live in heaven; a divine Person has come to live on earth.

We often find the world and our circumstances in it perplexing, and we groan within ourselves, v. 23, while unknown to us the whole creation also groans, v. 22. But, we now learn that a divine Person, the Holy Spirit, who has been living on earth since the day of Pentecost, sympathizes with our suffering. Although He sympathizes with our perplexity, He does not share it, as He is fully aware of the will of God for our lives and this world. God searches our hearts, not to find sin or failure in us, but to know 'the mind of the Spirit' for us, v. 27. The intercession of the Spirit is made in a language which is not understood on earth and may seem to be only 'groanings', but this language is spoken and understood in heaven, 2 Cor. 12. 4.

And so, as we are being daily helped by a divine Person living on earth who shares our experiences, 'we know that all things work together for good'. We are further assured of this when we learn that we are 'the called according to his purpose', v. 28. It is impossible for the purpose of God to fail and it is therefore impossible for our part in that purpose to fail.

On earth, however, the believer's lot remains one of suffering and tribulation. Sometimes, in the midst of suffering and difficulty, the believer may think that there is a distance between him and heaven. But no one has ever experienced tribulation, distress, persecution, famine, nakedness, peril, or sword in the way our Saviour has. Satan, our enemy, may think he can introduce distance between the believer and Christ through trial. But our suffering only makes His love more real to us.

We are delivered from condemnation in Adam, the service and wages of sin, and law-keeping as a means of sanctification. All this would have made us 'wretched'. The intercession and love of Christ enables us to be 'more than conquerors'. Divine love overcomes every force and foe in the universe both now and in the future.

October 12th

Romans 9. 6-24

WHAT SHALL WE SAY THEN? IS THERE UNRIGHTEOUSNESS WITH GOD?

The apostle has clearly established in chapter 3 that 'there is none righteous, no, not one'. It would therefore be sheer audacity for men to attribute unrighteousness to God. And yet, there is no truth that seems to provoke men to challenge God more than His sovereignty in blessing men. Some have even suggested that this chapter contains only history and that God does not intervene to bless one man rather than another!

The chapter is indeed full of history but Paul shows Israel that they must accept God's sovereignty, or all the promises made to them as a nation will be lost. And, if they accept His sovereign movements, they must understand that He means to extend blessing to the Gentiles. If blessing came only through history, it would be necessary for God to accept all Abraham's descendents, including Ishmael and Esau. But, if 'they which are the children of the flesh' are not the 'children of God' and only 'the children of the promise are counted for the seed', history is set aside and blessing stands only on God's sovereign choice of the individual.

The charge of unrighteousness could not be made by a people whose own history in the wilderness had brought them to the brink of destruction, 'I will come up into the midst of thee in a moment and consume thee', Exod. 33. 5. And yet, even in that day, God's sovereignty triumphed over man's history and He had mercy and compassion on whom He willed.

And, if the objectors persist, they meet the rebuke, 'Who art thou that repliest against God?' Clay has no intrinsic value: it can only become a vessel unto honour in the potter's hands. Carefully, Paul does not say that God makes a man to dishonour but that He has the *power* to do what He pleases. Men, like Pharaoh, persist in a pathway of disobedience and become 'vessels of wrath', fitting themselves for destruction. But God has made known 'the riches of his glory on the vessels of mercy, which he hath afore prepared unto glory'. Their eternal theme of thanksgiving will be, 'Except the Lord . . . we had been as Sodoma and made like unto Gomorrha'.

October 13th

Romans 10. 1-13

BUT WHAT SAITH IT? THE WORD IS NIGH THEE

Paul's opening prayer for the national salvation of Israel is not yet answered. It was the desire of the apostle's heart but he knew in his mind that God is not offering national salvation today. We live in a dispensation where God is offering personal salvation to Jew and Gentile alike.

The Jews divided the Old Testament scriptures into three parts: the law, the prophets and the psalms. Paul quotes in chapter 10 from each division to show that God's present dealings with men are not inconsistent with His past word.

Salvation is *available*, 'The word is nigh thee, even in thy mouth, and in thy heart', v. 8; Deut. 30. 14.

Salvation is *individual*, 'Whosoever believeth on him shall not be ashamed', v. 11; Isa. 28. 16.

Salvation is *universal*, 'their sound went into all the earth and their words unto the ends of the world', v. 16; Ps. 19. 4.

The gospel reveals that God is now offering righteousness on the basis of the death of Christ. Belief in Christ brings to an end any thought men may have of law being a means of obtaining righteousness. Jews must decide either to accept 'God's righteousness' and be saved, or seek to 'establish their own righteousness' and be lost.

Paul takes his readers back to Deuteronomy chapter 30 where Moses assured Israel that even if they were dispersed amongst the nations for their disobedience there was a way of recovery. This would not require ascending into heaven to bring down the law again, nor would it involve crossing over the sea to return to Jerusalem. They could turn to the word of God just where they were, accept its terms, confess their need of Him, and be blessed.

And so today, man is not asked to bring Christ down from heaven: God did this at the incarnation. Man cannot bring Christ out of the grave: God did this at the resurrection. God has done everything for us. And, if God has accepted the work of Christ by raising Him from the dead, all that remains is for the sinner to accept it, believe unto righteousness, and confess unto salvation. Salvation is near to all – 'the word is nigh thee'.

October 14th

Romans 10. 14-20

HOW SHALL THEY HEAR WITHOUT A PREACHER?

The Lord Himself confirmed that the gospel message is universal in its scope, 'He said to them . . . ye shall be witnesses unto me both in Jerusalem, and in all Judea and in Samaria, and unto the uttermost part of the earth', Acts 1. 7-8. The divine intention to reach mankind was further confirmed by the salvation of three men who represented the division of the nations of the earth after the flood: the Ethiopian (son of Ham), Saul of Tarsus (son of Shem) and Cornelius (son of Japheth).

The divine means of reaching mankind with the gospel is remarkable. There are an 'innumerable number' of angels who could come into the world and declare, as Gabriel once did, 'a Saviour, which is Christ the Lord'. But God has entrusted the message to the preacher, a mere man, who tells his fellow men about the way of salvation. God may not send the preacher into the world with an advertising budget, a marketing strategy, choirs and musicians, a promise of stadiums filled with hearers, or even a guarantee of success. But they are engaged in a beautiful work and their preaching can lead a sinner to hearing, believing, and calling on the Lord for salvation.

The New Testament preacher followed in the path of the Old Testament prophet. The great Isaiah had been one of those who pointed forward to the coming of a Messiah who would be 'wounded for our transgressions'. But his report has not been received by the Jews and so the weak link in the chain of events leading to salvation was the attitude of the hearer to the message. The prophets had fulfilled their commission, as their words had reached 'unto the uttermost part of the world'. The report had been heard but not believed.

Israel may object that the preaching was unclear and therefore the way of salvation could not be known. Paul reveals that even Moses in his day had to warn the people that God would turn from the unbelieving nation to the 'no people' of the Gentile nations. Isaiah, too, had learned of God's intention to bless the nations who sought Him not and asked not after Him. The long day of the Old Testament had been characterized by Israel's disobedience and gainsaying.

October 15th

Romans 11. 1-12

I SAY THEN, HATH GOD CAST AWAY HIS PEOPLE?

Since Israel had proved to be a 'disobedient and gainsaying people', the natural and logical conclusion would be that God has 'cast away his people'. But human logic has no place in the sovereign purpose of God. Paul himself was a proof to the nation that God had secured from among them 'a remnant according to the election of grace'. This had been foretold in the days of Elijah when that great servant of God felt that he had been left alone in a day of darkness and unbelief. Men object to the truth of election on the ground that it seems to limit divine blessing, but Elijah learned that, although he had thought in terms of one, electing grace had reached out to seven thousand!

Israel 'unto this day' is judicially made blind and deaf because of their repeated rejection of divine revelation. Instead of enjoying the Lord's table and feeding on Christ, they have made their own table. The Jew has been ensnared by material wealth at the expense of spiritual gain, and their history in the world since rejecting Christ is one of 'bowing down their back always' to other nations.

Israel has fallen and seems to the natural mind to be beyond recovery. They had judged themselves unworthy of everlasting life and so the gospel had been preached to the Gentiles 'and as many as were ordained to eternal life believed', Acts 13. 46, 48. But the God whose ways are 'past finding out' is using this day of opportunity for the Gentiles to provoke Israel to jealousy. They see others enjoying a blessing that was rightfully theirs.

The prophets had clearly taught that God intended to bless the nations through Israel. The Epistle opened with the promises of the holy scriptures 'concerning his Son Jesus Christ our Lord, which was made of the seed of David', Rom. 1. 2-3. God will keep His promises: Israel has not been 'cast away'.

And so, Paul concludes that, if today we see that 'the fall of them be the riches of the world', what will be the extent of blessing to the world when Israel is seen during the millennium in 'their fulness'? Even Egypt and Assyria will be counted as 'my people' and 'the work of my hands' in the day when Israel is established as 'mine inheritance', Isa. 19. 25.

October 16th

Romans 11. 13-24

HOW MUCH MORE SHALL THESE . . . BE GRAFFED INTO THEIR OWN OLIVE TREE?

As far back as the days of Noah, the olive tree was a testimony to the mercy of God. 'And the dove came in to him in the evening, and, lo in her mouth was an olive leaf pluckt off: so Noah knew that the waters were abated from the earth', Gen. 8. 11. God's intention to show mercy to the nations was founded in Abraham and is fulfilled in Christ. The olive tree bears testimony to a God who has 'concluded them all in unbelief, that he might have mercy upon all'. It is a sphere where men profess to be partakers of 'the root and fatness of the olive tree'. To be in the olive tree is to take the place of privilege and profess that we have accepted the testimony and promises of God. The warnings of verses 20-22 show that being in the olive tree is not synonymous with being in the body of Christ.

Consistently, we have seen that Paul presents election and sovereignty as God's means of introducing the greatest possible number of men into blessing. If so many Gentiles, who are wild branches, can be blessed through grafting them into a 'good olive tree', who can estimate the blessings that will come to Israel when they, as the 'natural branches', will be grafted into 'their own olive tree'? And so 'the seed of Abraham' will be saved by Christ 'the Deliverer' that shall come out of Sion. Election secures the future blessing of the nation, despite its unbelief, and enables God to remain faithful to the 'gifts and calling' promised in the past.

Paul concludes by showing that, just as we Gentiles were shown mercy when we did not believe, Israel's present unbelief will bring them into mercy. It is all of mercy! And, while chapters 9, 10 and 11 contain teaching that is dispensational, it is intended to have a profound impact on us. Our reasoning and logical arguments are to be drowned in the depths of the wisdom and knowledge of God. We will be careful to acknowledge that His ways 'are past finding out'. We will not be like Job and his friends 'who have not spoken of me the thing that is right', Job 42. 7. If we understand anything of these scriptures we will spend our days ascribing to God 'glory for ever'.

October 17th

Romans 11. 25-36

WHO HATH KNOWN THE MIND OF THE LORD?

The rhetorical questions at the end of Romans chapter 11 display the immensity of God's thoughts in comparison with man's feeble thinking. The Lord's wisdom goes beyond human understanding. He is described as 'God only wise', Rom. 16. 27, and possessed wisdom from the beginning, Prov. 8. 22. The unparalleled genius of the divine mind is only fully appreciated, however, as one contemplates His redemptive work towards individuals, as well as Israel and the church corporately.

Man's wildest imaginations could never produce a scheme like the Almighty's plan for His creation. Instead of consigning the planet's inhabitants to destruction after Adam's fall, God sent His only Son to die as a propitiatory sacrifice, thereby satisfying His just anger against sin. This enabled Him to righteously forgive sinners, Rom. 3. 25-26. Having removed the holy wrath which their iniquities deserved, He reconciled them to Himself, providing an eternal standing of peace based on faith in Christ who died and rose again, 5. 1-11. He still was not finished, for He also liberated the believers from sin's slavery by freeing and sanctifying them. Moreover, He will one day deliver them from sin's presence through the Lord's coming, and they will share in His glory, 8. 17-30.

God's astounding plan goes beyond individual blessing and includes a solution for the intractable separation between Jews and Gentiles, eventually bringing salvation to both groups. To look at the first-century Jews who disbelieved in Christ – or their modern kinsmen – one might erroneously assume that the Lord had abandoned them in their apostasy. Nevertheless, Paul points out in Romans chapters 9 to 11 that He has not cast them away, 11. 1-2, and that He will reconcile them to Himself at His return to earth, vv. 25-27. Meanwhile, during Israel's estrangement from the Lord He is mercifully saving the Gentiles, who had no claim to His promises, 9. 23-25. He uses Israel's past rejection to offer salvation to the nations, and their future restoration to demonstrate His grace to the world. This fulfilment of God's promises to Israel, assure the church that He will also fulfil His word to them.

October 18th

Romans 13. 1-7; 1 Peter 2. 13-17

WILT THOU THEN NOT BE AFRAID OF THE POWER?

'Question authority!' is the cry of many western thinkers. Marx and Engels famously told the workers of the world that they had 'nothing to lose but their chains', betraying a negative view of the societies of their day. Dissent and political upheaval are the order of the day in many nations. Nonetheless, Romans chapter 13 and 1 Peter chapter 2 exhort Christians to obey the authorities. This command stems from God's establishment of human governmental powers; accordingly, they possess the divinely-given means of punishing evildoers, Rom. 13. 2-4, and so must be feared by their citizens. What is more, Christians are to testify to their submission to the righteous God by adhering to the laws of the land, 1 Pet. 2. 15. Those who accuse the saints of being hypocrites or libertines will be silenced by their obedience to the authorities. If, however, the government enjoins believers to do something contrary to the Bible's teaching, then, like Daniel and the apostles, they 'ought to obey God rather than men', Acts 5. 29; Dan. 6.

The Lord Jesus is the best example of godly citizenship. He advocated love toward one's enemies, Matt. 5. 44, and instructed His disciples to go beyond the standards of Jewish and Roman society, 5. 20-42. He taught His followers to pay taxes, 22. 21. Furthermore, no one was able to point out any misdeeds in His actions, John 8. 46, because He never broke any human or divine laws. He was sinless and impeccable. During His hearings before Pilate, the Jews accused Him of 'perverting the nation', through royal pretensions which encouraged tax evasion, Luke 23. 2. Rather than respond in kind, the Lord was respectful. Although He could have called on more than twelve legions of angels to defend Him, He voluntarily went with a lynch mob, Matt. 26. 53. Nor did He permit His servants to establish His kingdom by force, John 18. 36. Instead, 'when he was reviled, he reviled not again; when he suffered, he threatened not; but committed himself to him that judgeth righteously', 1 Pet. 2. 23. Christ was an obedient, good citizen, who never compromised the truth. He was unjustly executed by men, yet glorified God by His righteous behaviour.

October 19th

Romans 14. 1-17

BUT WHY DOST THOU JUDGE THY BROTHER?

The world cynically demands, 'Who are you to judge?' Sometimes it is necessary to judge that one may approve what is excellent, Phil. 1. 10. Clearly, matters involving moral or doctrinal sin require judgement, 1 Cor. 5. 1-8. As for personal piety, believers are to examine themselves regarding their fellowship with the Lord before coming to His Supper, 11. 28, 31. Therefore, Christians are commanded to judge good and evil, their personal relationship with the Lord, and moral and doctrinal issues so that they may be holy and obedient to God.

People find it easy to criticize one another. By focusing on another's shortcomings, one can shift attention away from one's own failings. Unfortunately, scrutinizing another's faults for personal aggrandizement is not merely an error perpetrated by the lost. Christians also find it perilously easy to judge their brothers and sisters. Romans chapter 14 contemplates an even more troubling situation: believers who are judging their fellows' personal convictions.

Sitting in judgement on fellow believers' convictions undermines key elements of Christianity. First, each believer is the Lord's servant, and is chiefly accountable to Him for his attitudes and behaviour. Thus, the believer's conduct is to be regulated in relation to the Lord's opinions, not those of other Christians. Many who were saved out of Jewish backgrounds struggled with completely abandoning the food aversions and holy days of their past. They did these things believing that they were honouring the Lord thereby. Meanwhile, other believers who had no conscience about the type of meat they ate enjoyed this liberty as unto the Lord. Whether one abstained or partook, the action was to be done in keeping with what one believed God would have them do. Dependence on Christ is the hallmark of the Christian life. One day each saint will give an account to the Lord at His judgement seat for his own conduct, Rom. 14. 12. Instead of criticizing one another, believers must make sure that their liberties do not place any stumblingblocks in the way of their fellow Christians by carelessly trampling on their sincere convictions, v. 13.

October 20th

1 Corinthians 1. 10-17

IS CHRIST DIVIDED? WAS PAUL CRUCIFIED?

The Corinthian church was notable for its conspicuous strengths and weaknesses. On the positive side, they came 'behind in no gift', 1 Cor. 1. 7. As for the negative side, criticism of Paul's authority, chs. 4 and 9, tolerating sexual immorality, ch. 5, law-suits between believers, ch. 6, idolatry, ch. 10, disorder in the meetings, chs. 11-14, and heresy, ch. 15, all necessitated stern correction. As an antidote to each of these problems, the apostle directed the saints' minds back to the Saviour and His gospel. Significantly, 1 Corinthians first deals with the basic problem of disunity among the Christians. The solution lay in looking away from great personalities and back to the Lord.

If Christians are to give the Lord His proper glory, they must remember what He did for them and what He means to them. Their identity lies in the historic propitiatory death of Christ and in the spiritual body which it created – commonly called the church. By his deft use of rhetorical questions the apostle reminds them that no one else died for them or is capable of being their Lord and Saviour, v. 13. As important as Paul was to the Corinthians, he was unable to redeem them, let alone lay claim to their ultimate allegiance. Christ died for them and they were baptized in His Name. By this act in their past experience, the saints demonstrated the reality that they died with Him, were buried with Him, and rose again with Him.

The Lord Jesus is supremely important in God's plans. To identify oneself with a mere man obscures His importance to the believer. Colossians chapter 3 verse 4 does not exaggerate when it refers to Christ as 'our life'. Christians must never elevate men – however gifted or used of the Lord – above the Head of the church Himself. For all their accomplishments, Paul, Cephas, and Apollos were simply His servants, 1 Cor. 3. 5. Furthermore, the body of Christ acts inconsistently with its unified nature when it divides and forms sects based on outstanding personalities and gifts. Christ unites Jews and Gentiles, slaves and free, rich and poor, Gal. 3. 27-28; His people must maintain that unity within the church.

October 21st

1 Corinthians 1. 18-25

HATH NOT GOD MADE FOOLISH THE WISDOM OF THIS WORLD?

Through the centuries, thoughtful people sought to discover ultimate reality by philosophical speculation and scientific investigation. Questions of human origin, the meaning of life, and the destiny of man have perplexed the great minds of philosophers and sages. Nonetheless, their rigorous logical probing failed to reveal the God who created everything and 'worketh all things after the counsel of his own will', Eph. 1. 11. What humans could not do by mental exertion, the Almighty did by revealing Himself through the preaching of the cross of the Lord Jesus Christ – a message which sets aside man's wisdom altogether in favour of the divine plan of the ages.

Every man-made religion suggests ways for people to reach God through their own efforts. Whether they labour to enter heaven, moksha, paradise, or nirvana, people believe that they can do it through their own strength. The same idea permeates Christendom with many so-called Christians mixing faith in Christ with their works, sacraments, and ceremonies. Implicit in such thinking is the confidence that man knows the truth and can achieve his own salvation.

Christ's cross contradicts this humanistic tenet, for it leaves no room for human effort. At Calvary, men vented their venomous hatred towards God and His Son, subjecting the Saviour to calculated indignity and torture. Their statements, 'We will not have this man to reign over us', Luke 19. 14, and, 'Away with him, away with him, crucify him', John 19. 15, aptly summarized their attitude towards Him. The sin for which Christ died was man's only contribution to the work that He performed at Golgotha. His propitiatory death and victorious resurrection need no addition from man; in Christ, God has made a complete salvation apart from human wisdom and work. In the cross, we see a holy God judging sin to the fullest extent. Simultaneously, He extends grace to fallen man by providing deliverance from divine wrath, sin's tyranny, and eternal perdition. God's wisdom offers this through that which is an affront to human thinking, faith in the crucified and risen One.

October 22nd

1 Corinthians 2. 6-16

FOR WHO HATH KNOWN THE MIND OF THE LORD?

In philosophy-loving Corinth, Paul asserted God's perfect knowledge. 'Who hath known the mind of the Lord, that he may instruct him?' 1 Cor. 2. 16, quoting Isa. 40. 13, rhetorically refers to His omniscience. The Almighty does not need advice from sages and pundits! The gospel offered the Corinthians the revelation of God's preordained purposes which were hidden from thinkers through the ages, but now were taught by the Holy Spirit, vv. 10, 14. His brilliant programme will continually be a source of wonder through the ages to come, as He displays the riches of His grace in His redeemed and glorified saints, Eph. 2. 7; 3. 10.

The cross manifested God's incomparable wisdom over human thinking. Doubtless, the Lord Jesus' enemies supposed that no one dared adore such a disgraced teacher. To first-century people, crucifixion was a method of execution reserved for the lowest sort of criminals. The Jews in particular equated such a death with a divine curse, Deut. 21. 23. No human imagination would ever dream of using this instrument of cruelty and shame as the centrepiece of a story of deliverance. Only an all-wise God could turn this ignominious object of pain into one of hope and salvation. If the rulers of this world had realized that their actions would ultimately destroy themselves and grant the victory to Christ, they would not have crucified Him, 1 Cor. 2. 8.

Better than access to the faculties of Socrates, Plato, or Seneca, believers possess 'the mind of Christ', v. 16. The Spirit of God faithfully reveals the things of the Father and Son to them, John 16. 13-15. Christians are thus brought into truths that were formerly concealed to the most astute human brains, v. 7, which 'eye hath not seen, nor ear heard, neither have entered into the heart of man, the things which God hath prepared for them that love him', v. 9. These mysteries are now manifested to the saints for their enjoyment and edification. Man's thoughts pale in comparison with the magnificent design that the Creator has in store for His universe. Through the Lord's death, resurrection, and ascension He has secured a glorious future for His redeemed children – a destiny to which they are already privy.

October 23rd

1 Corinthians 3. 1-9

ARE YE NOT CARNAL AND WALK AS MEN?

The Christian life is a spiritual one, for believers are indwelt by the Holy Spirit, who leads them into 'the deep things of God', 1 Cor. 2. 10. In spite of this position of privilege in Christ, many of the Corinthian saints were not behaving consistently with their calling and blessings. Instead of conducting themselves spiritually, they were acting in keeping with their old, fallen lives. Paul wanted to instruct them in deeper truth, but their immature condition restricted him to imparting simpler things to them – 'milk' instead of 'meat', 3. 2. The tell-tale signs of their carnality were clearly on display: jealousy and strife, v. 3.

'Envy' – often rendered 'jealousy' – is coupled with 'strife' four times in the New Testament. They both appear on the notorious list of the works of the flesh, Gal. 5. 20. Romans chapter 13 verse 13 exhorts believers to 'walk properly, as in the day; not in revelry and drunkenness, not in lewdness and lust, not in strife and envying' NKJV. These negative features are characteristic of this sinful world; when they appear among God's people there is something seriously amiss. 'Envy' emphasizes desire for position and benefit in the church. 'Strife' is rendered 'contentions' in chapter 1 verse 11. This word shows that the assembly was afflicted by infighting, party-spirit, and the jostling of outsized egos. Rather than considering 'others better than themselves', Phil. 2. 3, they were behaving carnally and walking as men – that is to say, they lived according to the common behaviour of fallen humanity, 1 Cor. 3. 3.

Clearly, these negative attitudes were a serious impediment to the Corinthians' progress in the Lord's things. Like the sordid politics of this world, the assembly became the arena for conflict between the devotees of gifted men, v. 4. Paul called them to consider things from a more spiritual viewpoint. The men that they revered were merely servants who laboured for God. The Lord was the operative power behind their accomplishments, vv. 6-7; apart from the True Vine, the branches were powerless, John 15. 1-8. Christians are to work together for the glory of God, eschewing envy and strife.

October 24th

1 Corinthians 3. 10-23

KNOW YE NOT THAT YE ARE THE TEMPLE OF GOD?

The Lord is building the church as a spiritual edifice, Eph. 2. 20-22; 1 Cor. 3. 9-10, and the Corinthian believers were acting inconsistently with their identity as members of it. Paul reminded them that corporately they were the temple of God because the Holy Spirit indwelt them, v. 16. Such a privilege meant that the church was to be a holy sanctuary, adorning the doctrine of God and reflecting His character. When the church loses its understanding of its true God-given role – as in Corinth – it falls prey to the error of becoming a human-centred entity. Destroying His temple by pride, carnality, self-centredness and immorality inevitably brings the holy Lord's judgement against the perpetrators of this impious outrage, v. 17.

As God's temple, the church offers up spiritual sacrifices to its Maker and Head, 1 Pet. 2. 5, as described, 'By him therefore let us offer the sacrifice of praise to God continually, that is, the fruit of our lips, giving thanks to his name. But to do good and to communicate forget not: for with such sacrifices God is well-pleased', Heb. 13. 15-16. As in the other divinely-designed sanctuaries like the tabernacle and the temples of Solomon's and Ezra's days, its service and gatherings are motivated by, and focus on, God. The host at the weekly Supper is the risen Lord Jesus Himself. The substance of the church's preaching is the inspired word of God. Furthermore, its prayers and worship are offered up by the Son as intercessor in the power of the Holy Spirit and directed toward the Father's throne of grace. In short, it is designed to be a God-centred temple, edifying the members and reaching out to the lost.

In Corinth the focus sadly drifted away from the Head of the church towards various men. Some of them, like Paul, did not approve of this; nonetheless, the believers' minds turned from God to men as the primary object of their attention. Others were engaging in unholy activities, like envy and strife, 1 Cor. 3. 3, and were causing divisions in the congregation. These actions impaired the local church in its true function and jeopardized its effectiveness with God and men.

October 25th

1 Corinthians 4. 1-13

WHAT HAST THOU THAT THOU DIDST NOT RECEIVE?

Self-confidence and ingratitude are symptoms of the deeper malady of human pride. These unseemly traits thrive within the fallen heart. They deny the source of man's existence and ongoing physical maintenance, for God is the Creator and Sustainer of mankind, Acts 17. 28. They are foreign to the mind of Christ which believers ought to exhibit, Phil. 2. 5-8. If believers would bear in mind the question at the head of this page, it would fill them with humility and thankfulness towards the Lord who has given them 'all things richly to enjoy', 1 Tim. 6. 17.

There was a definite incongruity in the Corinthians' boasting. Since everything that they possessed was God-given, how could they take credit for it? It would be absurd for the recipient of a birthday gift to claim superiority because of the generosity of someone else. If there is any merit apportioned it should go to the giver – who in this case was God, the Giver of every good and perfect gift, Jas. 1. 17. Yet they gloried in their abundant spiritual gifts, and revered dynamic preachers, instead of glorifying the Source of these blessings. Paul vividly describes their lavish lifestyles with effective hyperbole, 'Now ye are full, now ye are rich, ye have reigned as kings without us', 1 Cor. 4. 8. He goes on to contrast their easy lives with the difficult pathway of the apostles, vv. 9-13. Instead of suffering for Christ by taking up their cross, they were seeking exaltation and comfort in this age, rather than in the coming one.

Believers receive no material or spiritual benefits independently of God's gracious distribution. The gift of His Son at Calvary manifests the extent of His loving provision for mankind. Such a matchless gift assures the saints that the divine largesse is unlimited, 'He that spared not his own Son, but delivered him up for us all, how shall he not with him also freely give us all things?' Rom. 8. 32. To be given so much obliges Christians to act as stewards of God's endowments, superintending them for His glory and pleasure. Rather than boasting, they should give thanks to the Lord and seek to use all of their blessings in a manner that demonstrates the riches of His grace to the world.

October 26th

1 Corinthians 4. 14-21

SHALL I COME . . . WITH A ROD, OR IN LOVE?

Paul's first letter to the Corinthians exudes parental concern, for they were his children in the faith, 1 Cor. 4. 14-15. There is a hint of sarcasm in his comment, 'Though you have ten thousand instructors in Christ', v. 15, for it is likely that they boasted in the number of gifted teachers under whose ministry they regularly sat. An instructor might impart information without truly caring for their souls, but, as a father, he was writing out of interest for their spiritual growth and well-being. In this role, however, he could also exercise discipline in order to correct them when they erred. In their current situation Paul could come to them either with the chastening rod, or 'in the spirit of meekness', v. 21 – the choice was theirs.

The unhappy experience of being perpetually scrutinized by others was Paul's common lot in Corinth. In his second epistle to them, he referred to self-proclaimed 'super-apostles' who habitually compared themselves to him and others, 2 Cor. 10. 12-14; 11. 5. They asserted that he wrote tough-sounding letters to compensate for his poor physique and unimpressive oratorical talents, v. 10. What he was in letter, however, he was also in person. As an apostle he had great authority, and was not afraid to use it when the occasion warranted. If they persisted in their proud and divisive ways, he would come with the correcting rod. If they repented, he would keep his strength in check and display gentleness among them. Doubtless, the apostle preferred to visit the Corinthians with the latter approach, demonstrating tenderness and love. If they would heed his warning, they would spare themselves unpleasant discipline.

The conquering Christ will bring the rod at His second coming, Rev. 19. 15, to set up His thousand year reign; thus, in wielding this tool, Paul resembled the Lord, 2. 27. Christ is the Good Shepherd who applies the rod perfectly. He is never too harsh or too lenient, but always disciplines appropriately – the correction fitting the error. Likewise, Christian brethren should meekly act to restore sinning believers if they are repentant, Gal. 6. 1-2, or discipline them more gravely if they are unresponsive to reproof, 1 Cor. 5. 9-13.

October 27th

1 Corinthians 5. 1-13

KNOW YE NOT THAT A LITTLE LEAVEN LEAVENETH THE WHOLE LUMP?

A tolerant attitude toward sin is extremely dangerous for a local church. If, as in Corinth, the believers begin to take a light view of immorality, then holy living is immediately imperilled. Paul illustrated this by pointing to an example from the culinary world: leaven permeating a lump of dough. Once leaven is added, it diffuses itself through the entire lump and affects the whole. In the moral sphere, it is the same. Tolerate open sin in the congregation and it will progressively degenerate into a licentious mixed multitude of false professors and indolent, backsliding believers. In such situations, those faithful saints who try to live holy lives will be frustrated by the libertine pew-sitters in their midst who care nothing for the will of the church's Head.

Just as the Old Testament Passover was linked to the Feast of Unleavened Bread, so those redeemed by the Lamb of God must 'keep the feast, not with old leaven, neither with the leaven of malice and wickedness, but with the unleavened bread of sincerity and truth', 1 Cor. 5. 8. The Lord Jesus' sacrificial death as Passover Lamb demands that the saints live holy lives. Israel was purchased out of judgement by blood in order to live for God's glory. In like manner, Christians today are freed from His coming wrath in order to please the Lord. Those who are redeemed through Christ's blood must put away the practices of the old life in favour of the sincere and truthful way of living that reflects their Redeemer's character.

The church's tolerance of fornication was as disturbing as the sin itself. Instead of displaying the appropriate 'mourning' in the presence of iniquity, they were 'puffed up' and glorying, vv. 2, 6. Sin is not to be trifled with. It brings forth death, Jas. 1. 15, and, in a believer's conduct, it is unbecoming and opposed to eternal life in Christ. Purging the leaven out of the Corinthian assembly meant removing the incestuous member from their fellowship by way of excommunication. He was to be barred from the meetings, as well as from social interaction with the believers, vv. 5, 11. The assembly must be holy, for God purchased it at tremendous personal cost, Acts 20. 28.

October 28th

1 Corinthians 6. 1-8

DARE ANY OF YOU, HAVING A MATTER AGAINST ANOTHER, GO TO LAW BEFORE THE UNJUST?

The modern world is a litigious place with people permitting no infringement whatsoever upon their rights. Frivolous cases abound: for instance, if someone dislikes something they may sue to try to change it. On a more serious note, from the world's perspective being cheated in business is certainly good ground for taking someone to court. In fact, if one were defrauded by another most people would say he is insane for not rectifying the matter before the law. Nevertheless, for Christians aggrieved with one another, lawsuits are not an option. The Lord has ordained other methods in the church in order to right wrongs between believers.

In the light of the saints' future destiny, some of the Corinthian Christians' rush to secular law-courts was illogical. Paul reminds them of their future participation in Christ's reign, 'Do ye not know that the saints shall judge the world? And if the world shall be judged by you, are ye unworthy to judge the smallest matters? Know ye not that we shall judge angels? How much more things that pertain to this life?' 1 Cor. 6. 2-3. Given that they will have such great responsibilities, adjudicating between fractious members of the assembly is completely within their capabilities. More to the point, for all of its problems the local assembly was their law school, preparing them for service in the future administration of the King of kings.

When Christians have seemingly intractable problems with one another they should take it to the assembly's spiritual brothers for resolution. If one party refuses to bow to this process, then the other should willingly suffer loss for the sake of the testimony before the other believers and the world, vv. 6-8. To sue fellow-believers is a denial of the common family of God to which they belong: Christians are brothers and sisters, v. 6. In the early centuries of the gospel, it is written that people said of Christians, 'Behold how they love one another, behold how they die for one another'. As the Lord Jesus expressed it, 'By this shall all men know that ye are my disciples, if ye have love one to another', John 13. 35.

October 29th

1 Cor. 6. 9-11

KNOW YE NOT THAT THE UNRIGHTEOUS SHALL NOT INHERIT THE KINGDOM OF GOD?

The Lord Jesus Christ changes lives. He defined eternal life in terms of a relationship with the Father and Himself, John 17. 3; therefore, it is no surprise that the recipient of His gift of eternal life demonstrates personal qualities that reflect Christ's character. Conversely, if unrighteousness is the defining characteristic of someone's life then it is apparent that he does not possess life in Christ and thus will not inherit the kingdom of God, John 3. 3; 1 Cor. 6. 9. The Corinthian church needed to conduct itself with an eye on the future reign of the King of kings. If they did so, then a clear distinction would be made between those who were walking consistently with their Christian profession and those who were inconsistent pretenders.

The chief modern virtue among the unconverted is tolerance. Contemporary thinking reasons that one can say and do whatever one pleases, so long as it puts no burden upon anyone else. For instance, if someone says he is a Christian, then his profession should be accepted uncritically, even if his behaviour makes a mockery of Christian living. As Paul affirmed in the title question of this devotional, the unrighteous will not inherit the kingdom. The Lord Jesus agreed, saying, 'Not everyone that saith unto me, Lord, Lord, shall enter into the kingdom of heaven; but he that doeth the will of my Father . . . Many will say to me in that day, Lord, Lord, have we not prophesied in thy name? And in thy name have cast out devils? And in thy name done many wonderful works? And then will I profess unto them, I never knew you: depart from me, ye that work iniquity', Matt. 7. 21-23; see also Rev. 21. 8.

God's cleansing, sanctifying, and justifying power ensured that some of the Corinthians who had formerly lived in the way described in verses 9-10 were now completely changed and would one day inherit the kingdom. The Lord can and does save people from lives of sexual perversion, covetousness, idolatry, and violence. Nevertheless, He refuses to justify the impenitent and give the unrighteous admittance into His future kingdom. He is holy and will not tolerate sin in His presence.

October 30th

1 Corinthians 6. 12-20

KNOW YE NOT THAT YOUR BODY IS THE TEMPLE OF THE HOLY GHOST?

Modern people have a twisted perspective towards their bodies. On the one hand they are obsessed with fitness, diet, and appearance. On the other hand, their moral actions are a matter of indifference to them. 'It's my body', they reason, 'I can do with it as I please'. This is a fallacy, for the God who created them cares deeply about their bodies and how they are employed. The Christian's body is claimed by the Lord and reserved for His special plan; He demands that it be kept pure, Rom. 12. 1.

It is the prerogative of the Creator to determine the proper function of His creation. This divine purpose is clearly stated, 'Now the body is not for fornication, but for the Lord; and the Lord for the body', 1 Cor. 6. 13. When one remembers that God is also the one who providentially sustains the body – 'the Lord for the body' – it gives further justification for His prescription for the human body's proper use. What is more, God intends to raise it up in a glorified form in a future day, v. 14; 15. 50-57. A body with such a destiny must be maintained in purity.

Contrary to the contemporary world's way of life (and that of the ancient Graeco-Roman world, for that matter), believers are to abstain from fornication. Today, if one refrains from this type of sin he is considered abnormal, or even aberrant. Light is called darkness and darkness light, as during a notorious low-point in ancient Israel's history, Isa. 5. 20. Christians are united to Christ in a spiritual union; they belong to His body, 1 Cor. 6. 15; John 14. 20; 17. 21-23, and so should not join themselves to a harlot. Furthermore, since they are indwelt by the Holy Spirit their body is His temple, 1 Cor. 6. 19. It is unthinkable that Christ's body would be associated with sexual immorality or that the sanctuary of one of the Persons of the Trinity would be defiled in this way. The saint's body must be chaste for the Lord, and the temple must be preserved from uncleanness. Lastly, their bodies were purchased by our Redeemer at the cross; consequently, they are not their personal property. As verse 19 states, 'Ye are not your own . . . therefore glorify God in your body, and in your spirit, which are God's'.

October 31st

1 Corinthians 7. 12-16; 1 Peter 3. 1-2

FOR WHAT KNOWEST THOU, O WIFE, WHETHER THOU SHALT SAVE THY HUSBAND?

The gospel of the Lord Jesus Christ divides people. As He expressed it, 'Think not that I am come to send peace on the earth: I came not to send peace, but a sword. For I am come to set a man at variance against his father, and the daughter against her mother, and the daughter in law against her mother in law. And a man's foes shall be they of his own household', Matt. 10. 34-36. Sometimes the good news comes to a family and every member receives it, Acts 16. 31-34. As the above-quoted verse from Matthew indicates, on other occasions some believe and others reject it. 1 Corinthians chapter 7 envisages the scenario of a married couple divided: one is born again, the other is not. Certainly, this poses real difficulties for the Christian spouse; nevertheless, the Lord can still work in such mixed marriages to bring the lost member to Christ.

The question at the top of the page particularly contemplates the believing wife's situation. If her unbelieving husband chooses to leave, she cannot prevent him, 1 Cor. 7. 15; nonetheless, if he wants to remain married she is to stay in the relationship, v. 13. Beyond the issue of remaining together or not, the Christian wife can influence the relationship in a way that brings about a change in her man. 1 Peter chapter 3 verses 1-2 instructs her regarding her significant method of persuasion, 'Likewise, ye wives, be in subjection to your own husbands; that, if any obey not the word, they also may without the word be won by the conversation of the wife; while they behold your chaste conversation coupled with fear'. If he does not listen to the scriptures, there can still be a wordless testimony, as he sees his godly wife submitting to him. Her pure and respectful behaviour may induce him to consider the change that God has made in her life since she received Christ. Conversely, if she is insubordinate, unfaithful, or cantankerous, this would dissuade him from any further interest in the gospel. Living together in such intimacy provides the Christian woman with an unparalleled witnessing opportunity. She has the quiet power to lead him to the Lord by letting His light shine through her life.

November 1st

1 Corinthians 7. 17-24

ART THOU CALLED BEING A SERVANT?

This part of First Corinthians is taken up with the call of God and how it might affect the social circumstances of those who are called. Paul teaches that in this situation the salvation of one partner in a marriage, for example, does not break the marriage bond. Indeed, if anything it should strengthen it! Nor does the question suggest that the new Christian should be ashamed of, or seek to hide the circumstances he was in when called. In verse 21 there is the particular question as to whether someone saved while working as a slave should now seek to leave that position of servitude. After all, it might be argued that it is not acceptable to be in material and physical bondage while one enjoys a new spiritual freedom in Christ. In New Testament times many slaves were converted and no doubt at least some of them felt that should, as of right, ensure their freedom from the bondage of physical slavery.

Verses 23 and 24 teach that such, originally the servants of men, had now become the servants of a higher Master, the Lord Himself. An understanding of that fact should reassure the convert that he was not really bound to man but to God and had become a participant in a higher service. The tasks that previously were performed solely for the earthly master are now seen to be performed primarily for the Lord. This would encourage the slave to work diligently so that he need not spend his days dreaming about freedom. On the other hand, however, should a slave for some reason be offered freedom then it would be right for him to accept that situation as of the Lord who may have a different plan to be put into operation.

Slaves called by the gospel were spiritually the Lord's freemen and others called while free in society became the Lord's bondslaves. In effect, therefore, there was no difference between the bond and the free and no reason for either to insist on changing his circumstances. If the Lord wished to change the circumstances then He would do so. Today, believers are often able to choose and to change their employment at will and are thus given the opportunity of judging whether their employment is compatible with, or antagonistic to, their Christian profession.

November 2nd

1 Corinthians 8. 1-13

THROUGH THY KNOWLEDGE SHALL THE WEAK BROTHER PERISH?

The background to the question in verse 11 (or is it a statement?) is that the believers in the assembly in Corinth had a significant problem and they raised it in a letter to Paul, hoping that his advice would declare one party to be wholly right and the other completely wrong. There was a difference of opinion about the rights and wrongs of eating, or even buying, meat which had been offered to idols in sacrifice in heathen temples. Such meat was freely available to purchase in the marketplace and at the tables of neighbours. Some said that idols really did not exist at all; they were 'nothing'. Therefore, there should be no problem in eating and any who could not see this had not been freed from pagan bondage! They in turn recalled from bitter personal experience that behind dead idols were living demons and therefore, surely, it must be wrong to eat such meat. The issue was divisive and clear instruction was needed.

Paul, probably much to their surprise, indicates that the answer to the question should be based on love and not on knowledge. Knowledge, which is limited in any case, puffs up but genuine love to God and to one's fellow Christian must be the basis for action in this matter. Paul re-affirms that an idol is indeed 'nothing', in that there is but one God. He is, however, very aware of the conscience of the weak brother (the one who feels that to buy or to eat such meat is wrong) mentioning it four times in these verses, describing it as 'weak' and open to potential defilement. He now declares the meat in itself to be 'nothing'. In being offered to an idol it has not changed in any way – it has not been defiled nor has it acquired any evil spiritual qualities – it is simply meat.

So a believer who has no conscience about eating may indeed eat; but if in so doing he wounds the conscience of the weak brother, then out of love for the one for whom Christ died he should forgo this liberty. And certainly, he must not compel the weak brother to eat as that could destroy him. In all such matters, love rather than knowledge is to be the sole basis for the decision. This motive should control our actions at all times.

November 3rd

1 Corinthians 9. 1-18

WHAT IS MY REWARD THEN?

I like to call 1 Corinthians chapter 9 'The 20 Questions Chapter' because in it the apostle through the guidance of the Holy Spirit makes his points by asking that number of questions, the one we are to consider here being the nineteenth. The whole chapter is taken up with the question whether preachers of the gospel, a free message, should accept financial support for preaching it. The answer is a clear 'Yes', though Paul waives his right to do so because he has discovered a better, and for him, more appropriate way. In verse 1 he speaks of his freedom and then of his apostleship. In the Revised Version freedom comes first and then service, as it does in real life, and his apostleship is proven by the fact he had seen the Lord on resurrection ground and the success of his work in Corinth was further evidence of it.

He asserts that as a free man is able to make choices: whether to eat and drink, or not to; whether to marry or remain single; whether to do physical work as well as spiritual, or not to. He then points out that a soldier is paid for fighting for his country, a vineyard owner expects to consume some of its produce and a shepherd will drink of the milk of the flock. Further, he goes back to the Old Testament to show that both priests and Levites took their designated share of the offerings. In verse 11 he concludes that those who sow spiritual things have a right to reap carnal things. So, the Lord has ordained that those who preach the gospel may live of the gospel. This is a general statement but each individual servant must come to his own personal decision as to how to proceed and Paul now shares with us what he feels is right for him.

When he preaches the gospel he anticipates no financial reward for doing so. His reward is the joy and peace of knowing that he has preached a free message freely. This joy is his reward! Paul chose to draw on his own skill set as a tentmaker to pay his way through life, and only in the direst of circumstances did he accept gifts from the saints. Seeking continuous support in the Lord's service should perhaps be an action of last resort. Individuals and assemblies should consider this passage carefully, weighing what is permissible, but also what is preferable.

November 4th

1 Corinthians 10. 1-22

THE CUP OF BLESSING . . . IS IT NOT THE COMMUNION OF THE BLOOD OF CHRIST?

In this chapter, part of which comprises the reading for today, Paul draws comparisons between the nation of Israel of old with the church and uses these to demonstrate that believers should not be involved in the offering of sacrifices to idols. While all understand that the idol is nothing it is also clear that behind the idols are demons and no believer should be involved with them. He draws attention to the fact that Israel displeased God throughout their wilderness journey. They had been saved corporately out of Egypt, yet in spite of this miraculous deliverance they became entwined in idolatry and fornication; additionally they tempted God and constantly murmured. In the end they were almost all destroyed. We are warned not to jeopardize our Christian blessings by living in disobedience and sin. We need to be humble and not consider ourselves untouchable by sin. We may stand today, but must take heed lest we fall.

The Israelites, because of their worship of God and involvement in the sacrifices, were viewed as one nation. The believers, in meeting together at the Lord's Supper, share the cup which speaks of the blood of Christ and the bread which speaks of His body. We bless God for the symbols and especially for the One of whom they speak. Because it is one cup and one bread it also signifies the unity of all those who partake, 'We being many are one', v. 17. The message is that being involved in the body and blood of Christ we are together as one and each must consider the good of others in the same fellowship, see v. 24. As we consider this we realize that all things may be lawful (allowable) but all things may not be expedient (appropriate).

Being together as 'one', the strong believer needs to consider the conscience of the weak and endeavour not to give offence in the matter of association with others outside the church. There is to be a separation; I seek not my own will but carefully consider the potential loss of confidence, peace of mind and even the confusion that may come to others as a result of my actions. Clearly, partaking of the bread and wine at the Lord's Supper has many implications outside participation in the feast itself.

November 5th

1 Corinthians 10. 23-33

WHY IS MY LIBERTY JUDGED OF ANOTHER MAN'S CONSCIENCE?

Liberty and conscience are two themes of this section; they are compatible, not contrary the one to the other. Two situations are discussed here: is it right for a believer to buy food in the market-place that may or may not have been offered to idols? The problem is that he really has no way of knowing whether or not it was. Secondly, if a believer is invited to dine with his unsaved neighbour should he run the risk that the meat set before him may have been associated with idol worship before his neigh-bour bought it? These are to us interesting questions but to them they were real practical everyday difficulties.

Paul points out that all things are lawful for the Christian, i.e. all things associated with the problems being discussed. In any wider context his words would conflict with scripture! So, while to eat may be lawful it may not be helpful and if it is unhelpful it should be avoided. Discrimination is necessary as the outcome must be the building up of others and not just to suit one's convenience. Regarding meat offered for sale in the market, the believer is free to buy and to eat. This is because in eating he gives God thanks and is aware that the real source of the meat is God and that it is provided by Him for human consumption. If it had been offered to heathen idols on the way to the table it was not contaminated by that. So he eats without fear.

The second situation is somewhat different. Meat provided in someone's home is subject to the same rule unless and until someone points out or asks whether it was associated with idols. If this is confirmed then the weak brother's conscience will suggest he should not eat it. He will watch to see the strong brother's reaction to the information. This latter feels free to eat but if he does so he may destroy his brother so he decides not to do so. Does that mean, our question asks, that one's liberty is controlled by another's conscience? If so, surely that would be wrong? The answer is that by not eating the strong brother is exercising his liberty in Christ and has chosen not to eat. His liberty has been exercised and has nothing to do with being con-trolled by another. Liberty and conscience work in harmony.

November 6th

1 Corinthians 11. 1-16

IS IT COMELY THAT A WOMAN PRAY UNTO GOD UNCOVERED?

The short answer to this question is, 'No, it is not at all comely (suitable, proper, desirable)'. However, in this chapter, Paul takes time to set out the reasons why, when prayer or prophesying takes place in a church setting, women should be covered and men uncovered. Even though he does so there appears to be confusion in some minds about coverings. We note that it is coverings and not veils which are in question. The latter covers the face but the former covers the head. In the Jewish setting men covered their heads but in a Christian context men should be uncovered. This is a truth acknowledged and accepted by the Christian world and submitted to even by unbelievers. If people see a man inside a church building with a covering on his head they feel instinctively that it is wrong. The Bible supports that natural feeling.

This is because headship is involved. The divine order is: God – Christ – man – woman. Just as Christ is not inferior to God, neither is the woman inferior to the man. They are equals but divine order requires that the woman submit to the man and that is demonstrated in the wearing of a covering. Women are naturally given to have long hair and men short hair. Some deduce that the long hair is in itself sufficient covering but that is not so. Her long hair is a God-given covering but the teaching is that she should willingly cover it with a second covering. If she feels disinclined to do so, then says scripture, she should go the whole way and have her head shaven. But that is not an attractive proposition because that is what temple prostitutes and others did. Discarding the second covering negates the natural one.

Paul, having shown that scripture requires a woman to have her head covered, now shows that nature itself teaches the same thing. Long hair for a man is inappropriate and effeminate. Short hair for a woman is unsuitable and improper. An uncovered head for a woman, i.e. wearing no second covering, is not becoming and presumably also dismays the angels who monitor obedience to God and His word. We should always accept that 'in church' men should have no covering; women should.

November 7th

1 Corinthians 11. 17-34

HAVE YE NOT HOUSES TO EAT AND DRINK IN?

The section of scripture before us today sets forth a description of the Lord's Supper, or the breaking of bread gathering of the saints. It is a time of remembrance, reverence, fellowship, and godly fear. We recall the Person of Christ and His birth, life, death, and resurrection while at the same time enjoying fellowship with like-minded believers. These awesome truths should humble us and cause us to be thankful for the mercies of God. A great attraction of the feast has always been, and still is, its simplicity – aptly expressed in the words of the hymn, 'The bread and wine are spread upon the board; The guests are here, invited by the Lord; Why come they thus? Why tarry for a space? But for Thy presence, O Thou King of grace'.

However, we are shocked to read that in the church at Corinth there were very evident divisions, heresies, greed, drunkenness, partiality, and excess of many kinds. Surely, these could not be happening in the breaking of bread services? The breaking of bread, as well as being a remembrance of the Lord Jesus Christ, is also a declaration of the unity of saints; the exact opposite of what seemed to be happening here. It would appear that in the early days of assembly testimony there was a separate but associated love feast which the saints attended bringing their own refreshments. Some brought little because they did not have much to bring while others went over the top in the abundance they provided. The rich shared with each other but not with the poor. While meeting in the Lord's Name this gathering became destructive and was doing more harm than good. It was here that the ugly vices of verses 18-21 raised their heads.

This gives rise to the question, 'Have ye not houses to eat and drink in?' Paul's question should not be taken to mean that such behaviour is all right behind the closed doors of private homes, but it is most certainly inappropriate and unacceptable in an assembly gathering. With love feasts now a thing of the past we must be on our guard lest the evils associated with them become even worse by invading the Lord's Supper. Behaviour which may be acceptable in the home may not be appropriate in the assembly. Reverence is paramount.

November 8th

1 Corinthians 12. 12-26

IF THE WHOLE BODY WERE AN EYE, WHERE WERE THE HEARING?

The question above is one of a number posed in this chapter. It draws attention to the fact that eyes and ears co-exist and for the proper functioning of the body are dependent on one another. The truth taught in this section of the Epistle demonstrates the oneness of the church universal. Believers through all ages were baptized into this one body on the Day of Pentecost, and in it there are no divisions, not even between Jews and Gentiles nor bond and free; it is one body. The local assembly is representative of this basic teaching; it too is one. The human body has some prominent parts, like the head, hands, eyes, etc., and many less prominent, even hidden parts which for proper bodily function are indispensible, which work unseen or in obscurity.

To perform efficiently as a body the various individuals in an assembly must work together harmoniously and where there is any defect, or something not functioning, the rest of the members strive to compensate for that. All parts work together for the benefit of the whole. Humanly speaking, the foot may be somewhat less dexterous than the hand but without a foot the body is severely impaired. The ear may be less prominent than the eye, but if there is no hearing the whole body is debilitated. If all parts of the body became eyes then it would be hideous.

God has given the human body its various parts and their individual responsibilities, and He has put together the local assembly in the same way. Each member should be content with his position and gift and all must work together continuously for the benefit of the whole. There would then be no schism in the local church and when there is, it is most probably because one member has become discontent with his position and aspires to something greater: the ear wishes to become the eye, but the skill set of an ear does not allow it to function as an eye. The result is disaster for both, and for the whole. We describe such happenings as 'personality clashes' and that is precisely what this section's teaching is aimed at. When your assembly next suffers as the result of a personality clash you will perhaps recognize the envy that caused it.

November 9th

1 Corinthians 14. 1-12

WHAT SHALL I PROFIT YOU?

Chapter 13 of this Epistle has shown that the greatest of all things is love. Paul now encourages the believers to pursue love and together with it to cultivate a desire for spiritual gifts, especially the gift of prophecy. This desire is of course subject to the limitations discussed in the previous study where each is to be content with his God-given gift. The gift of tongues was active at this time and many judged it superior to others. There seemed to be something attractive, even mysterious, about it and its users, but if there were no foreign language speakers present and no interpreter then it became a waste of time. It was flashy and bold, and whether or not people understood the message it seems they were impressed by the display!

On the other hand the gift of prophecy resulted in edification, exhortation, and comfort because the message could easily be understood. So, prophecy ought to be regarded as far more worthwhile than tongues. The question which is the subject of this meditation is in verse 6. Paul supposes that he comes to the assembly and speaks in a tongue, yet if he were to do so without an interpreter even the effort of this uniquely gifted speaker would be to no effect. However, should he speak plainly then all would learn and all would be comforted. Thus, if he had a revelation from God he would not use tongues but prophecy to announce the revealed truth and apply it to the hearers. If he wished to share his knowledge of God and His ways with the saints then he would do so plainly in teaching. Even at this time there was not much to encourage speaking in tongues. Paul said he would rather speak five words in prophecy or teaching than ten thousand words in an unknown tongue.

It is clear that the profiting of the assembly has precedence over everything else. Where the saints are built up God will be glorified. It is therefore important that preachers and teachers resist the temptation to display their gifts and concentrate on the profiting of the hearers in the things of God. Tongues are for a sign to unbelievers, especially Jews; prophecy and teaching is for the saints. They should not be intermingled, then or now!

November 10th

1 Corinthians 14. 26-40

CAME THE WORD OF GOD OUT FROM YOU? OR CAME IT UNTO YOU ONLY?

In this section the apostle deals with the subject of the word of God and divine order in the assembly. As the saints gather there is to be exercise and liberty so that the different gifts may operate within the limitations and conditions set down here. This applies to tongues, interpretations, and prophecies where we have the instructions, 'two or three', 'one', and 'one by one'. If disorder arose this was the fault of those taking part; obviously they were not in control of themselves. God is not the author of confusion but of peace. Then we have teaching that women must be silent in the church and not take part audibly as individuals. They may participate with others in audible praise and heart worship; not in teaching nor in any other prominent role.

It would seem that the assembly at Corinth was tolerating such things: an exercise of tongues that was out of place in that no foreigners were present and no interpreter was there either. Furthermore, the prophets were so anxious to speak that one could scarcely wait until another had finished; and to cap it all women were uncovered and taking part publicly. Now the assembly at Corinth was autonomous and directly responsible to the Lord Himself. They could say that what they did was nobody else's business, as their responsibility was solely to the Lord. Yet, while this is true, each assembly in its practices should be in line with apostolic teaching. But they were not; neither were they in line with the practices of other assemblies; but did that matter? They were autonomous.

In addressing this Paul asks the two questions above. The first implies that perhaps it was the Corinthian elders and prophets who were the real authors of scripture. Truth was based solely on their ideas and practices. They therefore really knew the truth better than any, including God. The second implies that perhaps the only people God had given His message to was them, so other assemblies did not know how to interpret and apply the truth. However, it does matter what other assemblies practice and if Corinth is out of line with clear Bible teaching and the practices of other churches then Corinth is wrong.

November 11th

1 Corinthians 15. 12-34

HOW SAY SOME AMONG YOU THAT THERE IS NO RESURRECTION?

In the first part of chapter 15 the apostle Paul sets forth the importance of the resurrection of Jesus Christ in salvation. He preached it, they received it, stand in it, and are saved by it! He then details some of the occasions on which the Lord appeared to His disciples on resurrection ground. So, the gospel and the salvation it offers are based upon the firm conviction, and positive evidence, that Christ did indeed rise from the dead.

It would seem that some Corinthians were saying that after death there would be no bodily resurrection of believers. This is rather strange thinking because if there were to be no resurrection the whole message of the gospel would be without foundation and the lives of believers without motive or incentive. The only benefit to be achieved would be the pleasure of living a moral life on earth. 'Not so', says Paul, as he details seven different consequences of not believing in the bodily resurrection of the dead: Christ is not risen; our preaching is vain; your faith is vain; ye are yet in your sins; those fallen asleep are perished; we are without hope; we are of all men most miserable, or to be most pitied. We live in a day when it is comforting to many to believe that there is no such thing as resurrection; that when they die that is the end of everything. But it is not so. Thousands of years ago Job declared that 'in my flesh shall I see God'; a statement in support of the truth of bodily resurrection. After death there is resurrection and there is judgement.

As believers, we joyously accept the evidences of the resurrection of Jesus Christ. We believe that He is the firstfruits and that in the same way as God raised Him from the dead, 1 Thess. 4. 14, He will raise the saints from their burial grounds. This is a truth to rejoice in and it should be as motivational for us as it was for Paul. If there were no resurrection what would be the point of being baptized for the dead? As older Christians die, and perish why would others hurriedly take their place only to perish also? If there were no resurrection why would Paul and his companions put their lives in jeopardy? 'But now is Christ risen' and His followers will be raised. There is a resurrection!

November 12th

1 Corinthians 15. 35-49

HOW ARE THE DEAD RAISED UP? AND WITH WHAT BODY DO THEY COME?

Accepting the fact of bodily resurrection for believers the Corinthians now pose two further questions, 'How are the dead raised up? And with what body do they come?' These are indeed interesting questions that are answered with limited knowledge. We do not know every detail of the resurrection but we are sure of the general principles. Looking at the first question, 'How?', we realize that the power of God is at work. Perhaps the questioner had in mind, 'How is it possible that a dead, buried, decayed body consisting perhaps only of bones, or maybe not even that, should be put together again?' Good question! The answer is that the body that will be raised is not the same as was buried – it will be different! In what way? Paul teaches that we should observe how God works in nature. A seed is sown, described here as 'bare grain, perchance of wheat or of some other grain'. It is dead and buried. But due to the power of God some time later there is a 'resurrection' and something different comes up! It is raised a fully-fledged plant such as wheat, and it is so different to the seed that was sown in the soil that we marvel at the change. The key to the first of these two questions is that the raised body is 'different'.

Regarding the second question, 'With what (kind of) body do they come?', the questioner is accepting that there will be a bodily resurrection and that body will be different, but now wonders in what way it will be different. Paul deals with this by showing that bodies of all kinds are formed to be appropriate for the environment in which they normally function. For example, beasts must live outdoors and fight for their daily food. They are equipped of God to do so. Birds fly in the air, fish swim in water. Crops mature in soil. Each is fearfully and wonderfully made to enable it to do so perfectly.

The body we have is right for life on earth; it is physical and material. In heaven will we need a different body – a spiritual body – specially suited for life there. 'It is sown a natural body; it is raised a spiritual body', 15. 44. As 'difference' answers the first question, so 'suitability' answers the second.

November 13th

1 Corinthians 15. 50-58

O DEATH WHERE IS THY STING?
O GRAVE WHERE IS THY VICTORY?

Here we see the normal process of sin and death, 'Sin, when it is finished, bringeth forth death', Jas. 1. 15. Firstly, there is a sting – sin; the inevitable result of this sting is death, as decreed by the law of God. On this basis as all have sinned, so all must die. This is a principle, or a law, it cannot be avoided or evaded. It would therefore appear that sin and death must have ultimate victory over humanity; all sin, all die, end of story! But this is not so. As we think of bodily resurrection as described in 1 Corinthians chapter 15 we are forced to ask two further questions, 'O death, where is thy sting?', 'O grave, where is thy victory?' On resurrection ground neither the sting nor its results are anywhere to be seen, praise God!

We appreciate that these questions, really, I suppose, statements are made in the light of the corruptible having put on incorruption and the mortal having out on immortality, v. 53. These are amazing facts and we must look at them more closely. Firstly, man is mortal, i.e. he must die. Indeed all men from the beginning of time have done so, with only a couple of exceptions. Every living person is, or certainly should be, aware that the day will come, sooner or later, when he or she will pass away. Yet, in the aftermath of the rapture it will become clear that millions will have safely entered heaven without dying! Those who were mortal will have cheated death and entered glory by another way. The mortal puts on immortality. Similarly, many millions more who were both dead and buried and whose bodies have decayed and corrupted in their various burial places will find that they have been raised, incorruptible!

It is therefore clear that those believers in our Lord Jesus Christ who are still alive at the Lord's coming have been stung by sin; yet the sting has been dealt with in the death of Christ, our Substitute, thus death has no claim on them. Equally, for all who have died and been buried, the grave which claimed their bodies is now dispossessed of them. The victory is theirs and their Lord's. Sin and death are rendered powerless and at last the people of God are forever free!

November 14th

2 Corinthians 1. 23-24; 2. 1-11

WHO IS HE THEN THAT MAKETH ME GLAD?

In 1 Corinthians chapter 5 we are told that a particularly grievous sin had taken place and a brother from the assembly was involved in it. Apparently, the facts of the case were common knowledge but the assembly had chosen to ignore the talk, and the sin, and to continue as if nothing had happened. The news had travelled and Paul became aware of the situation. He had been wanting to visit the assembly in Corinth but now feared that if he did so he would have to speak out publicly about the sin and even to personally take action against it. This he did not want to do, preferring that assembly deal with it in the proper way. So, instead, he wrote to them the letter now known as 1 Corinthians and in it told them plainly what they should do. And they acted! The offender was put away by 'the many', v. 6.

Furthermore, to God's glory, the offender had repented and put things right insofar as they could be righted. Paul, aware of that, now besought the assembly to be forgiving, to show the brother compassion lest if they delayed over-long in receiving him back to fellowship advantage would be handed to Satan. Indeed, Paul now had such confidence in the believers and their judgement that he said that if they exercised forgiveness so also would he, v. 10. All this meant that a visit by Paul for fellowship and ministry would be a time of blessing and rejoicing and not of grief all round, as it might otherwise have been. When he had made them 'sorry' by his first letter he was himself made sorry also. He had shed many tears as he thought about the sin and the failure to deal with it and he wanted them to know that these tears were the outcome of his deep love for all concerned in the affair. But now, as they were glad that all had been satisfactorily and scripturally resolved, their gladness became his! He could look forward to seeing them in full fellowship; Satan's temporary advantage had been wrestled back from him.

The lessons are clear: sin, where it is known, should be judged; excommunication is effected in love and has always the objective that the offender will be restored. That should happen as soon as is possible after repentance lest the offender be overcome with grief and be lost forever to the saints.

November 15th

2 Corinthians 2. 12-17

WHO IS SUFFICIENT FOR THESE THINGS?

Coming daily upon the apostle Paul was what he described as 'the care of all the churches'. The church at Corinth certainly seemed to cause him many problems and anxiety of spirit. There had been the sin we thought about in our previous meditation, then he was very concerned indeed as to how the believers there would react to his letter condemning them for the way things were going. Would they write him off and have no further fellowship with him? Would they do as he had told them in these matters of church practice and fellowship?

So he sent Titus to visit Corinth and to report back to him as soon as possible as to how his letter had been received. Apparently, he had arranged a rendezvous at Troas so that he could be updated. But Titus did not show up. Fearing bad news, Paul abandoned his gospel preaching there and rushed off to meet Titus whom he hoped would be travelling along the usual trade route through Macedonia. Eventually they met and Titus gave Paul his report. The saints had received the letter and acted on it and they desired to see Paul again. The apostle could scarcely contain himself. He was relieved and delighted and said, 'Now thanks be unto God which always causeth us to triumph in Christ'. Thinking again of the gospel which he had not preached in Troas he recalls that in the gospel, as well as in ministry to the saints, those who bring God's message are to some a savour of death unto death and yet to others of life unto life!

To be God's messenger with God's message is sometimes a heavy burden and the messenger may feel such a responsibility is just too much to bear. Paul preached sincerely, v. 17, and did not take his responsibilities lightly. No mere human being is up to the challenge of a message that has eternal implications for saints and sinners, hence the big question, 'Who is sufficient for these things?' Self-sufficiency is not an option, but adequate sufficiency is to be found in the Person of the Lord Jesus, as Paul said, 'I can do all things through Christ that strengtheneth me'. We too are often faced with seemingly intractable problems and we are quick to acknowledge our weakness, yet like Paul, our sufficiency is found in Him. Praise His Name!

November 16th

2 Corinthians 3. 1-11

DO WE BEGIN AGAIN TO COMMEND OURSELVES?

In this epistle Paul is under personal attack. Lurking behind our question is the suggestion that he was prone to self-praise. Paul utterly refutes that charge. He had never engaged in self-commendation and had no intention of doing so. His spiritual character and zealous service did not need to be boosted by self-promotion. 'For it is not the one who commends himself who is approved, but the one whom the Lord commends', 2 Cor. 10. 18 ESV.

The source of the trouble was a group of visitors from Jerusalem. They had arrived with glowing letters of commendation and expected impressive testimonials when they left. Paul and Timothy needed no such introduction to the Corinthians and no commendation from them. The Corinthians were themselves their letter of commendation. They were Paul's apostolic credentials, 1 Cor. 9. 2. He was their father in Christ, 4. 15. Their new life in Christ was the living evidence that Paul was a genuine apostle.

The Corinthians were a letter written by Christ. He was the divine Author. Paul was only a human penman. The message was written not in ink but by the Holy Spirit. Their transformed lives displayed the grace and power of the Lord Jesus. His image was engraved upon them. When others look at us do they see the unmistakeable impress of Christ? Do we display features that can have come only from Him?

Such features in Christians are written by the Spirit deep in the centre of personality. No longer are God's requirements impressed externally on stone tablets, Exod. 24. 12; 31. 18. In the new covenant they are internalized in the hearts of His people, Jer. 31. 33; Ezek. 11. 19-20; 36. 26-27.

God had displayed His glory when He gave the law, a covenant of death. The new covenant is one of life by the Spirit. The law was a ministry of condemnation, the gospel one of justification. Thus the glory of the new covenant far excels that of the old. The old has passed away. The new is permanent. What a privilege to be a minister of the new covenant, enabled by the all-sufficiency of God!

November 17th

2 Corinthians 6. 14-18; 7. 1

FOR WHAT FELLOWSHIP HATH RIGHTEOUSNESS WITH UNRIGHTEOUSNESS?

This passage commands us not to become involved in an unequal yoke with unbelievers. The picture is taken from the prohibition of ploughing with an ox and a donkey together, Deut. 22. 10. This scripture does not forbid all association with non-Christians but the forming of close relationships. These are incongruous alliances because there is an absolute difference between those who are in Christ and those who are not. In God's eyes that is the only real distinction.

Paul demonstrates this fundamental difference in five questions, posing five contrasts. 'No' is the only possible answer to each of them. He then quotes scripture to support his argument, gives us some wonderful divine promises, and concludes with a challenging application. We can almost 'catch an echo of Paul the preacher', HUGHES.

The first question contrasts righteousness with lawlessness. Christ loved righteousness and hated lawlessness, Heb. 1. 9. He offered Himself to redeem us from all lawlessness, Titus 2. 14. Before conversion, lawlessness was our lifestyle. Now we are challenged to live righteously, Rom. 6. 19. No partnership between righteousness and lawlessness is possible. Nor can there be fellowship between light and darkness. Once we were darkness, now we are light in the Lord, Eph. 5. 8. God has shined in our hearts giving the light of the knowledge of His glory in the face of Jesus Christ, 2 Cor. 4. 6.

The next contrast is between the Light of the world and the prince of darkness. Since Eden, Christ and Belial have been locked in deadly conflict. There can be no accord between them. The loyalties of a believer and an unbeliever are entirely different. One still belongs to Satan, Eph. 2. 1; the other owes allegiance to the Lord Jesus. The final distinction is between God's temple and idols. These can never reach agreement. Christians are the temple of God and they must flee idolatry, 1 Cor. 10. 14.

Let us avoid all dangerous alliances and indeed 'whatever cannot abide the holy eye of God', DENNEY.

November 18th

2 Corinthians 11. 1-15

HAVE I COMMITTED AN OFFENCE IN ABASING MYSELF THAT YE MIGHT BE EXALTED?

Paul writes here with deep irony. He feels forced to defend himself from attacks from Jewish teachers who had arrived in Corinth. They boasted of high spiritual status. They presented themselves as 'super apostles', 2 Cor. 11. 5 ESV. Actually they were 'false apostles', masquerading as apostles of Christ, v. 13.

A specific charge was that Paul had accepted no financial support in Corinth. The intruders argued that this proved how dubious Paul's standing was. Was not a teacher's prestige 'weighed by the price he could command', CARSON? Surely a labourer was worthy of his hire, Luke 10. 7?

Paul had made it clear that he had waived his right to support from the Corinthians, 1 Cor. 9. 12, 15, 18. Was it a sin for him to humble himself so that the Corinthians might be elevated? Obviously not! He had refused to stand on his dignity and had resorted to manual toil so that the Corinthians could be lifted from idolatry and immorality. Paul's lifestyle was modelled on Christ. His Lord had become poor so that His people by His poverty might become rich, 2 Cor. 8. 9.

Paul's practice of not accepting remuneration was to demonstrate that his preaching was 'free of charge', 11. 7 ESV. 'His payment was to receive no payment', BARNETT. The freeness of God's grace must never be 'obscured by the merest suggestion of a price to be paid', DENNEY. Freely we have received, freely we must give, Matt. 10. 8.

Paul was going to keep on maintaining this strategy. Even when in need he had not burdened the Corinthians. Rather he had accepted unsolicited gifts from other churches where he was not currently serving. This was no sign of a lack of love to the Corinthians. God knew his deep affection for them. It was designed to undercut the claim of the false teachers that they stood on the same level of ministry as Paul. They greedily sought payment for their services, 2 Cor. 2. 17 NKJV. Paul never did. The utter contrast in financial practices clearly showed who truly had the right to claim to be an apostle of the risen Christ. True servants of Christ are not motivated by worldly gain.

November 19th

2 Corinthians 11. 16-27

ARE THEY HEBREWS? SO AM I

'Answer a fool according to his folly', Prov. 26. 5. In Paul's assessment the interlopers in Corinth were 'fools'. He answers them in their own language. Triumphalist boasting was their hallmark. Paul cringes in embarrassment as he starts to boast as well. He is conscious that he is 'not talking as the Lord would' 2 Cor. 11. 17 NIV. Nothing is more unlike Christ than arrogant bombast. Yet boast Paul must. The false apostles were overbearing bullies, seeking to dominate the Corinthians. Yet impressed by their arrogant claims, they were willing to let them humiliate and abuse them. By kowtowing to these men they were surrendering gospel freedom for religious slavery.

In three rhetorical questions Paul takes up the first boast of his foes. Are they Hebrews, of the purest Jewish stock? Are they Israelites, members of the old covenant people of God? Are they Abraham's seed, heirs of God's unique promises? If so, Paul declares, so am I. He had as many Jewish qualifications as they had, indeed more. His heritage was at least as prestigious. Yet he counted all such claims as utter loss compared with the surpassing gain of knowing Christ as Lord, Phil. 3. 4-9.

'Are they servants of Christ? I am a better one', 2 Cor. 11. 23 ESV. Paul takes their profession at face value in his argument. Why was he better? Not because he had established more churches or preached to bigger crowds with greater results. Not because of his exploits and victories but because of his sufferings and defeats. It is in these that he boasts.

These deeply moving verses show that 'the sign of true apostleship is massive suffering in the service of Christ', CARSON. The boasters were left with nothing to say. Paul had been beaten by Jews and Romans. He had often been imprisoned. Once he had suffered stoning. Three times he had endured shipwreck, once adrift at sea for a day and a night. He was constantly in danger. Deprivation was often his lot. Frequently he was surviving below the poverty line. These were his credentials as a servant of Christ. The scars on his body were the brand marks of the Lord Jesus, Gal. 6. 17. Such unconditional devotion to the Saviour should stir us to the depths of our being!

November 20th

2 Corinthians 11. 28-33

WHO IS WEAK, AND I AM NOT WEAK?

Paul continues with paradoxical boasting. Besides all the suffering he details and much more he omits, he also has the daily pressure of concern for all the churches. He views this anxiety as 'the climax of his trials', CARSON. This burden is at least as great as the immense afflictions he had endured for Christ's sake. When we consider the spiritual energy he expended on the churches of Galatia or on Corinth we begin to understand a little of what he means. Paul's pastoral care extended beyond the churches he had planted to all the fledgling assemblies.

This was no professional administration, applying principles of business management. Paul was willing to travail in birth until Christ was formed in his converts, Gal. 4. 19. He was mother and father spiritually to new Christians, 1 Thess. 2. 7, 11. Most gladly he would spend and be spent for their souls, 2 Cor. 12. 15. He was willing to pour his own life into the lives of others, 1 Thess. 2. 8. Ultimately it was all about 'a deep involvement with people', CARSON.

Two passionate rhetorical questions tell us how much this cost Paul. They focus on individuals, living people and how fully the apostle made himself one with them. 'Who is weak, and I am not weak?' Whenever any Christian had reached a spiritual low point with their hoarded resources of strength exhausted Paul empathized deeply. 'In the fullness of his Christ-like strength he lived a hundred feeble lives', DENNEY. Paul practised what he taught. He upheld the weak, 1 Thess. 5. 14. Like the Lord Jesus he would not break the bruised reed or quench the dimly burning flax, Isa. 42. 3.

What of those who came to spiritual harm? If any are made to stumble and sin, then I feel pain in my heart like a burning fire, Paul says. He shared the deep indignation of Christ at those who led any of His little ones into sin, Matt. 18. 6. This explains his vehement reaction to false teachers. He burned inwardly when any believer was seduced from their devotion to Christ.

How dare we treat any of our brothers and sisters with indifference or unconcern! How unlike Paul! How unlike the Lord Jesus!

November 21st

2 Corinthians 12. 14-21

DID TITUS MAKE A GAIN OF YOU?

Paul turns his mind to a plan to revisit Corinth. He wants his readers to know that he has no intention of changing his policy of declining to accept their financial support. He had always waived these rights in Corinth. He was not going to start burdening them now. What he wanted was not the Corinthians' money but themselves, their devotion to Christ, and their personal affection. A parent spares no expense for his children so Paul will give unstintingly his time and energy for their spiritual growth. He had drunk deeply of the spirit of Christ. He was coming to Corinth not to be served but to serve. Yet he yearned for a response of love from the Corinthians. Already in this letter he had appealed to them to widen their hearts to make room for him. They were restricted in their affections, 2 Cor. 6. 11-13, 7. 2. Their base ingratitude must have hurt the apostle deeply.

His spirit was even more harshly wounded by a wicked accusation that his financial independence 'was a cunning front that masked his financial corruption', CARSON. Paul, it was said, did not take support openly and directly but extracted it by guile, using his associates. His opponents insinuated that Paul was crafty and unscrupulous. They suggested that at least a cut of the collection for the impoverished believers in Jerusalem being taken up by Titus and another close associate of Paul was going to find its way to Paul's back pocket. It is hard to imagine more harmful and hurtful charges. They said the apostle was both a hypocrite and a thief. He was willing to exploit the Corinthians by trickery. He was prepared to use the device of the offering for Jerusalem in this base scheme. Worst of all, these accusations implicated Paul's friends. How low had the Corinthians sunk to believe such blatant untruths, even for a moment!

Paul's answer is to appeal to the character of his colleagues, especially to the unimpeachable integrity of Titus. Could anyone imagine him taking advantage of the Corinthians? That was also true of Paul himself. It is crucial in the financial side of Christian work that the highest standards of honesty and transparency are always maintained.

November 22nd

Galatians 2. 11-21

WHY COMPELLEST THOU THE GENTILES TO LIVE AS DO THE JEWS?

Today's reading records a regrettable episode in Peter's life. Our text is Paul's searching question to Peter when he confronted him. Antioch was the first church with a Gentile presence. When Peter spent time there, he happily enjoyed meals with Gentile believers, ignoring the food rules of Judaism. Those rules maintained segregation between Jew and Gentile. However, when stricter Jewish believers appeared Peter changed his practice. He withdrew from social fellowship with Gentiles because he was afraid of Judaizers.

Peter's behaviour was hypocritical. If his former practice was right, to abandon it under pressure was two-faced. Why was he now insisting on Gentiles living like Jews before he could have fellowship with them? Peter, of all people, knew that the dietary restrictions of the law had been set aside by God. A voice from heaven had told him three times, 'What God has made clean do not call common', Acts 10. 15-16 ESV. Peter was disobedient to that revelation. He was acting a part he knew to be false. We need to be true to our convictions.

Peter's behaviour was influential. Tragically, all the Jewish believers followed his example. They separated themselves from Gentile Christians as well. Their action even swept Barnabas away. He took the same course even although he had been so greatly used in building up Jews and Gentiles alike, Acts 11. 22-24. We must be careful how we influence others.

Peter's behaviour was destructive. It undermined the foundations of the gospel. Jew and Gentile stood on exactly the same platform in sin and salvation. Only faith in Christ justifies, not the works of the law. To try to be justified by the law is to say that Christ died for no purpose. We must hold firmly to these essential truths.

Peter's reaction to Paul's rebuke was commendable, 'Faithful are the wounds of a friend', Prov. 27. 6. Many years later, he calls Paul 'our beloved brother', 2 Pet. 3. 14. Clearly, he did not hold this episode against him. We should thank God for Paul's insight and courage in defending the truth of the gospel.

November 23rd

Galatians 3. 1-14

O FOOLISH GALATIANS, WHO HATH BEWITCHED YOU?

In this searching question, Paul recalls the Galatians to reality. They had found the teaching of the visiting preachers exceptionally persuasive. Malign spiritual influences lay behind it. Legalism had operated on the minds of the Galatians like a magic charm. The attack on the purity of the gospel was satanic. Its pernicious effect was to seduce them from their devotion to the truth. The apostle's aim is to break the spell.

Paul reminds the Galatians of the message he had proclaimed to them. His language had been vivid. No one could misunderstand it. With broad strokes, he had painted a placard which unmistakably displayed the crucified Saviour. Today we need a renewed emphasis on the centrality of the cross in our evangelistic proclamation. In language as clear and contemporary as possible, we must express the unchanging truth of the gospel.

Paul also recalls their response to the message. In five rhetorical questions he underlines their first Christian experiences. By simply hearing and believing and not by works they had received the Holy Spirit, the crown of salvation. How foolish to think then, that they could progress to Christian maturity by a fleshly religion of performance and achievement. Were all their early trials in vain? God was still supplying them with the Spirit's grace and power in response to faith. From first to last, the Christian life is lived by grace alone and by faith alone.

Paul also explains that by their faith in the gospel they had received exactly the same blessing as Abraham. He had been counted righteous by God because of his belief. So had they. To rely on the law brings cursing and not blessing because no one can keep all of it all the time. Deliverance from that awful curse comes through Christ who bore it for us by His death on the tree. Then the dread sentence on the law-breaker was executed on Him. He stood in our place, cursed that we might be blessed. United to Christ, every Christian receives the wonderful blessings of justification and the gift of the Holy Spirit. The cross is the only basis of salvation; faith alone receives it.

November 24th

Galatians 3. 15-29

WHEREFORE THEN SERVETH THE LAW?

An answer to this question is demanded by the argument of the paragraph, the doctrinal heart of Galatians. Our passage begins by emphasizing that the law of Moses cannot supersede God's covenant with Abraham. It ends by explaining that Christians receive the blessings of that covenant through union with Christ, Abraham's seed.

In everyday life, a later will cannot nullify an earlier one which is already in effect. So the law cannot abrogate God's promises to Abraham, because it came 430 years after He confirmed them. God made His covenant with Abraham directly with no intermediaries. It was emphatically a covenant of promise. Its obligations rested on God alone. When the law was given, angels represented God and Moses represented Israel. Its obligations rested on the people. In promise, God says, 'I will'. In law, He says, 'You shall' and 'You shall not'. The fulfilment of the promise depends on God. The fulfilment of the law depends on failing people.

Paul then asks our question, 'Why then the law?' ESV. The law's role was temporary, lasting only until the coming of the Promised Seed. Its God-given function was negative, revealing that we deliberately break God's commands. God never designed the law to save, only to condemn. It could not bestow the spiritual life needed to meet its own demands. Only Christ can deliver from sin's guilt and power.

Paul gives two illustrations of the law's role. The law is a prison warden, keeping men under lock and key. Under it, men were strictly confined until faith in Christ released them. It is also like a child leader (literal translation) harshly supervising his youthful charges. Under it, men were severely restricted until the Lord Jesus brought them to spiritual adulthood. By faith we are free and no longer prisoners. By union with Christ we are adults and no longer infants. Every believer has received mature sonship in Christ. We all share equally the highest possible spiritual blessings and privileges. The law has fulfilled its purpose. Belonging to Christ, we are the seed and heirs of Abraham.

November 25th

Galatians 4. 1-11

HOW TURN YE AGAIN TO THE WEAK AND BEGGARLY ELEMENTS?

This is an astounding question, revealing how much was at stake in the spiritual battle in Galatia. The readers were in the balance. They were on the verge of submitting to the law. They had already started to keep the Jewish festivals. Paul was afraid that his gospel labours for them had been a tragic waste of time and effort.

To accept the legalistic demands meant enslavement. The different gospel was presented as a great advance to deeper spirituality. Actually it was a retreat to slavery, little different from what the Galatians had known as pagans. Once they had lived by rote under elementary principles of worldly religion. They had worshipped idols with no reality. They had been liberated by coming to a personal knowledge of God. Better still, He knew and loved them. What was being pressed upon them was the same system that had been the ABCs of religion to the Jews before the coming of Christ. For Gentiles to accept it now was to revert from liberty to slavery, and from maturity to infancy.

To submit to the law meant enfeeblement. The system they were about to accept lacked all spiritual power 'to rescue man from condemnation', LIGHTFOOT. It brought neither forgiveness for the past nor empowerment for the future. The gospel had given them both.

To be persuaded by the Judaizers meant impoverishment. Their message was beggarly or 'worthless', ESV. It brought 'no rich endowment of spiritual treasures', LIGHTFOOT. The Galatians possessed such treasures already by grace. By the Son, they had been redeemed. By the Father, they had been adopted. By the Spirit, they had a personal consciousness of intimacy with God as Abba, Father. Each one of them individually was a son and heir.

Why would anyone want to accept such a message? It was because the Galatians 'could still feel the attraction of slavery', MORRIS. Slavery meant taking no personal decisions. Free men and women in Christ enjoy the privilege and face the challenge of making responsible choices for themselves.

November 26th

Galatians 4. 12-31, 5. 1

TELL ME, YE THAT DESIRE TO BE UNDER THE LAW, DO YE NOT HEAR THE LAW?

With this question Paul challenges his readers. If they desire to be under the law, let them listen to it. We need to check all the messages we hear against the inerrant standard of God's word. It has absolute authority over all our thinking and living. 'To the law and the testimony', Isa. 8. 20, must be our motto.

Paul has already shown that the gospel fulfils the covenant with Abraham and that the law cannot supersede that covenant. Now he demonstrates that 'legal bondage and spiritual freedom cannot co-exist', BRUCE.

He does this by using the story of Hagar and Sarah and their sons, both born to Abraham, as an allegory, spiritual truth embodied in actual events. Hagar was a slave. Sarah was free. Ishmael was born to Hagar by the operation of the flesh. Isaac was born to Sarah in fulfilment of God's promise. Hagar stands for Sinai and the system of bondage centred in earthly Jerusalem. The adherents of the law are still enslaved. Sarah stands for the heavenly Jerusalem, the free mother city to which God's people belong and which sustains them. Isaac represents all Christians, Jews and Gentiles alike. They are freeborn sons by God's promise and His Spirit. The teenage Ishmael had taunted the infant Isaac. So the devotees of the law persecuted those who believed the gospel. Ishmael's sneers led Sarah to demand the casting out of the slave woman and her son. She knew Ishmael would always be a threat to Isaac's inheritance. There could be only one heir, not two. Paul quotes her words as scripture. Legalism was enslavement and a deadly threat to the spiritual inheritance of the Galatians. They must totally reject it.

In the stirring exhortation which encapsulates the message of this mighty epistle, Paul underlines that we owe our spiritual freedom to the work of the Lord Jesus on the cross. He is the divine Emancipator. He set His people free so that we might live in freedom with its tremendous privileges. We must stand firm in the liberty He has gained for us and never submit to the encroachments of any form of spiritual slavery. Liberation is a key note of the Christian gospel and of the Christian life.

November 27th

Galatians 5. 2-15

WHO DID HINDER YOU THAT YE SHOULD NOT OBEY THE TRUTH?

The Christian life is a race. Paul is very fond of this athletic metaphor. He uses it to describe his own service in Gal. 2. 2. The race continues from conversion to the end of our lives. It is a marathon, not a sprint. The focus is on the heavenly goal, the prize of the high-calling of God in Christ Jesus, Phil. 3. 14. To gain that eternal reward is worth any sacrifice. Attaining it should be our all-consuming ambition, 1 Cor. 9. 24. Winning demands endurance, Heb. 12. 1. Each runner must hasten on with all his strength, focussed on the finishing line. We must persevere, refusing to give in to fatigue. The wreath of victory from the Lord Jesus, the heavenly Umpire, is the noblest award of all. To win it we must finish the race, 2 Tim. 4. 7-8; it is finishing well that counts.

The Galatians had started well, Gal. 4. 14-15. Paul commends them for continuing well. They had made steady progress. Would they finish well? Sadly, someone had hindered them. 'Hindering' originally meant breaking up a road to make it impassable. It may carry that background here, or refer to runners who cut in across other contestants, or even trip them up. Whatever word picture is used, the result was that the Galatians had stopped running for God.

Our rhetorical question has its obvious answer – the legalistic teachers. They were the road-wreckers or the cheating athletes. Behind them stood Satan. The enemy of our souls takes a wicked delight in impeding our progress. If our running has been hampered we must ask ourselves Paul's question. Perhaps we need to lay aside the sin which clings so closely to us or the weights which hold us back, Heb. 12. 1. Certainly, any hindrance in the Christian race has nothing to do with the will and purpose of God who has called us to Himself.

The false teachers had hindered the Galatians by persuading them not to continue to obey the truth which they had once warmly received. Positively, spiritual progress and perseverance in the heavenly race demands that we should be eager to obey God's truth. Thus we shall win the glorious prize.

November 28th

1 Thessalonians 2. 13-20

FOR WHAT IS OUR HOPE, OR JOY OR CROWN OF REJOICING?

Paul pens this passage with 'the eloquence of a loving heart', HIEBERT. It pulsates with deep affection for the young converts in Thessalonica. You, the Thessalonians, say Paul, Silas and Timothy, are our hope, joy and crown of exultation in the presence of the Lord Jesus at His coming. Indeed, 'Who could it be if it is not you?' HIEBERT. Nothing can disguise the pride and delight the missionaries took in their spiritual children who had become so dear to them.

Their dear Thessalonian friends filled the hearts of Paul and his companions with hope. They were convinced that the converts would not disappoint them. By God's grace, the high hopes they cherished for them would be fulfilled. They had seen them turn to God from idols, accepting their message as the word of God. Now that divine word was working in their hearts bringing them to spiritual maturity. They were steadfastly enduring persecution. Clearly God was at work in their lives. In the great day to come He would present them faultless before the presence of His glory with exceeding joy, Jude 24.

These new Christians caused Paul and his companions to thrill with 'joy in the evident genuineness of their faith', BRUCE. The Thessalonians were displaying the work of faith, labour of love, and patience of hope. Their divine election was proved by their response to the gospel. Now they themselves were spreading God's message far afield. Indeed they had become a model church. Like the Lord and His servants, they had experienced joy amid affliction.

The converts produced exultation in Paul and his friends as they looked forward to appearing with them, the fruit of their service, at Christ's judgement seat. They anticipated receiving the soul-winner's crown surrounded by those they had led to faith. The Thessalonians would themselves be their laurel wreath of victory. Their presence in glory would be the evidence that Paul and his companions had fulfilled their commission. Their dear Thessalonians would be their prize, proof that they had not run or laboured in vain, Phil. 2. 16.

November 29th

1 Thessalonians 3. 1-13

FOR WHAT THANKS CAN WE RENDER TO GOD AGAIN FOR YOU?

Paul and Silas had received the very best news. They had sent Timothy to encourage the Thessalonians. He had returned, reporting that their faith was steadfast and their love fervent amidst affliction and satanic assault. They were as eager to see the missionaries again as they were to see the saints. These tidings removed Paul's anxiety. His heart overflowed. It was vibrant life for him if the Thessalonians stood fast in the Lord. Nothing gave him greater joy. Immediately he writes to encourage them further and instruct them more fully in belief and behaviour.

Paul cared deeply for individuals. He had an affectionate interest in all those he sought to serve. No ministry is effective without genuine love. Paul yearned for reciprocal affection. He desired no other reward. The Thessalonians gladly gave him a place in their hearts. He had given up all his earthly ties for Christ. The Lord compensated him with the love of his brothers and sisters in the family of God.

Paul and his companions were men of prayer. Their prayers were thankful. Their immediate reaction to the news Timothy brought was to express their thanks to God for the Thessalonians and all the joy they had given them. Their constancy was due to God's upholding grace. Yet our question shows that the missionaries were well aware that words were only a poor and inadequate repayment of the debt of gratitude they owed to God. Their prayers were persistent. During the silent hours of night and the busy hours of day they lifted up their voices for the Thessalonians. Beseeching God for others was their constant practice. The very strong adverb 'exceedingly' or 'superabundantly' shows that their prayers were 'the spontaneous outflow of their hearts', Hiebert. They were in earnest. There was nothing half-hearted in their prayers. Their chief longing in the life of prayer was the spiritual blessing of others. They pleaded with God for an opportunity to visit the Thessalonians again to seek to bring them to greater maturity in their faith. Do I have a genuine interest in others and in their spiritual growth? Do my prayers bear any resemblance to prayers like these?

November 30th

1 Timothy 3. 1-7

IF A MAN KNOW NOT HOW TO RULE HIS OWN HOUSE, HOW SHALL HE TAKE CARE OF THE CHURCH OF GOD?

The churches of the New Testament shared a common pattern of leadership. Each assembly was led by a plurality of spiritually mature men called elders, Acts 14. 23. These same men were termed overseers, Acts 20. 17, 28. Their work was to watch over and guard the believers. This pattern remains the model for churches today.

In this passage Paul underlines the qualities needed in those who aspire to the noble task of overseership. A remarkable number of them focus on a man's family life. God requires an elder to be faithful in marriage. He should practise hospitality. He should govern his children with dignity and be a good manager of his home. Our question shows 'the necessity and importance of this requirement', STRAUCH.

These issues are stressed because the church is a family – the family of God. Fathers are expected to meet the needs of their household. Elders are to meet the needs of the local church. The home is the proving ground for the church. A man's leadership in his own household prepares him for leadership in God's.

Our question describes spiritual leadership as taking care of the congregation of God's people. It is not domineering control. The biblical style of leadership is shepherding. This demands sensitivity and sacrifice. The flock of God must be led by example, not driven by force, 1 Pet. 5. 2-3.

An elder must show such leadership to his own family. He must 'govern his children graciously and gravely', GUTHRIE. He should rule his household in a dignified way seeking to gain and maintain the respect of his children and their submissiveness to his direction. An elder's approach to his children will manifest itself in his approach to the assembly members. His relationship to his family will be the model of his relationship to the church fellowship. 'A biblical elder is best tested by how well he handles his children, not by how rich, successful or well-known he may be', STRAUCH.

December 1st

Philemon 1-22

PERHAPS . . . RECEIVE HIM FOR EVER?

The delightful letter from Paul to Philemon has been described as a model of Christian courtesy, and so it is. The same writer who would sometimes use his apostolic authority to command a particular course of action, here speaks in tones of tenderness, consideration, and sincere encouragement, never mentioning his apostolic calling. He is writing to Philemon, a wealthy resident in the city of Colossae whose conversion to Christ had been through the preaching of the apostle. This we know from Paul's words in verse 19, 'Thou owest unto me even thine own self besides'. Apphia was possibly the wife of Philemon and they, with Archippus (whose relationship to the others we do not know, but possibly he was their son) opened their home for the believers to meet in local assembly fellowship.

Onesimus, a servant of Philemon, had run away from his master and gone to Rome where Paul was imprisoned. There, somehow, he had come under the sound of Paul's preaching and been gloriously saved. We can imagine the pleasure on Paul's part, and the immediate fear on the part of Onesimus, when it became evident that Paul not only knew the master of the runaway slave but had also led him to Christ in Colossae. Was this simply a wonderful coincidence? Not at all! Paul, recognizing the sovereign hand of God at work, told Onesimus that he must return to Philemon but that he, Paul, would give him a personal letter of commendation. It would seem from Colossians chapter 4 verses 7 to 9 that Paul entrusted Onesimus and the letter to Philemon into the care of Tychicus who also carried Paul's epistle to the Colossians as he returned to that city.

The question raised by Paul in verses 15 and 16 was intended to focus Philemon's mind on the sovereign dealings of God with Onesimus. The expression 'he therefore departed' suggests that Onesimus 'was parted' from Philemon rather than he had simply run away. In the sovereign purpose of God, a slave and his master had become brethren in Christ, and Philemon now had opportunity to show the love of God in receiving Onesimus as such. An unprofitable sinner had fled, but it was a profitable saint who came home.

December 2nd

Hebrews 1. 1-5

WHICH OF THE ANGELS . . . THOU ART MY SON?

The question posed at the outset of the Epistle to the Hebrews was intended to focus the minds of the readers on the supremacy of the Lord Jesus over all the angelic realm. We frequently hear it stated that chapter 1 of the epistle establishes the deity of Christ and chapter 2 His humanity, but such a statement is a little simplistic. Remember, the letter begins with the glorious truth that God has spoken 'in Son', the fullest possible declaration of God to man. Previous divine statements had used the ministration of angels, particularly where the giving of the law was concerned. Stephen, speaking of the nation, said, 'Who have received the law by the disposition of angels, and have not kept it', Acts 7. 53. The Jews attached great importance to angelic glory, but now it has been revealed that a Man has surpassing glory! In assuming perfect manhood, the Lord Jesus never relinquished anything of His essential deity. True, He veiled the glory of His deity in flesh, but He never became less than what He eternally is. He is the eternal Son of God, Creator and Upholder supreme, and He became Man, absolutely and impeccably, in order to fully declare the Father.

Referring to Psalm 2 verse 7, the writer asks the rhetorical question, 'For unto which of the angels said he at any time, Thou art my Son, this day have I begotten thee?' It may be remarked that angels are referred to as sons of God in Genesis chapter 6 verses 2 and 4, and again in Job chapter 1 verse 6 and chapter 2 verse 1, but that description is always collective, never individual. In thinking of the Lord Jesus as Son of God, no thought of genealogy is in view. A true son displays the character of his father, something clearly taught by the Lord Jesus, John 8. 31-47. As Son of God the Lord Jesus manifested the Father in the fullest possible way, John 14. 9, something no angel could ever do.

'This day have I begotten thee' is a phrase used by some to deny the eternal sonship of the Lord Jesus. The day referred to is not the day of His incarnation but the day of His resurrection out from among the dead. Paul's preaching recorded in Acts chapter 13 verses 26-37 should be studied to confirm this fact.

December 3rd

Hebrews 1. 6-14

WHICH OF THE ANGELS . . . MY RIGHT HAND?

The first chapter of the Epistle to the Hebrews has seven quotations from the Old Testament scriptures to confirm the supremacy of the Lord Jesus over all principalities, powers, and angelic spirits. Might we say, reverently, that the final quotation is the greatest of them? Is there a clearer confirmation anywhere in scripture of the eternal deity and greatness of the Lord Jesus than to hear David say by the Spirit, 'The Lord said unto my Lord, Sit thou at my right hand, until I make thine enemies thy footstool', Ps. 110. 1? (Remember that this quotation, like all other Old Testament quotations in the Epistle, is taken from the Greek version known as the 'Septuagint'. This often explains why such quotations are not always as they appear in the Old Testament).

The inspiration of scripture by the Holy Spirit is the only explanation for the exactness of Psalm 110. David wrote of the return of the Lord Jesus to heaven after His rejection by men, and the assurance He was given by God that, in the fullness of time, all His enemies would be subdued beneath His feet. Without pausing, David continued to write verse 2 of Psalm 110, 'The Lord shall send the rod of thy strength out of Zion: rule thou in the midst of thine enemies'. What David could not have understood was that between verses 1 and 2 of the psalm there would be a period of time stretching out more than 2000 years! Verse 1 describes the Lord's return to heaven at His ascension and verse 2 describes His return to the earth to establish His millennial kingdom in power and great glory.

But to which of the angels did God say at any time, 'Sit on my right hand, until I make thine enemies thy footstool?' Clearly the answer is 'none'! They were created as ministering spirits, not rulers, Heb. 1. 14, 'For unto the angels hath he not put in subjection the world to come', 2. 5. There was one angel, Lucifer, who aspired to the throne and he was cast down. His end will be the lake of fire, whilst the kingdom and the glory of universal dominion will be given to the one blessed Man who is entitled to it all, our Lord Jesus Christ. God has said, 'Yet have I set my king upon my holy hill of Zion', Ps. 2. 6.

December 4th

Hebrews 2. 1-9

HOW SHALL WE ESCAPE . . . ?

In seeking to understand the urgency of this first warning passage in the Letter to the Hebrews, we do well to remember that the main purpose of this epistle was to exhort the readers. As the writer concludes his rich ministry, he says, 'And I beseech you, brethren, suffer the word of exhortation: for I have written a letter unto you in few words', Heb. 13. 22. In fact, the word rendered 'beseech' in this verse is itself the word 'exhort', so he is exhorting them to heed the exhortation. In Romans chapter 12 verses 7 and 8 we learn that teaching and exhortation are two different things, so the Letter to the Hebrews was intended not so much to teach as to exhort. Teaching imparts knowledge of things formerly unknown to the hearers, but exhortation calls those who know things to live in the good of them. The recipients of the Letter to the Hebrews knew through apostolic preaching the truth of the Person and work of the Lord Jesus. Hence the writer says, 'We ought to give the more earnest heed to the things which we have heard, lest at any time we should let them slip', 2. 1. Divine truth stands fast, but there is a danger that, through neglect, we can drift away from things once heard and believed. That is the warning with which chapter 2 begins.

The writer now uses the natural tendency of the Jew to venerate angels as a lever to persuade them to action. God had used angels as messengers of His word in the past, and every pronouncement had stood fast. Angels spoke to Moses, Lot, and Daniel amongst others, and if the word conveyed by these created beings was attended to intently, knowing that just recompense would always ensue, how much more should men respond when the Lord Himself not only speaks but is the very Word? There was a time, recorded in Matthew chapter 22, when the Lord Jesus told a parable concerning a king who made a marriage for his son. When his servants went out with the message of invitation there were those who 'made light of' the king's kindness. The words 'made light of' are rendered 'neglect' in our passage today. To make light of so great salvation is to provoke divine anger, for these things were spoken by the Lord and His apostles. There can be no escape!

December 5th

Hebrews 3. 1-19

WITH WHOM WAS HE GRIEVED FORTY YEARS?

The writer's purpose in posing this question is to provoke fear, according to the first verse of chapter 4, 'Let us therefore fear, lest, a promise being left us of entering into his rest, any of you should seem to come short of it'. Note the use of the words 'us' and 'you' in this verse. The fear and the promise are common to 'us', says the writer, but the danger of coming short of it applies to 'you', a select number. The specific case in the Letter to the Hebrews concerned those with a background steeped in Judaism who had now heard the gospel. Through the enlightening work of the Holy Spirit they understood that God had finished with the old order of things and the divine demand was now repentance toward God and faith in our Lord Jesus Christ. Nevertheless, some hovered in indecision, preferring that which was seen to that which was not. It was a question of faith, an active belief in, and obedience to, the living God. To press home the point, a well-known episode in Israel's history is recalled.

The events recorded in Numbers chapters 13 and 14 make very sad reading. God had brought His people out of Egypt so that He might bring them into a land prepared for them, a land 'flowing with milk and honey'. Their estimation of the same land, however, was that it was occupied by giants who could not be defeated. They believed the evil report of the ten spies and, for this lack of trust in the living God, they were doomed to perish in the wilderness. It was their unbelief that provoked God to anger, because unbelief (the word means 'no faith') is not only a refusal to obey God's word but is also a terrible slur on God's character and trustworthiness. Through lack of faith, all over the age of twenty years who came out of Egypt, except Joshua and Caleb, died in the wilderness. These were not ignorant Gentiles, but the people of God who had seen His miracles! Later in the epistle the writer will tell his readers, 'Without faith it is impossible to please him', Heb. 11. 6.

Unbelief is evil, 3. 12, and deprives people of blessing they would otherwise receive. What blessing the Saviour would have brought to those of 'his own country', but 'he did not many mighty works there because of their unbelief', Matt. 13. 54-58!

December 6th

Hebrews 7. 1-25

WHAT FURTHER NEED . . . ANOTHER PRIEST?

'And in those days, when the number of the disciples was multiplied . . . a great company of the priests were obedient to the faith', Acts 6. 1, 7. It is very possible that this company of the priests was the primary readership of the Letter to the Hebrews. Certainly, the writer supposes a knowledge not only of Jewish things in general, but of Levitical procedure especially. Notice how, in chapter 4, he speaks of the word of God being sharper than any two-edged blade that can merely divide between joints and marrow. As priests, his readers knew what it was, with consummate skill and sharp knives, to swiftly dismember a beast and expose all to the view of God. They now learned that the word of God was doing the same to them, dividing soul and spirit, thoughts and intents of the heart, so that 'all things are naked and opened unto the eyes of him with whom we have to do', Heb. 4. 13.

In speaking of Melchisedec in chapters 5 and 7, the writer is not so much revealing new truth but causing his readers to consider scriptures they knew well but had never properly grasped. They supposed that the priesthood of which they had been part, the priesthood headed by Aaron, was the ultimate. But if the Aaronic priesthood had been able to achieve eternal salvation and total sanctification for the people, why did the Old Testament scriptures speak of another priest arising, one after the order of Melchisedec? They had only to give the matter some thought to realize that Melchisedec pre-dated Aaron, so his was the original priesthood. The priesthood headed by Aaron was only ever intended to be temporary until the time should come in the purpose of God that a priest of a different kind should arise who, by one sacrifice, and that of Himself, should do away with all that was under Aaron in one stroke.

Perfection, that is, completion of purpose, had manifestly not been achieved by the Aaronic priesthood. The priests themselves were subject to death and the sacrifices they offered could never take away sins. Why then did the readers of the letter want to cling so tenaciously to an imperfect system? They must let it go and cleave to Christ alone.

December 7th

Hebrews 9. 1-22

HOW MUCH MORE . . . THE BLOOD OF CHRIST?

The Day of Atonement with all its ritual and purpose forms a backdrop to much of the Letter to the Hebrews. This fact is a strong reason for Christians having a good understanding of the Old Testament scriptures. Some say that the Old Testament, and the first five books especially, are difficult to understand and irrelevant to the practical life and experience of a Christian today. A lot of the difficulty in understanding will disappear with repeated reading, just as we have all proved, probably, in secular studies. As to Old Testament truth being irrelevant, no statement could be more wrong. Without a knowledge of Genesis, Exodus, and Leviticus in particular, the Epistles to the Romans, the Galatians, and the Hebrews will never be properly understood. In turn, that means our knowledge of the gospel, our liberty in Christ, our sanctification, and priestly ministry before God and men, will never be rightly understood. But these are the very doctrinal precepts that underpin our practical living! Dear reader, prayerfully and diligently study the whole Bible!

In our passage today, the efficacy of the blood of Christ is contrasted with the blood of animal sacrifices under the old order of things headed by Aaron. On the Day of Atonement the high priest went alone into the holiest of all, first to atone for the sins of himself and his family, Lev. 16. 6, and then 'to make an atonement for the children of Israel for all their sins once a year', v. 34. Huge limitations are immediately apparent. First, the man representing the people was a sinner. Second, the blood he took into the holiest of all was incapable of *taking away* sins, Heb. 10. 4. The most the blood could do, and that by divine grace, was to *cover* the sins of the people. Third, the incapability of the animal blood meant that the guilty consciences of the people were never purged. Fourth, the ineffectiveness of the whole ritual meant that it had to be repeated annually.

Ah! How wonderful the truth we have read, 'How much more shall the blood of Christ, who through the eternal Spirit offered himself without spot to God, purge your conscience from dead works to serve the living God?' The sacrifice of the Lord Jesus has put an end to futile Aaronic service for ever!

December 8th

Hebrews 10. 1-18

WOULD THEY NOT HAVE CEASED TO BE OFFERED?

With the procedure of the Day of Atonement still firmly in view, the writer relentlessly presses upon his readers the futility of the Aaronic order and all its ritual. The one thing the people desperately needed was the assurance that their sins had been dealt with, fully and finally. That assurance was something never possible in the whole sacrificial system of which the Day of Atonement was the pinnacle. The statement of verse 4 is stark and hard-hitting, 'For it is not possible that the blood of bulls and of goats should take away sins'. If it had been in any way possible, the writer explains, they would have ceased to be offered. How well ISAAC WATTS summed it up, 'Not all the blood of beasts on Jewish altars slain, could give the guilty conscience peace, or wash away one stain'.

If the Aaronic ritual was so manifestly lacking, yet was ordained of God, what was its purpose? The blood that could never take away sins could, nevertheless, provide atonement, that is, a covering for those sins. The atonement averted the gaze of a righteous God from the sins of the people. He saw the blood and acknowledged that necessary judgment had been borne by a substitute. It could not be a permanent thing because, principally, the victim had been utterly unaware of its part in the work. Not one sacrifice knew the reason why it was at the altar, so it could not intelligently give its own life for another. The life of an animal could provide relief from judgment for a little while, but then the whole thing had to be repeated.

When the Lord Jesus went to the altar of Calvary it was as an intelligent Victim. 'He took my sins and my sorrows, He made them His very own; He bore the burden at Calvary and suffered and died alone', CHARLES H. GABRIEL. Himself sinless, the Lord Jesus was morally qualified to be the perfect Substitute for repentant sinners. He exposed Himself consciously to the wrath of an offended God, accepting responsibility Himself for the sins that had attracted that wrath. Peter wrote, 'Who his own self bare our sins in his own body on the tree', 1 Pet. 2. 24. If Old Testament sacrifices could have done all this, 'would they not have ceased to be offered?' Heb. 10. 2.

December 9th

Hebrews 10. 19-39

HOW MUCH SORER PUNISHMENT?

The solemn context of this question, posed for emphasis upon the readers, is found in verse 26, 'For if we sin wilfully after that we have received the knowledge of the truth, there remaineth no more sacrifice for sins'. That is, if persons enlightened by the Holy Spirit as to their guilt before God and their need of salvation through faith in the Lord Jesus, if they consciously reject the truth, they place themselves beyond the reach of divine grace. They despise God's love, the blood of His Son, and the overtures of the Holy Spirit. If men so despised God in Old Testament days and died under summary and horrific judgement, 'Of how much sorer punishment, suppose ye, shall he be thought worthy, who hath trodden under foot the Son of God, and hath counted the blood of the covenant, wherewith he was sanctified, an unholy thing, and hath done despite unto the Spirit of grace?' Heb. 10. 29.

The American preacher, Jonathan Edwards, once preached, 'Thou hast despised the mighty power of God; thou hast not been afraid of it. Now why is it not fit that God should show the greatness of His power in thy ruin? What king is there who will not show his authority in the punishment of those subjects that despise it? And what king will not vindicate his royal majesty in executing vengeance on those that rise in rebellion? And art thou such a fool as to think that the great King of heaven and earth, before whom all other kings are so many grasshoppers, will not vindicate His kingly majesty on such contemptuous rebels as thou art? Thou art very much mistaken if thou thinkest so. If thou be regardless of God's majesty, be it known to thee, God is not regardless of His own majesty; He taketh care of its honour, and He will vindicate it'.

If men of old were sorely judged for despising God's righteousness when it was revealed, how much more will men be judged who have seen His mercy, love, and kindness displayed in the giving of His Son, and who have contemptuously flung that gift back in His face? Take heed, for God is a God of vengeance who has said, 'I will recompense', v. 30. 'It is a fearful thing to fall into the hands of the living God', v. 31.

December 10th

Hebrews 12. 1-13

SHALL WE NOT . . . LIVE?

The writer of the Letter to the Hebrews has turned his attention to the real suffering being endured by many of those to whom he was writing. It is difficult for a Gentile mind to fully comprehend the consequences for a Jew, and especially a priest, renouncing Judaism and publicly confessing Jesus as Saviour and Lord. It was worse than death; it was a living death, separated from all that had once mattered, and now outcast, despised, and reviled. Very few, if any, of those reading this daily meditation have known suffering of that kind on account of faith in Christ. For judgement to fall upon the ungodly is a righteous thing. For those who, having once been enlightened but have now turned their backs on divine grace, to know God's wrath is an understandable thing. But why do those who seek to be faithful to God and His word endure suffering?

In answering this genuine question, the writer asks his readers to consider the days of their infancy when they were subject to their natural fathers. Did not their fathers correct them, and did not that correction involve chastening? Loving and responsible fathers recognize in their children a natural tendency to do that which is wrong, and for the good of their children they administer discipline and, if necessary, correction. Any chastisement involved does not show the father to be cruel but, rather, to be loving and mindful of his responsibility to the child. All this was done by our earthly fathers who 'for a few days chastened us after their own pleasure', Heb. 12. 10. The verse does not mean, of course, that our fathers took delight in chastising us, but that any such correction was according to their standards and their attitude to child-rearing.

Seeing we gave respect to our earthly fathers and their corrective discipline, 'shall we not much rather be in subjection to the Father of spirits, and live?' In contrast to 'the fathers of our flesh', God is the 'Father of spirits' from whom all life flows. In their exercise of discipline, all our fathers had flaws, but our Father in heaven knows exactly the chastening we need to bring us into conformity with His will. It may not be pleasant at the time but, if we are exercised by it, it will result in fruitfulness.

December 11th

James 2. 1-13

ARE YE NOT THEN PARTIAL IN YOURSELVES?

The short passage in James' Epistle that deals with respect of persons lies between two references to the law of liberty. 'But whoso looketh into the perfect law of liberty, and continueth therein, he being not a forgetful hearer, but a doer of the work, this man shall be blessed in his deed', Jas. 1. 25. 'So speak ye, and so do, as they that shall be judged by the law of liberty', 2. 12. In the first reference, the link is between hearing and doing. In the second, the link is between speaking and doing. The law of liberty describes the practical effect on the life of a believer when the word of God is read and obeyed. The word of God is described as a mirror in chapter 1, and two kinds of men look into it. One looks into it with a view to admiring himself, the other looks into it to see if there are flaws revealed. The first walks away completely unaffected, but the second, acting upon what he has observed, is liberated from whatever it was that spoiled the reflection.

In the metaphor of the glass in chapter 1, two men observe themselves. In the incident James refers to at the start of chapter 2, two men are observed by others. The scene is swiftly set. The assembly is gathered and two visitors arrive in quick succession. It seems from the overall context of the chapter that the visitors are fellow believers in the Lord Jesus. The first visitor quite clearly is a rich man. His clothes, his ornamentation; all proclaim his wealth. Those responsible as doorkeepers follow a natural inclination to ingratiate themselves with the man, showing him to a chief seat and making much of him. The second visitor is noticeably poor, his vile raiment, that is, poor quality clothing, not necessarily dirty, testifying to his poverty. He is made to stand or else sit like a dog at somebody's feet.

Ask any of those believers if they are convinced of the truth of the body of Christ and they will answer in the affirmative. Yet their actions belie what they profess to believe. Hearers they may be, but doers they are not. They are partial, making wrong and divisive judgements, those judgements the product of evil thoughts. How important it is that we honestly practise what we profess to believe!

December 12th

James 2. 14-26

BUT WILT THOU KNOW, O VAIN MAN?

Perhaps the first thing to strike us about the question, 'But wilt thou know, O vain man, that faith without works is dead', is that James exposes the sin of selective belief. Effectively, he is saying to his readers, 'You tell me you believe the gospel. You tell me you believe there is one God. There is no credit for you in announcing you believe these things, for the demons believe them too. Are you prepared to believe this, however, that faith without works is dead?' This teaching is immensely practical, touching the very core of Christian life and experience. Faith without works is dead! We delude ourselves and others if we teach that people can quietly and personally know God's salvation but it does not necessarily affect the way they live. If their works do not justify their profession of faith, then faith is not there. Faith, like mercy and grace, is seen in action. If a person professes salvation but there is no change in his life, consistently no desire for God's word or His people, the lack of works declares that faith is dead. Mental assent to truth is not faith. Philosophy is not faith. Believing and obeying the living God is faith, and it will always be accompanied by works that declare its reality and its character. Are we prepared to believe that? Such is the question posed here by James.

The two examples cited by James, of faith being seen in works, concern a man and a woman, Abraham and Rahab. In the long list of well-known Old Testament characters, these two stand at opposite ends. Yet, they are united in this one thing – they believed God and they obeyed at potentially great cost to themselves. True faith takes people out of their comfort zone and casts them upon God and His promises. This is why verse 21 asks, 'Was not Abraham our father justified by works, when he had offered Isaac his son upon the altar?' We know that a man is justified by faith, Rom. 5. 1, but the reality of that faith is justified, demonstrated, by subsequent works. How do we know if a person's profession of faith is genuine? Not by an eloquent testimony or an insistence on being able to state when, where, and how they trusted Christ. The true evidence of faith is the fruit of the Spirit seen in the life, Gal. 5. 22-26.

December 13th

James 3. 1-12

A FOUNTAIN . . . SWEET WATER AND BITTER?

Once again, inspired by the Spirit of God, James takes us to the heart of practical Christian living. We can be so prone to assess spirituality by people's adherence to accepted church practice, by the way they dress, or their reputation for hospitality. These are all important things, without doubt, and we do not demean them for one moment. One very good test of a person's spirituality, James teaches us, is how well they control their tongue! The man who gains mastery of his words is a spiritually complete man, a spiritually mature man. If he can control his tongue, we can be sure he can control his whole body, Jas. 3. 2.

James uses several illustrations to bring home to his readers the impact of the tongue upon the life. A large horse is turned this way and that by means of a small bit put into its mouth. An ocean-going vessel has its direction controlled by a rudder that is comparatively tiny and unseen. Large objects directed by small ones, but that is not the whole point. The bit and the rudder are being controlled by the horseman and the helmsman respectively. But, if the tongue can direct, it can also destroy! A small fire can eventually destroy an entire forest, and undoubtedly the fire does the damage. But who started the fire?

James is teaching us that we should first be aware of the capacity of the tongue to direct and damage, but his main point is the way the tongue is controlled. An aggressive horseman, through the bit, can cause the horse to fall. An inattentive helmsman, via the rudder, can run the ship onto rocks. Is the bit at fault? Is the rudder to blame? Not at all – the control of those things is the problem. That is why James speaks of a fountain, a source of water. It is not possible for a fountain to send forth, at the same place, sweet water and bitter. Note the words, 'at the same place'. Water that is sweet at its source can be polluted further downstream, but at its source it can only be either sweet or bitter. So what kind of spirit controls my tongue? Do I connect my old nature or my new nature to that powerful member? The tongue will always obediently follow the inputs given to it. I am like the horseman. I am like the helmsman. The responsibility for controlling the tongue is mine.

December 14th

James 3. 13-18

WHO IS A WISE MAN . . . AMONG YOU?

In yesterday's meditation we looked at the dangers associated with the tongue in a general way. There is necessary teaching in the epistle for every believer. As we look today at the question in chapter 3 verse 13, however, we need to note that James was particularly addressing those who would be teachers of the Lord's people. Chapter 3 begins, 'My brethren, be not many masters, knowing that we shall receive the greater condemnation', v. 1. The word 'masters' is better understood as 'teachers', and James, a teacher himself, reminds those who would stand before the saints as teachers that such a dignified privilege brings with it a much greater responsibility before the Lord. Then comes the teaching about the dangers of the tongue when not properly controlled.

So how can a truly able teacher of the word of God be recognized? Is it by his power of oratory, or by a certain presence? Is it by his ability to sway an audience this way and that, from laughter to tears and back again? Emphatically no! Knowledge alone is not enough, it must be accompanied by wisdom. We could define wisdom as that ability to apply knowledge in the right way and at the right time, but James takes it further. Just as faith without accompanying works is dead, so a teacher who does not live out the things he teaches is no true teacher at all. His manner of life must commend his teaching, and his attitude must be one characterized by the meekness that godly wisdom will bring, v. 13. There is a wisdom that belongs to this world, and there is a wisdom that is from above. The word of God handled with worldly wisdom can be destructive. Paul told the Corinthians, 'For Christ sent me not to baptize, but to preach the gospel: not with wisdom of words, lest the cross of Christ should be made of none effect', 1 Cor. 1. 17. Sadly, assemblies of believers have been spoiled and divided, not by false teaching, but by the word of God being handled without that wisdom from above.

Believers are very quick to detect whether true wisdom is there when men handle the word of God. A true teacher will be truly wise, and will exemplify his own teaching.

December 15th

James 4. 1-10

FROM WHENCE COME WARS . . . AMONG YOU?

That such a question has to be asked of believers in the Lord Jesus is a great shame indeed. Our unity by grace with the Man of peace should, in the ideal, make every gathering of His redeemed people on earth a foretaste of heaven itself. But we know in our hearts that the question is a needful one and, pushed to give an answer, we might venture one. Why is there strife in the assembly of which you are part? Ah, you might say, there is a particular brother who is out to make trouble. Or, you might say, there is a sister who has waged a vendetta against another for a long time. The answers would be as varied as our faces, but would any of us dare to come out with the answer that James gives? He says that the lusts that war in *your* members, and the lack of grace because of pride, are the real reasons for strife and battles. The emphasis he makes is upon individual responsibility. It may well be true that the current problem you are facing is caused by the unspiritual behaviour of another, but there is little you can do to correct another. If each of us learned of God the real character of the old nature within, and humbly submitted to the power of the indwelling Spirit of God, each heart would become a place where the fires of envy and enmity cease to burn out of control. We must be honest: has there not been terrible damage done to individuals and local assemblies because men who claimed they were contending for the truth have fought each other in a carnal way until the very thing they were trying to preserve has been destroyed around them? How true it is that the wars and fightings among us are born of the lusts that war in our members!

If the war that is within each of us is not to break out in war among us, what is to be done? First, we have to acknowledge the effect of worldliness upon us, Jas. 4. 4. It de-sensitizes us to sin and makes us brash and arrogant. We have to return to our God in true humility to seek the grace that we otherwise lack, v. 6. The devil, whose allies we so easily become against one another, must be resisted, and we must draw nigh to God for cleansing, v. 8. Are we prepared to humble ourselves before God, or must the wars and fightings continue?

December 16th

James 4. 11-12; Matthew 7. 1

WHO ART THOU THAT JUDGEST ANOTHER?

These verses are frequently quoted out of context and given a meaning that was never originally intended. It was not the purpose of the One who gave us the critical faculty that it should lie dormant, but rather that it might be exercised as instructed by the word of God and the Spirit of God. Indeed, the New Testament makes it clear that there are certain things that must be judged, such as sinful behaviour in the local church, 1 Cor. 5. 12, also, our 'love should abound more and more in knowledge and in all judgment', so that we 'may approve things that are excellent', Phil. 1. 9-10. Discrimination is actively encouraged so that as we try and test things that differ, and approve that which is excellent, we may be 'sincere and without offence till the day of Christ'.

The verses we have read today are, of course, not speaking about that true wisdom which distinguishes things that are different but relate to the possibility of having a critical and censorious spirit towards others. This is something we have no right to have. In Matthew chapter 7 our Lord indicates just how inappropriate it is for one to seek to pull out of his brother's eye a mote (a tiny piece of straw or wood, which might blow into the eye) when he has not attended to the beam (such as might be used to support the roof of a building) that is in his own eye. Not only is this hypocritical in the extreme but the Saviour reminds us that the standard of judgement that we may apply to others in such a situation will be that by which we ourselves will be judged. Accordingly, He urges self-judgement. The apostle Paul engaged in this necessary exercise and was able to say that he knew nothing against himself. However, he recognized that he was not thereby justified and lived knowing that 'he that judgeth me is the Lord', 1 Cor. 4. 4.

Romans chapter 14 teaches in forthright terms that we have no right to stand in judgement on the servant of another, particularly in relation to the motives and scruples he has: the judgement seat of Christ is the only place where right judgements will be made and we shall all appear there. Self-judgement now will ensure a more joyful time then.

December 17th

James 4. 13-17

FOR WHAT IS YOUR LIFE?

The Lord has purposes for the lives of each of His children. The apostle Peter was made aware of this when the Lord Jesus told him how he would glorify God in his death and when he asked concerning John, 'Lord, and what shall this man do?' our Saviour answered, 'If I will that he tarry till I come, what is that to thee? follow thou me', John 21. 18-22. James now reminds us that there ought to be conscious, daily recognition that our lives are to be lived in ready submission to that will and the good it plans for us.

At the same time James is also teaching us that it is not wrong for us to make plans. Sometimes believers feel that planning is somehow contrary to the concept of there being a divine will but we learn here that plans made subject to the will of the Lord are appropriate and, no doubt, lead to a more ordered life. Note also that James is not considering that a desire to do the Lord's will should lead to major, undue anxiety: rather, he is simply indicating that when plans are made they should be formulated in recognition of the fact they will only come to fruition 'if the Lord will'.

His instructions in this matter arise from the proud way in which people were saying *we will* 'go into such a city, and continue there a year, and buy and sell, and get gain' rather than saying in a humble fashion *if the Lord will* 'we shall live, and do this, or that'. Their boasting failed to take account of the fact that life is transient. As the early morning mist, so heavy at times, is soon dispelled by the burning sun so our lives on earth are brief, passing and unpredictable.

To plan things subject to His will recognizes that He is in control but also acts as a regulator so that no course of action is decided upon that would dishonour Him. How important it is, therefore, to be prepared to submit to the will of the Lord in all things in our lives and to endeavour to fill them for His glory. And when our desires and aims are painfully disappointed, when the circumstances of life or the intervention of death abruptly thwart our plans, may we have grace to submit to the will of the God who always plans the best for His people!

December 18th

James 5. 13-18

IS ANY AMONG YOU AFFLICTED?

In life's rich tapestry the colours are not always bright. Afflictions accompany all men but the Christian is especially prone to feel their weight because of the added spiritual dimension to his experience in this fallen world. Elsewhere the word is translated 'endure hardness', 2 Tim. 2. 3, and 'suffer trouble', v. 9. These times should take us into the presence of our God in supplicating and prevailing prayer.

Life is not all dark, however, and prayer in the difficult times should be counterbalanced by praise in the singing of psalms when we are cheered. This does not mean that we are restricted to the use of Israel's hymn book but rather that we should express to God our thanks by singing to Him. Our singing might be sharp or flat but God is well pleased with a heart that is attuned to His praise.

At other times we might be sick. As believers we are not immune from physical weakness and, indeed, this passage seems to teach that believers might be more prone to enfeeblement than others. It is interesting to note that James wrote his epistle in the earliest days of this era when there were those living who had the gift of healing but he instructs the man, who in this passage is described as weak or feeble, verse 14, and weary in his mind, verse 15, to call not for the healer but for the elders of the church. It appears that there is a spiritual dimension to the man's ailment and in this connection it is worth noting that the possibility that he has committed sin is suggested, as is the need to confess faults.

It is well documented in scripture that if the believer sins, or thinks that he has sinned, there can be consequent physical and mental enervation; Psalm 32 describes such an occurrence. David had committed adultery and arranged for the death of princely Uriah. As a result, his bones waxed old and his moisture was turned into the drought of summer. It is not for one to say of another that sin is the cause of such weakness (the man called for the elders rather than the other way round), but where we experience it we do well to examine ourselves in order that there might be a restoration. 'The Lord shall raise him up'.

December 19th

1 Peter 3. 8-18

WHO IS HE THAT WILL HARM YOU?

The believer ought to be a follower of that which is good. Indeed, it is an evidence of new life and natural to the new man. Peter does not leave us in any doubt, either, as to what that 'good' is to which he refers. Having compassion, loving as brothers, full of pity and courteous, blessing those who are evilly disposed and who rail, speaking no guile, eschewing evil and seeking peace are all qualities that should characterize those who follow the One in whom is perfect goodness.

The quotation from Psalm 34, which is found in 1 Pet. 3. 10-12, would have reminded Peter's first readers that though they might have many enemies who would force them into the crucible of affliction they could not ultimately harm them. The Lord's eyes were upon them, His ears were open unto their cries and His face was against them that did evil to them. It is a sign of the depths of evil within the heart estranged from God that goodness in the believer can so often be the cause of the worst calumnies and enmity. It was thus with our blessed Lord, whose goodness and righteousness was requited by bitter hatred, 'They hated me without a cause', John 15. 25. Before He went to the cross He indicated that if they hated Him they would also hate those who belong to Him, and in Peter's day they were feeling that hatred in full measure in their fiery trial.

This, then, is an encouraging word. Having become followers of that which is good they might well suffer at the hands of foes who would seek to intimidate them, bringing them into fear, but they could never be ultimately harmed by them. In fact Peter indicates, rather, that suffering would bring them happiness. He had experienced this himself with the other apostles, 'rejoicing that they were counted worthy to suffer shame for his name', Acts 5. 41. 'Blessed are ye, when men shall revile you, and persecute you, and shall say all manner of evil against you falsely, for my sake. Rejoice, and be exceeding glad: for great is your reward in heaven: for so persecuted they the prophets which were before you', Matt. 5. 11-12.

What paradoxes there are in the pathway of faith! May the Lord help us to do unflinchingly that which is good.

December 20th

1 Peter 4. 12-19

WHERE SHALL THE UNGODLY . . . APPEAR?

In considering the fact that the righteous are scarcely saved we should be careful to guard against thinking that God has any difficulty in the matter of our salvation, for 'the gospel of Christ is the power of God unto salvation', Rom. 1. 16. When a person believes on God's Son he is immediately and eternally saved so that not all the powers of hell, however much they rage, can reverse what God has done. None can lay anything to the charge of God's elect and none is able to condemn them.

The thought in the righteous being saved with difficulty is, rather, to do with the circumstances in which those who believe are found. Both before and after salvation's day there are difficulties. The road to faith in Christ will often pass through at least one deep valley and while it is true that conversion brings gladness, Acts 2. 41, there are obstacles to overcome on the pathway that can cause deep distress of soul. After conversion there are new and remarkably difficult experiences to deal with. The Christian life is not one continuous crest of the wave: there are deep troughs resulting from internal conflict between the flesh and the Holy Spirit, and from the external enemies of the world and the devil. Additionally, the chastening hand of the Father is upon us as judgement begins at the house of God, compare 1 Cor. 11. 32; Ezek. 9. 6; Amos 3. 2.

Despite this we rejoice in our salvation and especially so when we consider the two rhetorical questions posed in these verses, 'What shall the end be of them that obey not the gospel of God?'; 'Where shall the ungodly and the sinner appear?' The unbeliever is apt to judge everything by present conditions and, regrettably, many believers have been tempted to do the same instead of committing themselves to God in the time of their suffering. Those disobedient to the gospel often look at those who are saved and see that their circumstances have not been helped by their faith, concluding that it is pointless to trust in the Lord. They are dangerously wrong, however, as there is an end to consider, which will be the outcome of ungodliness and sinfulness. The questions are left hanging but let no one underestimate the complete awfulness of eternal perdition.

December 21st

2 Peter 3. 1-7

WHERE IS THE PROMISE OF HIS COMING?

Second epistles, and none more so than Peter's, are generally populated by those who depart or apostatize. He particularly calls attention to the fact that in the last days scoffers would mock at the notion of the coming again of our Lord Jesus Christ. As they sneer that everything has always continued just as it is now, they live life fulfilling their own lusts, without regard to future judicial intervention in the earth by the Lord. It is an amazing description of these closing days of the dispensation in which uniformitarianism underpins geology and other branches of science and in which it is openly said that as 'there is probably no God, go out and enjoy the rest of your life'.

There is a great irony in that, in the very source of truth, the Bible, which is so derided by the atheistic and agnostic philosophers of science, they and their acolytes are depicted and foretold! How marvellous then is the longsuffering of God, for the one thing above all others that has meant that the promise of His coming is long delayed is His desire that none should perish, but that all should come to repentance.

The believer has a sure resource in the face of such contempt for the Lord. He is to remember the words of the holy (Old Testament) prophets and the commandments of the apostles of the Lord and Saviour. By the word of God the heavens and the earth were prepared for the judgement of the flood and by that same word are now reserved unto fire and the 'day of judgment and perdition of ungodly men'. Man's puny mind, in which he so often boasts, is limited by time and sense yet the eternal God, to whom one thousand years and one day are not dissimilar, is not so bound.

All of this is to have a marked effect in our lives. Our patient waiting for Christ and our confidence in the word of God should not be abandoned because of the jibes of the immoderate boasters of a materialistic philosophy. The increasing sinfulness of the age should not diminish our preaching of repentance and efforts to spread the gospel. Our behaviour should be holy and godly as we remember that everything down here will be burned up.

December 22nd

2 Peter 3. 8-13

WHAT MANNER OF PERSONS OUGHT YE TO BE?

The revelation in holy scripture of future events has not been given for mere intellectual stimulus, interesting though it is. God intends that our daily living should be in the light of what shall be when His prophetic calendar turns to its next page. Another has said, in thinking of the day of Christ, that the apostle Paul lived every 'this day' in the light of 'that day'. Present service for the Lord and faithfulness to Him will all be revealed and tried at the judgement seat of Christ and the realization of this will surely regulate our motives and devotion to the Lord.

Enoch's crisis at the age of sixty-five years, Gen. 5. 21-24, happened coincidentally with the birth of his son Methuselah, whose name means, 'when he is dead it shall come'. He died just before the flood and it seems that when Enoch got to know that the world in which he lived was heading for judgement he turned and walked with God. An event which actually lay nearly a thousand years in the future had a critical and immediate impact on his life.

This planet, on which we live, and the universe in which it is found are to be burned up. The power of that divine judgement is truly awful but it is a necessary precursor to the coming of the day of God. In the millennial kingdom righteousness will ***reign***: there will be an imposition of its just demands on all. The day of God is different. In that eternal day righteousness will ***dwell***; the sin of the world will have been taken away by the Lamb of God, John 1. 29, and will never again trouble or disturb. We long for that day and therefore it is right that our conduct in this present age be commensurate with what shall then pertain.

Accordingly, we ought to be marked by holy behaviour, the outcome of that proper attitude to God that the Bible calls godliness. If that is an obligation placed upon us we also must be diligent to 'be found of him in peace, without spot, and blameless', 2 Pet. 3. 14. As the days grow darker and as the standards of behaviour among the Lord's people diminish, let us determine that as nothing down here has abiding value we will live for the Lord and His glory, and by His grace reproduce that beautiful moral character seen perfectly in the Lord Jesus.

December 23rd

1 John 2. 18-28

WHO IS A LIAR?

John wrote his Gospel to establish the deity of the Lord Jesus Christ, 'These are written, that ye might believe that Jesus is the Christ, the Son of God; and that believing ye might have life through his name', John 20. 31. In his First Epistle, however, John establishes that our Lord is truly man. The apostles had heard Him, seen Him, looked upon Him and handled Him, 1 John 1. 1. Interestingly, as he establishes Christ's deity in the Gospel he underlines time and again our Lord's true humanity; and as he establishes Christ's humanity in the Epistle he repeatedly underlines His deity. It is clear that in John's day there was serious error abroad regarding Christ's glorious Person.

The person who denies the deity of our Lord by disavowing that Jesus is the Christ and denying the doctrine of the Father and the Son is a liar and is of the character of antichrist. This was not an unbelief that was vague, nor did it arise from ignorance, but it was a definite refusal to aver and confess the truth. John actually says he is '**the** liar' and as such we may be sure that such denial is diabolically inspired. The devil 'was a murderer from the beginning, and abode not in the truth, because there is no truth in him. When he speaketh a lie, he speaketh of his own: for he is a liar, and the father of it', John 8. 44.

In contrast to those who denied the deity of the Lord Jesus even the infants in the family of God had received an anointing (the result of receiving the Holy Spirit) from the Holy One (the Lord Jesus Christ). Where there is true faith the youngest believer is given intuitive knowledge which enables him to have an understanding of the truth. This does not mean that the Bible is redundant, of course, but where error raises its head he will intuitively know that it is a lie and will not be seduced by it. That which he heard from the beginning of hearing the gospel will abide in him so that he will continue in the Son, and in the Father, 1 John 2. 24, and he will abide in Christ, v. 27.

As believers, we rejoice in the Lord Jesus Christ who, by virtue of His unique relationship with the Father, properly represents and manifests Him, 'The only begotten Son, which is in the bosom of the Father, he hath declared him', John 1. 18.

December 24th

1 John 3. 7-12

WHEREFORE SLEW HE HIM?

The reason why Cain slew Abel was that his own works were evil while his brother's were righteous. The two brothers were totally different in character. Abel was a man of faith, 'By faith Abel offered unto God a more excellent sacrifice than Cain, by which he obtained witness that he was righteous, God testifying of his gifts', Heb. 11. 4. Cain, on the other hand, was of 'that wicked one'. Believers have overcome him, 1 John 2. 13, 14, and are outside of his reach, 5. 18, but Cain bore his character, 3. 12. It is no wonder that the world system that was started by Cain in Genesis chapter 4, in estrangement from God, blissfully lies asleep in the lap of the wicked one, 1 John 5. 19.

The sacrifices which the brothers brought bore the character of the offerer in each case. Abel came to God as a man of faith: even before he brought his sacrifice his works were righteous. Cain pictures the man of the flesh, blinded by Satan, who by his own efforts seeks to persuade God, against all the evidence, that he is righteous. The only possible result was that Abel's blood sacrifice was accepted whereas Cain's bloodless offering was refused.

It would be easy to think that Cain killed his brother simply because of the refusal of his sacrifice by God but in fact that rejection served to display the true character of the man, 'He that hateth his brother is in darkness', 2. 11; 'He that loveth not his brother abideth in death', 3. 14; 'No murderer hath eternal life abiding in him', v. 15.

Here, then, is demonstrated a feature of the writings of the apostle John. A person's characteristic behaviour will show whether or not he is a child of God or a child of the devil, and there is no middle ground. We walk either in the light or the darkness; we either keep his commandments or we do not; we love or hate (in an assumed relationship) our brother. The believer's righteous character will always attract and arouse the world's hatred but it will also lead him to love his brother in accordance with the message which was heard from the lips of our Lord Jesus Christ, 'Beloved, let us love one another: for . . . every one that loveth is born of God, and knoweth God'.

December 25th

1 John 3. 13-18

HOW DWELLETH THE LOVE OF GOD IN HIM?

Through diligent contemplation of Calvary we have come to know the highest expression of love in the Lord Jesus Christ laying down His life for us. 'He' is in stark contrast to 'us' and in a deliberate, voluntary act He revealed the greatness His love. Standing in contrast to Cain, who murdered his own brother, He is the great example to those who share His life in that they have a moral obligation, if the necessity arises, quite literally to lay down their lives for the brethren.

The laying down of His life will always have elements about it which we could not emulate, for His sacrifice was propitiatory in its nature, but in that it involved the satisfying of the supreme obligation of love we ought to be like Him. The measure of His love for us should be the standard of our love for one another.

The laying down of our life for another would only occur *in extremis* but 1 John chapter 3 verse 17 speaks of everyday events. We might not ever be called upon to make the supreme sacrifice for our brother, but if we have been blessed by some of this world's goods when, at the same time, our brother is in need we cannot shut up our affections from him and at the same time think that the love of God dwells in us.

'If there be among you a poor man of one of thy brethren within any of thy gates in thy land which the Lord thy God giveth thee, thou shalt not harden thine heart, nor shut thine hand from thy poor brother', Deut. 15. 7. The need was immediate and it was not permissible under the law to deny the needy that which he required, even if there were extenuating circumstances, such as the near approach of the year of release. Our obligation under grace is so much greater. The Macedonian churches knew this; 'in a great trial of affliction the abundance of their joy and their deep poverty abounded unto the riches of their liberality', 2 Cor. 8. 2. To shut up our 'bowels of compassion' is to determine not to help the need of another despite having the ability to meet it, and is a denial of God's love in us.

'For ye know the grace of our Lord Jesus Christ, that, though he was rich, yet for your sakes he became poor, that ye through his poverty might be rich', v. 9.

December 26th

1 John 5. 1-6

WHO IS HE THAT OVERCOMETH THE WORLD?

'He that believeth that', 1 John 5. 5, and 'He that believeth on', v. 12, are two expressions that need careful consideration. Indeed, it is not overstating the case to say that there is such a difference between the two ideas that our soul's salvation depends upon it! The mere intellectual acceptance of facts about divine persons never saved anybody. Agrippa believed the prophets but by his own admission he was not a Christian. A person is saved when he acknowledges as true all that scripture reveals about the Son of God (he believes in His Name) and consequently puts unreserved and unconditional faith in Him. To believe on Him is to rely on Him, to put confidence in Him, to depend upon Him, and it is therefore an act of trust. It is possible to 'believe that' without 'believing on' but wherever Christ personally is the object of trust the believer believes all that is revealed about Him in God's word.

All the overcomers in John's writings are believers and all believers are overcomers. A person is either an overcomer or an unbeliever. Faith, v. 4, in an abstract way, overcomes the world system from which God and Christ are excluded, looking beyond all that is tangible, temporal and prevailing over it, but verse 5 indicates that the person who overcomes by faith is a person who believes that Jesus is the Son of God. It should be carefully noted that John is not saying that this is a minimum requirement for salvation, but that all who are genuinely saved believe this glorious truth. Similarly, in verse 1, people who are born of God did not become so by believing that Jesus is the Christ, as if that is the sole requirement: rather, a proof of new birth having taken place is that a person so believes.

It is a truly glorious thing to have overcome the world and to continue to do so. The world would have us conform to its verdict on our Lord, but faith sees Him who is now invisible to mortal eyes and rises above all that would otherwise attract us down here. We cannot love the world and the Father. Let us not love it, therefore, but recognizing its true character as evil may we live by faith in the Son of God, being careful for nothing but His interests down here.

December 27th

Revelation 5. 1-14

WHO IS WORTHY?

The Lord created all things for His pleasure, Rev. 4. 11. This expresses the fact that the universe was created because of His will and He is worthy therefore to receive it for Himself. Although sin has spoiled, marred, tainted and corrupted His creation, the Lord will reclaim it in a manner consistent with His righteous character. As the events begin to unfold which will lead to this, the question is asked as to who is worthy to open that seven-sealed book, which has been described as containing the title deeds of the universe.

The question is heard throughout the universe but whether search is made in celestial, terrestrial or infernal spheres, no one is found who can step forward to open the book. John's tears at this fruitless search are stayed, however, as he is told that One has prevailed and He is worthy. He has a *legal right* for He is the Lion of the tribe of Judah, Gen. 49. 8-12. He also has a *personal right* for He is not only the offspring of David, Isa. 11. 1, but also the Root of David. In addition, He has a *moral right* to take and open the book: as John turns he sees a young Lamb, slain but standing in all the power of resurrection life. The Lamb of Calvary stands ready to act in the interests of the throne. He has been seated at the right hand of God but now the 'until' of Psalm 110 is about to be completed: all His enemies will be made His footstool. Omnipotent (He has seven horns) and omniscient (He has seven eyes), He stands in glorious contrast to all others who have tried to take the reigns of universal government and without a word, even as at Calvary, He comes to the throne to take the book.

This causes an outpouring of praise and adoration. It is started by the four living creatures and twenty-four elders. The redeemed in heaven raise the song of His worthiness. Myriads of angels, though they have no personal experience of redemption, join in praising the slain Lamb who is worthy. The choir is still not complete for to it there is added the voices of every creature, in anticipation of the deliverance they shall know through the opening of the title deeds. Let us sing the song even now, that will be newly sung in heaven, 'Lord, thou art worthy'!

December 28th

Revelation 6. 1-11

HOW LONG, O LORD?

The slain Lamb who is worthy begins, seal by seal, to open the seven sealed book and as He does so dreadful judgements begin to issue from the throne. The fact that later judgements seem to be more severe should not cause us to think that these seal judgements are minor. Multitudes will be killed by wars, famines, pestilences and wild beasts, so that death will pervade the earth.

The fifth seal brings to our attention those who have died in another way. They were 'slain for the word of God, and for the testimony which they held'. These are not martyrs of this church era, of course, for by the time the seals are opened they will already be in heaven, represented among the twenty-four elders. After the rapture God will still have a testimony on earth but they will be fearful days for those connected with it. This company is referred to in Revelation chapter 20 verse 4 where we learn that they 'were beheaded for the witness of Jesus, and for the word of God'. Truly, their blood had been shed.

It is not the character of our present day that those who suffer for Christ's sake call for righteous retribution. The apostles rejoiced that they were counted worthy to suffer for Him. If a fiery trial was to try them the Christians were to rejoice, 1 Pet. 4. 12-13, knowing that in the day when His glory is revealed they will be glad with exceeding joy as being partakers of His sufferings. Such is the calling of a heavenly people, but for those who will then look for the establishment on earth of Messiah's kingdom it is rather different. In echoes of the imprecatory psalms the souls under the altar cry for the judging of those who dwell on the earth and for the avenging of their blood.

They call upon the One who is the *'despotes'*, the Sovereign Master. All is under His control. From Him they are assured that judging and avenging will take place, but not yet: others must first die in like manner to them, and so they must rest a little season. In fact, beyond what they prayed or anticipated, they are going to be among those who will live and reign with Christ a thousand years, Rev. 20. 4, and will thus share in the heavenly side of that coming kingdom.

December 29th

Revelation 7. 9-17

WHAT ARE THESE . . . ARRAYED IN WHITE ROBES?

God is not limited in His purpose to what He is doing at this present time. Even after the moment when the Lord Himself comes to the air to raise the dead in Christ and catch them up together with those who at that time are living and remaining, there will be mighty saving work done on the earth.

Revelation chapter 7 forms a parenthesis between the opening of the sixth seal, Rev. 6. 12, and the seventh, 8. 1. While the judgements are going on God allows us to peep through the window, as it were, and see that there are people here who are safe in His keeping during the great tribulation and who will be manifested publicly in due course. Chapter 7 does not say when this will be but simply notes that it will happen.

The different companies in the chapter have to be noted and distinguished, if we are to understand who these are who are arrayed in white. The first half of the chapter speaks of Jews who are sealed and the number of them is counted. They are a remnant from God's ancient people, Israel, unlike the innumerable multitude who come from all nations, kindred, people and tongues. In turn, these are to be distinguished from the angels, the elders, and the four living creatures noted in verse 11. Those arrayed in white are not the church, for the church is represented in the elders already crowned and surrounding the throne of God in heaven. Also, the distinction between Jew and Gentile is done away in this present church era in which the church is 'one new man', Eph. 2. 15. God is not now dealing with Jews and Gentiles as such but clearly He will do so in that future day.

After the rapture, and as a result of the preaching of the gospel of the kingdom, this great multitude will be saved and enter the millennial kingdom. There will be a huge ingathering but let no one take any comfort from thinking that if he does not believe the gospel now he will at least have the opportunity to be saved then, 'God shall send them strong delusion, that they should believe a lie: that they all might be damned who believed not the truth', 2 Thess. 2. 11-12. There is an urgent imperative contained in the gospel, 'Now is the day of salvation', 2 Cor. 6. 2.

December 30th

Revelation 13. 1-10

WHO IS LIKE UNTO THE BEAST?

The fact that this question is raised points to the extreme wickedness that will be on the earth in the days of the tribulation period. Questions, or statements, in this form belong to the Lord. Having been redeemed from Egypt, Moses asks in his great song, 'Who is like unto thee, O Lord, among the gods? who is like thee, glorious in holiness, fearful in praises, doing wonders?', Exod. 15. 11. Three further similar statements in the Psalms, Pss. 35. 10; 71. 19; 113. 5, confirm the appropriateness of declaring the uniqueness of God. Those who know His Name ascribe to Him unrivalled glory, praise and honour.

In the seventieth week of Daniel's prophecy, when God resumes His dealings with Israel, the apex of man's wickedness will be reached. A triumvirate of evil in the form of the devil and the two beasts of Revelation chapter 13 will mimic the Godhead. The devil, the dragon who gives power to the beasts, will be worshipped. The first beast will speak against and oppose all that is good, and will exalt everything that is evil, and all those who live on the earth, with the exception of those whose names are written from the foundation of the world in the slain Lamb's book of life, will worship him.

The beast is undoubtedly a man but he is at one with the empire he represents and leads. This empire is the feet and toes of the image in Nebuchadnezzar's dream, Dan. 2. 40-43, and the fourth beast, 'dreadful and terrible', in Daniel's dream, 7. 7, 19-28. It is the last of four world empires in the times of the Gentiles, cruel, strong, devouring, and destroying; unlike anything that has gone before it. Its leader is the 'prince that shall come', 9. 26. His people, the Romans, were responsible for the destruction of Jerusalem in 70 AD and the slaughter of over a million Jews, and in that future day he will make war with the saints.

Our Lord will summarily answer the question. He is the Heir of all things and will claim that which is His. The beast's dominion will be taken away and he will be cast alive into the lake of fire but our Lord shall set up a kingdom that will fill the whole earth and stand for ever. Who is like unto the Lord?

December 31st

Revelation 15. 1-8

WHO SHALL NOT FEAR THEE, O LORD?

The singers of this song have known great conflict. In the terrible days of the beast, with whom they were contemporaneous, they had been victorious because they had neither bowed to his image nor received either his mark or the number of his name. Now, however, they stand in peace and tranquility upon a sea of glass. They did not need the purification that the molten sea of Solomon's temple would afford the priests, 2 Chr. 4. 6, but stood on a glassy, fiery sea in a purity that nothing could defile.

The fact that 'they sing the song of Moses' immediately reminds us of the salvation side of the Red Sea. Having come on dry land through the divided waters Moses and the children of Israel sang the first song in the Bible, Exod. 15. 1. They sang it in the good of the redemption they had just experienced. The song of Moses is also the last song in holy scripture. The vast majority of this earth's songs are empty and vain but the twin themes of the works and ways of God occupied both Moses and this company standing on the sea of glass. 'He made known his ways unto Moses, his acts unto the children of Israel', Ps. 103. 7, is paralleled by, 'Great and marvellous are thy works, Lord God Almighty; just and true are thy ways, thou King of saints', Rev. 15. 3.

Revelation is about to record the outpouring from vials which are filled up with the wrath of God. These will cause men on earth to blaspheme the God of heaven but this company recognizes that God is to be feared and that His ways are just and true. His judgements are not capricious nor arbitrary, and in any event are tempered with mercy. Such is the thought that He is holy. The word used indicates not simply that God is entirely separate from evil and is righteous in all His ways, but also that He is gracious and merciful. Even in His wrath there is that in which His mercy may be seen.

As the year draws to its close let us, also, be taken up with the character of God and live in His fear. Let our songs not be those which are filled with the endlessly repetitive subjectivism of much that is popular, but with the greatness and glory, the justice and truth of the One whom all nations will worship.